'Flann O'Brien' was one of the two pseu
Brian O'Nolan – the other being 'Myles
name he wrote a famous column in the
novels in English, *The Third Policeman*
Swim-Two-Birds and *The Hard Life*, as well as the famous work in
Irish, *An Béal Bocht*, now translated as *The Poor Mouth*. He was
born in County Tyrone in 1911 and died in Dublin in 1966. His
reputation is constantly growing.

Myles na Gopaleen
(Flann O'Brien)

The Best of Myles

A selection from 'Cruiskeen Lawn'

Edited and with a Preface by Kevin O Nolan

PICADOR
Pan Books London and Sydney

First published in Great Britain 1968 by
MacGibbon & Kee Ltd
Third impression 1975 by Hart-Davis, MacGibbon Ltd
This Picador edition published 1977 by
Pan Books Ltd, Cavaye Place, London SW10 9PG
© Evelyn O'Nolan 1968, 1971, 1975
ISBN 0 330 24855 3
Printed in Great Britain by
Richard Clay (The Chaucer Press) Ltd, Bungay, Suffolk

ACKNOWLEDGEMENTS

THE publishers would like to express their thanks to the Editor and Proprietors of *The Irish Times*, in whose pages the contents of this book originally appeared, for their co-operation and help.

CONTENTS

PREFACE

THE 'Cruiskeen Lawn' column started in *The Irish Times* twenty-nine years ago, and continued until the author's death in 1966. Indeed it was resumed after his death in the form of reprinted articles under the heading 'The Best of Myles'. The column was at first wholly in Irish but shortly it came to be written in English on alternate days. This continued for several years after which it appeared mainly in English. The daily contribution was often quite long, and the topic of one day might be resumed on a subsequent day. This serial form was acknowledged in later years where an identical caption was often followed by I, II, III, and so forth.

In the present selection articles are separated by asterisks. Where the topic was continued, the continuation follows the asterisks. Accordingly the asterisks denote the conclusion of an article or a lapse of time before resuming. Apart from single or continued articles the selection includes shorter extracts, also isolated by asterisks.

It seemed worth while, for the convenience of readers, to attempt some classification. But it is not rigid. Many waifs and strays have been bundled into the Guard's Van under 'Miscellaneous'. Nor are the other compartments specially reserved. A Keats and Chapman anecdote may be found lurking elsewhere than in their allotted space, or the Plain People of Ireland may find themselves hopelessly embedded in some alien context. But this reflects the reality of the column, where innovation and surprise were no rare ingredients, where the reader was unceremoniously hauled within brackets (for greater privacy), or addressed not in English or Irish but in a strange-looking mixture, English through the phonology of the Irish alphabet. In later years some of the author's adventures were related wholly in Latin. With regard to Keats and Chapman, the author once listed among his happiest moments the hypothetical occasion of being assured 'that I will never meet Keats in the hereafter.'

The selection covers about the first five years, mostly the period of the Second World War. The American critic Richard Watts, writing in the *New York Herald Tribune* (in the summer of 1943) summarised the scope of the column: 'As "Myles na gCopaleen" he writes a daily column for the conservative and Anglo-Irish newspaper,

Preface

The Irish Times . . . a column devoted to magnificently laborious literary puns, remarkable parodies of De Quincey and others, fanciful literary anecdotes, and erudite study of clichés, scornful dissection of the literal meaning of highflown literary phraseology and a general air of shameless irony and high spirits. No one can build up a pun more shamelessly. No one can analyse the exact meaning of a literary flight of fantasy more devastatingly. He is at his best when telling absurd anecdotes, which he usually attributes to Keats and Chapman.'

Regular readers of *The Irish Times* may notice that the present selection does not represent the tone of the column throughout its whole history. In its more recent years the tone was often more sombre, more fiercely satirical, and many passages of savage denunciation deserve resurrection. Perhaps a further selection may give this *saeva indignatio* its place.

1968   KEVIN O NOLAN

PUBLISHER'S NOTE

IT HAS not been thought advisable to delete from the following pages the occasional references to the original appearance of these articles in a daily newspaper. The author, for example, sometimes indicated by arrows or a pointing finger his references to other contributions in the paper, either a leading article with which he disagreed or some contribution in the social column. He was for many years a committed newspaperman and it would distort the tone of this book if all indications that these articles were written against a deadline, or that his own column was part of the greater whole, were to be deleted.

THE BEST OF MYLES

Waama, etc.

I HAVE RECEIVED by post a number of papers inviting me to become a member of the Irish Writers, Actors, Artists, Musicians Association, and to pay part of my money to the people who run this company. I am also invited to attend a meeting in Jury's Hotel on Sunday week. Foot I will not set inside that door; act, hand or part I will not have with that party.

At one of the preliminary meetings of this organisation, I bought a few minor novelists at five bob a skull and persuaded them to propose me for the presidency. Then I rose myself and said that if it was the unanimous wish of the company, etc., quite unworthy, etc., signal honour, etc., serve to the best of my ability, etc., prior claims of other persons, etc., if humble talents of any service, etc., delighted to place knowledge of literary world at disposal of, etc., undoubted need for organisation, etc.

To my astonishment, instead of accepting my offer with loud and sustained applause, the wretched intellectuals broke up into frightened groups and started whispering together in great agitation. From where I sat in my mood of Homeric detachment I could distinctly hear snatches of talk like 'never sober', 'literary corner-boy', 'pay nobody', 'Stubbs every week', 'running round with a TD's wife', 'skip with the Association's assets', 'great man for going to Paris', 'sell his mother for sixpence', 'belly full of brandy and unfortunate children without a rag', 'summoned for putting in plate glass window in Santry', 'pity unfortunate wife', 'half the stuff cogged from other people', 'sneer at us behind our backs', 'use Association's name', 'what would people think', 'only inviting attention of Guards', 'who asked him here', 'believe he was born in Manchester', 'probably fly-boy', 'cool calculated cheek': and so on, I regret to say. Subsequently a man with glasses got up and mumbled something about best thanks of all concerned, proposal somewhat premature, society not yet wholly formed, bring proposal forward at later date, certain that choice would be a popular one, with permission of company pass on to next business, disgraceful sweat rates paid by broadcasting station . . . I thought this was fair enough, but think of my feelings a few days afterwards on hearing that Mr Sean O Faoláin had been elevated to the same Presidency. One shrinks from gratuitous comparisons, but man for man, novels for novels, plays for plays, services to imperishable Irish nation for services to i. I.n., popularity as drawingroom raconteur for p. as d.r., which was the better choice? I leave the answer not only to my readers but also to a betrayed posterity who may yet decide that Dermot MacMurrough was not the worst.

QUESTIONABLE AIMS

In any event, I was completely opposed to some of this organisation's aims. For instance, it is proposed to secure 'improved rates for all literary work'. This simply means an even heavier deluge of unpardonable 'poetry', more articles entitled 'Big John: A Sketch', and a premium on mediocrity generally. It is also sought to have 'concerted agreement on copyrights, contracts, etc.' What sort of an agreement is a 'concerted agreement', or is there such a thing as a unconcerted, disconcerted, or misconcerted agreement? 'Special rates for radio scripts.' Why? They all bore even my thick wife. Reduce the rates and you'll get less of them making a clack in your ear. 'Free legal advice.' This will disemploy several worthy solicitors, a fiery celtic breed that I admire. 'Recovery of fees.' Yes, but minus ten per cent. Get your money in your hand before you put pen to paper, that's what I say.

Also, having regard to the categories mentioned, membership seems to be open to every man, woman and child in Ireland. Even my wife could claim to be a 'commentator' (whatever they mean by that word) and everybody knows that all these organisations are really formed in order to give people a pretext for getting away from their families. So what's the use?

FURTHERMORE

This is the land of Ireland and now that WAAMA is in existence and in active operation, it is time that a 'split' was organised and a rival body formed. Would any person who thinks that he or she has not had a fair deal from WAAMA please communicate with me at this office? We will form our own organisation, with better aims and heavier annual dinners. Pretty girls will be admitted free and nobody will be bored with guff about Sigrid Undset or James Joyce Cabell. How about it, lads? I am determined to be president of something before I die—of Ireland itself, if need be.

* * *

MY SUGGESTION the other day that the lines to be spoken in a new play at the Abbey should be displayed on banners suspended from the balcony and read off by the players as they go along, has won me golden opinions from the acting clique in WAAMA. They say that they are frequently asked to perform in very bad plays, and that no torment is so terrible as that of being compelled to commit muck to memory. An authoritative spokesman in official circles also stated last night that there appeared to be 'no objection' to my plan. That, of course, pleases me. Had his reaction been otherwise, I should have been compelled to 'view' his pronouncement 'with concern'.

Yes, the plan is a good one. There would be no necessity to tell the actors beforehand what play they are appearing in. They just come out on the stage, peer into the auditorium, and then come out with some dreadful remark about 'Old John', or 'Brigid, his wife'.

My plan has another great advantage in these nights of rushing for last 'buses. Supposing it is a case of missing the end of the play or missing your 'bus. Being possessed of reason, you are damned if you'll miss your 'bus. But neither is it necessary to go home wondering what happened. You simply turn round and peer up at the balcony. Admittedly, it would look queer near the end of the play to have half the audience sitting with their backs to the stage and spelling out in loud whispers what the actors are going to say when they get a chance. Anything, however, is better than walking home in the rain. In an extreme case the entire audience might agree to take the rest of the play 'as read', and clear out *en masse* in the middle of the last act, thus releasing the tired actors and given them a chance of getting a lift home also. For the actors are human, too. Each had a mother.

BUCHHANDLUNG

A VISIT that I paid to the house of a newly-married friend the other day set me thinking. My friend is a man of great wealth and vulgarity. When he had set about buying bedsteads, tables, chairs and what-not, it occurred to him to buy also a library. Whether he can read or not, I do not know, but some savage faculty for observation told him that most respectable and estimable people usually had a lot of books in their houses. So he bought several book-cases and paid some rascally middleman to stuff them with all manner of new books, some of them very costly volumes on the subject of French landscape painting.

I noticed on my visit that not one of them had ever been opened or touched, and remarked the fact.

'When I get settled down properly,' said the fool, 'I'll have to catch up on my reading.'

This is what set me thinking. Why should a wealthy person like this be put to the trouble of pretending to read at all? Why not a professional book-handler to go in and suitably maul his library for so-much per shelf? Such a person, if properly qualified, could make a fortune.

DOG EARS FOUR-A-PENNY

Let me explain exactly what I mean. The wares in a bookshop look completely unread. On the other hand, a school-boy's Latin dictionary looks read to the point of tatters. You know that the dictionary has been opened and scanned perhaps a million times, and if you did not know that there was such a thing as a box on the ear, you would conclude that the boy is crazy about Latin and cannot bear to be away from his dictionary. Similarly with our non-brow who wants his friends to infer from a glancing around his house that he is a high-brow. He buys an enormous book on the Russian ballet, written possibly in the language of that distant but beautiful land. Our problem is to alter the book in a reasonably short time so that anybody looking at it will conclude that its owner has practically lived, supped and slept with it for many months. You can, if you like, talk about designing a machine driven by a small but efficient petrol motor that would 'read' any book in five minutes, the equivalent of five years or ten years' 'reading' being obtained by merely turning a knob. This, however, is the cheap soulless approach of the times we live in. No machine can do the same work as the soft human fingers. The trained and experienced book-handler is the only real solution of this contemporary social problem. What does he do? How does he work? What would he charge? How many types of handling would there be?

These questions and many more I will answer the day after tomorrow.

* * *

THE WORLD OF BOOKS

YES, this question of book-handling. The other day I had a word to say about the necessity for the professional book-handler, a person who will maul the books of illiterate, but wealthy, upstarts so that the books will look as if they have been read and re-read by their owners. How many uses of mauling would there be? Without giving the matter much thought, I should say four. Supposing an experienced handler is asked to quote for the handling of one shelf of books four feet in length. He would quote thus under four heads:—

'Popular Handling—Each volume to be well and truly handled, four leaves in each to be dog-eared, and a tram ticket, cloak-room docket or other comparable article inserted in each as a forgotten book-mark. Say, £1 7s 6d. Five per cent discount for civil servants.'

'Premier Handling—Each volume to be thoroughly handled, eight leaves in each to be dog-eared, a suitable passage in not less than 25 volumes to be underlined in red pencil, and a leaflet in French on the works of Victor Hugo to be inserted as a forgotten book-mark in each. Say, £2 17s 6d. Five per cent discount for literary university students, civil servants and lady social workers.'

A RATE TO SUIT ALL PURSES

The great thing about this graduated scale is that no person need appear ignorant or unlettered merely because he or she is poor. Not every vulgar person, remember, is wealthy, although I could name . . .

But no matter. Let us get on to the more expensive grades of handling. The next is well worth the extra money.

'De Luxe Handling—Each volume to be mauled savagely, the spines of the smaller volumes to be damaged in a manner that will give the impression that they have been carried around in pockets, a passage in every volume to be underlined in red pencil with an exclamation or interrogation mark inserted in the margin opposite, an old Gate Theatre programme to be inserted in each volume as a forgotten book-mark (3 per cent discount if old Abbey programmes are accepted), not less than 30 volumes to be treated with old coffee, tea, porter or whiskey stains, and not less than five volumes to be inscribed with forged signatures of the authors. Five per cent discount for bank managers, county surveyors and the heads of business houses employing not less than 35 hands. Dog-ears extra and inserted according to instructions, twopence per half dozen per volume. Quotations for alternative old Paris theatre programmes on demand. This service available for a limited time only, nett, £7 18s 3d.'

ORDER YOUR COPY NOW

The fourth class is the Handling Superb, although it is not called that —*Le Traitement Superbe* being the more usual title. It is so superb that I have no space for it today. It will appear here on Monday next, and, in honour of the occasion, the *Irish Times* on that day will be printed on hand-scutched antique interwoven demidevilled superfine Dutch paper, each copy to be signed by myself and to be accompanied by an exquisite picture in tri-colour lithograph of the Old House in College Green. The least you can do is to order your copy in advance.

And one more word. It is not sufficient just to order your copy. Order it *in advance*.

* * *

IT WILL BE remembered (how, in Heaven's name, could it be forgotten) that I was discoursing on Friday last on the subject of book-handling, my new service, which enables ignorant people who want to be suspected of reading books to have their books handled and mauled in a manner that will give the impression that their owner is very devoted to them. I described three grades of handling and promised to explain what you get under Class Four—the Superb Handling, or the Traitement Superbe, as we lads who spent our honeymoon in Paris prefer to call it. It is the dearest of them all, of course, but far cheaper than dirt when you consider the amount of prestige you will gain in the eyes of your ridiculous friends. Here are the details:

'Le Traitement Superbe'. Every volume to be well and truly handled, first by a qualified handler and subsequently by a master-handler who shall have to his credit not less than 550 handling hours; suitable passages in not less than fifty per cent of the books to be underlined in good-quality red ink and an appropriate phrase from the following list inserted in the margin, viz:

Rubbish!
Yes, indeed!
How true, how true!
I don't agree at all.
Why?
Yes, but cf. Homer, Od., iii, 151.
Well, well, well.

Quite, but Boussuet in his Discours sur l'histoire Universelle has already established the same point and given much more forceful explanations.

Nonsense, nonsense!

A point well taken!

But *why* in heaven's name?

I remember poor Joyce saying the very same thing to me.

Need I say that a special quotation may be obtained at any time for the supply of Special and Exclusive Phrases? The extra charge is not very much, really.

FURTHERMORE

That, of course, is not all. Listen to this:

'Not less than six volumes to be inscribed with forged messages of affection and gratitude from the author of each work, e.g.,

'To my old friend and fellow-writer, A.B., in affectionate remembrance, from George Moore.' 'In grateful recognition of your great kindness to me, dear A.B., I send you this copy of The Crock of Gold. Your old friend, James Stephens.'

'Well, A.B., both of us are getting on. I am supposed to be a good writer now, but I am not old enough to forget the infinite patience you displayed in the old days when guiding my young feet on the path of literature. Accept this further book, poor as it may be, and please believe that I remain, as ever, your friend and admirer, G. Bernard Shaw.'

'From your devoted friend and follower, K. Marx.'

'Dear A.B.,—Your invaluable suggestions and assistance, not to mention your kindness, in entirely re-writing chapter 3, entitles you, surely, to this first copy of "Tess". From your old friend T. Hardy.'

'Short of the great pleasure of seeing you personally, I can only send you, dear A.B., this copy of "The Nigger". I miss your company more than I can say . . . (signature undecipherable).'

Under the last inscription, the moron who owns the book will be asked to write (and shown how if necessary) the phrase 'Poor old Conrad was not the worst.'

All this has taken me longer to say than I thought. There is far more than this to be had for the paltry £32 7s 6d that the Superb Handling will cost you. In a day or two I hope to explain about the old letters which are inserted in some of the books by way of forgotten book-marks, every one of them an exquisite piece of forgery. Order your copy now!

* * *

BOOK HANDLING

I PROMISED to say a little more about the fourth, or Superb, grade or book handling.

The price I quoted includes the insertion in not less than ten volumes of certain old letters, apparently used at one time as bookmarks, and forgotten. Each letter will bear the purported signature of some well-known humbug who is associated with ballet, verse-mouthing, folk-dancing, wood-cutting, or some other such activity that is sufficiently free from rules to attract the non-brows in their swarms. Each of the letters will be a flawless forgery and will thank A.B., the owner of the book, for his 'very kind interest in our work', refer to his 'invaluable advice and guidance', his 'unrivalled knowledge' of the lep-as-lep-can game, his 'patient and skilful direction of the corps on Monday night', thank him for his very generous—too generous—subscription of two hundred guineas, 'which is appreciated more than I can say'. As an up-to-the-minute inducement, an extra letter will be included free of charge. It will be signed (or purport to be signed) by one or other of the noisier young non-nationals who are honouring our beautiful land with their presence. This will satisfy the half-ambition of the majority of respectable vulgarians to maintain a second establishment in that somewhat congested thoroughfare, Queer Street.

The gentleman who are associated with me in the Dublin WAAMA League have realised that this is the off-season for harvesting the cash of simple people through the medium of the art-infected begging letter, and have turned their attention to fresh fields and impostures new. The latest racket we have on hands is the Myles na gCopaleen Book Club. You join this and are spared the nerve-racking bother of choosing your own books. We do the choosing for you, and, when you get the book, it is *ready-rubbed*, ie, subjected free of charge to our expert handlers. You are spared the trouble of soiling and mauling it to give your friends the impression that you can read. An odd banned book will be slipped in for those who like conversation such as:—

'I say, did you read this, old man?'
'I'm not terribly certain that I did, really.'
'It's banned, you know, old boy.'
'Ow.'

There is no nonsense about completing a form, asking for a brochure, or any other such irritation. You just send in your guinea and you immediately participate in this great cultural uprising of the Irish people.

CONSTRUCTIVE CRITICISM

Occasionally we print and circulate works written specially for the Club by members of the WAAMA League. Copies are sent out in advance to well-known critics, accompanied by whatever fee that is usually required to buy them. We sent one man ten bob with a new book and asked him to say that once one takes the book up one cannot leave it down. The self-opinionated gobdaw returned the parcel with an impudent note saying that his price was twelve and sixpence. Our reply was immediate. Back went the parcel with twelve and sixpence and a curt note saying that we were accepting the gentleman's terms. In due course we printed the favourable comment I have quoted.

But for once we took steps to see that our critic spoke the truth. The cover the volume was treated with a special brand of invisible glue that acts only when subjected to the heat of the hands. When our friend had concluded his cursory glance through the work and was about to throw it away, it had become practically part of his physical personality. Not only did the covers stick to his fingers, but the whole volume began to disintegrate into a viscous mess of treacly slime. Short of having his two arms amputated, putting the book down was an impossibility. He had to go round with the book for a week and submit to being fed like a baby by his maid. He got rid of the masterpiece only by taking a course of scalding hot baths that left him as weak as a kitten.

That's the sort of customers we of the WAAMA League are.

Letters have been pouring in in shoals (please notice that when it is a question of shoals of letters they always pour) regarding the book-handling service inaugurated by my Dublin WAAMA League. It has been a great success. Our trained handlers have been despatched to the homes of some of the wealthiest and most ignorant in the land to maul, bend, bash, and gnaw whole casefuls of virgin books. Our printing presses have been turning out fake Gate Theatre and Abbey programmes by the hundred thousand, not to mention pamphlets in French, holograph letters signed by George Moore, medieval playing cards, and the whole paraphernalia of humbug and pretence.

There will be black sheep in every fold, of course. Some of our handlers have been caught using their boots, and others have been found thrashing inoffensive volumes of poetry with horsewhips, flails, and wooden clubs. Books have been savagely attacked with knives, daggers, knuckle-dusters, hatchets, rubber-piping, razor-blade-potatoes, and every device of assault ever heard of in the underworld. Novice handlers, not realising that tooth-marks on the cover of a book are not accepted as evidence that its owner has read it, have been known to train terriers to worry a book as they would a rat. One man (he is no longer with us) was sent to a house in Kilmainham, and was later discovered in the Zoo handing in his employer's valuable books to Charlie the chimpanzee. A country-born handler 'read' his books beyond all recognition by spreading them out on his employer's lawn and using a horse and harrow on them, subsequently ploughing them in when he realised that he had gone a little bit too far. Moderation, we find, is an extremely difficult thing to get in this country.

OUR NEW SERVICE

That, however, is by the way. A lot of the letters we receive are from well-off people *who have no books*. Nevertheless, they want to be thought educated. Can we help them, they ask?

Of course. Let nobody think that only book-owners can be smart. The Myles na gCopaleen Escort Service is the answer.

Why be a dumb dud? Do your friends shun you? Do people cross the street when they see you approaching? Do they run up the steps of strange houses, pretend they live there and force their way into the hall while you are passing by? If this is the sort of a person you are, you must avail yourself today of this new service. Otherwise, you might as well be dead.

OUR SERVICE EXPLAINED

Here is how it happened. The WAAMA League has had on its hands for some time past a horde of unemployed ventriloquists who have been beseeching us to get them work. These gentlemen have now been carefully trained and formed in a corps to operate this new escort service.

Supposing you are a lady and so completely dumb that the dogs in the

street do not think you are worth growling at. You ring up the WAAMA
League and explain your trouble. You are pleased by the patient and
sympathetic hearing you get. You are instructed to be in attendance at
the foyer of the Gate Theatre that evening, and to look out for a tall,
distinguished-looking gentleman of military bearing attired in immaculate
evening dress. You go. You meet him. He advances towards you smiling,
ignoring all the other handsome baggages that litter the place. In an
instant his moustaches are brushing your lips.

'I trust I have not kept you waiting, Lady Charlotte,' he says pleasantly.
What a delightfully low, manly voice!

'Not at all, Count,' you answer, your voice being the tinkle of silver
bells. 'And what a night it is for Ibsen. One is in the mood, somehow.
Yet a translation can never be quite the same. Do you remember that
night . . . in Stockholm . . . long ago?'

THE SECRET

The fact of the matter is, of course, that you have taken good care to
say nothing. Your only worry throughout the evening is to shut up and
keep shut up completely. The trained escort answers his own manly questions in a voice far pleasanter than your own unfeminine quack, and gives
answers that will astonish the people behind for their brilliance and
sparkle.

There are escorts and escorts according to the number of potatoes you
are prepared to pay. Would you like to score off your escort in a literary
argument during an interlude? Look out for further information on this
absorbing new service.

'Well, well, Godfrey, how awfully wizard being at the theatre with
you!'

'Yes, it *is* fun.'

'What have you been doing with yourself?'

'Been trying to catch up with my reading, actually.'

'Ow, good show, keep in touch and all that.'

'Yes, I've been studying a lot of books on Bali. You know?'

'Ballet is terribly bewitching, isn't it? D'you like Petipa?'

'I'm not terribly sure that I do, but they seem to have developed a
complete art of their own, you know. Their sense of décor and their general
feeling for the plastic is quite marvellous.'

'Yes, old Dérain did some frightfully good work for them; for the Spectre, I think it was, actually. Sort of grisaille, you know.'

'But their feeling for matière is so profound and . . . almost brooding. One thinks of Courbet.'

'Yes, or Ingres.'

'Or Delacroix, don't you think?'

'Definitely. Have you read Karsavina?'

'Of course.'

'Of course, how stupid of me. I saw her, you know.'

'Ow, I hadn't realised that she herself was a Balinese.'

'Balinese? What *are* you driving at?'

'But—'

'But—'

EXPLANATION

This ridiculous conversation took place recently in an Irish theatre. The stuff was spoken in loud voices so that everybody could hear. It was only one of the many fine things that have been done by the Dublin WAAMA League's Escort Service. The League's horde of trained ventriloquists can now be heard carrying out their single-handed conversations all over the city and in the drawing-rooms of people who are very important and equally ignorant. You know the system? If you are very dumb, you hire one of our ventriloquists to accompany you in public places, and he does absolutely all the talking. The smart replies which you appear to make will astonish yourself as much as the people around you.

The conversation I have quoted is one of the most expensive on the menu. You will note that it contains a serious misunderstanding. This makes the thing appear extraordinarily genuine. Imagine my shrewdness in making the ventriloquist misunderstand what he is saying himself! Conceive my guile, my duplicate duplicity, my play on ignorance and gullibility! Is it any wonder that I have gone into the banking business?

SUFFERERS HELPED

I want now to turn to something rather more important. Some ladies have approached me for advice. They are in trouble with their ballet. They are too fat to lep the requisite six feet and have been sternly warned that they will be expelled from the corps unless they can show better 'altitude'—the latter a technical term that is used by Dublin teachers. Could I help them?

'Yes, yes, yes. The 'Myles' Patent Ballet Pumps meet and demolish this difficulty. Each shoe is fitted with three diminutive land mines, one in the heel and one in each side of the front foot. If you give a little hop and take care to land on one mine (e.g., land with the full weight on the ball of the foot or the heel) the mine will go off and you will be sent flying

after

THE "MYLES" PATENT BALLET PUMPS

through the air with the greatest of ease. When you land, there is another explosion and away up with you again. If you don't want a second super-lep, you simply take care to land on the spent or exploded mine, and there you are. The pumps ensure at least six terrific jumps in the one performance and refills, of course, can be had very cheaply. The audience may think it strange that a dancing piece should be punctuated by loud detonations followed by smoke and the acrid stench of dynamite and gun-powder, but they will not mind if they are assured that it is the usual thing in Russia. Your foot, of course, is protected by a steel shield, but I am afraid the stage—

The Plain People of Ireland : That's a fine looking lump of a girl. What's her address?

Myself : I was wondering how long I'd have to wait for that question. Her address is none of your business.

But I am afraid the stage will be full of holes. I have for disposal a limited number of cork bungs suitable for stopping up the holes, price four shillings per dozen while they last. Bungs, pumps and all in a presentation casket with a suitable greeting card, twenty-eight bob, post free.

Remind me to come back to this subject.

* * *

'HEAR YOU were at old Lebensold's bottle do the other night. How was it, sticky and all that?'

'Pretty average grim, actually. Old Peter Piper was there.'

'Not that intoxicatingly witty painter person?'

'Sorry, one hadn't thought of him as a painter, actually. His work irritates one, you know, so derivative and all that.'

'I do quite definitely agree, but personally I trace his influences more in sorrow than in anger.'

'You do mean more in Seurat than in Ingres, old thing, I s'ppowse.'

This is just a sample of the very special dialogues that our WAAMA League ventriloquist escorts have prepared for the round of Christmas parties. The extra charge is paltry.

And do not think that an escort will humiliate you by making you crack smart jokes like the one above after it has already been cracked at several other parties. Each service is exclusive. The same build-up will be retained (you can't have everything different) but the names in the last line will be changed. For instance, if the 'conversation' is on a philosophic topic, the names will be Suarez and Engels. If on a literary topic, Thoreau and Béranger. And so on, until every reference book and guide to this and that has been ransacked.

Mark your envelope 'Christmas Escort' and enclose two pounds.

SERIOUS SITUATION

Desperate is the only word that will do when it comes to describing the latest developments of the WAAMA League Escort Service. Several 'incidents' (using the word practically in the Japanese sense) have occurred in recent weeks, and it is now practically certain that we may expect unsavoury court sequels. Such a prospect makes me shudder, because the presence of even one small Escort in the High Court could lead to unheard of complications. Soon the nation may be faced with a vast constitutional crisis arising from pronouncements made (or, at all events, distinctly heard to have been made) by the princes of the bench and all sorts of lesser judicial dignitaries. I am afraid the astonishment on His Honour's own face will not be accepted as evidence to the contrary. Nor will a plea of gross-feasaunce be valid either.

Briefly, the ranks of my respectable and loyal Escorts have been infiltrated by cheats and disaffected elements who have, however, surpassing competence at the game of voice-throw. Extraordinary utterances have been made in public places, but nobody knows for certain who made them. Worse, intelligent and perfectly genuine remarks made by dowdy young women have been completely ignored by the person to whom they were addressed, whose first instinct is to turn round and search the faces of inoffensive strangers to find the 'genuine' speaker.

I will have more to say on this matter in a day or two.

* * *

THE ESCORT MESS

THE TROUBLE I referred to the other day began like this. A lady dumbbell hired out what she took to be a genuine WAAMA League Escort, and went with him to the Gate Theatre. Before the play and during the first interval dozens of eavesdroppers were astounded at the brittle cut and thrust of the one-man conversation. The lady herself, who barely knew how to ask for her porridge, was pleased at the extraordinary silence that was won by her companion's conversational transports. Quite suddenly he said loudly:

'By the way, old girl, is that your old woman's dress you are wearing tonight?'

Simultaneously, the unfortunate client found a printed card shoved under her nose. It read:

'Don't look round, don't move, and don't scream for the police. Unless you sign on the dotted line promising to pay me an extra fiver for tonight, I will answer in the affirmative, and then go on to talk about your wretched tinker-woman's blouse. Play ball and nobody will be hurt. Beware! Signed, the Black Shadow.'

The poor girl, of course, had no alternative but to accept the proffered pencil and scrawl her name. Instantly she was heard to say in her merry twinkling voice:

'Really, Godfrey, it's the first time I ever wore the same gown twice, why must you be so quaint! One must make forty guineas go a bit further nowadays, you know, tightening the belt and all that.'

WORSE TO COME

After the show there was an extraordinary scene in the foyer. The lady's husband called to fetch her home, and was immediately presented with her IOU by the 'Escort'. The demand for £5 out of the blue made his face the colour of war-time bread. He roared at his wife for an explanation. Floods of tears and mutterings was the best she could do. Then the husband rounded on the escort and denounced him as one who preyed on women, an extortionist, and a blackmailer of the deepest dye.

'And you over there with the whiskey face on you,' he added, apparently addressing a well-known and respected member of the justiciary, 'I don't like you either, and I've a damn good mind to break your red neck!'

The flabbergasted jurist (not that he was one whit less flabbergasted than the excited husband) turned the colour of cigar-ash and ran out into the street in search of a Guard. In his absence the husband began to insult the wife of another bystander and to 'dar and double-dar' her companion to hit him. This favour was no sooner asked for than received. The unobtrusive 'Black Shadow' gallantly ran forward and picked up the prostrate figure, adroitly extracting in the process every item of silver and notes in his pockets. It was a chastened warrior that was delivered in due course into the arms of the rain-glistening Guard.

All this, I need hardly say, is only a beginning. Horrible slurs on our civilisation were to follow.

THOSE ESCORTS

LET ME give some further details of the Escort mess I mentioned the other day. When it became generally known that a non-union man had succeeded in extracting a five-pound note from a client by menaces, hordes of unscrupulous ventriloquists descended upon the scene and made our theatre foyers a wilderness of false voices, unsaid remarks, anonymous insults, speakerless speeches and scandalous utterances which had no known utterer. Every second person wore a blank flabbergasted expression, having just offered some gratuitous insult to a stranger, or, perhaps, received one. Of course, blows were exchanged. Innocent country visitors coming to the theatre for the first time, and unaware of the situation could scarcely be expected to accept the savage jeers of some inoffensive bystander. Nor was the boot always on the same foot. The visitor's first impression of our intellectual theatres was all too frequently a haymaker in the belly, the price of some terrible remark he was heard to have made as he pushed in through the door.

Practised theatre-goers have trained themselves to listen for the almost imperceptible little pause between the genuine answer to a question and the bogus addendum of some ill-disposed ventriloquist. Thus:

'Have a cigarette?'

'No, thanks (pause), you parrot-clawed, thrush-beaked, pigeon-chested clown!'

'Do you like the play, Miss Plug? (pause) I'm only asking for politeness, because how an illiterate slut like you would presume to have an opinion on anything is more than I can understand!'

'The first act was wizard, actually. (Pause). There's egg on your tie, you pig!'

And so on, I regret to say.

MOREOVER

Several people prefer to remain inside at intervals nowadays. They are afraid of their lives of what they might blurt out if they ventured forth for a little air. This means, of course, putting up with the quieter and more deadly snake-bites of the seated malcontents, living in a phantom world of menacing mumble, ghost-whisper, and anonymous articulations of the most scandalous character, not to mention floods of threatening postcards. This sort of thing:

'Slip me a pound or I will see that you ask the gentleman beside you where he got the money to pay for his seat. Beware! Do not attempt to call for help! Signed, The Grey Spider.'

'Empty everything in your handbag into my right-hand coat pocket and make sure that nobody sees you doing it! Otherwise you will spend the evening plying strangers with salacious conundrums, even in the middle of the play. Don't think too hard of me, we all have to live. I have a wife and ten children. I do this because I have to. Signed, The Firefly.'

'Pay me 25s instantly or I will make a holy show of you. Be quick or you're for it. No monkey work! Signed, The Hooded Hawk.'

'This is a stick-up. Slip off that ring and drop it in the fold of my trousers. Otherwise you are going to heckle the players in the next act and think of what Hilton will have to say. Signed, The Mikado.'

This is merely the background of this ramp. What happened afterwards is another day's story. Just imagine Lord Longford saying: 'Has anybody here got a handball? I challenge any man here to a moonlight game above in the gardens, against the gable of the Nurses' Home!'

*   *   *

'PUT FIVE single bank-notes in an envelope and stick the envelope under your seat with chewing gum before you leave the theatre for the first interval. Stay out for at least ten minutes. No monkey-work, mind. Fail me in this and I will fix your hash for you. Signed, the Green Mikado.'

The somewhat scared lady who showed me this mysterious missive at the Abbey the other night asked me what she was to do. Naturally, I counselled courage and no truck with the evil voices that were infesting the national theatre like plague-nits in a rat's back. I promised her the assistance of my genuine WAAMA League Escorts, in ever-growing volume, until the stream became a torrent. Grievous and sombre as the prospect was, I assured her, our mighty and illimitable resources would be marshalled towards the common-end. I then telephoned for my ace-escort. His wife said that he was out, but that she would send a message to him. I knew that he had no wife. He arrived just as the curtain was going up.

DRAMATIC INCIDENT

My lady friend had bravely ignored the threat and all of us sat down for the second act with some little trepidation. Just how would the dread Mikado strike? What did he mean by his threat to settle my friend's hash? I was waiting every moment to hear her make some horrible remark, of which she would be as innocent as the child unborn.

Quite suddenly the blow fell. It happened that there was a lengthy pause in the play where the story had reached a stage of crisis. A pause, but not silence. A player standing on the left of the stage electrified the audience by saying:

'Do you know, I have been wondering all night who in the name of Pete that fat cow in the fur coat is. The one second from the left in the third row!'

I turned to my own escort, thunderstruck.

'It's all right,' he whispered. 'Your lady friend is fifth from the right. The addendum was mine. I was expecting this. It is common Leipzig practice.'

Meanwhile, the unknown victim was being assisted out, the theatre was in uproar, the curtain had been rung down and the livid husband was already on his way behind the scenes to ask the reason why.

* * *

HORRIBLE DEVELOPMENTS have taken place in the Escort scandal. One particular theatre has become a bedlam of 'voices' and coarse badinage, notwithstanding the foolish rule of the management that 'no one who looks like a ventriloquist is to be admitted.' If you say something, no one will believe that you said it. Even a simple 'what-time-is-it?' simply evokes a knowing smile and an involuntary search of the nearest bystander's countenance; that or some extraordinary reply like 'Pie-face!' 'Who wants to know?' or 'Time we were rid of a hook like you!'

Meanwhile, decent people are taking steps to protect their interests. I was at a play the other night and could not help overhearing a scandalous monologue that was apparently being recited by my neighbour on the right, a very respectable-looking elderly man. I watched him through the corner of my eye and saw the hand go into an inside pocket. Was he searching for his card? Was he The Black Dragon about to shove some printed threat under my nose? Yes, yes, the small white card was in his claw! In a second it was held adroitly for my gaze. Imagine my astonishment when I read it:

> 'I give you my solemn word of honour that I am a civil servant and that the appalling language that you hear coming from me is being uttered by some other person. Signed, JUST A MINOR STAFF OFFICER.'

You see the point? He was afraid to *say* this. Because if he did, his explanation would be instantly followed up with a coarse insult to my wife, who was sitting beside me.

EACH WITH HIS OWN CARD

I had further evidence of this later in the foyer. I was standing smoking when a small gentleman said to me: 'Excuse me for addressing a stranger, but I cannot help assuring you that it is only with the greatest difficulty that I restrain myself from letting you have a pile-driver in your grilled steak and chips, me bucko?' Instantly he produced a card and handed it to me:

> 'So help me, I am a crane-driver from Drogheda, and I have not opened my beak since I came in tonight. Cough twice if you believe me. Signed, NED THE DRIVER.'

I coughed and walked away. Just for fun I said to a lady who was standing near: 'Hello, hag! How's yer ould one?' Her reply was the sweet patient smile that might be exchanged between two fellow-sufferers from night starvation. What a world!

Next day I want to tell you about the lady who hired out two Escorts, thinking that each would keep the other down.

A CLASH AT HEADQUARTERS

THERE WAS HELL and holy bedlam at a recent meeting of the inner council of the Myles na gCopaleen WAAMA League. Our horde of literary ventriloquists sent in a demand for more pay. I agreed to hear a deputation from them, although determined to take my stand on Order 83 and to die rather than concede a blue farthing. They were barely in the room when I heard myself saying: Well, gentlem'n, I'm not surprised to see you, I may say right away that I recognise that your wages are ridiculously low and that an increase of fifty per cent is the least I would have the effrontery to offer you.

Before I had recovered from my astonishment, the spokesman said that such a response was disappointing, but that they were prepared to accept the increase under protest and without prejudice to their right to re-open the matter after consultation with their union. Then they filed out. The whole matter was over and done with before I had an opportunity of opening my beak. I mention the humiliating episode only because I see in it the idea for a new and exclusive WAAMA League service. Why not make my ventriloquists a bulwark of the Trade Union movement? Why not use their unique gifts to bring the parasite boss class to heel? Why not arrange beforehand, beyond yea or nay, that you will get the answer you are looking for? I'm talking to Mr O'Shannon.

* * *

My little engraving today is intended to help you through life. It shows, and very plainly, too, how to cross a river without letting your top hat get wet. You use your cane, see. Of course, you are finished if a clap of rain comes when you are in mid-stream. All this is surrealist stuff. The

Senegalese tiger will eat the tri-coloured bread. Observe that small cottage in the picture. It is an old Land League cabin. Valuation: On land, 15s; on other hereditaments, 13s. Arrears of rates payable to the County Council, £84 8s 0d. A tall farmer is sitting inside the cottage, sucking his hollow tooth. His wife, daughter, and nine strong sons are in Amerikey. There is not a stick of furniture in the house, no fire, no food, no other living thing, unless you want to count eleven gaunt rats. But the man is happy, he smiles to himself and keeps fiddling absently for a watch-chain that is long gone. A sharp fox's smile flits on his old face. He is undoubtedly suffering from an incurable disease. There are weals on his legs from the whipping of the wind, his trousers have no seat. Long-standing suppurations of the joints have elongated his thin fingers. But he is happy, his mind is pleased. He is a member of WAAMA.

A recent visit to the 'Plough and the Stars' set me thinking. Here is the old play re-vitalised and re-done by new players. It is better, perhaps, but different. Could it not be ordained that a play shall be played by the same players so long as they live? If after the years one or two have died, a brief programme note could explain the absence of the missing characters and the remaining players could work in suitable gags. 'Ah, sure it was here poor ould Fluther used to come in the good ould days, the Lord be good to him, the place has never been the same since he went.' Picture the Covey as an old man of seventy, the sole survivor of the original caste, trying desperately to carry on the play single-handed, muttering all sorts of explanations and blessings on the departed in between his own lines.

Possibly when the last player has gone to his reward, I might be prepared to hear of an entirely new company being recruited to do the play. But not until then.

AT THE PLAY

'To within five minutes of the fall of the curtain on the first act people were streaming into the reserved seats, requesting those already seated to divulge the numbers of the seats they were occupying, to arise to let them squeeze past, and frequently to arise again to let them struggle back on their discovering they had entered the wrong row and invariably the wrong end. The stage was completely blocked from the view of those behind; the tip-up seats were banged up and down, and the 'tut-tuts' 'shushes' and more robust imprecations frustrated all hopes of listening to the play.'

From a letter to the *Irish Times*.

Yes, yes. I know. I have been campaigning on this matter for many years. Please see my design for a doorless theatre in the 'Irish Engineer and Builder', June 1933. My idea is that the patron should approach his seat through a trap-door situated where he keeps his feet when seated. The patrons approach the building through a cellar and locate their seats before they enter the theatre at all. They then mount velvet-runged ladders and reach their seats with the minimum fuss and interference. Take your stand at the back of such a theatre and watch the audience arriving. There is no door, entrance or exit of any kind. All is silence and soft light. After a time you hear a gentle click and, hey-presto, a solitary bald head has appeared in the middle of the parterre. One by one, heads appear silently throughout the vast auditorium. The usual hot-tempered, wrangling about seats and ticket stubs is going on hell for leather in the cellar, but not a word of it reaches the sacred cathedral of the drayma.

Occasionally, if you like, a wit will book a seat and hoist a sack of potatoes instead of mounting the ladder himself. This will not make much difference unless it is done on a large scale. A 'house' that is composed mainly of solemn sacks of spuds would probably have a bad effect on the players and even offend a certain type of female playgoer, who is fastidious about what she is asked to sit beside. The knobby shoulder of a bag of Kerrs Pinks would not appeal to many ladies, excepting possibly our hand-ful of native Marxy-arxies, the little girls who read what they are told to read by the Left Book Club. But please excuse such a boring digression.

ANOTHER THING

Incidentally, I don't know that it is fair to complain about the row made by an audience without also adverting to the clatter that comes not in-frequently from the stage. Often in the theatre I can hardly hear myself talking or assuring my doxy that so-and-so is the same fellow that played so-and-so in so-and-so, he's very good, he's a civil servant in the Depart-ment of Agriculture, I met a sister of his in Skerries, and so on. Actors should conduct themselves like the rest of us and practise the unobtrusive intonation of the gentleman.

As regards the correspondent's other complaint about loud feeding during the course of an important play, this can be got over by hoisting trays of grub through the trap-doors at half-time. The humiliating exodus for whiskey (how is it so few can stand a play cold sober?) could also be prevented by sending up rubber tubes through which our middle-aged sucklings could draw their golden pap without leaving their seats and inconveniencing eccentric people who don't drink.

And think of this. You are sitting comfortably in your seat when you feel some ignorant clown (too lazy to look carefully at the number on his ticket) pushing his way up through *your* trap-door. Lift your feet quickly off it until his head is halfway up. Then smash the trap-door down with every ounce of weight and strength you can command. Listen for the remote thud of his falling body then resume giving your attention to Micheál.

Excuse me.

Round to the Gaiety there last week (I say 'round' because I live on the NCR and my approach was necessarily more circuitous than tangential) to see a piece of Mr Mac Liammóir's entitled—if memory fools me not— 'The Packed Ewer of Doreen Grey'. There was not much in it that I would criticise. Or should I say criticize? For the piece was described in the programme as 'a dramatization of Oscar Wilde's only Novel'. Wilde I never met; though the father and I were close friends in the early daze.

One thing rather puzzles me. Wilde wrote a number of plays and also this 'only' novel. Unless he was mad, he must have intended to write 'Doreen Gay' *as a novel*, otherwise he would have done what was for him the customary thing—written it as a play. Since, however, a man of the calibre of Mr Mac Liammóir does not hesitate to reverse Wilde's judgment in this regard, I fear we are faced (unless we also are mad—a thing that would not astonish me in the least) with the theory that Wilde fully intended to write it as a play. He couldn't think of the word, went ahead writing, and the thing turned out to be a novel!

But . . . is there not then a complementary theory? If Wilde mixed up the dissimilar modes of play and novel, how can we be satisfied that he did not intend to be a novelist only—that his plays were so written in error? If his novel (and we do not admit it is a novel, m'lud) if his novel be a play . . . em . . . a play *manqué*, then why not a novelization of his 'plays'?

I am terribly serious about this, because it involves a major problem in aesthetics. I go to an exhibition of 'paintings'. I am astounded by what I appear to see with my (own) eyes. The 'message' of this or that canvas eludes me, sometimes I am distressed by the frames. (You see, I too am an artist.) It does not follow that I denounce the author of these . . . these . . . practices. This painter, I say, can it be that he is a novelist? A poet? A worker in exquisite enamels? A musician in the manner of Ravel? For certain it is, that painter he is not.

There can be a *fusion* of artistic activities directed towards the communication of a single artistic concept. Example: a song—a poem sung to an air. But is artistic function interchangeable? Can a play be made a novel? Some people are chronically incapable of appreciating a thing in terms of itself. (My wife thinks I am a husband, for example—whereas, of course, I am a philosopher.) Show a cobbler a cow. Note his trade union obtuseness in relation to all kine! He simply cannot see how fine they are! 'Ah yes,' he will say, 'there's many a fine pair of shoes in that animal.' Show this or that patriot an equestrian statue and he will say 'Hah! Pretty big job that. That'd take the 24-foot ladder and a double-handled gauge-4 saw.' Tell a Hollywood man about the Kabbala, or the Koran, and he will ask you whether you could get 34 thousand feet out of it. Show a certain type of funny (?) writer something sincere, serious, and he will mutter: 'I wonder how we can make a laugh of this.'

You see? The problem is everywhere. No Irish farmer appreciates his young strapping son for the attractive healthy agricultural type he is (and must intrinsically remain). The Irish farmer sees his son as a potential Higher Executive Officer, Grade II, Temporary, Unestablished, full of grievances about bonus.

Do engine drivers, I wonder, eternally wish they were small boys?

I have not been to the Abbey since the decline set in, nor indeed has Blythe sent me the customary free pass since the day we had words about the terminology adopted in the program when plays in Irish are being presented. You have been there, of course, you have noticed that for the word 'stall' (costing 3/6, I think) they say: *steallai.*

My point was that such a term is recherché, difficult and obviously mined out of Dinneen and that there is no justification at all for using it when you have in Irish—every chisler in Dublin knows it—(PS. O'H. please note spelling of chisler) the simple word: *stól.*

I might as well be talking to the wall, of course, though this phrase has always seemed strange in view of the belief that walls have ears. Equally fruitless was another effort I made about the title of the theatre. They call it 'Amharclann na Mainistreach', although everybody knows that 'mainistir' means monastery. Do they not then know the Irish for 'abbey'? Are they too stuck-up to ask some one who does?

It follows from the opening sentence above that I have not seen Mr Tomelty's play, 'The End House'. I couldn't go, of course—it would never do to hear theatre-going 'wits' (foyer-flies if you like) making terrible jokes about 'the house'.

'Was there a good house last night?'

'O just the same—the end house.'

A slogan that interests me immensely is that one that they came out with some months ago and still have despite its decrepit syntax—'Late-comers not admitted until end of First Act.' It has several undesirable implications. First, that every play must have not only acts but even a first act! (Nay, a First Act). What would, say, Rouault think of such unenterprise? Is it also suggested, forsooth, that every play must have a last act? I have several plays (opens drawer, points in, hastily covers half-exposed bottle, slams drawer shut) and competent people who have read them certify that there is neither beginning nor end to them. Some of them have no characters—I did not say *character*, mind—some are without 'climaxes', 'plots' and other dreary journeyman paraphernalia. As for Aristotle's unities of thyme, plaice and auction—faugh! There are enough earnest souls observing *them*, we have a plenitude of knaves tricking with rules made by people who have not had the advantage of . . . of . . . being present for a couple of thousand years.

The second deplorable implication of the 'late-comer' slogan is that while those who are in at the beginning will not be disturbed during the first act they will not necessarily be undisturbed during subsequent acts. You can't barge in in the middle of the first act but you can arrive in the middle of the second or third act, start tuning the piano, decide you haven't enough light and stagger out with the thing on your back. What they really mean, you say, is 'Patrons not admitted between the acts.' But not quite. Because if that were the rule, nobody would ever get in. The . . . interval, shall we call it, before the first act is not, within the meaning of the statute, 'between the acts.'

The Abbey should think of a more precise and literate slogan, something catchy—like this:

The National Theatre Society
Likes promptness and sobriety,
No patrons will be admitted
Unless promptly stalled (or pitted).

The real trouble is, of course, that too many of the patrons have learnt their manners from characters on the Abbey stage. *Gach éan mar a adhbha!*

The Brother

THE BROTHER is making a great job of the landlady.

I beg your pardon?

Says he'll have her on her feet in another week.

I do not understand.

She was laid up, you know.

Is that a fact?

Ah, yes, she got a very bad attack on New Year's Day. The rheumatism was at her for a long time. The brother ordered her to bed, but bedamn but she'd fight it on her feet. The brother took a very poor view and said she'd be a sorry woman. And, sure enough, so she was. On New Year's Day she got an attack that was something fierce, all classes of stabbing pains down the back. Couldn't move a hand to help herself. Couldn't walk, sit or stand.

I see.

Of course, the brother took command as quick as you'd order a pint. Ordered the whole lot out of the digs for the night, sent for the married sister and had the landlady put to bed. A very strict man for doing things the right way, you know, although he's not a married man himself. O, very strict.

That is satisfactory.

Well, the next day she was worse. She was in a fierce condition. All classes of pains in the knees, knuckles swollen out and all this class of thing. Couldn't get her breath right, either, wheezing and moaning there inside in the bed. O, a desperate breakdown altogether.

No doubt a doctor was sent for?

Sure that's what I'm coming to man. The unfortunate woman was all on for calling in Doctor Dan. A son of the father, you know, round the corner, a nice young fellow with all classes of degrees after his name. Well, I believe the brother kicked up a fierce row. Wouldn't hear of it at any price. Of course, the brother was always inclined to take a poor view of the doctors, never had any time for them at all.

I see.

If you want to hear the pay given out in right style, get the brother on to the doctors. Fierce language he uses sometimes. Says half of those lads never wash their hands. Now say there's some ould one down the road laid up with a bad knee. Right. She sends for the doctor. Right. But where are you in the meantime? You're laid up, too. You're inside in your bed with a bad cold. Right. You send for the doctor, too. Right. In he comes and takes your pulse and gives you some class of a powder. Next morning you're feeling grand. The cold is gone. Fair enough. You think you'll get up. You hop out of bed like a young one. The next minute you're on your back on the floor roaring out of you with all classes of pains. What's happened?

I fear I have no idea what's happened.

The knee is gone, of course. Your man has cured the cold, but given you a knee that's worse than the knee the ould one had. Be your own doctor, that's what the brother says, or get a good layman that understands first principles. That 'flu that was going round at the Christmas, the brother blames the doctors for that, too.

What happened the landlady?

O the brother started treatment right away. Stuck above in the bedroom half the day working away at her. Running up and down stairs with big basins of scalding water. Of course the brother believes that the whole secret is in the circulation. It's the blood all the time. Well do you know, the third day the landlady was very much improved.

That is remarkable.

Very . . . much . . . improved. But did the brother let her up?

I should not imagine so.

Not on your life man. O no. He still keeps working away at her and puts her on a special diet, milk and nuts and all this class of thing. And now she's nearly cured. The brother is going to let her up for a while on Sunday.

That is very satisfactory.

Of course the married sister was under the roof all the time, if you know what I mean.

I understand.

Ah yes, the brother has fixed up harder cases than that. Weren't you telling me that you had some class of a stiffness in one of your fingers?

I had.

Would you like to show it to the brother?

Thank you very much but the trouble has since cleared up.

I see. Well, any time you think you're not feeling right, you've only to say the word. No trouble at all. Begob, here's me 'bus.

Good-bye and thank you again.
Cheers now.

YES, INDEED

HELLO. Yes.

Ah, yes. Certainly.

Who? WHO?

Ah, not at all. No. No.

Begob he'd touch a man in a shroud for a tanner.

Cork? Yes. What?

WHAT?

I can't hear you.

I CAN'T HEAR YOU.

Yes, the wife is a Cork girl, a right flighty article. Yes. Let me know the whole story. Yes. See you at the smoker Saturday. Goodbye. Cheers. WHAT? No, I said Goodbye. GOODBYE!

These telephones are indistinct occasionally.

Yes, that was the brother. There's a new Guard moved into the station near the digs and the brother is having inquiries made. Who, where and what, you know. Show me your companions and I'll tell you what you are. He likes to know who he's living in the same street with. Believes in keeping his weather-eye on the Guards. *Necessitas compellibus*, you know. He's just had an inquiry put through to Cork.

I see.

He got a Guard transferred in 1924. Was lifting the little finger too much for the brother's taste.

I see. Quis custodiet ipsos custodes and so on.

The very thing. Do you know what I heard the brother once called? What?

'An Iron Disciplinarian.' It's a good job somebody's keeping the Guards right. Because, do you know what I'm going to tell you, they take a bit of watching. Of course there's a white and black sheep in every fold.

An acute and penetrating observation.

Yes. BEGOB HERE'S THE 'BUS. Cheers!

* * *

THE BROTHER had them all in stitches above in the digs the other night. *Is that a fact?*

Gob he was in right form. Sits down to his tea and has a go at the jam. Then he gives the old man a nudge and says he: Do you know, says he, it's well for that crowd Williams and Woods.

I see.

The old man, of course, only that the eyes do be movin' in his head you'd think he was a corpse. A desperate man for readin books and all that class of thing. Takes no notice of the brother at all. Then the teacher asks why. The landlady begins to laugh out of her, too well she knows the brother. Then the lad from the bank asks why. Begob in two ticks they were all laughing and waiting for the word from the brother. Of course, he goes on chawing and takes no notice.

I understand.

After a while he looks up. WHY IS IT WELL FOR WILLIAMS AND WOODS? BECAUSE, says he (and begob there wasn't a bit being touched or swallyed be this time) BECAUSE, says he, THEY GET MONEY FOR JAM! Well lookit. The roarin and laughin was something fierce. The old man begins to choke and the landlady laughs so much she takes her left hand away from her chest where she keeps it when she's drinkin tea. Not a smile out of your man the brother, of course. A face on him as long as a hare's back leg.

Most amusing. Your relative would do well to take up one or other of the music hall avocations or even consider writing humorous matter for the newspapers.

Ah yes, he is great sport when he is in form. And the great thing is this, that every joke is RIGHT if you know what I mean. The brother is very strict about that class of thing. The youngest baby in all Ireland could be there and no danger of anything that isn't right coming out in front of it. Yes. Well, here's where I lave yeh.

Bye bye.

* * *

PRAY CAST your eye across the street. Our mutual friend with the cap. Going down there for a quick one unless I'm very much mistaken. I have frequently observed you in converse with him. And I'll bet you a shilling that he talks to you about his brother because damn the thing else he can ever talk about to man or layman. Is he a personal friend?

I should classify him as an acquaintance.

Well I am glad to hear it because if you would take a tip you will make it your business to be on the other side of the street accidentally on purpose when you observe him on the distant horizon. Because do you know what

I am going to tell you, he's not the simple man that he lets on to be, faith he isn't, he was down in a certain public house one night last week with some hop-off-my-thumb from the County Wicklow on a rogue's errant with two softies that have a quarry out on the south side, the pair of them being bested out of their property by the two boyos with the kind assistance of General Whiskey and Major Porter, IOU's passing to and fro like a snowstorm, make me your partner, and you'll get five pounds a week for life and here, sign this, thanks very much. The Lord knows what the unfortunate men signed away, crooked drunk inside in the back snug and a certain detective that you know and that I know standing at the bar winking the other eye, waiting for his twenty-five per cent as usual, fresh and good-looking from getting five motor-cars across the border for a certain man in Phibsborough that I know and that you know. Faith now I would play cagey-cannon while that gentleman is in the offing because he would take the shirt off your back and put a cheaper one in its place and you would notice sweet nothing. Himself and his brother. I would not be surprised to hear that he has no brother at all.

That is a shocking thing to say.

That is my honest opinion, take it for what it is worth. I passed smarter boyos than that through my fingers, they get away with little with yours truly, I can smell them a mile off. 'That letter about the rates that you wrote to the papers was very well done, it was the best thing I read for a long time, could you lend me half a crown.' This class of thing. O faith many's a time he has tried it on. But I'm ready for him and ready for them all.

He never asked me for money.

Ah but give him time, give him time. When it comes you will find it will be a real knock. A five pound note if you please, the mother was taken bad and had to be brought off to Jervis Street, you'll have your money back on Thursday next at half-past two. Nolly may tango is the motto. 'I am unwilling to be touched.' Follow?

I understand.

And talking of hospitals, tell me this much. The good lady. Is she . . . ?

O very well, thanks very much.

Was it . . . ?

Yes, but it is all right now, she is feeling grand.

Well do you know, I am very glad to hear it because these things can be very awkward. Very awkward. Yes. And now let me put a question to you. What is your private opinion about this war or is it going to end at all in our time and generation?

I fear it is a world-wide upheaval the end of which no man can foresee.

Well I am with you there, truer word than that was never said. And do you know, it is a judgment from heaven on the world. There is a very bad class of young person going now, no time for anything but the dance halls and the pictures and the Lord knows what devilment. And they are all destroyed with this dole, they wouldn't work if you paid them. Well here we are. Would you join me in a small Redbreast to keep the life in us this cold day?

Thank you, I never drink before six.

And a wise rule for those that have their health. Goodbye to you and please remember me to the good lady.

I will indeed. Goodbye!

* * *

THE BROTHER has it all worked out.

What?

The war. How we can get through the war here in the Free State. I mean the rationing and brown bread and all that class of thing. The brother has a plan. Begob you'll be surprised when you hear it. A very high view was taken when it was explained in the digs the other night.

What is the nature of this plan?

It's like this. I'll tell you. We all go to bed for a week every month. Every single man, woman and child in the country. Cripples, drunks, policemen, watchmen—everybody. Nobody is allowed to be up. No newspapers, 'buses, pictures or any other class of amusement allowed at all. And no matter who you are you must be stuck inside in the bed there. Readin' a book, of course, if you like. But no getting up stakes.

That strikes me as a curious solution to difficulties in this dynamic iron age.

D'ye see, when nobody is up you save clothes, shoes, rubber, petrol, coal, turf, timber and everything we're short of. And food, too, remember. Because tell me this—what makes you hungry? It's work that makes you hungry. Work and walking around and swallying pints and chawin' the rag at the street corner. Stop in bed an' all you'll ask for is an odd slice of bread. Or a slice of fried bread to make your hair curly, says you. If nobody's up, there's no need for anybody to do any work because everybody in the world does be workin' for everybody else.

I see. In a year therefore you would effect a saving of twenty-five per cent in the consumption of essential commodities.

Well now I don't know about that, but you'd save a quarter of every-thing, and that would be enough to see us right.

But why get up after a week?

The bakers, man. The bakers would have to get up to bake more bread, and if wan is up, all has to be up. Do you know why? Because damn the bit of bread your men the bakers would make for you if the rest of us were in bed. Your men couldn't bear the idea of everybody else being in bed and them up working away in the bakery. The brother says we have to make allowances for poor old human nature. That's what he called it. Poor old human nature. And begob he's not far wrong.

Very interesting. He would do well to communicate this plan to the responsible Government department.

And you're not far wrong there yourself. Bye-bye, here's me bus!

I noticed an interesting reference to Handel in this newspaper recently. 'He died,' I read, 'on the anniversary of the first performance of his greatest Oratorio, and is fitly buried in the Poets' Corner of Westminster Abbey, for he is, indeed, the Milton of English musicians.'

That makes James Joyce the Don Bradman of English literature and Oscar Wilde the Constable of English music-hall.

* * *

INTERCHAT

WHO IS going to win beyond? Which of the pair would you back?

I do not know.

The brother says your man is going to win. But begob I don't know. It'll be a long time before your other man hands in his gun.

That is true.

Your man is smart, I'll agree with the brother there. And he doesn't take a jar, that's another thing that stands to him. And of course he bars the fags as well. But does that mean that your other man is a buff?

Scarcely.

Oh indeed begob it doesn't. It certainly does not. Because your other man gets up very early too. It wasn't yesterday or the day before your other man came up.

He has undoubtedly certain qualities of adroitness.

Of course the brother looks at it the other way. He is all for your man and never had any time for your other man. Says no good could ever come

out of the class of carry-on your other man has been at for the last ten years.
There's a lot in that, of course. The brother certainly put his finger on it
there. But it's not all on the wan side. Your man was up to some hooky
work in his time too.

No doubt.

There's a pair of crows in it. And I think your other man is six to four
on. Do you know why?

I do not.

Because he knows the place backwards, every lane and backyard in it.
Lived there all his life, why wouldn't he. And of course your man doesn't
know where the hell he is. And do you know why I wouldn't be sorry to
see your other man coming in first?

No.

Because it would be great gas to prove the brother wrong for once.
And you'll live to see it too. Because do you know what I'm going to tell
you?

What?

Your man is using the whip. Do you know that? YOUR MAN IS USING
THE WHIP.

Is that a fact?

I'm telling you now. Begob here's me 'bus. Cheers!

Bye bye.

The brother is having terrible trouble with the corns.

Is that a fact?

Ah yes. Sure the corns has nearly finished him with the ball-dancin.

Is that the way?

Not that he complains, of course. Word of complaint is a thing that
never passed his lips. Never was KNOWN to pass his lips. A great man for
sufferin in silence, the brother. Do you know what I'm going to tell
you?

No.

A greater MARTYR than the brother never lived. Do you know that?
Talk about PAINS! He's a great example to all of us.

How is that?

Number one, the eyes isn't right. Can't see where he's goin or who's
shoutin at him half the time. Number two, he does have all classes of
shakes in his hands of a mornin. Number three, he does have a very bad
class of a neuralgia down the left side of his jaw and a fierce backache in

the back as well. And of course the bag does be out of order half the time. But do you know a game he does be at?

I do not.

He does spend half the day eatin pills. He does have feeds of pills above in the digs.

I see.

And you do know why? Because he bars the doctors. He'd die roarin before he'd let them boys put a finger on him.

That is a singular prejudice.

And of course half the pills he does be swallyin is poison. POISON, man. Anybody else takin so many pills as the brother would be gone to the wall years ago. But the brother's health stands up to it. Because do you know he's a man with an iron constitution.

Is that a fact?

He's a man that would take pills all his life and not be killed by them. In wan night I seen him takin' three red pills, four white pills and a blue one. All on top of one another. Well of course a man that could do that could have a feed of arsenic for his breakfast and damn the feather it'd take out of him.

No doubt.

Cheers now.

*   *   *

I'VE A QUARE bit of news for you. The brother's nose is out of order.

What?

A fact. Some class of a leak somewhere.

I do not understand.

Well do you see it's like this. Listen till I tell you. Here's the way he's fixed. He starts suckin the wind in be the mouth. That's OK, there's no damper there. But now he comes along and shuts the mouth. That leaves him the nose to work with or he's a dead man. Fair enough. He starts suckin in through the nose. AND THEN DO YOU KNOW WHAT?

What?

THE—WIND GOES ASTRAY SOMEWHERE. Wherever it goes it doesn't go down below. Do you understand me? There's some class of a leak above in the head somewhere. There's what they call a valve there. The brother's valve is banjaxed.

I see.

The air does leak up into the head, all up around the brother's brains.

How would you like that? Of course, his only man is to not use the nose at all and keep workin' on the mouth. O be gob it's no joke to have the valve misfirin'. And I'll tell you a good one.

Yes?

The brother is a very strict man for not treatin himself. He does have crowds of people up inside in the digs every night lookin for all classes of cures off him, maternity cases and all the rest of it. But he wouldn't treat himself. Isn't that funny? HE WOULDN'T TREAT HIMSELF.

He is at one there with orthodox medical practice.

So he puts his hat on his head and talkes a walk down to Charley's. Charley is a man like himself—not a doctor, of course, but a layman that understands first principles. Charley and the brother do have consultations when one or other has a tough case do you understand me. Well anyway the brother goes in and is stuck inside in Charley's place for two hours. And listen till I tell you.

Yes?

When the brother leaves he has your man Charley in bed with strict orders not to make any attempt to leave it. Ordered to bed and told to stop there. The brother said he wouldn't be responsible if Charley stayed on his feet. What do you think of that?

It is very odd to say the least of it.

Of course Charley was always very delicate and a man that never minded himself. The brother takes a very poor view of Charley's kidneys. Between yourself, meself and Jack Mum, Charley is a little bit given to the glawsheen. Charley's little finger is oftener in the air than annywhere else, shure wasn't he in the hands of doctors for years man. They had him nearly destroyed when somebody put him on to the brother. And the brother'll make a job of him yet, do you know that?

No doubt.

Ah yes. Everybody knows that it's the brother that's keepin Charley alive. But begob the brother'll have to look out for himself now with the nose valve out of gear and your man Charley on his hands into the bargain.

Is there any other person to whom your relative could have recourse?

Ah, well, of course, at the latter end he'll have to do a job on himself. HAVE TO, man, sure what else can he do? The landlady was telling me that he's thinkin of openin himself some night.

What?

You'll find he'll take the razor to the nose before you're much older. He's a man that would understand valves, you know. He wouldn't be long puttin it right if he could get his hands at it. Begob there'll be blood in the bathroom anny night now.

He will probably kill himself.

The brother? O trust him to look after Number One. You'll find he'll live longer than you or me. Shure he opened Charley in 1934.

He did?

He gave Charley's kidneys a thorough overhaul, and that's a game none of your doctors would try their hand at. He had Charley in the bathroom for five hours. Nobody was let in, of course, but the water was goin all the time and all classes of cutthroats been sharpened, you could hear your man workin at the strap. O a great night's work. Begob here's me 'bus!

Bye bye.

* * *

HALF THE CROWD above in the digs are off to Arklow for a week Tursda. On their holliers, you know.

I see. Is your relative travelling also?

The brother? Not at all man. Yerrah not at all. Shure the brother can't leave town.

Is that a fact? Why not?

The brother has to stop in town for the duration of the emergency. The Government does be callin the brother in for consultations. Of course that's between you and me and Jack Mum. The brother gave a promise to a certain party not to leave town during the emergency. He has to stand by. Because if something happened that could only be fixed up be the brother, how could your men be chasin after him on the telephone down to Strand Street, Skerries, where he goes every year to the married sister's?

Admittedly it would be awkward.

Sure you couldn't have that, man. You can't run a country that way.

I agree.

You couldn't have that at all. And do you know what I'm going to tell you, if ould Ireland isn't kept out of this business that's goin on, it won't be the brother's fault. And all the time he'll keep the Guards right, too. The ould weather-eye never leaves them boyos, no matter what consultations he's called in on. They needn't think they can take it easy because he's busy. He has the eye at the present time on a certain boyo in plain clothes.

I see.

I was thinking of takin a week myself in August. Down as far as Bettys-town with Charlie. Would you say that'd be all right?

I think the nation would be reasonably safe, especially since your relative has undertaken to remain in the capital.

Begob I think you're right, I think I'll chance it. Here's me bus. Cheers.

* * *

THE BROTHER can't look at an egg.

Is that so?

Can't stand the sight of an egg at all. Rashers, ham, fish, anything you like to mention—he'll eat them all and ask for more. But he can't go the egg. Thanks very much all the same but no eggs. The egg is barred.

I see.

I do often hear him talking about the danger of eggs. You can get all classes of disease from eggs, so the brothers says.

That is disturbing news.

The trouble is that the egg never dies. It is full of all classes of microbes and once the egg is down below in your bag, they do start moving around and eating things, delighted with themselves. No trouble to them to start some class of an ulcer on the sides of the bag.

I see.

Just imagine all your men down there walking up and down your stomach and maybe breeding families, chawing and drinking and feeding away there, it's a wonder we're not all in our graves man, with all them hens in the country.

I must remember to avoid eggs.

I chance an odd one meself but one of these days I'll be a sorry man. Here's me Drimnagh 'bus, I'll have to lave yeh, don't do anything when your uncle's with you, as the man said.

Good bye.

If you keep this column reasonably clean and return it to me when used, I will allow you a halfpenny on it. Think not too ill of me, I am young, my nails are broken and it is years since I amused myself by rubbing them on slates.

* * *

I WAS OUT in a boat with the brother down in Skerries, where he's stopping with the married sister. On his holliers, you know. A great man for the sea, the brother.

Indeed?

Ah yes. If the brother had his way, of course, it's not here he'd be but off out with real sea-farin men, dressed up in oil-skins, running up and down ropes and all the rest of it.

I see.

The brother was givin out about the seals. 'Tumblers', he called them. The brother says all them lads should be destroyed.

That would be a considerable task.

They do spend the day divin and eatin mackerel. If them lads had their way, they wouldn't leave a mackerel in the sea for you and me or the man in the next street. They do swally them be the hundred, head an' all. And the brother says they do more than that—they do come out of the water in the middle of the night-time and rob gardens. You wouldn't want to leave any fancy tomato-plants around. And you wouldn't want to leave one of your youngsters out after dark, either, because your men would carry it off with them. The brother says they do take a great interest in the chislers. They do be barkin out of them during the day-time at chislers on the beach.

That is most interesting.

The brother says the seals near Dublin do often come up out of the water at night-time and do be sittin above in the trams when they're standin in the stables. And they do be upstairs too. Begob the brother says it's a great sight of a moonlight night to see your men with the big moustaches on them sittin upstairs in the trams lookin out. And they do have the wives and the young wans along with them, of course.

Is that a fact?

Certainly, man. The seals are great family people, always were. Well then the brother was showin me two queer lookin men with black and white feathers on them and black beaks, out sittin there in the water.

Two birds?

Two of the coolest customers I ever seen, didn't give a damn about us although we went near enough to brain them with the oars. Do you know the funny thing about them lads?

I do not.

Them lads takes a very poor view of dry land. Never ask to go near the land at all. They do spend their lives sittin on the sea, bar an odd lep into the air to fly to another part of it. Well do you know what I'm going to tell you, I wouldn't fancy that class of a life at all. Because how would you put in your time or what would you do with yourself, stuck there out on the water night an mornin? Sure them lads might as well be dead as have a life like that. Annyway, it wouldn't suit me and that's a certainty. Would *you* fancy it?

Scarcely, but then I am not a bird. Birds have ideas of their own.

Begob they've a poor time of it, say what you like, no comfort or right way of livin' at all. Sure they do have to lay their eggs out in the sea.

Do they?

Certainly they do. The brother says the mother-hen has some kind of pocket in under the wing. Nobody knows how she whips the egg into the pocket when she lays it. Do you know what the brother called it? ONE OF THE GREAT UNSOLVED MYSTERIES OF THE SEA.

I understand.

ONE OF THE GREAT UNSOLVED MYSTERIES OF THE SEA. And of course there wouldn't be anny need for anny mystery at all if they had the sense to land on the shore like anny other bird. That's what I'd do to lay me eggs if I had anny. But no, the shore is barred, they do take a very poor view of everything but the water. Begob, here's me 'bus. Cheers!

Good bye.

*   *   *

DID YOU ever meet our friend's dog?

Whose dog?

Your man's.

But whose?

The brother's.

No.

Well that animal's an extraordinary genius. Do you know what I'm going to tell you, he could take you out and lose you. There's nothing he can't do bar talk. And do you know what?

What?

Who said he can't talk?

I thought you said so yourself.

Don't believe a word of it man. The dog talks to the brother. He does be yarnin with the brother above in the digs of a Sunday when everybody's out at the first house of the pictures. Believe me or believe me not now.

Upon what subjects does this animal discourse?

Sure luckit. I seen meself on a day's walk with the brother off out in Howth last March. Your man was with us and the three of us went for a ramble.

Who was with you?

Arthur. The dog. Well here was I in front, suckin in the fresh air and exercisin meself and payin no attention. What happens? I hear the brother chattin away behind me and been answered back. Then the brothers gives a laugh at some joke d'other lad was after makin' Then there's more laughin and chattin. I look back but the brother's hidden be a bend. I wait there unbeknownst and I see the brother comin into sight laughin his head off and your man beside him gruntin' and growlin and givin chat out of him for further orders. Course I was too far away to hear what was goin on. And when the pair sees me, the laughin stops and the two gets serious. It wouldn't do, of course, to say annything to the brother about a thing like that. He wouldn't like that, you know. An extraordinary pair, Arthur and the brother.

I see.

But I'll tell you what takes me to the fair. Your men above in the park. The fellas that's tryin to hunt the deer into a cage. Sure the brother and Arthur could take charge of them animals, and walk every wan of them up to Doll Erin of a Monda mornin if there was anny need for them to go there.

I see.

Sure luckit here man, I seen meself out in Santry four years ago when the brother had Arthur out on sheepdog trials and I'll go bail no man ever seen a dog parcel up sheep the way Arthur done it. There was a hundred of them in it if there was wan. Did Arthur start jumpin and scootin about an' roarin out of him? Did he start bitin and snarlin, snawshilin and givin leps in the air with excitement?

I deduce that quite the contrary was the case.

O nothin like that atchall. Not a sound out of him but a short step this way, a step maybe that way, the nose down in the ground, the tail stuck sideways, just enough to put the fear of God into your men the sheep. You'll see the right ear go up. That means a sheep two hundred yards away is thinkin of makin a dash out. Does he do it after Arthur puts up the ear? He certainly does NOT.

I understand.

He stops where he is and he's a sound judge. But I got on to the brother about them deer. Why is it, says I, that you and Arthur don't take a walk up there some fine day and march the deer in instead of having your men above there makin exhibitions of themselves with their lassoos and five bar gates and bicycles? Do you know what the brother said?

I do not.

THE DEER, says the brother, IS MAN'S FRIEND. The deer is man's friend. That's what he said. And he's right. Because when did the deer harm you?

Never, I assure you.

And when did they take a puck at me?

Never.

When did they try to ate your men on the bicycles?

Never.

Then tell me why they're tryin to slaughter them.

I am sorry I do not know. I perceive my large public service vehicle approaching. Good bye.

Your bus? OK. Cheers.

* * *

DO YOU KNOW that picture by George Roll* that was banned be the gallery?

I think I understand your reference.

Well the whole thing was gone into in the digs the other night. The brother was layin' down the law about pictures and art and all this class of thing. The brother says that any picture done be a Frenchman must be right.

Admittedly there is a widely held opinion that the French excel in artistic pursuits.

The brother says the French do be at the art night and mornin'. They do have it for breakfast, dinner and tea.

Is that a fact?

The brother says some of them lads thinks nothing of being up in the middle of the night-time workin' away at the pictures. Stuck inside a room wearin' the hair off a brush. Very mad-lookin' stuff some of it is too, so the brother says. But very INTERESSTIN' stuff. O very interesstin'. Very . . . very . . . interesstin'.

I see.

Then other lads does be stuck below in cellars makin' statues. There's a quare game for you now. They do be down hammerin' away in the middle of the night-time.

Surely not the most healthy of occupations.

Ah, yes. Well then do you know what goes on in the mornin-time in a French house?

* Rouault. *See Criticism, Art Letters.*

I do not.

They do all come down for breakfast, ready to tuck into a damn fine feed of rashers and black puddin'. Starvin' with the hunger, do you understand, after been up all night workin' at the art. What happens?

I take it they eat their meal.

Notatall. In marches your man of the house with overalls on him. Will yez all come in here, says he, into this room, says he, till I show yez me new picture. This, of course, is something he was after runnin' up in the middle of the night-time. So in they all march and leave the grub there. And be the time they're finished lookin' at that, your man below in the cellar is roarin' out of him for them all to come down and take a look at what HE'S after doin'. Do you understand? No breakfast. But plenty of art, do you know.

That is a rare example of devotion to the things of the intellect.

The brother says it's what they call art for art's sake. Well then do you know what goes on on Sunda?

I do not.

The brother says that beyond in France they have a big palace be the name of the Tweeleries. The Tweeleries was built in the days of the French Revolution be Napolean Bonipart himself and built be slave labour too. None of your one and fourpence an hour with time and a half on Saherdas. Well annyway all around the Tweeleries they do have fancy gardens and parks. What would you say is in the gardens?

Root crops, one should hope, in keeping with these stern times.

I'll tell you what's in the gardens. The gardens is full of statues. And of a Sunda the Frenchmen do be walkin' around the gardens havin' a screw at the statues.

I see.

They do be up early in the mornin' waitin' for the gates to be opened. And then nothin'll do them all day only gawkin' out of them at the statues. They'll ask nothin' better than that. As happy as Larry lookin' at them first from this side and then that. And talkin' away in French to one another. And do you know why?

I do not.

Because the statues is art too. The brother says the statue is the highest form of art. And he's not far wrong because even look at the height of some of the ones we have ourselves above in the Phoenix Park.

The effigy of Nelson also ranks high.

Ah yes, great men for the art, the French. Sure the brother says a man told him they do be sellin' pictures in the streets. Here's me 'bus. Cheers now.

Cheers.

* * *

THE BROTHER is thinkin of goin up.

Going up what?

The brother is thinkin of standin.

Standing what? Drinks?

The brother is thinkin of having a go at the big parties.

Do you mean that your relative is considering offering himself as a candidate when a general election becomes due by reason of constitutional requirement?

The brother is thinkin of goin up at the elections.

I see.

Of course it's not the brother himself that is all mad for this game. He's bein pushed do you understand me. Certain influential parties is behind him. They're night and mornin' callin' to the digs and colloguin with the brother inside in the back-room with the brother givin orders for tea to be made at wan in the mornin'. Any amount of fat oul' fellas with the belly well out in front, substantial cattle-men be the look of them. No shortage of the ready there. And do you know what I'm going to tell you?

I do not.

It's not today nor yesterday this business started. Months ago didn't I catch the brother inside in the bed with the Intoxication Act they had all the talk about. He was havin' a rare oul' screw at it, burnin the light all night. Says I what's this I see, what's goin on here? Do you know what the answer was? Says he I'm makin—wait till you hear this—I'm makin, says he, COPIOUS NOTES. That's a quare one. Copious notes is what the brother was at in the bed.

I understand. Your relative no doubt realises that the study is the true foundation of statesmanship.

And I'll tell you a good wan. The brother has books under the bed. I seen them.

The love of books has been a beacon that has lighted the way in our darkest hour.

Sure wasn't the landlady getting on to the brother for havin the light on till four and five in the mornin. Of course the brother doesn't mind the landlady.

I see.

The brother takes a very poor view of the Labour Party. Cawbogues he calls them. And what else are they?

I do not know.

Not that the brother fancies the other crowd either. Begob wan day there came a collector to the digs lookin for election money. This is years back, of course. Well do you know what, he walked into it. Everybody thought the brother was out and the crowd in the digs was all for payin up and lookin pleasant. But begob the next thing the brother comes marchin down the stairs. I need'nt tell you what happened. Your man was humped out on his ear. A very strict person, the brother. He's not a man to get on the wrong side of.

I do not doubt it.

Well then the brother was workin away at figures. Do you know what it is, says he. I think I can see me way to pay every man woman and child in the country four pounds ten a week. That's a quare one. Four pounds ten and no stamp money stopped.

That is quite remarkable.

The brother was a bit worried about the ten bob for a day or two. But he got it right in the end. He'll be able to manage the four-ten. Begob I had to shake him be the hand when he told me the news. It'll be changed times when the brother's party gets in. And do you know what? Certain proof that the brother is goin places . . .

What?

The brother was down the kays the other day pricin' clawhammers.

An excellent omen.

Here's me bus. Cheers!

* * *

DO YOU know what it is, the brother's an extraordinary genius.

I do not doubt it.

Begob he had them all in a right state above in the digs.

Is that a fact?

Comes in wan night there, puts the bike in the hall and without takin off coat, cap or clips walks into the room, takes up the tea-pot, marches out with it without a word and pours the whole issue down the sink. You should see the face of her nibs the landlady, her good black market tay at fifteen bob a knock!

An extraordinary incident.

But then does your man come back and explain?

I should be astonished if he did.

O not a bit of it. Marches upstairs leavin the lot of them sittin there with the eyes out on pins. They do be easily frightened be the brother.

A natural reaction to this unusual personality.

Well annyway the brother is upstairs for half an hour washin and scrubbin himself and smokin fags in the bathroom. And the crowd below sitting there afraid to look at wan another, certain sure they were all poisoned and not knowin which was going to pass out first.

I see.

Well after a while the brother marches downstairs and gives strict orders that nobody is to drink any more water. Gives instructions to the landlady that there's to be no more tea made until further notice. The brother then goes out to the kitchen and makes a dose of stuff with milk and some white powder he had in the pocket and makes them all drink it. The whole lot might be dead only for the brother.

Your relative will no doubt be compensated elsewhere for his selfless conduct.

Well next mornin he's off on the bicycle up to the waterworks at Stillorgan and comes home with bottles full of water. He was above in the waterworks carrying out surveys and colloguin with the turncocks—never lettin on who he was, of course, just chattin and keepin th'oul eye open.

I understand.

And the crowd in the digs livin on custard and cocoa made with milk, the unfortunate landlady crucified for a cup of tea but afraid of her life to make a drop or even take wan look at the tap.

Quite.

Well annyway up with the brother to the bathroom with the bottles of water and he's stuck inside there for hours with the door locked. The brother was carryin out tests, d'y'understand.

I do.

Down he comes at eight o'clock, puts on the hat and coat and begob you should see the face. The brother was gravely concerned. Very gravely concerned. He doesn't look at anyone, just says, 'I'll have to see Hernon to-morrow.' Then out with him.

A most ominous pronouncement.

The next mornin the brother comes down in the blue suit and gives orders that if anybody calls he's above in the City Hall with Hernon and that he'll be back late and to take any message. Well do you know I never seen the digs so quiet after the brother left. And that night at tea-time there wasn't two words said be anybody. The whole crowd was sittin there waitin for the brother to come back from Hernon. Seven o'clock and he wasn't back. Eight, Nine. Begob the suspense was brutal. BRUTAL.

I can quite imagine.

At half nine the door opens and in comes the brother. I never seen a man lookin as tired. And would you blame him, fifteen hours non-stop stuck up in the City Hall?

Undoubtedly a most arduous exertion in the public interest.

Well annyway the brother sits down and starts takin of the boots. And then without liftin the head, he says: 'From tomorrow on,' says he, 'yez can have your tea.'

Indeed.

Well begob there was nearly a cheer. But the brother just goes upstairs without another word, tired to the world. He was after fixin the whole thing and puttin Hernon right about the water.

Undoubtedly a most useful day's work.

* * *

WELL, do you know the brother's taken to the books again.

You do not say so.

Comes home to the digs wan day a month ago with a big blue one under d'arm. Up to the bedroom with it and doesn't stir out all night. The brother was above havin a screw at the book for five hours non-stop. The door locked, of course. That's a quare one.

Odd behaviour without a doubt.

Well wan Sunda I see the brother below in the sittinroom with the book in the hand and the nose stuck into it. So I thought I'd get on to him about it. What's the book, says I. It's be Sir James Johns, says the brother without liftin the head. And what's the book about, says I. It's about quateernyuns, says the brother. That's a quare one.

It is undoubtedly 'a quare one'.

The brother was readin a book about quateernyuns be Sir James Johns.

A most remarkable personality, your relative.

But I'll tell you another good one. The brother does be up in the night-time peepin at the moon.

I see.

What do I see wan night and me comin home at two in the mornin from me meetin of the Knights only your man pokin the head out of the window with the nightshirt on him. Starin out of him at the stars.

A practice beloved of all philosophers throughout the centuries.

Well I'll tell you this, mister-me-friend: you won't find yours truly
losing sleep over a book be Sir James Johns. Damn the fear of me been up
peepin out of the window in the night-time.

I accept that statement.

Well then another funny thing. The brother does be doin sums. The
digs is full of bits of paper with the brother's sums on them. And very hard
sums too. Begob I found some of the brother's sums on me newspaper wan
day, written all down along the side. That's a quare wan. Workin away at
sums breakfast dinner and tea.

Proof at least of perseverance.

Of course all the brother's sums isn't done in the digs. He does be
inside in a house in Merrion Square doin sums as well. If anybody calls,
says the brother, tell them I'm above in Merrion Square workin at the
quateernyuns, says, he, and take any message. There does be other lads
in the same house doing sums with the brother. The brother does be
teachin them sums. He does be puttin them right about the sums and
the quateernyuns.

Indeed.

I do believe the brother's makin a good thing out of the sums and the
quateernyuns. Your men couldn't offer him less than five bob an hour and
I'm certain sure he gets his tea thrown in.

That is a desirable perquisite.

Because do you know, the brother won't starve. The brother looks after
Number Wan. Matteradamn what he's at, it has to stop when the grub-
steaks is on the table. The brother's very particular about that.

Your relative is versed in the science of living.

Begob the sums and the quateernyuns is quickly shoved aside when the
alarm for grub is sounded and all hands is piped to the table. The brother
thinks there's a time for everything.

And that is a belief that is well-founded.

Here's me bus. Cheers now.

* * *

DID YOU hear the latest about Eugene?

Who is Eugene?

The brother's dog.

I did not hear the latest about Eugene.

The brother is gettin Eugene fixed up.

I do not understand.

He was above in the park chattin Kissane for five hours a Monda.

Who is Kissane?

The head–buck–cat in the Guards. The brother was inside with Kissane colloguin in a back office about Eugene's prospects. Kissane takes a very high view of the brother. He does often be gettin advice from the brother about managin the Guards. Do you know what Kissane calls the brother?

I do not.

Kissane calls the brother AN IRON DISCIPLARIAN.

I see.

Kissane does be sendin the brother out an odd time to keep th'oul eye open, chattin Guards at night when they do be out on their beats. The brother and Kissane is very strict about the Guards smokin fags in doorways or nippin into pubs at ten o'clock to get the crowd out and then swallyin a couple of pints on the q.t. when nobody's lookin. Great men for keepin the Guards right, Kissane and the brother.

I have no doubt of it.

Fierce men for maintainin order.

I quite understand.

And of course very strict men for seein that the Guards is kept honest. If Kissane or the brother catches a Guard pinchin stuff, the Guard has to go. Matter a damn what else, the Guard has to go.

How do these considerations affect your relative's dog.

The brother is gettin Eugene into the Guards.

I see.

The Guards is lost for an animal like Eugene. The Guards could be lookin for something for six months where Eugene would find it in two minutes. A great man for sniffin and usin the nose, Eugene. That dog has a nose on him that would save the Guards five thousand pounds a year.

That is a considerable sum.

Of course Eugene does be smellin things out on his own. The brother and Eugene do take turns doin private police work. And an odd time the brother sends Eugene off on a special job. No sign of Eugene in the digs for four or five days. And the growlin and barkin that goes on between himself and the brother when he comes back is something fierce.

I see.

Well, anyway, the brother has it fixed up with Kissane that Eugene is to go up to the Depot a Tuesday for an interview. Kissane, do you see, is tied up be the regulations. You can't get into the Guards without havin an interview and then into a back room to be stripped be the doctor. That's why Eugene has to have his interview a Tuesda.

I understand. A bureaucratic formality.

Kissane is for makin Eugene a sergeant but the brother won't have this at all. The brother wants Eugene to start from the bottom like anybody else. The brother is very strict about wire-pullin and favours. Wouldn't have that at all, even if it was his own mother. But of course Eugene won't get anny pay, so it doesn't matter. Begob I'll jump this one! Cheers!

Good bye.

* * *

THINGS IS movin in great style above in the digs. The brother has the landlady humped down to Skerries.

This is scarcely the season for seaside holidays.

Wait till you hear what happened man. This night, d'y' see, the landlady is for the pictures. Has the black hat and the purple coat on and is standin in the hall havin a screw at the glass and puttin on the gloves. The shoes polished and shinin like an eel's back, of course. All set.

I understand.

Then the key is heard in the hall door and in comes the brother. He's half turnin into the room when he gives a look at her nibs. Then he stops and comes back and starts starin like a man that was seein things. The landlady gets red, of course.

A not unnatural reaction in the circumstances.

Well annyway the brother orders the landlady into the room where he can see her in the light. He puts the finger on the landlady's eye and starts pullin the lids out of her to get a decko at th'inside. Begob the poor landlady gets the windup in right style. Then the brother starts tappin her chest and givin her skelps on the neck. Inside ten minutes he has her stuffed into bed upstairs with himself below in the kitchen makin special feeds of beef-tea and the crowd in the digs told off to take turns sittin up with the landlady all night. That's a quare one for you.

It is undoubtedly a very queer one for you.

And th'unfortunate woman all set for the pictures thinkin' she was as right as rain. Wasn't it the mercy of God the brother put his nose in at that particular minute?

The coincidence has that inscrutable felicity that is usually associated with the more benevolent manifestations of Providence.

Well the next day the brother gives orders for the landlady's things to be packed. What she wanted, the brother said, was a COMPLETE REST. The brother said he wouldn't be responsible if the landlady didn't get a complete rest.

I see.

So what would do him only pack the landlady down to the married sister in Skerries. With strict orders that she was to stop in bed when she got there. And that's where she is since.

To be confined to bed in midwinter in that somewhat remote hamlet is not the happiest of destinies.

Of course the brother does things well, you know. Before he packs the landlady off in a cab for the station, he rings up Foley. And of course Foley puts the landlady on the train and sees her right t'oblige the brother.

I see.

A great man for lookin after other people, the brother. Ah yes. Yes, certainly . . .

I quite agree. And now I fear I must be off.

Ah yes . . . I'll tell you another funny thing that happened. Queer things always happen in pairs. I was goin home late wan night and I was certain sure I was the last in. I'm lying there in the bed when I hear the door been opened below. Then the light is switched on in the sittin-room. Next thing begob I think I hear voices. So not knowin what's goin on, I hop out of bed and run down in me peejamas.

A very proper precaution in these queer times.

I whip open the sittin-room door and march in. What do I see only the brother leppin up to meet me with the face gettin a little bit red. This, says he, is Miss Doy-ull.

A lady?

The brother was with a dame on the sofa. I suppose he was chattin her about banks and money and that class of thing. But . . . do you know . . . if the landlady was there . . . not that it's my place to say annything . . . but her nibs would take a very poor view of women been brought into the digs after lights out. Wouldn't fancy that at all.

That is the fashion with all landladies.

Well the brother does have Miss Doy-ull in every night since. They do work very late into the night at the bankin questions. I couldn't tell you when she leaves. A very hard-workin' genius, the brother. I was askin' him when he's goin to let the landlady get up below in Skerries. A thing like this, says he, will take a long time, but I might let her up for half an hour a Sunday.

Care is necessary in these delicate illnesses, of course.

You're right there, but it's not the first breakdown the brother pulled the landlady through. Begob here's me bus!

Good-bye.

*   *   *

Hullo, kaykee vill too!

Atá sinn folláin et ar dheagh-shláinte maille le toil Dé.

Taw shay mahogany gas-pipe. An vill Gwayleen a gut?

Is eol dúinn an chanamhain mhín mhilis mháthardha atá fós le clos a ccríoch Bhriain na mbuinneadh ngeal, in Éirinn, i bhflaitheas Ír, Éirimoin agus Éibhir.

Taw Gwayleen eg an dreehaar.

Cúis meisnigh et mór-mheanmhan dúinn an ceileabhar binn íbéirneach a bheith go beacht ag an té sin atá gaolta libh.

Taw an dreehaar ee Gloon na Booey ogus insan Kunra ogus insan Crayv na Hashery. Ack neel na deeney shin dareeriv galore do'n dreehaar.

Binn linn díoghrais et deagh-bheartacht an té sin atá ina bhráthair agaibh.

Jer an dreehaar nock tigin na deeney shin an Gwayleen hee gcart ogus nock mbeen an grawmayr goh creen a-cuh. Jer an dreehaar goh vill na deeney shin golayr ass Bayl Fayrstcheh ogus goh vill an Bayrla goh dunna a-cuh freshen. Neel na foomanna carta a-cuh ins an Gwayleen naw ins an Bayrla. Jer an dreehaar nock faydir loe ayn changa do lowirt goh creen. Jer an dreehaar goh vill an cheer lawn deh deeney as Bayl Fayrstcheh. Been sheed hee gconey eg kynt ogus eg baykfee hee druck-Gwayleen ogus druck-Bayrla.

Dar linn a blas féin a bheith ar an mhín-chanamhain mháthardha do réir mar is loc-labhartha di, i grad gonta grinn ins an áird thuaidh agus mall múinte mín-fhuaimeach sa taobh theas, acht cheana í máthardha milis ion-mholta pé di theas nó thuaidh.

Well taw an dreehaar eg moona Gwayleen ogus Bayrla doh na deeney shin golayr er agla goh n-ahvyoke sheed rud aygin nock Gwayleen naw Bayrla ay. Shin an ubar wore ataw aw yayniv eg an dreehaar er sun na cheera ogus na changin.

Is é ár nguidhe go bhfuighidh an té sin atá gaolta libh díol agus cúiteamh as ucht a shaothair agus má's amhlaidh é ina n-éaghmuis sin ar shroichtin dhó foirceann na beathadh saoghalta is é fós ár nguidhe go mbeidh an díol sin agus an lán-chúiteamh ag dul dó sa chrích allmhurdha ainglidhe anaithnid.

Taw farg et an dreehaar lesh an illskull.

Ní iongantach linn go dearbhtha é sin go léir.

Jer an dreehaar goh mbeen reenkee goulda er shool gock eeha insan illskull ogus nock vill Gwayleen eg an ooctarawn.

Tá a theist sin ar an fhoirgneamh fíorfhada dá ngoirtear a nGaedilg Coláiste na hollscoile agus ag Sacsaibh University College Dublin a Constituent College of the National University of Ireland.

Kirin a lehayd shin farg er an dreehaar. Taw an drechaar ogus Gloon na Booey eg erry rang Gwayleena do cur er shool san illskull leh high na moistree avawn. Boh vah lesh an dreehaar veh eg moona Gwayleena des na moistree gock eeha.

Dar linn gur geal an chuspóir í sin, gur binn, gur breágh agus gur buntáisteach.

Och taw an dreehaar hee gcroocoss. Taw shay roe-gayluck leh dul ischack insan oitch goulda shin in aykur, neer vah lesh a kussa doh hala. Daw vree shin nee fulawr des na moistreee chackt amack go jee tig an dreehaar kun go moona shay an Gwayleen doyv.

Is é ár nguidhe nach saoth leo an turas tráthnónamhail sin go h-aitreabh agus buan-bhaile bhur mbráthar.

Beg na moistree eg chackt kun an dreehaar an vee shoh hooin, jer an dreehaar nock lecky an nawra doyv gan chackt. Taw agla er na moistree anish taraysh an ree-raw avee ins na pawpayree tamal ohin. Taw agla er na moistree goh gcalyah sheed na pustana dassa ataw a-cuh.

Dar linn gur mithid agus gur trathamhail a n-aithrighe.

Begob, shoh kooin mo bhus. Slawn lat anish!

Go soirbhighidh Dia daoibh, agus go bhfuighidh an té sin atá gaolta libh cuideadh agus coimirce san obair mhór atá ar láimh aige dochum onóra na hÉireann.

* * *

THE BROTHER'S bag is out of order.

Is that so?

Going round like a poisoned pup. ⸱ets the pain here look. A great man for taking care of the bag, the brother. But where does it get him?

Nowhere, apparently.

I mean to say, I wouldn't mind a man that lifts the little finger. Whiskey puts a lining like leather on the bag, so a man from Balbriggan was telling me. But the brother doesn't know what to blame. Hot water three times a day if you please and this is what he gets for his trouble. All classes of pains in the morning.

I am sorry to hear it.

Breakfast on top of the wardrobe in the bedroom and then *what's that smell* months afterwards.

A familiar situation with topers.

Now you're talking man. Who's going to believe that a sour bag is the trouble. You know the way they talk above in the digs. O him? Drunk night and morning. Can't look a breakfast in the face.

A very unjust judgment.

I'm telling you now, if the bag is in good order be thankful for it.

I am thankful.

Because there is nothing so bad as a bad bag.

* * *

I'LL TELL you a good wan.

Indeed?

I'll give you a laugh.

How very welcome.

The brother's studyin the French. The brother has the whole digs in a right state and the nerves of half of the crowd up there is broke down.

How truly characteristic of your relative.

The brother comes down to breakfast there about a fortnight back, ten minutes late. And I'll tell you a good wan. What be all the powers had the brother up here at the neck.

I do not know.

A bow tie begob.

I see.

A bow tie with spots on it. Well luckit. I nearly passed out. I didn't know where to look when I seen the bow tie. You couldn't . . . say anythin, you know. The brother wouldn't like that. The brother takes a very poor view of personal remarks. Did you not know that? Shure that's well-known.

I did not know that.

Well anyway the crowd tries to pretend to be goin on with the breakfast and pay no attention to your man but of course there wasn't wan there but was shook in the nerves be the appearance of the brother. Gob now the atmosphere was fierce. What does your man do? Does he sit down and start eatin?

I should be astonished to learn that he did.

Not at all man, over with him to the mantelpiece and starts workin and pokin and foosterin at the clock, he was squintin and peerin and peepin' there for five minutes and then he comes along and starts lightin matches to see better, manipulatin and cavortin there for further orders, you'd swear he was searching for the hallmark on it. He was openin the glass . . . and shuttin it . . . and opening it . . . and slammin it shut again—you'd need the nerves of an iron man to sit there and swally the grub. It was fierce.

I have no doubt.

There we were the whole crowd of us sittin waitin for the blow to fall, the landlady changin colour like something you'd see in a circus. The only man that wasn't sweatin there was meself. Bar meself, the nerves of the crowd was in flitters.

Pray proceed to the dénouement.

At last begob the blow fell. Without turnin round at all, the brother speaks in a very queer voice. I don't see any Hair Dev, says he. *I don't see any Hair Dev.* Well luckit. Do you know what it is?

What is it?

The crowd nearly passed out. The poor ould landlady—there was tears in her eyes. What's that, says she. But the brother doesn't pretend to hear, sits down very cross-lookin and starts swallyin tea, you could see the bow tie waggin every time your man swallied a mouthful. There wasn't another thing said that fine morning.

I see.

Next thing off with the poor landlady down town to Moore Street, tried every shop in the street lookin for the brother's fancy feed but it was no use, she didn't know whether it was sold loose or in a bag or in a tin. The nearest French stuff she could get was the French beans. So what does she do only have a feed of them things laid out for the brother's breakfast next mornin. What's this, says the brother. Them's French garden vegetables, says the landlady. *The land of France*, says the brother, *never seen them things.*

That is what one would call 'a quare one'.

Thing's is gone from bad to worse. The brother now had a jug of Hair Dev bought be himself above in the bedroom. Breakfast in bed *and drinkin tay out of a glass!* And the bow tie never offa the neck!

And one assumes that is only a beginning.

The brother says he doesn't know why he lives in this country at all. Takes a very poor view. Here's me bus! Cheers!

Cheers!

*   *   *

WELL, BEGOB is it yourself! How's thricks?

It is and they are well.

How did you get over the Christmas?

Safely, thank you. May I ask how you find the new white bread?

Hah?

The white bread?

The white bread? Why, did you not hear?

Hear what?

Sure me dear man the brother wouldn't have that stuff in the digs at all. Wouldn't hear of it . . . at anny price. So I never got a chance of puttin' it in me mouth at all.

I see.

Takes a very poor view. Begob there was ructions there a fortnight back. Skin an' hair flyin' above in the digs. A fierce heave wan mornin'. Her nibs the landlady got herself into very serious trouble with the brother.

One sympathises with the lady.

The day before the white bread is due, the brother issues ordhers to all hands. No white bread . . . in anny circumstances. The brother said that he was after goin into the whole thing personally, analysin and workin at the chemical ends of it above in d'Upper Castle Yard with a man be the name of Wheeler. The brother says the white bread is poison, wouldn't hear of annybody puttin it into his mouth. And begob her nibs the land-lady with her tongue hangin out waitin' for the white loaf the next morning!

One again sympathises with that lady.

So the white bread is barred. But begob about a week ago the brother comes down to breakfast and starts into the French Hair Dev that he does

have in a special jug of his own above in the bedroom. Suddenly begob
he puts down the spoon and says he: WHAT'S THIS I SEE?

And what did he see?

Wasn't there a white crumb on the table cloth. Well luckit.

I am looking.

If you seen the face the brother put on him. WHO IS RESPONSIBLE FOR
THIS, says he in a fierce voice. No answer, of course. I wouldn't like to be
the one to say yes to that, would you?

I would not.

So up with the brother without another word and out to the kitchen.
The crowd could hear him rootin and searchin and foosterin around
the suddenly the landlady goes the colours of the rainbow when she hears
him pullin over a chair to have a screw at the top of the dresser. Sure
enough in he comes with the half of a white loaf in the hand. Well luckit.

I still am looking.

It would frighten you to look at the brother's face. WHICH OF YEZ IS
RESPONSIBLE FOR THIS, says he, lookin hard at the landlady. I am, says
she in a terrible watery voice. Then gettin the wind up from the brother's
face, she says No, I mean I'm not, it was left here be the married sister
that lives below in Skerries. Wasn't that a good wan. The brother's married
sister.

An excellent one, in fact.

The brother pokes up the fire, puts the loaf in it and then away upstairs
with him. Down again with the coat and hat on and in the hand a dose
he was after makin up in a glass, desperate-lookin red tack. HERE, says
he to the landlady, THROW THIS BACK. Her nibs, of course, has no choice.
NOW, says the brother, I'M ON ME WAY TO SKERRIES AND I'LL BE BACK
TO-NIGHT. IF THINGS ISN'T SERIOUS. Begob he's hardly out of the door
when the landlady takes bad. Starts gripin' and moanin' and goin' pale
in the face. The crowd in the digs has to cart her upstairs to bed, sixteen
stone begob. Fierce work.

I have no doubt of it.

Well she's lyin there all day in a terrible condition but of course nobody
was goin to chance calling a docthor. The brother wouldn't like that, you
know. The brother takes a very poor view of the docthors.

So I recollect.

Well annyway when the brother comes home at night, I tell him the
landlady took bad after the red dose. IS IT ANNY WONDHER SHE'S TOOK BAD,
says the brother, AFTER PUTTIN THAT WHITE POISON IN HER MOUTH.

DIDN'T I WARN YEZ ALL. IT'S A GOOD JOB I TOOK HER IN TIME, says he. And then up to start dosin' her again, black stuff this time. She's above in the bed still. Gob, me bus. Cheers!

Good-bye.

* * *

YOURSELF, is it? Fit an' well you're lookin. I'll tell you a good one. I'll give you a laugh.

Do.

I'll give you a laugh. The digs was in the front line for near on a fortnight. Martial law, begob. It was a . . . thremendious business. Fierce.

One divines a domestic crisis of unexampled gravity.

Some was for handin in the gun after the first week and runnin off on holidays, muryaa, off down to Skerries or Arklow where they were sleepin five in a bed and not a place to be had for love or money. All hands was losin weight be the pound. It was a . . . most . . . thremendious . . . war of nerves.

No doubt your relative was the author of this tension?

Tuesday fortnight was D-Day. The brother comes down to breakfast without the mark of a shavin-razor on the jaw. The brother—!

Indeed?

A man . . . a man . . . that was never known to put the nose out of the room of a mornin without everything just so—the handkerchief right, the tie right, and never without a fierce smell of shavin-soap off him. An' the hair-oil standin out on the head like diamonds!

One cannot always maintain such an attitude neque semper tendit arcum Apollo.

Of course the crowd starts eatin an' takin no notice. There would be no question of anybody passin remarks, you know. There was very ferocious eatin goin on that morning. The brother just reads the paper and then off to work. He only opens the beak once. Goin out he says to the landlady 'Pardon me but I may be delayed to-night and there is no necessity for you to defer retiring.'

A most considerate thought.

The next mornin the crowd is sittin at the table as white as a sheet, all waitin for the brother to come down. Begob you would think they were all for the firin-squad. And down comes the brother. Do you know what I'm goin to tell you?

I do not.

The face was as black as a black-faced goat. I never seen a more ferocious-lookin sight. Begob there was hair on him from the ears to the neck. The crowd begins to feed like prisoners given thirty second to swally their stew. The landlady's face gets red and out she comes in a big loud voice with a lot of chat about the war. The secret was out! He was tryin to raise wan.

Trying to raise what?

To raise a whisker. Your man was puttin up a beaver!

Curious that any activity so ancient should be considered reprehensible!

I couldn't tell you how the crowd in the digs lived through the next ten days. You wouldn't know your man to look at him. A fierce lookin sight, comin in and sittin down as bold as bedamned. Starts enlargin the bridgehead from wan day to the next. An' not a word out of him but Pardon me this an' Pardon me that. O a very cool customer, say what you like. And no remarks passed, of course. Do you know what it is?

I do not.

If the brother came down without a face on him at all, there wouldn't be wan that would pass a remark. The heads would go down, the chawin and aytin would go on and the landlady would pass the brother the paper. A nice crowd begob.

A remarkable character.

After a fortnight the brother got himself into a condition I never seen a man in in me life. There was hair hangin out of him behind the ears an' there was hair growin into the eyes. The strain was terrible. The digs was about to crack. It was H-Hour. Then begob the big thing happened. Next mornin the brother comes down with his face as smooth as a baby's, sits down and says Parding me, ma'am, but I think that clock is four minutes slow be the Ballast Office. Well luckit.

I am looking.

The crowd in the digs goes off their heads. They all start chattin an' talkin and roarin out of them about the time and peepin at their watches and laughin and cavortin for further orders. I think we'll need more tea, the landlady says, gettin up to go out. Do you know what it is?

I do not.

I'll give you a laugh. Her nibs was cryin.

Not unusual in such an emotional crisis.

I never put in such a fortnight in me life. Begob here's a 52. Cheers!

Cheers!

* * *

BEGOB is it yerself?

It IS myself.

I see where the Christmas is on. Things is in full swing.

It cannot be denied.

I'll tell you a good wan.

Pray, by all means do so.

I'll tell you a good wan about the brother. The brother is holdin a conversasioney in the digs, Sahurda. All hands is to report for duty. A hand of cards, thrifle, plum puddin and a bit of a sing-song. No jars, of course, bar a few bottles of stout in the pantry for the hard chaws. An ould-fashioned conversasioney, that's what the brother calls it. Ladies present, o'course.

I see.

Do you know why?

I do not.

The brother is for keepin the crowd in over the Christmas. Have your life if you looked for a pass-out to mooch off down-town aSahurda.

One admires the preservation of ancient customs.

The brother was makin' inquiries about the pubs. Peepin' in here and there, askin an odd question, chattin the curates, maybe takin an odd sip for himself on the Q.T. Do you know what the brother says?

I do not.

The brother says there's stuff been got ready.

Indeed?

The brother says there's special stuff been got ready for the Christmas.

You mean inferior and poisonous potions?

The brother says there's lads below in cellars at the present time gettin stuff ready be the bucketful. They do be below in the daytime mixin stuff in firkins. Whiskey by yer lave. For the Christmas. Two bob a glass.

Surely the police should be informed?

There's mixtures been made up that was never made up before. This year it's goin to be the works altogether.

Surely the reputable houses in their own interest should communicate with the police?

I'll tell you another thing. The brother says there's a black market in turps.

Indeed?

Yer men use a lot of turps for the mixtures, you know. Turps, sherry-wine and a drop of the Portugese brandy that was brought in early in the war. That's yer glass of malt. And I'll tell you a funny wan. Do you know what a glass of fine old brandy is, three and six a knock?

I do not.

Turps and sherry-wine.

You astound me.

The brother says the North of Ireland crowd is goin to be sorry men.

You mean the undiscerning stranger will be poisoned?

And there's wan particular crowd gettin their own cigars and cigarettes ready, the brother says. Word'll be sent round that so-and-so has bags of cigarettes and your men will all march in and do their drinkin there. First they'll get the sherry-wine and the turps. Then on top of that the special fags got ready downstairs be the boss himself. And goin out, a half-naggin of turps for the morning.

I sincerely hope you exaggerate.

That's why the brother is gettin up the conversasioney for the Sahurda. Here's me bus. Happy Christmas now and mind yerself!

Good-bye, and thanks!

Cheers now.

* * *

YOURSELF begob! How did you get over the Christmas?

Excellently, thank you.

There was fierce goins-on in the digs over the Christmas.

Indeed?

The brother got up a conversationey for the Christmas Eve so as to keep the crowd out of the pubs where there was turps, and sherry-wine got ready as a Christmas present for all-comers. I'll tell you a damn good wan.

Do.

The brother invites the uncle from Skerries up for the Christmas. Your man arrives up on the Thursday night. The brother takes out a bottle of sherry-wine. A very broad-minded customer, the brother. Offers the uncle a glass. But not on your life. The uncle puts up the hands, makes a terrible face, wouldn't touch it. Thanks very much but not for him. A very abstemious character, the uncle. Next thing he's off up to bed.

Admirable.

Next day is the Frida. Landlady up at eight o'clock, reports the uncle missin. A note on the hall table, 'Very important appointment, back at twleve.' Is he back at twleve?

I would hazard the opinion that he is not back at twelve.

He certainly is not back at twelve. Nor at wan. Nor at two. Nor at four. *Extraordinary behaviour.*

And the dinner stuffed in the oven. Begob at six there's a report that your man's coat is on th'hallstand. One of the crowd goes up and peeps into the bedroom. Here is me bould man asleep, dead to the world. *Eccentric is scarcely the word for such behaviour.*

The brother hears the story when he gets home. Says nothin' but you could see he was takin' a poor view. Goes up, takes a look at th'uncle, comes down, says nothin' but starts with David Copperfold. *An ominous reaction.*

Annyway next mornin'—this is the Christmas Eve, mind—th'uncle wakes up very tired and asks for a feed of Farola for breakfast. Says he had a busy day with appointments, buyin stuff an' all the rest of it, and that he's for stoppin in bed all day. The crowd in the digs start readin and snoozin and gettin ready for the conversationey. Twelve twenty-five, th'uncle's coat is reported missin'. *My goodness!*

The brother starts a sort of martial law in the digs. The crowd arrives for the conversationey but certain parties is ordered to keep a watch. Believe me or believe me not the coat is back at six and not a soul's seen it comin! *Here one is almost tempted to suspect the machinations of the occult.*

And the bould uncle stuffed above in the bed. You won't believe the next thing that happened. Eight o'clock the crowd is workin' away at the charades when word comes in that the coat is gone again—AND the brother's bike! *Well, well, well!*

Begob I never seen such a look on the brother's face. Makes a signal for the crowd to carry on, on with the black velour, and out. Next thing that happens—ten o'clock Christmas Eve—a message is sent up be the Guards that the brother is stretched on one of the Guard's beds. Dead to the world. Do you know what happened? *I do not.*

Goes into a boozer lookin for th'uncle. Thinks he'll chance a drop to make things look natural. Gets an extra special dose for himself offa one of the curates. *You mean this lethal mixture of turpentine and sherry?*

Not at all man. The turps gave out at five. Do you know what he got? *I do not.*

Paraffeen!

Surely you are not serious?

Paraffeen and sherry-wine. And th'uncle was never heard of since. Cheers. Here's me bus! Happy new year!

* * *

I'LL TELL you another man that the brother fixed up—Jamesie D. Now there was a man that wasn't getting his health at all. When he came to the brother he was a cripple. And look at him now.

In what condition is he now?

Sure wasn't he picked for a trial with Rovers Seconds and couldn't turn out because the ould mother beyond in Stepaside was taken bad on the Friday. A great big gorilla of a man.

And what was his trouble?

Arthreetus, so the brother said. It was a very poor glass of water, I'm telling you. But the brother got it in time.

That was fortunate.

Ah yes, if you don't put it off too long the brother can work wonders. He does be often giving out about people that don't come to him in time.

And what happened in connexion with that gentleman you mentioned?

Jamesie D.? Ah poor Jamesie had a bad time. The joint of the elbow went out of order with his arthreetus. He could no more lift a pint than he could lift a fog. The poor man took it very badly, hardly ever came down to the smoker of a Friday. A man remember that could play Ave Maria on the piana to bring the tears to your eyes. To tell you the truth he was half poisoned by the doctors. All classes of pills and bottles. And one doctor gave him the machine.

I beg your pardon?

As true as I'm here, strapped him down to some class of an electric chair and turned on the juice. Poor Jamesie thought it was the end. He thought your man was a maniac, you know, passing himself off as a doctor. Begob, what the chair did for him was to give him a bad ankle. It was after that that he went to the brother.

I see.

Well do you know what I'm going to tell you. The brother got that arthreetus at the elbow, he chased it up the arm to the shoulder, then down the back, over across to the other leg and down the thighs. He got it just above the knee. It took him two years but he got it in the end. He killed it just above the knee. And it never came back.

I see.

No, it never came back. Well, here's me wagon. Good luck now and back no horses, as the man said.

Farewell, friend.

The Plain People of Ireland

SEVERAL PEOPLE have written to compliment me on my drawings and to express astonishment at the variety of styles I can adopt. Particularly have I won golden opinions, not to say encomia, as a result of my mastery of the old-time craft of the woodcut.

It is true that my drawings are fine things. They satisfy the human appetite for what is pleasing and well-made. It is no lie to say that they are delightful.

How do I do it?

I cannot say. Genius, take it how you will, is an odd thing. Talent, yes—that can be analysed and explained. But not genius. I am myself as much an astonished spectator of my own work as any reader. When my fingers begin drawing I often find myself giving involuntary gasps of surprise and excitement. A few quick strokes and the thing is done. The whole thing is over in a moment. Every line is in its place, every delicate little shade exquisitely delineated.

And those fingers! You should see them. They are rich with rings, crusted with exotic opal, lapis lazuli, Benghazi myrmum, incomparable cheznook and fahr from the Orient. They are long, nervous and beautifully shaped, the fingers of an artist. Please notice their white translucent skin of perfect grain, the perfectly kept nails, pink suffusion of pale quick under pearly shell, the delicate, almost feminine, rounding of the thumb. My face, too—

The Plain People of Ireland: Could we hold the face over till tomorrow?

Myself: Certainly.

CONVERSATION PIECE

The Plain People of Ireland: If it's all the same, we'd prefer to have you by instalments.

Myself: Fair enough.

Well, what do you think of the war?

Nothing. I never think of the war.

The brother was across to the other side last week. He said we have no idea.

Have we not?

The brother says you'll see the Americans in before the New Year. And do you know what I'm going to tell you?

I do not.

The Swiss are thinking of having a go at the French. There's bad blood there, you know, always was. Some of your men in Switzerland speak French, but don't run away with the idea that that makes them Frenchmen.

I rarely run away with such ideas.

The brother takes a poor view of the situation above in Africa. He says that class of thing can't last—couldn't last. He says you'll see a republic there before the New Year. He gives them to Christmas to blow up.

This is very kind of him.

Another crowd that aren't happy at all, so the brother says, is the Swedes. A desperate crowd of men for going off to sea. Close up the area with mines and torpedo boats and where are you? You're in for trouble.

That makes it simple.

The brother was saying that he has eighteen pounds of tea stored up above in Finglas. He knew the war was coming five years ago. He said the thing couldn't last.

That reminds me that it is tea-time. Good-bye!

* * *

IN THE SERE THE YELLOW

LOOKING OVER my well-thumbed volume of Keats the other day ('First Prize for English Composition, Clongowes Wood College, 1888') I re-read the sonnet on the four seasons of man.

> 'He has his summer, when luxuriously
>   Spring's honeyed end of youthful thought he loves
>   To ruminate, and by such dreaming nigh
>   Is the nearest unto heaven; quiet coves
>   His soul has in its Autumn, when his wings
>   He furleth close . . .'

This is largely hearsay or guesswork on the part of Keats, who died when he was a boy. All the same, he was not far out. I am old enough myself to know what Autumn is, and I find that my habits are of the order imagined by the poet. There is nothing I like better than an evening with a few quiet coves in the dimmer corner of a pub, murmuring together in friendship the judgements of our mature minds. As regards furling my wings close, that is also true enough. To spend a whole bob or a tanner in one go entails physical suffering. My little pension is woefully inelastic. A wing or two saved in ordering porter instead of stout is not to be despised. A borrowed match, a cadged filling of the pipe, all small things mount mightily in a year.

The Plain People of Ireland : Did you really go to Clongowes?

Myself : Certainly.

The Plain People of Ireland : Isn't that a fancy place, gentlemen's sons and all the rest of it.

Myself : It is. That's what I mean.

The Plain People of Ireland : Um. Did they teach you spelling there at all?

Myself : They taught me anything you like to mention.

The Plain People of Ireland : Then how about the word 'judgement' above? Unless we are very much mistaken, that should be JUDGMENT.

Myself : It is unthinkable that you should be very much mistaken, but if you take the trouble to look up any dictionary, you will find that either form is admissible, you smug, self-righteous swine.

(*Half to Myself :* The ignorant self-opinionated sod-minded suet-brained ham-faced mealy-mouthed streptococcus-ridden gang of natural gobdaws!)

* * *

A FEW WEEKS ago I was interrupted when about to give the public my long-awaited description of my own face. Several anxious readers have written in asking when they might expect it. My answer is that they may expect it to-day. Let us take the features one by one and then stand back, as one stands back from a majestic Titian or Van Gogh, and view the whole magnificent—

The Plain People of Ireland : Is this going to be long?

Myself : Not very.

The Plain People of Ireland : How long roughly?

Myself : Well, say ten lines for the vast Homeric brow, the kingly brow that is yet human wise and mild. Then the eyes, peerless wine-green opal of rare hue, brittle and ebullient against the whiteness of Himalayan snow—

The Plain People of Ireland : Another ten lines?

Myself : Say seven each. That's fourteen altogether.

The Plain People of Ireland: Seven *each*! You don't say there's any difference between them?

Myself: Well, there's not exactly any difference, nothing that could be said to be repugnant or incompatible. Nevertheless, there is some slight divergence of *vivre*, some indefinable yet charming *indépendance*, some enchanting *drôlerie de la paupière—*

The Plain People of Ireland: And how about the gob and the snot?

Myself: If you mean the finely-moulded masterful—

The Plain People of Ireland: Did you ever hear this one: As a beauty I am not a star. There are others more handsome by far—

Myself: I did, I did. Stop!

The Plain People of Ireland: But my face I don't mind it, For I am behind it, It's the people in front get the jar!

Myself: Lord save us!

The Plain People of Ireland: Could we not leave the whole thing over to another time?

Myself: Very well. But heaven knows whom we are disappointing in this matter.

*   *   *

A SOLICITOR well known in the west—I do have jars with him on me holidays when the circus is in town—

The Plain People of Ireland: The *circus*?

Myself: Sorry. The circuit. But there's not much difference, really, when it gets on to midnight in the bar.

Well, this distinguished jurist has written to me asking whether an estate with remainders to the first and fourth sons in tail can be alienated without reversionary codicils terminating *pro tanto* all seignory advowsons in gross, the assumption being that appendant copyholds can be extinguished at will under the Land Transfer Act 1897.

Alas, the answer must be no. Any estate held as between coparceners without the inseisinment of freebench copyholds must stand in foeffment pending escheat of all incorporeal rent-charge bars, subinfeudations in frankalmoign *aperte*, mesne rights, copycharges presented *à prendre*, or devises held by chartered copybrokers *possessio fratris*, *pur autre vie*, or even *quousque*.

We have close analogy in the right of socage where it ranks for beneficial apportionment of any chattel-warrants engrossed with interfeudal *droit* in fee. The undercopy-holder has the advowson absolutely, *with uncommuted scutage and burgage rights where the estate subsists in petty serjaunty.* All engrossments must be registered, with the privity of the Lord Lieutenant; similarly with instruments of attornment, frankalcheigh, seisinfoimaunt, cesser of *cestui qui* caveats *en graund playsaunce du roi*, interfeudalated copywrit of cave, and recovenanted socage-bills subsisting part in petty serjaunty and part in foeff-frankalseignory *majeur*.

There, possibly, I might crave permission to leave the matter.

KEATSIANA

It is a considerable time since I related an anecdote from the life of John Keats. Here is one at last.

When the poet was eighteen he decided to make a journey to the American continent to pick up some of the potatoes that even the brazenest fraud can garner by lecture-touring. In Boston he met a pretty lady, fat and forty, but beautiful with the bloom of cash and collateral. The poet instantly laid siege, praised her expensive fancy hats, and called her his Dark Lady of the Bonnets. She accepted his advances after a fashion, but made no move to buy him a pair-in-hand, and would not consent to meet him anywhere but in the local park by day. Desperate with greed, he decided to stake all on a bogus offer of marriage. The lady's reply was peculiar.

'Have you ever read the works of our great writer, Thoreau?' she asked.

'Never heard of the lad,' Keats said.

'Well, you are hearing about him now,' said the lady. 'I happen to be his wife.'

'So what?' asked the poet.

'How could I marry you if I already have a husband?'

'Easy,' replied the great wit. 'Why not get a divorce a mensa et thoreau?'

OBJECTION

The Plain People of Ireland : Lord save us!

Myself : That's nothing. Listen to this.

Some years before the present war I met a lady called Lottie and fell deeply, even exquisitely, in love. We used to keep nightly tryst near the house of Dr Mahr, who was in charge of the National Museum before he returned to Germany a few years ago.

The Plain People of Ireland : Where is the joke? What's funny in that?
Myself : Do you not see it? 'Pale hands I loved beside the Chalet Mahr.'
The Plain People of Ireland : Well—
Myself : Shut up, shut up. I'd give you another puck in the wind if I had the space.

* * *

WITH THE ever-hastening approach of winter there is a proportionate increase in speculation as to the outcome of the titanic struggle which is taking place in Russia. In that strange but distant land vast masses of men and metal are locked together in a battle-front which ranges from the Black Sea to the far-off Karelian isthmus, a span that embraces a great variety of terrain and even climate. When the Fuehrer first threw his *Panzerdivisionen* against Smolensk and embarked on the vast pincer operation which culminated in the bloody battle for the Dnieper, many observers predicted a long war. General Koniev, whose masterly strategy for the Allied successes in Moravia, has moved up considerable forces from the middle front, where the pincer 'claw', turning south, has brought the *Sturm und Drang* of battle to new and unexpected quarters. The—
The Plain People of Ireland : Isn't there some mistake. Surely, this is the leading article.
Myself : It is.
The Plain People of Ireland : But—
Myself : Yes, I am sorry, there is something wrong. My stuff is in the wrong place. Some fool has blundered.
The Plain People of Ireland : You don't mean to say you write the leading article?
Myself : I do, usually. We have another man who comes in when I am 'indisposed', if you know what that means. And there is no reason why you shouldn't, red-snouts.
The Plain People of Ireland : But— Well, dear knows. How do you find time to do the two things?
Myself : It's no trouble to me. In both cases it is the same old stuff all the time. You just change it round a bit.
The Plain People of Ireland : Do they pay you much for the leader? A couple of bar a knock, maybe?
Myself : I get half a guinea for the leading article and I throw in the other funny stuff for nothing because I enjoy publishing jibes at the

expense of people I dislike. I also write a lot of the For-Ireland-Boys-Hurrah stuff that appears in *The Leader* every week.

The Plain People of Ireland: Well, honestly! You're a wonderful man altogether. Don't you write plays for the Abbey, too?

Myself: Certainly.

The Plain People of Ireland: Well, Lord save us!

* * *

NEVER FORGET that tenure by sochemaunce seisined by feodo copyholds in gross and reseisined through covenants of foeffseignory in frankal-puissaunce—

The Plain People of Ireland: This sounds like dirty water being squirted out of a hole in a burst rubber ball.

—is alienable only by *droit* of bonfeasaunce subsisting in free-bench coigny or in re-vested copywrits of *seisina facit stipidem*, a fair copy bearing a 2d. stamp to be entered at the Court of Star Chamber.

Furthermore, a rent seck indentured with such frankalseignory or chartamoign charges as may be, and re-empted in Market Overt, subsists thereafter in graund serjaunty du roi, eighteen fishing smacks being deemed sufficient to transport the stuff from Lisbon.

The Plain People of Ireland: Where do the fishing smacks come in?

Myself: Howth, usually.

The Plain People of Ireland: No, but what have they got to do with what you were saying?

Myself: It's all right. I was only trying to find out whether ye were still reading on. By the way, I came across something very funny the other night in a public-house.

The Plain People of Ireland (*chuckling*): What was it?

Myself: It was a notice on the wall. It read: 'We have come to an arrangement with our bankers. They have agreed not to sell drink. We, on our part, have agreed not to cash cheques.'

The Plain People of Ireland: O, Ha Ha Ha! Ho Ho Ho! (Sounds of thousands of thighs being slapped in paroxysms of mirth.)

Myself: Good. I knew that would amuse you.

* * *

COME ON, LADS

SURE THERE'S nothing like it. It's the best idea of the lot for keeping us all out of the pubs and off the streets. Good clean healthy amusement. Come on, what's all the delay. Don't keep me waiting all day. Hurry up!

The Plain People of Ireland : What do you mean ? What's all this about ?

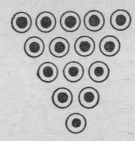

Myself : A game of snooker. We'll make it a foursome if you like. And I'll give you twenty-five.

The Plain People of Ireland (doubtfully) : Where are the cues ?

Myself : I'm afraid I forgot about them.

The Plain People of Ireland : And the colours ?

Myself : Well what a head I have on me. Smart boy wanted.

The Plain People of Ireland : Anyway, how could we play a game with them things ? Maybe this is a joke. Those aren't real balls.

Myself : I swear I'm serious.

The Plain People of Ireland : And they're not red.

Myself : Lend me a red pencil.

The Plain People of Ireland : This is some class of a fancy joke. If you're serious come down to Tommie's some night and we'll see who'll give twenty-five, there's a lad there called Rooney that'll show you something.

Myself : Fair enough.

* * *

I wish to take the opportunity of wishing all and sundry a happy new year and many happy returns.

The Plain People of Ireland : It's a bit late in the day.

Myself : If my simple and heartfelt greeting is to be questioned or discussed, I'll withdraw it.

The Plain People of Ireland : Go ahead and withdraw it.

Myself : It is now withdrawn.

The Plain People of Ireland : The cheek of some people.

* * *

A DEVISE of incorporeal rent secks which subsist in subwrit of coigny-bar, I do not mind telling you may rank for apportionment with appendant seignmoigns du petit playsaunce, quit-writs of *cestui que cave* and re-entered copy-warrants of grand attainder.

It was once urged (v. Bract, fo. 87a, 207a, Vinogradoff Hist. E. L. xvii Reg. v Shaughnessy et al.) that the devise of a rent-charged easement held in frankalchaise-a-moins with mesne bars inquoted was a lawful devise *having regard to fraundpuissaunce of charterfee*. Held by Pallas C. B. that

'. . . devises charged with consolidated quodwrits of quit-bar or seigny-poke subsist thereafter in fee of grossplaysaunce, notwith-standing all copyholds of mesnemanor, socagemoign, interfee, mort-lease, grand bastardy in copygross, sub-escheats of scutage *quousque*, refeoffed disseisor of sub-seisin in scignyfrankalpuis and vivmain of copycharged serjaunty.'

To-day, this may seem a somewhat staid—even a technical—pro-nouncement. Yet when it was made it was regarded by the Irish people as the most stirring vindication of their immemorial right to quit-scutage and sochemaunce—indeed, a wider charter of democratic self-determina-tion than the Local Government Act of 1898.

The Press Association managed to get the judgment down to Mitchels-town the day it was made. The excitement it caused was enormous. Great bonfires were kindled by willing hands, and patriotic speeches were delivered to the politics-demented people in the square.

Late the same night a corrupt peeler called Monk was presented by persons unknown with the father and the mother of a haymaker in the pit of the stomach.

The Plain People of Ireland : And good enough for him, too.

HINTS FOR SOTS

Day after day I receive letters calling for stuff that is more 'popular', 'more in touch with the ordinary people'. 'Give us,' a reader says, 'some-thing that may interest and help us in our daily lives.'

Very well. Let us admit openly that it is almost your nightly experience either to be brought home or to be saddled with the task of 'seeing' an inebriated friend 'right'.

Look at my picture. Your 'friend' has consumed forty-eight pints and has now fallen down on the broad of his back. To-day's Hint is this: DON'T lift his head as is being done in the illustration. Keep his body completely horizontal. If you lift his head and shoulders, you'll probably spill some.

GUFF

The Plain People of Ireland:

Myself: Stop pointing. It's rude.

The Plain People of Ireland: Who in heaven's name is that?

Myself: That's my pal, Mr Claude ffoney. He's a painter.

The Plain People of Ireland: A house painter?

Myself: O, indeed, no. 'The Poddle at Blessington', 'Market Place, Tours', and so on.

The Plain People of Ireland: Then why is he wearing a workman's pants?

Myself: Them's corduroys, and luscious purple articles they are, too.

The Plain People of Ireland (*doubtfully*) : It's very hard to be up to you intellectual lads.

Myself (*venomously*) : I think I am going mad! (Getting pale with passion, the voice rising to a scream). Do you hear me? Mad, *mad*, MAD!

* * *

IN NEW YORK'S swank Manhattan lives blond, smiling, plump James Keats, descendant of famous poet John. No lover of poetry, James Keats is director of the million-dollar dairy combine Manhattan Cheeses and ranked Number Three in the Gallup quiz to find America's Ten Ablest Executives. James lives quietly with slim dark attractive wife, Anna, knows all there is about cheeses, likes a joke like his distinguished forbear. Wife Anna likes to tell of the time he brought her to see the Louis-Baer fight.

'He just sat there roaring "Camembert, Camembert!" '

If the joke doesn't interest you, do you derive amusement from this funny way of writing English? It is very smart and up-to-date. It was invented by America's slick glossy *Time* and copied by hacks in every land. For two pins I will write like that every day, in Irish as well as English. Because that sort of writing is taut, meaningful, hard, sinewy, compact, newsy, factual, muscular, meaty, smart, modern, brittle, chromium, bright, flexible, omnispectric.

ANOTHER PROBLEM SOLVED

I am happy to announce that I have discovered a remedy for the cigarette and tobacco famine. No longer need you slink from shop to shop like a criminal.

It is simple. All you need is a pack of cards. Summon four or five friends to your house, seat them around you and deal out the cards for poker. First, though, make sure that the cards are arranged so that each person gets a 'full' hand, i.e. a straight, full house, and so on. Each player, when he sees what he has got, will have no alternative but to 'smoke'. If the cards are not re-dealt but each player permitted to retain his original hand all night, he can sit there and 'smoke' quietly until bed-time. With your own permission, he may even bring his hand home with him and 'smoke' in bed until he falls asleep.

If you have any odd playing cards, send them along to the Myles na gCopaleen Social Club. Our Ladies' Committee will arrange them into flushes, straights and full houses and send them to the troops, who are as much in need of a smoke as anybody.

The Plain People of Ireland : Talking of cards, there is nothing to beat a good game of solo, best game of the whole lot, hear young slips of girls talking about their bridge and all the rest of it make you sick.

Myself : Pray continue, you interest me strangely.

The Plain People of Ireland : To be stuck inside there in the back room of an evenin' with a few of the lads, a couple of dozen stout in the corner and ten or fifteen bob in the middle of the table, Lord save us, what more could a man ask?

Myself : Personally, I am never happy when I am away from my beloved books.

The Plain People of Ireland : And not a word spoken, every man for himself, every card counted, a trump down on the ace of spades as often as you like.

Myself : Ay indeed.

HAIRS WANTED

My Patent Beard Food is enjoying a considerable vogue. A well-known humbug (I am advised that I cannot mention his name because of some legal technicality) has ordered three of my special presentation Christmas cases of the stuff and is due to appear on the streets any day now bearded himself and accompanied by four bearded children. He insists that his children have 'talent' and show it early.

Some souls have written to ask whether the Food takes long to work. Not at all. My special illustration below shows what happens in the space of one hour.

Just think of it! Communism, Art, Poetry, even Submarine Experience, all in one hour! Why be smooth?

I SEE that the collected letters of Cézanne have been published. Believe me, they are not half as interesting as the letters of Manet, which I am editing for publication at present. The title of the volume will be 'Littera Scripta Manet'. Limited edition of 25 copies printed on steam-rolled pig's liver and bound with Irish thongs in desiccated goat-hide quilting, a book to treasure for all time but to lock away in hot weather.

By the way, Keats once had a female parrot which he called Tess. 'Toujours la Polly Tess!' he was wont to roar at her in his odder moments.

About the Manet book, absorbing revelations will be as abundant in it as wrinkles in an elephant's nose. The price will be very high. Watch this newspaper for further details. Or better, write to me for some information on the side. The jockey and the horse-trainer in me prefers to do business that way.

If the castors on your Steinway piano are rusty and in poor condition, you should lubricate them.

The Plain People of Ireland : With what?

Myself : Castor oil, of course.

Chopin's Ballade in G minor, a great favourite with Beverley and myself, will then sound many times sweeter.

Chopin, when moving, used to have his piano towed through the streets by a cart-horse while the composer was spread-eagled over the top of it playing downwards on the bumpy keys. This was no mean feat, because he had to use the wrong hand for the wrong side of the piano. Keats and Chopin had much in common; their work has the same sickly-sweet languor of disease, the same nachtschaft with night-forms, identical symbolosis of muscatel, the morning after the Christmas party in the workhouse. What are they carrying out now? A child's coffin, mister, observe the pathetic dimensions of the thing. Aged two months and ten days. Born and reared on the premises. Ah well.

TALENTED TENOR

An excellent tenor whose records you can buy is Sidney MacEwen. He is a good man and sings some of our own songs with greater distinction than my dear friend, God bless him. By his name he must be a member of the Scottish nation. His voice is rich and easy and smooth and he uses it with the grace and competence of the true artist. Observe him in his record 'She moved through the fair' and 'The lark in the clear air'. It is worth very much more than three shillings.

The Plain People of Ireland : Look, this is very mixed up to-day.

Myself : YWSK ryeamdklwo2&&J hu)O'&87! What do you think of that?

The Plain People of Ireland : That's worse.

Myself : Then shut your gobbogue!

* * *

I HAD intended that this column should appear today in glorious Technicolor but certain technical difficulties supervened. It is all rather difficult to explain without slides. Supposing I stand at the window here and close the shutters. We are then in darkness. Very good. But now I open the left-hand shutter. Light into the room.

The Plain People of Ireland: Light into the room? Isn't there a word left out there?

Myself : There is indeed. The word 'floods'. 'Light floods into the room.' By the way, do you mind if I put this explanation off to another time?

The Plain People of Ireland : O not at all, it's all right. What about a couple of good jokes?

Myself : I will have you in stitches by and by. In the meantime listen to this. One of the morbid sub-human pretences adopted by Keltured idiocated Dubliners is that Georgian Dublin simply must be preserved do you hear me, I mean these marvellous façades, exquisite squares, the foot and the cavalry were here then, and 500 Dublin people made a good living making military unyforms at sixty pounds a time. Fitzwilliam Square was a blaze of lights, the grand old Whig nobility, gracious way of living, Grattan's Parliament, the Beresfords lived here, stucco ceilings, classical iconography, civilisation, Gandon, Fwawnsees Johnston, Cassel, William Chambers, Ivory, Burlington, Cooley, fanlights, fenestration, the Wide Streets Commissioners, mellow old brickwork, observe how a century's weathering has modulated the first bright plum-flush to wan wine-hues incomparably nice.

Leave that shutter alone, when I close a shutter it is meant to be kept closed. But what are the facts about this Georgian ramp? I'll tell you (they'll get me for this but my public comes first) I'll tell you the inside guts of it. Dublin is a slum. Dublin is a slum do you hear me. At its best (in Fitzwilliam Square) a well-preserved flat-riddled professional slum. At its worst (in Bride Street, the Liberties, Summerhill, Mountjoy Square) a sprawling dung-hill on stilts, giving off a constant odourless vapour of rancid, unwashable profit-rents. Ah yes, it is all real Dublin, the old crowd are the best, I was born in this house and my father before me was born here and his father before him faith. Aye. Old Dublin is so picturesque that you can smell its nostalgic charm when the mail boat is ten miles out coming in by Lambay (do you remember the time we had a picnic there in the old days, poor George was alive then). When I come back to Dublin after Paris, I feel I am near to tears. Tears are always near when one contemplates a work of great art like the Pan in the Dresdner Muckschule or the exquisite figures at Orvicto, or the second quartet by Bloch.

Contemplate Little Britain Street bloch by bloch, Joe, and drop me a postcard telling me in your own words about the remote faded poignancy of elegant proportions, minute delicacy of architectural detail balanced against the rather charmingly squalid native persons who sort of provide a contrapuntal device in the aesthetic apprehension of the whole.

The Plain People of Ireland : How about those jokes.

Myself : Well wait till I see. Would you say that the cousin of the French Pretender is the Duc de Guise ?

The Plain People of Ireland : Whaa ?

Myself : And I wonder would he be annything to the Wild Geese ?

The Plain People of Ireland : Dear knows some people are very smart, these County Council scholarships to the universities above in Dublin do more harm than good, young gossoons walking around with their Sunday suits on them on week-days when they're home at Easter, ashamed to be seen out with their fathers and O no thanks, I'm not going to give *any* hand with the sowing, I have to attend to me studies, I've an exam in two months. And that reminds me, I want five pounds for books. Sure it's all madness. You say you'd like a joke or two for a bit of crack and the finger of scorn is pointed at you. It's madness, the country's in a right state. Madness. There's no other word for it. Madness.

* * *

SOME PERSON who has the time should set about making a collection of the fearfully-witty-I-mean-to-say pronouncements made about this country by immigrant scribes of one kind and another. One can almost smell the smugness, can almost hear oneself hoping that some of it will not drip down and stain the carpet. In a recent issue of 'The Tablet' Mr Christopher Hollis writes about being brought down and given a feed in Maynooth where everybody understands Latin, it's all frightfully Irish to say the least of it. Then this:

'I am told that the Irish are much better at English prose than they are at Irish prose. I cannot say if it is true, For there are very few people who can read Irish prose, and those that can read it can hardly ever read any other Irish prose than their own.'

Mr Hollis once wrote an inaccurate book about Lenin. I am told he understands no Russian. I cannot say if it is true.

'Thank heaven for the Film Society is all there is space to say of *La Femme du Boulanger*, sophisticated, witty, beautifully directed, acted and photographed.' *Irish Times* Critic.

You're right, you're right, shure there's nothing like th' oul French film, lovely stuff it is, you'd think you were in Paris where Maurice Chevalier comes from, bobbies with queer lookin' caps on them an' all.

For years they have been talking on the upper-class well-bred-lines about der film als kunst, this Hollywood thing is well I mean to say it is all right if you like that sort of thing but it's vulgar, old boy, it's vulgar, it's not Awrt. Look what they did to poor Eisenstein's *Que Viva Mexico*. There was I mean an oeuvre which would show his telekinetic treatment of over-tonality at its fullest maturity in his new alert awareness of the sound-track, I mean to say everybody knows that the comparative structural simplicity of acoustical events makes them most suitable for controlled use in the highest orders of the Eisenstein montage hierarchy. And wot did they do? They gave it to Sol Lesser, damn me, to 'edit', called it Thunder Over Mexico! (Thing would be laughable were it not so tragic.)

Yes. But the film is a great industry: it does not have to apologise to the unwashed uneducated artistic classes, the madolescents and peterpanjandrums for not being an art. Hollywood has brought up the best brains, the best technicians, the best cameramen and designers, the best actors in the world. When a good film is made, Hollywood makes it—and everyone can see that it's good. It earns millions of dollars. (Ah that's all right for you, I know the sort you are, but give me a private job that's shot on faded sepia sixteen millimetre stock with non-professional actors, epileptic cameramen, no story and dialogue in French *anny day of the week*.)

There is no reason in the world why a film should be addressed to a small clique; each film gives employment to armies of technical, sales and publicity people before it gets to the public and if it does that it must be better than the flickering fiddling avant-garde releases. In any event the film is merely spectacle and has nothing to do with what Mr Harris

Tottle chatted about. (But try and prove that to the velvet daddy-long-legses with greasy hair.)

The Plain People of Ireland : Another day gone and no jokes.
Myself : Yes, curse you.

* * *

I DO NOT suppose that there is a decent man within the four walls of Ireland who has not been annoyed by the publicity given to this stage coach gag. Self-respecting Irishmen (wherever they may be, on land, or sea or in the sky) will ask themselves what is the necessity for having, for instance, this horn-tooting business? It is colourful, you say. *Colourful?* And if you get half a chance you will undoubtedly come out with some old bit of chat about 'these drab times' and how 'cheering˙ the effect of 'a bit of colour' and (please don't hurt me too much) 'a bit of old-world romance'. Yes. I wonder in what baby's newspaper you read that. COLOURFUL? Every time I hear the word 'colourful' I reach for my revolver.

The Plain People of Ireland : Ah but shure 'tis grand, the old coaching days, you know, with the horn blowing and the scarlet coats and the ostlers and the potboys and the jars of hot punch inside in the pub. Shure it's like ould times man.

Myself : Aye, but could we not have Tom Mix or John Wayne galloping down from the Galtees and sticking up the coach with blunderbusses, your money or your life, throw out the bags of gold dust and put all your jewelry into that hat, nobody will get hurt unless—Oh no, you don't—BANG! Bang-bang-bang! BANG! They've got me, Jake—look after Cis when I'm gone. BANG! Bang! Bang! Bang! Wheeeeee—plop! And the little flash of funny stuff, a bullet has punctured the flask of the card-sharper drunk (played by your old pal Joe Kerrigan) and the booze, more prized than life-blood, drips tragically into the fine burning sand. Bang, bang, bang! But what's this—the clatter of a hundred hooves? They sweep into view with guns blazing—the Rangers! The Texas Rangers in the nick of time! The fearless Rangers, led by steel-faced Bill Boyd, otherwise known as Hopalong Cassidy.

The Plain People of Ireland : Oh they're saved, THEY'RE saved, Hurrah, good old Rangers!

Indeed, Adare* is not the only place where the far-from-funny collapse of our transport services is regarded as a pretext for whimsy and jolly

* A war-time coach service was started in the village of Adare.

pranks with red coats. Side-splitting jokes are made on the subject in other places. Look at this tragic swathe of twaddle that appeared the other day in—yes—this newspaper.

'Why not elephant and llama services, starting at the Pillar and running (or rather walking) to the nearer suburbs? Why not let the dromedary earn his keep? It might even be possible to run a special gala zebra-line to the current charity carnival.'

Well, two can play at that game, two can do that withering funny-man act, two can kill the *Irish Times* readers with that class of stuff. I mean, it would be only right that these services should be named after the various districts served; one can visualise (with a special premature dodderer's smirk) the Clonskeagh-Whitehallephant, the Ranellamagh, the Dundromedary and the elegant two-seater zebriolet (to Cabra or vice versa).

Go further (and fare worse). Would a tram drawn by emus be emusing? It you had a small dray drawn by a hot flapping phoenix, would it be permissible under the traffic regulations to let the phoenix park? Fox-rides to Foxrock? Monkey-trots to Monkstown?

Yes, it is a fine thing to make fun. But let the fun be gentle, *gentle*. Gentle and subtle. The world-weary and word-weary lips LaGiocondosely curved in tender amusement. Life is rather a lark, you knaow, fun is where you find it, humanity playing pitiful perspiring pranks and oozing with limp straw-coloured joy. But life remember has its sterner moments. The harvest, I mean, wheat, transport, economic holdings, an enlightened monetary policy and the Craobh Ruadh. We must work now and again, too, you know. Work is the man that will see us right at the latter end.

* * *

CONSIDER the word *wheat*. By its nourishment *wheat* gives you heat. And in addition to *heat*, *wheat* gives you something to *eat at t*. Get it? Wheat, heat, eat, at t. W-h-e-a-t. Take away the first letter of wheat and you get heat. Then take away the first letter of heat and you get eat. Then take away the—

The Plain People of Ireland: O fair enough! Good man, good man! It must be a desperate job thinking out things like that. Couldn't see it at first. Smart boy wanted.

Myself: I'm pretty deep, you know, sometimes.

The Plain People of Ireland: O it's very hard to be up to you be times, especially the days when you do have jawbreakers in the paper. Did you ever hear this one ? What tongue is it that frequently hurts you but never speaks a word?

Myself : I give up.

The Plain People of Ireland : THE TONGUE OF YOUR SHOE!

Myself : Ha-ha-ha, very good! Here's one I'll bet you don't answer. What trade is that at which a man will succeed only by sticking it?

The Plain People of Ireland (eagerly) : What is it?

Myself : Bill-posting.

The Plain People of Ireland : O, HA-HA-HA-HA-HA! (Sounds of thousands of thighs being slapped and the creak of coarse country braces as the body bends double in writhes of mirth.)

* * *

PEOPLE in my position get a queer view of life, as the cynical acrobat said when he was hanging upside down 200 feet from terra firma et incognita. I mean, people write to me. All classes of letters by every post. Can you tell me this or that? I can, of course. A Waterford lady tells me that her face is destroyed with freckles. Have I a remedy? I have. To remove freckles, take one ounce of lemon juice, a quarter of a drachm of powdered borax, and half a drachm of sugar. Mix and let stand for a few days in a glass bottle, then rub occasionally on the face and hands.

And listen to this from a Casanova in Belmullet. 'I am madly in love with eighteen girls and cannot make up my mind which of them to marry. Can you advise me?'

I can faith. Marry the fat fair dumpy one.

The Plain People of Ireland : How do you know there's a fat fair dumpy one among them?

Myself : How could you find a group of eighteen girls without a fair fat dumpy one among them?

The Plain People of Ireland : Um.

Myself : Sure didn't I marry a fair fat dumpy one myself?

The Plain People of Ireland : Did you? Any kids?

Myself : Nine.

The Plain People of Ireland : O fair enough.

* * *

WHAT WOULD you do before you'd write—sorry—before you'd sit down and write this stuff?

I'D ATE IT, D'YE HEAR ME, THAT'S WHAT I'D DO, I'D ATE IT FIRST.

What is like what you always said?

That the poor helps the poor.

What will that be out of you?

Enough.

What condition may be said to be the prerequisite for a fine day?

The condition that the rain keeps off.

To what variable horizon can some people not be trusted?

As far as you would throw them.

What tribe has unique rights to the epithet finny?

Your men the fish.

Feathered?

Your men the birds.

Lost?

Your men the Gaels.

What is the sole and true badge of nationhood?

The national language.

Without what also would it be idle to seek to revive the national language.

Our distinctive national culture.

The Plain People of Ireland : What is that you had up there about 'finny'? Fish aren't men, are they? Do you mean mermen?

Myself : I was referring to the denizens of the deep.

The Plain People of Ireland (very doubtfully) : Is that the way? (Brightening up) Did you ever read round the world in eighty days by Jools Vern?

Myself : I did faith.

The Plain People of Ireland (enthusiastically) : It's very clever the way your man makes a bet to get round in eighty days and then he thinks he's lost it, he's done it in eighty-one, but then he comes along and discovers that he's gained a day on the journey because of the Gulf Stream, you know, and the curvature of the earth and all the rest of it. He wins out in the latter end. Why don't you sit down and write a book like that?

Myself : For a very simple reason. I haven't got a chair.

The Plain People of Ireland : A chair?

Myself : Yes, a chair. How could I sit down and write a book without having a chair to do the sitting on?

The Plain People of Ireland : What happened all the chairs you had?

Myself : Had to sell them, the only course compatible with honour. The rates, you know. Do you know the story about a certain college where they speak Latin and where the use of tobacco is strictly ta—

Taboo.

Yes. Well, this prefect comes along and sees a student with a lump in his cheek as if he was chewing a certain forbidden commodity. Quid est hoc? says the prefect. Hoc est quid, says the man, as quick to make a smart retort as the apocryphal character, the next. That joke dates from 1873. In what do I trust it keeps you?

Stitches.

* * *

IT IS now sixteen or seventeen years since I saw the queen of France, then the dauphiness, at Versailles; and surely never lighted on this orb, which she hardly seemed to touch, a more delightful vision. I saw her just above the horizon, decorating and cheering the elevated sphere which she just began to move in; glittering like the morning star, full of life and splendour, and joy—

The Plain People of Ireland : Sure that wan went to the wall years ago, you must be mixin' her up with some other party.

Myself : For me the Queen of France never died.

The Plain People of Ireland : And if it's above the horizon you seen her, that's fair enough, many's a man seen more than the queen of France and him out in a boat fishin', coopers of stout and sandwiches, half fallin' out of the boat rotten fluthery-eyed drunk on porter and whiskey, sure is it any wonder you're seein' visions man? Sure Lord save us you'll be Napolean Boneypart himself next above in the Grange weedin' turnips.

Myself : I was at a wake the other night and every man jack was drunk —including the corpse.

The Plain People of Ireland : O faith now never mind the wakes, many's a better man than you was happy enough at home be the fire with Knocknagow or a good American cowboy story, there's a very bad type of person goin' around now that wasn't known in our fathers' day.

OVERHEARD

I tried to get it many a time. O many a time.

Well I could never see any harm in it.

I seen it once in a shop on the quays, hadn't any money on me at the time and when I came back to look for it a week later bedamn but it was gone. And I never seen it in a shop since.

Well, I can't see what all the fuss was about.

You read it, did you?

I couldn't see any harm at all in it there was nothing in it.

I tried to get it many a time meself . . .

There's no harm in it at all.

Many's a time I promised meself I'd look that up and get it.

Nothing at all that anybody could object to, not a thing in it from the first page to the last.

It's banned, o'course.

Not a thing in it that anybody could object to, NO HARM AT ALL IN IT, nothing at all anywhere in the whole thing.

O indeed many's a time I tried to get it meself.

*　*　*

DO NOT for that singular interval, one moment, think that I have been overlooking this new Intoxicating Liquor Bill. I am arranging to have an amendment tabled because it appears that there is absolutely nothing else you can do with amendment.

My idea is to have the hours altered so that public houses will be permitted to open only between two and five in the morning. This means that if you are a drinking man you'll have to be in earnest about it.

Picture the result. A rustle is heard in the warm dark bedroom that has been lulled for hours with gentle breathing. Two naked feet are tenderly lowered to the flower and a shaky hand starts foraging blindly for matches. Then there is a further sleepy noise as another person half-wakens and rolls round.

'John! What's the matter?'

'Nothing.'

'But where are you going?'

'Out for a pint.'

'But *John*! It's half two.'

'Don't care what time it is.'

'But it's pouring rain. You'll get your death of cold.'

'I tell you I'm going out for a pint. Don't be trying to make a ridiculous scene. All over Dublin thousands of men are getting up just now. I haven't had a drink for twenty-four hours.'

'But John, there are four stouts in the scullery. Beside the oat-meal bag.'

'Don't care what's in the scullery behind the oat-meal bag.'

'O, John.'

And then dirty theatrical snivelling sobbing begins as the piqued and perished pint-lover draws dressing gowns and coats over his shivering body and passes out gingerly to the stairs.

Then the scene in the pub. Visibility is poor because a large quantity of poisonous fog has been let in by somebody and is lying on the air like layers of brawn. Standing at the counter is a row of dishevelled and shivering customers, drawn of face, quaking with the cold. Into their unlaced shoes is draped, concertina-wise, pyjama in all its striped variety. Here and there you can discern the raw wind-whipped shanks of the inveterate night-shirt wearer. And the curate behind the bar has opened his face into so enormous a yawn that the tears can be heard dripping into the pint he is pulling. Not a word is heard, nothing but chilly savage silence. The sullen clock ticks on. Then 'Time, please, time. Time for bed, gentlemen.' And as you well know, by five in the morning, the heavy rain of two-thirty has managed to grow into a roaring downpour.

The Plain People of Ireland : Is all this serious?

Myself : Certainly it's serious, why wouldn't it be serious, you don't think I'd try to make jokes about anything so funny as the licensing laws, why would I bring turf to Newcastlewest?

The Plain People of Ireland : If you're serious so, it's only a trick to get more drink for newspapermen.

Myself : Nonsense. Newspapermen couldn't hold any more than they have at present. ˙

The Plain People of Ireland : O faith now, that's enough. That's enough about that crowd. Remember well, many's a county council meeting, fluther-eyed note-takers couldn't get the half of it, stuff that days was spent thinkin' out.

Myself : Hic!

The Plain People of Ireland : Faith indeed that was loud enough, well you may talk about putting down drink. Putting down is right.

Myself : Ut's only mey undajaschin, d'yeh ondherstawnd.

I can see even another domestic aspect of this new order. It is after midnight. The man of the house is crouched miserably over the dying fire.

'John! Look at the time! Are you not coming to bed?'

'No. I'm waiting for the pubs to open.'

* * *

ON A RECENT Thursday I went to the pictures and saw a tall gentleman called Randolph Scott in a film called 'The Spoilers'. At the end of the picture Randolph gets into a fight with another man in a pub. At the end of the fight there is no pub. The fight is so fierce that it is reduced to smithereens. Randolph, being the bad lot, gets a frightful thrashing, a frtfull throshou, a frajfyl tromaking, a fruitful . . .

The Plain People of Ireland : Whatsamatter?

Myself : Feel queer . . . dark . . . nase blooding . . . giddy . . . where am I?

The Plain People of Ireland : Ah sure you often meet that in the pictures, too—that's altitude. You're too high up. No oxygen. The pilots do often have a black out. Come on down lower in the page and you'll be game ball.

Myself : All right. Thanks.

The Plain People of Ireland : Are you OK now?

Myself : Yes, thanks, I'm feeling all right now. Well, as I was saying, Randolph gets a frightful hiding, he is a terrible mess when the picture ends. But the following night I happened to see the same Randolph in another picture called, I think 'The Texan'. All I can say is, fit and well he was looking after the hammering he got the night before.

The Plain People of Ireland : Will you have a bit of sense man. 'The Texan' is an old picture. A real ould stager man. But 'The Spoilers' is a new picture. It doesn't say because you see the one on wan night and then d'other on another—

Myself : Say no more. I realise I have been hasty. I will think before I shoot my mouth off next time.

Yes. Let me see. Not bad down here. Sort of . . . cool. The daddy was a steeplejack but I was never a man for heights. Though many's a time I bought an irish-timesful of chips from that Italian chap Vertigo.

What's this I have in me pocket? Dirty scrap of paper. Some newspaper heading I cut out. 'LANGUAGE IN DANGER.' Of course if I was a cultured European I would take this to mean that some dumb barbarous tonguetide threatens to drown the elaborate delicate historical machinery for human intercourse, the subtle articulative devices of communication, the miracle of human speech that has developed a thousand light-years over the ordnance datum, orphic telepathy three sheets to the wind and so on. But I know better.

Being an insulated western savage with thick hair on the soles of my feet. I immediately suspect that it is that fabulous submythical erseperantique patter, the Irish, that is under this cushion—beg pardon—under discussion.

Yes. Twenty years ago, most of us were tortured by the inadequacy of even the most civilised, the most elaborate, the most highly developed languages to the exigencies of human thought, to the nuances of inter-psychic communion, to the expression of the silent agonised pathologies of the post-Versailles epoch. Our strangled feelings, despairing of a sufficiently subtle vehicle, erupted into the crudities of the war novel. But here and there a finer intellect scorned this course. Tzara put his unhappy shirt on his dada (Fr. for hobby-horse as you must surely know), poor Jimmy Joyce abolished the King's English, Paulsy Picasso started cutting out paper dolls and I . . .

I?

As far as I remember, I founded the Rathmines branch of the Gaelic League. Having nothing to say, I thought at that time that it was import-ant to revive a distant language in which absolutely nothing could be said.

*   *   *

THE SON of Pharaoh's daughter was the daughter of Pharaoh's son. Know that old one?

The Plain People of Ireland: How could that be, man? How could a man's son be his daughter at the same time?

Myself: I said the son of Pharaoh's daughter was the daughter of Pharaoh's son. It's all right, as you will see if you work it out with algebra. Let x equal the son of Pharaoh. Go further—call him Mr X. Then what you have is Mr X's daughter was the daughter of Mr X, surely not an unlikely relationship in all the circumstances.

The Plain People of Ireland: Begob, you're right, never thought of that, smart boy wanted.

Myself: Don't go yet. There's another way of looking at it. Call Pharaoh's daughter Mrs Y. Then you have another story—the son of Mrs Y was Mrs Y's son. See it?

The Plain People of Ireland: That's one of the smartest things for a long time. You ought to put that into the paper.

Yes, the son of Pharaoh's daughter. Then the other one, your man is looking at a photo and says brothers and sisters have I none but that man's father is my father's son. Who's picture is he looking at? His own. Right. Then the other one, a fiddler in Cork had a brother a fiddler in Dublin, what was the fiddler in Cork to the fiddler in Dublin? Brother? No that's wrong, you're completely out there, the right answer is sister.

Remember the last time we played these little games when we were all together? Remember the yellow lamplight, 'Spot' with his torn ear, the shutters with the iron bar across them; the black kettle hanging from the

old smut-furred chain in the chimney and the delicate
cups made in Belleek? Poor George was alive then and
little girl, little thinking she was soon to marry. That wa
years ago, in Newcastle West, where daddy's column of t
was stationed. Dear old dead days, gone beyond recall.

Every time I start this flash-back act, I always com
That is because the past is . . . essentially . . . personal, y
part of it is mine. They can't take my memories away fr
me as they will. Do you recall reading this in the *Irish*

'If you answer the knock of a "gas-man" with a pa
clean-shaven, wearing a dark or navy suit, soft gr
rimmed spectacles, make sure that he is a gas man. I
says the police, a man going about the city represen
inspector from the Gas Company. He examines the
gets the chance, steals any money that may be lyin

I suppose you blame me. You don't hesitate to lie ba
guinea armchair that creaks from the weight of your
suet-padded body and denounce me to your even weigh
a fly-be-night, a sleeveen and a baucagh-shool. Cliché
that you are, you probably go through that absurd act of
of scorn at me. It only serves to show me how plu
nourished it is. But let me tell you that I, too, must live
day I may call, stuff you into your own oven, and roast y

*   *   *

I NOTICE these days that the Green Isle is getting
ulcerations resembling buds pit the branches of our tre
can be seen on the upland lawn. Spring is coming an
is thinking of that new Spring costume. Time will ru
Favonius re-inspire the frozen Meade and clothe in
and rose that have nor sown nor spun. Curse it, my mi
Heidelberg days. Sonya and Lili. And Magda. An
Georg Geier, Theodor Winklemann, Efrem Zimbalis
the accordion player Kurt Schachmann. And Doktor
of Irish princes. Ich hab' mein Herz/ in Heidelberg
lauen/ Sommernacht/ Ich war verliebt/ bis über beide/
Röslein/hatt'/ Ihr Mund gelächt or something hum
tumpty tumpty mein Herz it schlägt am Neckarstra

student melody. Beer and music and midnight swims in the Neckar. Chats in erse with Kun O'Meyer and John Marquess . . . Alas, those chimes. Und als wir nahmen/ Abschied vor den Toren/ beim letzten Küss, da hab' Ich Klar erkannt/ dass Ich mein Herz/ in Heidelberg verloren/ MEIN HERZ/ es schlägt am Neck-ar-strand! Tumpty tumpty tum.

The Plain People of Ireland: Isn't the German very like the Irish? Very guttural and so on?

Myself: Yes.

The Plain People of Ireland: People do say that the German language and the Irish language is very guttural tongues.

Myself: Yes.

The Plain People of Ireland: The sounds is all guttural do you understand.

Myself: Yes.

The Plain People of Ireland: Very guttural languages the pair of them the Gaelic and the German.

MY THOUGHTS

I was watching a hen walking about a garden recently. Occasionally it picked up dirt and ate it, but otherwise spent an hour of complete idleness. I fell to wondering why hens have two legs and later tried to reason out the pretext for giving a horse four of these useful jointed props. Why has a horse eight knees and a hen no knees at all? As to the legs, I decided that a horse has four because he is a draught animal and a beast of burden; his four legs give him more drawing power than two, just as four driving wheels enhance the utility of a locomotive. By why then has a rat four? Why not two-legged rats—(I seen them meself the day the new City Hall was opened in Cork)? Two-legged rats would probably roost like fowls and would perch on the rails of a bed rather than merely chew the wainscotting as they do every night at present. On the other hand, four-legged hens would present a problem as their roosting-perches would have to be made to measure individually according to the length of each fowl. Perhaps I'd better stop.

AN UNIDENTIFIED PARTY

'SIR-SIR W. BEACH THOMAS asks "Is any animal anywhere quite silent?" The most extraordinary instance of almost, if not complete, silence

in any land animal is the giraffe. It has been heard, I believe, to utter a
very slight bleat when teased with food.'

This letter appeared recently in the London *Spectator*. It reminds me
that I have been harbouring a strange little animal in my house for years.
It looks not unlike a monkey, but since it roosts at night it must be something else. The 'face' is extraordinarily withered and old. The creature is
covered with a coarse fur and has never uttered a sound. It feeds chiefly on
books and newspapers, and sometimes takes a bath in the kitchen sink,
cunningly turning on the taps with its 'hand'. It rarely goes out and is in
its own way courteous. I am afraid and ashamed to let anybody see it in
case I am confronted with some dreadful explanation. Supposing it's a
little man cunningly disguised, some eccentric savant from the East Indies
who is over here studying us. How do I know he hasn't it all down in a
little book?

The Plain People of Ireland : Yerrah man you'll find it's an over-grown
rake of a badger you have in the house. Them lads would take the hand of
you.

Myself : Indeed?

The Plain People of Ireland : Better go aisy now with them lads. Ate the
face off you when you're asleep in the bed. Hump him out of the house
before he has you destroyed man. Many's a good man had the neck clawed
off him be a badger. And badgers that doesn't be barkin out of them is
very dangerous.

Myself : Thanks for the warning.

The Plain People of Ireland : A good strong badger can break a man's
arm with one blow of his hind leg, don't make any mistake about that.
Show that badger the door. Chinaman or no Chinaman.

Myself : Thank you, I will draw his attention to that useful portal.

* * *

WHY CHAIRS? Consider that man was made before furniture. He was
therefore made to sit on the floor. If today he finds it uncomfortable to
sit on the floor, the inference is that the human body has been modified
and impaired by thousands of generations of rascally chair-makers. Women
have been altered in our own day by high heels. Between high heels and
chairs they are the sort of people one is chary to approach. But I'll tell you
something. No chair in this part of the world can compare for its adverse
effect on the human with a chair that has been invented by those Americans. I mean the electric chair. It's as much as your life is worth to sit in

that thing. (Yes, I know. In a distant part of the prison the lights are momentarily dimmed; Wallace Beery glances at Tyrone Power under his shaggy brows—both men being in the attire of lifers in the Big House—and mutters: Yeah, they got Joe. They got Joe, son. Joe was a swell guy. I gotta get out of here.) (And then that damn searchlight on the prison wall, the stutter of tommy guns, then escape, ESCAPE—

The Plain People of Ireland : Out into the jungle begob! Man-eaters an' rattle-snakes and pigs as big as cows with tusks hangin out of them! They'll never make it!

Myself : And supposing they do. Supposing they reach the coast, what then? The shark-infested Timor Sea!

The Plain People of Ireland : And your men out in motor boats pottin at them with tommy guns!

Myself : Yes faith.

PROBABLY A MISTAKE

I was looking into an English Dictionary (yes—the other day) and came across this mistake:

'Intelligentzia: the part of a nation (esp. the Russian) that aspires to independent thinking.'

Now why the assumption that every nation has two parts, one being Russian? I know it so happens that it's true of this country—you know that introspective crowd from Cork—but I see complaints in the newspapers regarding the position in England. Incidentally, what sort of thinking is dependent thinking? And look at the mess you get into if you apply this definition to Russia itself.

A bad business, opening dictionaries; a thing I very rarely do. I try to make it a rule never to open my mouth, dictionaries or hucksters' shops.

OUR SAD COUNTRY

I had an unfortunate and indeed chastening experience (well, yes—the other day). I ran into a characteristic Irishman and before I had time to run out again, he had taken me nappertandywise by the hand and started to talk. How were we to-day? And wasn't there a great stretch in the evenings? Playing desperately for time I switched the talk to theatre matters. Would he like to see a show? Certainly he would, there was nothing he loved better than to be sitting down quietly in the theatre of an evening. I had a few free passes which a theatre manager had given me to keep me from talking aloud about his theatre whiskey and I gave one of these to my 'friend'. Profuse thanks. He'd rush off now and be in time for the first curtain. Thanks thanks thanks. We parted but I was shocked to see this worm again in another place ten minutes later. He was deep in a persuasive conversation. Need I say that like his fathers before him, he was trying to sell the pass?

* * *

HER FACE was radiant. She looked up, sensing the passion that was written in every line of the taut, lean face. Their eyes met.

'Mary!' he cried.

He bent down and took her in his arms. How strong he was, how masterful! How utterly he crushed her frail body against his pounding heart!

'Mary!' he cried again, huskily this time.

Their lips met. Heaven and earth seemed to—

The Plain People of Ireland : What in the name of goodness is all this about?

Myself : It is a scene from my new serial, which commences in this column next week.

The Plain People of Ireland : But surely that isn't the beginning of it? That's no way to begin a story.

Myself : No, it's not the beginning.

The Plain People of Ireland : Then what—

Myself : Were you never at the pictures? This is the trailer. The trailer shows the high spots of the story.

The Plain People of Ireland (interested) : O, a trailer? Well, go on.

Myself : In a minute, when you cool down.

A BOUNDER PUNISHED

Derek closed the door and stood very still. The silence was ominous. It did not bode aught that was good to the cringing Carruthers, who rose from the sofa with a sickly smile.

'Hello, Sternleigh, glad to see you,' he stammered.

Derek did not answer. Mary's quiet sobbing made the muscles of his face stand out like whipcords. He went to her, assisted her to her feet and gently guided her faltering footsteps towards the door.

'Please wait in the next room,' he said softly. 'I have business to settle here.'

When she was gone he turned with steely menace to Carruthers, whose freshly-lit cigarette betokened a nonchalance that was belied by the shaking hand that held it.

'Now, Carruthers,' he rapped out, 'stand up! Surprised to see me here, eh? Thought I was killed when your hirelings threw me down that old well, eh? Thought it was safe at last to press your slimy attentions on Miss Shunk, eh? Stand up, you cad, and take what's coming to you!'

Carruthers made as if to rise but in a trice had bounded towards the fender where a massive old-world poker was reclining with the other fire-irons.

'O no, you don't!'

Derek's quick eye had sensed the manoeuvre. He cleared the intervening space in one athletic spring and with a well-aimed kick had knocked the deadly weapon flying from his adversary's hand. Pale with anger, Carruthers wheeled round. With deadly timing Derek stopped in his tracks. Then his famed left shot out like a piston, caught Carruthers on the point of the chin. Out cold, he crashed to the floor like a piece of stone or some inanimate thing.

The Plain People of Ireland : O, good man, good man! Good enough for the dirty dog!

Myself : Shut up! There's more.

AN UNSAVOURY ACCOMPLICE

Carruthers lay quite still. Derek stood looking down at him, contempt written on every line of the taut, lean face. Behind him the door opened noiselessly, to reveal the sinister form of Sloane, the rascally, yellow-faced billiard-marker, suspected to be a hireling of Carruthers. In his hand was a loaded cue. Noiselessly he stole across the carpet until he was behind the unheeding form of Derek Sternleigh. Without a sound the loaded cue was raised—

The Plain People of Ireland : Turn round! TURN ROUND!

Myself : Shut up! Don't you understand that that's the end of that? If you want to know what happened, you will have to wait and read the story. Did Derek know? Did he call into force his famed back-somersault, to confound and unnerve his cowardly assailant? Did Mary, perturbed by the ominous silence, return to open the door just in time to warn her lover?

The Plain People of Ireland : Well; did she?

Myself : Wait and see, wait and see. Order your copy in advance.

* * *

THE BALL climbs high into the air. It seems to pause, then to fall, falling slowly in the hot blue sky. Jamstutter races from Square Two, his inferior cotton 'flannels' pinned by the wind to his fleet thighs—a white smear of speed on the bright June grass. Will he catch the ball? He will. HE DOES! He reaches for it with clean avid fingers. HE HAS IT! Good man, good man. Good old Jamstutter!

Again it rises in a long gentle lob. Observe the glint of sun on the gold-faced lace-holes. Now it falls with a soft elegance of descent. Jamstutter races from Square Two and again—YES—again he has caught it with prim peerless ease.

Up again, higher this time, its soft brown hue of baby hogskin blotted to a blackness against the hard glare of the heavens. Again Jamstutter moves lithely to his task. Will he catch it this time? Will he make Square Two in time? He is flitting across the grass like a hare—

The Plain People of Ireland : What is this game and who is this man Jamstutter? It doesn't sound like an Irish name.

Myself : The game is—WAIT! He's got it! He's caught it again! O good man, good man! Good old Jamstutter!

The Plain People of Ireland : Whoever he is he is not as good as Patsy, the Tipp goalie that stopped 52 sure scores in the 1937 hurling final.

Myself : But Jamstutter has a wooden leg.

The Plain People of Ireland : O, that's different. If he has a wooden leg, fair enough. He must be good so. Certainly that's very smart work for a man with wan leg. He's O.K.

UNIQUE OPPORTUNITY

The other day at dusk on the outskirts of the Naul I caught a small verse-speaker. Myself and a friend stalked the little creature with nets for three hours. It was very exhausted when caught and offered hardly any resistance. We have it at present in the *Irish Times* office in a cage. It is nicely marked and would be a most acceptable gift for a member of WAAMA if you happen to be stuck for a wedding present. It may be inspected daily between the hours of 11 and 5. Ask for Miss Concordia Slush, my private secretary, who is in charge of the cage. There is no warranty, of course, as to the quality of the recitation or indeed that it will recite at all. If we fail to get a decent price the thing will be raffled.

I was once acquainted with a man who found himself present by some ill chance at a verse speaking bout. Without a word he hurried outside and tore his face off. Just that. He inserted three fingers into his mouth, caught his left cheek in a frenzied grip and ripped the whole thing off. When it was found, flung in a corner under an old sink, it bore the simple dignified expression of the honest man who finds self-extinction the only course compatible with honour.

CHAT

Docs Proust affect you terribly? Emotionally, I mean?

Nao, not rahlly. His prose does have that sort of . . . glittering te ure, rather like the feeling one gets from the best *émaux Limousins*. But na . . . his peepul . . . thin, yeou knaow, thin . . . dull, stupeed.

But surely . . . surely Swann . . . ?

Ah yes . . . If all his geese were Swanns. . . .

Research Bureau

A HANDY INSTRUMENT

THE ARTICLE illustrated to-day (did you guess?) is a snow-gauge. There are very few of them in Ireland at present. It is made of copper, and

consists of a funnel or catch-pipe for the snow, which widens inwardly, then drops eighteen inches, allowing the snow to fall into a pan beneath. A casing which can be heated with hot water surrounds the gauge and is used to melt the snow. By this arrangement the snow cannot escape; it melts and runs into the bucket beneath, where it is accurately gauged.

So what, you say. I will tell you what. There is one great advantage in having a snow gauge on your premises. Supposing some moon-faced young man who reads Proust happens to be loitering about your house, blathering out of him about art, life, love, and so on. He is sure to have a few cant French phrases, which he will produce carefully at suitable intervals as one produces coins from a purse. Inevitably the day will come (even if you have to wait for it for many years) when he will sigh and murmur:

'*Mais où sont les neiges d'antan?*'

Here is your chance. This is where you go to town. Seize the nitwit by the scruff of the neck, march him out to the snow gauge, and shout:

'Right in that bucket, you fool!'

I'll bet you'll feel pretty good after that.

HOME HINTS

Do you often think you are going to die in the middle of the night? Are your feet swollen? Is your blood choked with every manner of toxic rubbish? Are you looking your 'old self'? ('I seen him on the Monday, he was lookin' his old self, you'd have sworn . . .')

I have pleasure in illustrating to-day my patent Valetudinarian's

Vademecum. This ingenious little instrument may look like a greyhound hoodlum's stop-watch, but if you examine the dial closely you will realise that it is an ordinary thermometer. You wear it in an inside pocket, as near your skin as possible. No matter where you are it enables you to take your temperature without the least fuss 200 times a day. No matter whether you are in the mart, the dram-shop, glorious Killiney, or even Ballylickey, you just take out your 'watch'. Your temperature is already registered.

If you are absent-minded funny things can happen.

'What time is it, mister?'

'I am very ill. Excuse me. I must go home at once!'

The Vade-mecum costs from £2 to £7, depending on the metal it is made of.

* * *

'WANTED, WIFE, copper-faced, any length, capable of being bent. Box—'

This is an advertisement that appeared recently in an evening paper. It is obvious, of course, that 'wife' is a misprint for 'wire'.

To be honest for a change, I invented this advertisement out of my head. It did not appear in any paper. But, if any reader thinks that any special merit attaches to notices of this kind because they have actually appeared in print, what is to stop me having them inserted and then quoting them?

Nothing, except the prohibitive cost.

MYSELF AND THE EMERGENCY

I have been looking further into the problem of maintaining efficient railway services in these days of inferior fuel. My latest solution is expensive, but highly ingenious. My plan is that all the lines should be re-laid to traverse bogland only, and that the locomotives should be fitted with a patent scoop apparatus which would dig into the bog underneath the moving train and supply an endless stream of turf to the furnace. Naturally, it would be dried in the furnace before being burned. This principle is at present recognised in taking up water when the train is at speed, and must, therefore, be quite feasible.

Of course, there are difficulties—nobody sees them more clearly than myself. For example, unless care were taken, an express careering across a bog at full tilt might encounter a quagmire and disappear into the bowels of the earth, passengers and all. To prevent this, it would be necessary to precede every heavy train by a light engine fitted with a prodding apparatus. This would consist of a battery of steel poles, which would be fitted to the front of the engine. The poles would rise and fall as the engine proceeded, probing carefully into the nature of the bog strata and ringing bells in the driver's cabin where the resistance encountered was less than a given limit. When the bells are heard, the driver would press a button and set in motion another machine at the engine's rear. This rear machine would consist of mammoth pounders, which would descend on the bog, feed builder's rubble into it and pulverise it to a suitable firmness. Thus, by application and perseverance, our difficulties are surmounted.

FURTHERMORE

Another snag is the difficulty of finding continued bogland between, say, Dublin and Galway. Here, again, failure to recognise defeat will be invaluable. Our plan will be to follow the bog wherever we find it and get to Galway one way or another, even if we have to spend weeks in the train and wander through every county in Ireland. The unrelieved bogland scenery on such a journey would be a bit tedious to the eye, but telescopes could be supplied for viewing the more distant vistas.

Then there is another snag: After the train has been scooping along for a week or so, the trench between the rails will become gradually deeper, and there will be a tendency for water to drain into it, Nature being what she is. If the engine encounters a damp patch the scoop will deliver gallons of water to the firebox and put the fire out. Our obvious remedy here is an army of men equipped with giant sponges. Night and day these sponges must be used to drain the scoop-trench. If these men are face-tiously called 'spongers' it cannot be helped. I am often called the same thing myself. ('I say, old man, you're living beyond my means!')

DANGER!

Then, supposing the train ploughs into some of our bogland poteen deposits. A keg of the drastic brew is scooped into the fire and a blinding blue flash is seen to envelope the engine. The train pulls up and the passengers dismount to root madly in the bog with their nails, like the beasts of the field. When they have found any other kegs that may be buried in the vicinity and duly refreshed themselves they resume their journey amid brazen shouts from the engine crew that they are going to 'show a thing or two in the line of speed!'

The Great Northern Railway Company have courteously informed me that they are unlikely to operate my scheme, owing to the scarcity of bog-land in their territory. The Great Southern Company, however, are experimenting somewhere in Kildare. I almost feel justified in inviting the reader to watch this newspaper for an important announcement.

* * *

AN EMERGENCY PROBLEM

SOME SHORT TIME ago the Dublin City Manager, the Managing Director of the Gas Company, and the Chairman of the Electricity Supply Board asked me would I meet them to discuss the problem of conserving fuel. ~~y did not know me personally, but a friend, etc., etc. Admiration for my ingenious inventions, and great resourcefulness of intellect had prompted them, etc., etc. Necessity for all to pull together, etc., etc. Civic, not to say national, emergency, etc., etc. Take liberty of enlisting aid of great brain, etc., etc. Hoping for the favour of an early and favourable reply etc., etc. Beg to subscribe themselves, etc., etc.

Well, I had them in one evening. We went into the whole thing, facts and figures, pencil and paper. The public would not cut down their lights. Nobody in Dublin had the courage to take a bath in the dark. Everybody insisted on having an unnecessary light showing in the hall in case the neighbours should think that the supply had been turned off at the main for non-payment of the last quarter's bill. Light burning for two hours in Lizzie's room when she is going to bed. Papa up half the night tippling in the sittingroom. So on and so on. Could I find some way to make a large saving on *public* lighting to offset this? Dislike touching on money matters, but directors prepared to authorise generous fee, etc., etc.

MY SOLUTION

I told the gentlemen that money did not interest me, but that such small talents as I possessed were at their disposal, and, through them, at the disposal of the plain people of Ireland (from whom all authority is derived). I asked them to look in again in a week's time.

In a word, it is a plan for lighting the streets by sewer-gas. The mechanism shown on the right, built into the lamp-post, refines, vaporises and ignites

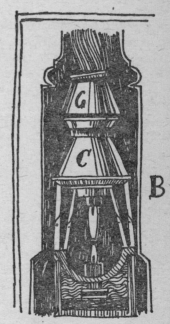

the sewer-gas, which is then transmitted to incandescent mantles in the globe higher up. It burns with a brilliant orange flame which is practically odourless.

I never saw three men go out with a lighter step.

* * *

THE MYLES na gCopaleen Central Research Bureau is working night and day on an invention that may mean the end of civilisation as we know it. Again, it is a new kind of ink, but nothing so footling as the other kind that disappears off cheques a few hours after you have written your signature with it. No, sir, this is something bigger, and when perfected will lead to a world-wide revolution, the end of which no man can foresee. It is provisionally called 'Trink', and looks for all the world like the ordinary black ink you can buy for twopence. 'Trink', however, is a very special job. When put on paper and dried, it emits a subtle alcoholic vapour which will hang over the document in an invisible odourless cloud for several days. A person perusing such a document is surrounded by this cloud. The vapour is drawn in with the breath, condenses on the mucous tract, gradually finds its way to the stomach and is absorbed in the blood. Intoxication ensues, mild or acute, according to how much reading is done.

Considerable difficulty has been encountered in perfecting the invention, not because of any major snag, but because our research workers emerge from the laboratory day after day in a hopeless state of inebriation and are unable to give any coherent account of their experiments. One of our best men has had to be put away; absenteeism is rampant among others, who cannot face two consecutive days' work owing to the paralysing hangover that is conferred by the first. This difficulty, however, is being taken care of. Soon a new type of gas-mask will be available and the great work will go on.

OUR AIM

Later, when 'Trink' has been perfected, the whole idea is to print the *Irish Times* with it. You will then get something more than a mere newspaper for your thruppence. You get a lightning pick-me-up not only for yourself and your family but for everybody that travels in your 'bus. Any time you feel depressed, all you need do is to read the leading article; if you want a whole night out, get down to the small ads.

I can see opposition: every great innovation must expect it. Vested interests, backstairs influence. The Licensed Vintners' Association will make a row; newsvendors will have to hold an excise licence or possibly the *Irish Times* will be on sale only in hostelries; the Revenue will probably clamp a crippling tax on every copy and compel us to print under the title 'Licensed for the Sale of Intoxicating News, 6 Days'. All that will not stop us, any more than the man with the red flag stopped the inevitable triumph of ~~the~~ motor car. And no power on earth, remember, can compel your copy of the *Irish Times* to close down at ten. You can read and re-read it until two in the morning if it suits your book, and even tear it in two and give your little wife a page.

I will have more to say on this subject and no wonder.

'TRINK' TO ME ONLY WITH THINE 'I's'

Our experiments with 'Trink', the new ink that exudes an insidious inebriating vapour, are proceeding apace. We are not yet at the stage when we can risk printing the *Irish Times* with it, but the other day we decided to use it for one or two posters intended for the country. The results, noted by our own plain-clothes narks who were on the spot, were quite satisfactory. A few people on their way to work in a certain town paused for a moment to spell out the placard (our educational system is weak remember) and to reflect for a moment on the news. The news was bad, as usual but the parties taking it in experienced a strange feeling of elation and well-being. They went on their way rejoicing and one of them, a staid school master, went into his class and straightway led them in a raucous rendering of 'Alexander's Rag-time Band', bashing out the time on his desk with a pointer. A loafer who had propped himself for the day beside the poster collapsed at 12.15 and was rushed to hospital.

In another town the papers failed to arrive at the shops from the railway station. A young man charged with delivering them was found stotious in a doorway with his papers under his head. He was instantly dismissed by his employers and is now earning £25 a week in a munitions factory abroad, a thing that will give each of us furiously to think.

Thus the pattern of life changes and we move into the new and better world that is being prepared for us by the Myles na gCopaleen Central Research Bureau.

* * *

AS REGARDS MARY, the Rose of Tralee, it will be recalled that it was not her beauty alone that won one; ah no, 'twas the truth in her eyes ever dawning. Bearing this in mind, it occurred to the Myles na gCopaleen Research Bureau the other day to try to ascertain whether the truth still dawns in the eyes of the ladies of to-day. An investigator was sent out with instructions to engage a hundred ladies in conversation and examine their eyes for traces of the truth, dawning, fully dawned, declining or otherwise.

He was away for a week and then returned to submit the following record of his researches:

45% Mild mydriasis, probably caused by the consumption of slimming drugs.

21% Ptosis of the lids due to defect in the oculomotor nerve, anisocoria, opthalmia, one or more small chalazions.

18% pronounced hyperthyroidism.

14% Evidence of retinal hemorrhages, papillary oedema, exophthalmos.

1% Mikulicz's disease.

1% Paralysis of the orbicularis oculi.

'No evidence of the truth ever dawning anywhere?' we asked.

'No,' he said, 'and what's more, I'm going to marry one of them.'

'Which one?' we asked.

'Mikulicz's disease,' he said, 'and she has three cute little yellow chalazions too.'

We agreed to put him on the married man's scale and changed the subject by putting that damn lovely thing by Toselli on the gramophone.

* * *

AN *Evening Mail* advertisement of a few weeks ago tells me that

'Sober workman will share room with same. 4/6 weekly.'

How sober are you if you insist on paying money to share a room with yourself? Don't worry, there's worse coming.

Though the Boyars and the old Tatar nobility no longer fill the higher cadres in the general staffs of the USSR's armies, nevertheless within the past year the Supreme Command has shown itself to be possessed of such dash and gallantry, such a mastery of strategy, tactics, camouflage, subterfuge, and all the wily arts of offensive and defensive war that one is tempted to believe that a new military herrenvolk is emerging—in fact, a Red Herrenvolk.

UPROOT THE YOUTH ROT!

This is an 'Irish Catholic' poster. But rot doesn't have any roots and even if it had, it wouldn't be any good pulling it up because it would come away in your hand.

Next to be shaved pleased!

No reasonable solution has been received to the conundrum as to the meaning of the phrase *Taisc do thicéad go seallfaidhe*, which appears on the Dublin Transport Company's tickets. I therefore keep my nice book prize. The phrase has no meaning but only schoolboys are slapped for this sort of thing.

Talking of transport, have our paunch-vested upper classes yet got over their first fine carless rapture?

The Myles na gCopaleen Research Bureau receives nearly a thousand letters a day (942 on Thursdays, however) from readers asking us to devise machines and engines that will solve their personal problems. Some of these problems are too intimate to be discussed here, but a Mitchelstown reader has approached us on what must be a fairly widespread difficulty. Nowadays it is nearly impossible to get matches and your cheap petrol lighter won't work in the middle of the night because it lacks the stimulation that is afforded by the heat of the body when carried round in the pocket all day. This means you cannot tell the time at night and do not know when to eat your nocturnal dose of pills—the pills your doctor warned you would be no good unless you could pull yourself together and lead 'a regular life'; and you know what I mean by that—please take the innocent smirk off your face.

Well, take a look at this apparatus we have devised. 'A' is an ordinary

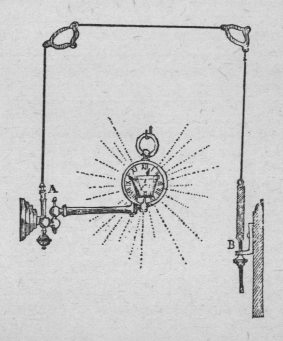

gas-jet with a modified vertical tap that is operated by a spring-loaded cord-pull ('B'), which is erected beside your bed. When going to bed (or 'retiring', if you prefer unctuous round-abouts) you light the gas, which is adjusted to afford a tiny and almost invisible fan-tail of light. You have already driven a stout nail into the polished teak panelling behind the light, and on this you have hung your watch. Everything is now in order. When you wake up and want to know the time, you just pull down the knob at 'B' and there you are.

The Plain People of Ireland : But shure that's no use. The gas is turned off at night, and in anny case there's no gas in Mitchelstown.

Myself : You err. To-morrow I will print a diagram showing how to make your own gas. In any case, I have often been told that there does be great gas in Mitchelstown.

The Plain People of Ireland : Listen, surely it's not that time! Lord save us, don't say it's twenty-five to one.

Myself : I'm a bit fast as a matter of fact.

The Plain People of Ireland : Oh, good. Thank heaven!

* * *

THE MYLES na gCopaleen Central Research Bureau is experimenting with the manufacture of intoxicating ice cream. The object of this step is to help to prevent the collapse of the national *moral* owing to the growing shortage of spirits and beer. (How can you talk of a thing 'growing' if you mean it is shrinking?) Several potent freezerfuls of a pink treacly mess have been produced but the preparation is still far from perfect. While it induces a pale wan languorous inebriation followed by unheard-of depression, it tastes like sludge from a tractor's sump, it cannot be digested even with the lavish assistance of enteric chemicals, and the fumes from it have a deadly effect on the optic nerve. This is not to say that the Bureau is giving up hope. Experiments continue night and day. Myles na gCopaleen, the da, has already decorated several employees for gallantry and distinguished conduct in the tasting room and has not scrupled to get them the best room in the hospital. In a moving address to them he said that however long the road, however sombre and bitter the setbacks they might encounter, they were determined to finish the task they had undertaken, they were resolved to rest neither night nor day until their objective was achieved and alcoholic ice cream had become a commonplace of Irish life.

By 'commonplace' he had in mind, no doubt, the daily court hearings of the future.

The sergeant stated that the defendant staggered badly after getting out of the car and smelt strongly of drink.

Defendant: I have not touched a drink for ten years.

District Justice: Did you have any of this new ice cream?

Defendant: Well, I had, your honour.

District Justice: How much had you?

Defendant: I had a twopenny wafer in Drogheda, your honour.

District Justice: Is that all?

Defendant: I felt a cold coming on me and had two cornets at Swords.

District Justice said he was determined to put down the growing practice of people driving around in motorcars and pulling up at roadside sweet-shops to consume ice cream. If such persons feel they need ice cream, they must leave their cars at home.

The Sergeant said that the defendant had a small freezer in the back of the car which bore the traces of fresh ice cream; the cushions also had traces of wafer-crumbs.

District Justice: No doubt he said 'Crumbs!' when he ran into the other car. (Laughter.)

Defendant stated that he had bad teeth and did not like ice cream but took it as a tonic and also to prevent himself getting colds. He realised now that he had been foolish and was prepared to take the pledge and drink only whiskey in future.

District Justice inquired what was defendant's capacity.

Defendant said he had often taken five or six cornets without suffering any ill effects or intoxication.

District Justice: Uneasy feels the head that's had six cornets. (Laughter.)

Defendant said he would lose his job and British Army pension if convicted.

District Justice said that defendant should have thought of that before indulging in the deadly potions of the freezer. The next time ice cream addicts were brought before him the sentence would be jail. In the present case he would give the defendant a stern warning and fine him forty shillings.

* * *

ANOTHER THING that is going short in the emergency is midnight oil. A friend who burns a considerable quantity of it tells me he is down to his last drum and his supplier (holds out) (little hope) of getting more. But pray do not think (for one moment) that the Myles na gCopaleen Research Bureau is asleep when the problem of this kind is confronting the nation. Advanced experiments are in progress with a patent midnight grease which is made from turf, whiskey, offals and cider. This mess burns with a pale blue flame and is quite satisfactory for illuminating midnight attics. The trouble (as I needn't tell you) is the smell. The smell is fearful. Already the Corporation has assured us that we are committing a nuisance by manufacturing the stuff. That, of course, is a scandalous charge (to lay) (at our door). Ireland must have midnight oil or a suitable substitute, otherwise it will disappear from civilisation. Without midnight oil the Irish Academy of Letters will (find it impossible to function) and even I will have to put aside my (monumental) work on Inorganic Geometry. Anybody who has a B.A. will not be able to proceed with his (or her) plan of reading the entire works of Dusty Evsky this winter. Chaos (will reign). Light-starved students will riot in the streets. Midnight-oil-tankers standing in the docks will be looted. Labour will challenge a general election.

That is why we are going to keep on trying to de-stink our inflammable treacle.

FURTHERMORE

Burners of midnight oil are not the only class who are suffering. The (acute) shortage of plate glass is causing serious embarrassment to people who live in glass houses, and our Research Bureau has been (inundated) with (shoals of) letters imploring us to see about manufacturing a substitute, 'opaque, if necessary.'

'It's like this,' a prominent person who lives in a glass house said to me the other day, 'by (exercising the greatest restraint) I can let six days of the week go by without . . . well . . . doing what we people who live in glass houses find it impossible to resist doing. On the seventh day (with the best will in the world) nothing will stop me from rushing out and firing a stone. Just one stone. And you know the result. Showers of stones and filth and brickbats descend on my glass house and smash twenty or thirty panes. My glazier tells me that after next week he will have nothing more for me. Putty has been cornered and can only be got in the black market at scandalously (inflated) prices. What am I to do? What's (going to become of me)?'

I mumble something about try to see what we can do, all for the best, stern and trying times, all must (be prepared to make sacrifices), war over in another year, crisis of civilisation.

'It's all very well' (voice now shrill) 'but we have to live too. What is the Government doing? The Government will have to (wake up and) do something because we are the most numerous class in the community. There are at least 400,000 people in Eire living in glass houses. Are their (claims) to be ignored? Do they (count for nothing)?'

And so on. Even that shifty class, wire-pullers, are complaining of the shortage of wire. Our Bureau these days is put to that essential accessory of its collar, the pin.

*   *   *

THE RESEARCH BUREAU is facing up to the problem posed by the jam shortage. The proposal to generate jam from second-hand electricity is being thoroughly investigated and a spokesman prominent in industrial jams—perhaps too prominent—revealed last night that experiments show that the inquiry 'will not be fruitless'. At present it is impossible to say more but an official spokesman stated that it is 'not unlikely' that the ESB and the sugar-beet people will be approached not to secure their co-operation but with a view to securing their co-operation in this vital industry. At the outset it is believed that a small army of collectors, recruited by competitive examination, will be sent out all over the country collecting, grading and cataloguing all sorts of electrical refuse (and fuse, of course). This 'raw' material will be absorbed by a factory (to be built somewhere in Ireland) where the new 'jam' will be degenerated into immense watts, pardon me, vats. Black and red currant will probably be the most popular varieties, though, at a later date, it may be possible to manufacture a limited quantity of alternating. In addition it is proposed to establish a cottage industry, probably in Donegal, where ohm-made jam will be produced for the carriage trade. A great advantage of the scheme is that it by-passes the bottling and carton problem since the new confiture will be distributed on the mains. Also the jam will be broadcast three times daily over wave-lengths to which only the purest fruit juice will be added. There is some talk of a secret plumb jam, a savoury but perpendicular mess which it is rumoured will be extracted from the uprights of old doors. (Here, according to taste insert a wretched joke about traffic jams, or if an educated person, murmur:

'Jam! Jam! (Non domus accipiet te laeta, neque uxor
Optima, nec dulces occurrent oscula nati
Praeripere et . . .')

RESEARCH BUREAU

BEFORE the leaves of autumn fall, the Research Bureau, spurred on by the exhortations of Sir Myles na gCopaleen (the da) will have provided new patent emergency trousers for the plain people of Ireland. These garments, conventional enough in appearance, will be fitted with long eel-like pockets reaching down to the ankles. The pockets will be the exact diameter of a bottle of stout and not by any coincidence, for they are designed to deal with the nuisance of those brown-paper Saturday-night parcels. It will be possible to stow four stouts in each leg. At first, walking in the 'loaded' position will necessarily be rather slow and straight-legged but practice will tell in the long-run, which should be undertaken only after short runs have been mastered.

What will happen if a man gets an accidental blow in the leg and has his bottles smashed? Nothing. The pockets are stout-proof and the beer will lie safely in the bottom until it can be syphoned into a jug, or even into a guest's mouth, in the privacy of the home. Indeed, many men, disdaining the rather precious affectation of bottles, will have their trousers filled with draught stout or porter and saunter home on their puffy, tubular and intoxicating legs. Where bottles are discarded, however, one must be careful to avoid overcrowded trams and 'buses. Should a fat lady sit down beside you and crush you with her great girth to make way for her loud children, great cascades of stout may emerge from your pockets, ascending to the roof and drenching everybody with the frothy brew.

On a long journey a small flexible tube may be carried. This can be unobtrusively inserted into the pocket, and then, after the face has been discreetly obscured by the *Irish Times* or other interesting national news-paper, the nozzle can be put between the lips and an innocent potation indulged in.

*   *   *

INCIPIT Crusculum Lan: sciant universi per presentes inso sios quod haec sunt vera indubitata agus authentica priathra miulesij copleansis videlicet primus fer et naem praeclarissimus & imperator ocus taisech Hiberniae alias Ierne alias Foley alias Bonbo alias sauioeurstut herend alias ould oireland alias iarm Breatane alias crioch Fheidhlim alias gort Neill alias clar righ-Eibhir alias clar Chriomhthain alias fod Eachaidh alias Tulcha Fail alias Fuinn Tuthail alias Craobh Chonnla alias Fuinn Fhoinidh alias Roe-Sheen Doo alias Catch Knee Guire alias Trimming Done Jeelish ocus tsar et paterculus gacho ruisse & ananamday a loqgteoir sechain an drochmhnai .i. in serpens ocus an ahair neimhe adapertamar Finuiot (A creak, son?)

Tri coindle furrowsnot cork drochnas, fear, agony, tetanus, Firkin annso. We could do with one, too—put it up on the piano, get four glasses and a knife to take the froth off.

RESEARCH BUREAU

There was a fearful row at the Bureau the other day. Sir Myles na gCopaleen (the da) arrived unexpectedly and it was obvious to all present that he wasn't feeling himself. (Truth to tell, he was feeling the tyres of his bicycle, fearing he had so stained a slope puncture.) He gave the savants he employs there a dressing down, a going over and a word in season, not to mention those pleasing but none too plentiful domestic

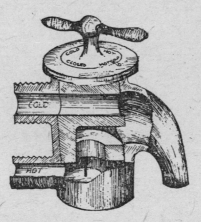

veracities, a few home truths. In brief, he complained that they had not done a tap for months. This charge was bitterly re-scented by the scientists. The charge hand (whose name happens to be George Shand) went to his drawing board and in two ticks had run up the blue prints of the tap mentioned. (He found he couldn't run down again and had to be rescued with a ladder.)

Irish faucet factors should study this drawing very closely. Not only does it give you two taps in one, thus saving metal in the emergency, but enables you to draw either hot water or cold water *or both simultaneously, mixed to a desired temperature.* If you think this is an effete and decadent convenience, there is nothing to prevent you from connecting the cold water pipe to a barrel of good Irish malt and providing yourself and your family with scalding punch for drinking and washing purposes. Think of the fine affectation of having handsome decanters full of water to pass to your guests so that they may adulterate what they get from the tap.

* * *

RESEARCH BUREAU

RECENTLY I referred briefly to a new type of telephone patented by the Research Bureau. It is designed to meet an urgent social requirement. Nearly everybody likes to have a telephone in the house, not so much for its utility (which is very dubious), but for the social standing it implies. A telephone on display in your house means that you have at least some 'friend' or 'friends'—that there is somebody in the world who thinks it worthwhile to communicate with you. It also suggests that you must 'keep in touch', that great business and municipal undertakings would collapse unless your advice could be obtained at a moment's notice. With a telephone in your house you are 'important'. But a real telephone costs far too much and in any event would cause you endless annoyance. To remedy this stay tough affairs the Bureau has devised a selection of bogus telephones. They are entirely self-contained, powered by dry batteries and where talk can be heard coming from the instrument, this is done by a tiny photoelectric mechanism. Each instrument is fitted, of course, with a bogus wire which may be embedded in the wainscoting. The cheapest model is simply a dud instrument. Nothing happens if you pick up the receiver and this model can only be used safely if you are certain that none of the visitors to your house will say 'Do you mind if I use your phone?' The next model has this same draw-back but it has the advantage that at a given hour every night it begins to ring. Buzz-buzz, buzz-buzz. You must be quick to get it before an obliging visitor 'helps' you. You pick up the receiver and say 'Who? The Taoiseach? Oh, very well. Put him on.' The 'conversation' that follows is up to yourself. The more expensive instruments ring and speak and they are designed on the basis that a visitor will answer. In one model a voice says, 'Is that the Hammond Lane Foundry?'

Your visitor will say no automatically and the instrument will immediately ring off. In another model an urgent female voice says 'New York calling So-and-So'—mentioning your own name—'Is So-and-So there?' and keeps mechanically repeating this formula after the heartless manner of telephone girls. You spring to the instrument as quickly as possible and close the deal for the purchase of a half share in General Motors. These latter instruments are a bit risky, as few householders can be relied upon to avoid fantastically exaggerated conversations. The safest of the lot is Model 2B, which gives an engaged tone no matter what number is dialled by the innocent visitor. This is dead safe.

Some people may think it a snag that one's name won't be in the telephone book. In a way that is nonsense because there is nothing so refined as having a telephone and not being in the book. In any case, if you have the Bureau's model that always gives the engaged tone, it might be possible for you to induce the Post Office to insert your name in the book, putting opposite it the telephone number of the Department of Supplies. PS might arrange it in exchange for a couple of old books.

* * *

SOME sat her daze ago I picked up this newspaper (hopeless business trying to read it on the floor) and read '. . . genuine European. How often do we hear the concept of "Europe" bandied about, and how rarely is it used by a writer who makes us feel that he really has Europe in his bones . . .'

This, of course, is a nasty dig at meself; thanks heavens I'm too big to pretend to notice. Go on.

'From the time when, in his early twenties, he first met Emile Verhaeren, he was constantly sensitive to "The Heart of Europe".'

Hmmmmm. Verhaeren. Hoho. *Verhaeren*. I have to laugh. Do you remember porridge . . . and and . . . treacle, and . . . Lyle's Golden Syrup out of the strong cometh forth sweetness . . . and brown sugar . . . and when the good Nanny is not looking . . . an enormous pat of butter. Hah? When you were a chisler, of course. Then pains all night and roars and Oh God please don't kill me this time I'll be good I'll be good. Well, if you remember what that felt like you'll have a faint idea of the texture, colour, sensibility of this small-town bill-poster. Here's a little bit of his 'work':

> 'Le monde entier travaille et l'Europe debout
> Là-bas, sur son tas d'or millénaire qui bout.

> Du fond de ses banques formidables, préside
> A ces trafics captés par des cerveaux lucides,
> Chiffre à chiffre, dans les mailles de leurs calculs.'

An esquisite image, Mac—— eh? (Cerveaux lucides is good begob).
European my hat. All on the strength of laborious steamship catalogues
the like of Et les voici tanguer, surs leurs vaisseaux, ces hommes dont
l'âme fit Paris, Londres, Berlin et Rome (if you or me wrote that, of course,
it would be called pantomime jingle). And then this schedule stuff—
prêtres, soldats, marins, colons, banquiers, savants . . .

Don't be talking man. It is rather significant, I hold, that this European
(?Euro-peon) was ran over be a goods loco at the heel of the hunt. Honest
engine!

What then is *my* Europe? It is in the mind, Resource, cunning, inventiveness. Brightness, life. Overcoming obstacles. Take my Research Bureau. There you have men who are truly European. *They know life.* They take steps to guard against it. Not for them filthy 'poetry', drivel and pretence. What profit have you in that, they say, if your skull is ripped open by a falling stove pipe? But they do not stop at this rhetorical query.

Here is what they conceive to be one of the perils attending life in a decaying city like Dublin. Gutters, pipes, chimney-pots falling on the citizens from immense altitudes. Bricks, slates, window sills and iron balconies. And what is the remedy? Simple as can be:

A hat with a patent spring top that instantly wards off the missile and projects it for a distance of twenty or thirty yards.

Personally, I would not feel very European if I was afraid to go out in a storm—or is it suggested that in Europe there are no storms? Bah!

*   *   *

RESEARCH BUREAU

IGNORANT people sometimes complain about the 'footling' character of some of the Bureau's inventions. Than this there were no more unjust accusation. *Every invention helps some poor fellow mortal . . . somewhere.* Some of the inventions, however, have a unique general utility for all mankind. Day and night, somewhere on the earth men are hoisting weights and wasting time and energy on futile grappling devices. They have to tie this knot or that, or make fast the other. Consider, however, this thing I illustrate:

Examine carefully the innovation at the top of the hook. It is a movable steel loop with just sufficient clearance to permit the hoisting-rope to pass through. In this case, you tie nothing. You simply pass the rope through and begin to hoist. The weight will cause the steel loop to tend to move up vertically and will thus catch the rope in an unshakeable vice.

Most difficult job, thinking out these things.

A NEW PROJECT

The Bureau is not, of course, solely occupied with mere mechanics. Vaster things are brewing. You have, no doubt, heard of the Hidden-Ireland. Professor Corkery has written a book on the subject and Mulhausen and I went rather deeply into the thing in 1933. And now, in conjunction with the Bureau, I have been trying to interest some people with money in a scheme— pretty ambitious, perhaps, but well worth it— a scheme that should win the support of all right thinking citizens. *Hide Ireland again*! Hmmmmm? Could be done war or no war, take my word for it.

* * *

RESEARCH BUREAU

AH WELL. You are of course, very ill with that disease of yours, yet doctors will not hear of it. You know (who better?) that there is nothing for it but hyperpyrexia. You fix on therapeutic malaria, stuff yourself into bed and send the son out for a jug of benign tertian parasites. Very good, these parasites you 'take' intravenously and the four or five dull days of incubation you pass by reading 'War and Peace', Lafayette's great novel of the American civil war. You know the *time* of the first paroxysm is most important. You know also (who better?) that the sequence of malarial paroxysms can now be regulated (remember my monograph in *The Lancet* (there) last year?) by sodium bismuth thioglycollate. You must watch the time so that a paroxysm will not come upon you unawares and prevent you giving yourself an injection at the right time. My sketch shows the Research Bureau's ingenious device for having the right time all night—and so big that you will grasp it even when debilitated by ten febrile paroxysms and crippled by quinine. The watch is fixed upside-down at the back of the projector, which is operated by an oil lamp and the

powerful lens can then be focussed to throw the image on a screen of frosted glass.

Therapeutic malaria can kill unless the paroxysms are timed and spaced properly. Why risk perilous dehydration or anorexia for the want of this magic lantern article? The whole, complete, 25 guineas.

* * *

THE RAILWAY WORLD

Same old boring story, as if anybody but themselves could be interested in their dividends. My picture (opposite) shows G.S.R. shareholders washing the Company's dirty linen in public.

* * *

SOME CHAPS who work in the Liffey Junction Tunnel came to us the other day complaining that they frequently have the clothes nearly torn off them by Rafferty, who 'coasts' on 493 and is nearly on top of the plate-laying gang before they have time to jump out of the way. They have no oil for their lanterns and cannot see the ruffian approaching when he is some distance off. They have tried putting detonators on the tracks but Rafferty has got wise to this and pumps out flange lubricant, thus destroying the squibs. Somebody will be killed, they say, unless a way can be found to best Rafferty. We went into the matter, of course, at the Bureau. Most steam men are aware that every tunnel suffers from what is called 'ground-damp'; this is an unpleasant moist breeze that blows along the bottom half of the tunnel. No naked flame could live in it. The problem was solved, of course, and the solution is illustrated overleaf. It is a patent tunnel-man's 'pin'. It is used to hold a candle and the whole point is that the candle can be stuck high up near the roof of the tunnel, where the

flame will burn without disturbance, even when a train is passing. A further advantage is that the spike can be reversed when not in use and the device carried conveniently in the pocket or hand-bag.

The Cruiskeen Court of Voluntary Jurisdiction

OWING TO (pressure) (of work) in the courts of justice, withdrawal of judges, electric heaters, bicycle-crime and other matters, the public-spirited Myles na gCopaleen Central Research Bureau has persuaded several impatient litigants to bring their differences before the Cruiskeen Court of Voluntary Jurisdiction. This institution conducts its proceedings in English and 'recognises' only those statues which are 'recognisable for the purposes of the court'. Since nobody knows what this means, the 'lawyers' do not like to spend too much time rehearsing jargon and citing 'cases', fearing that the whole spiel will be ruled out as 'inadmissible'. Hence, justice is rough, not to say ready.

The first case was called the other day before His Honour, Judge Twinfeet, who was attired in a robe of poplin green. He 'opened' that abstraction, the 'proceedings', by expressing the hope that there would not be too much jargon. 'Justice is a simple little lady,' he added, 'not to be overmuch besmeared with base Latinities.'

In the first case the plaintiffs sought a plenary injunction for trespass, a declaration of fief in agro and other relief. The defence was a traverse of the field as well as the pleadings and alternatively it was contended that the plaintiffs were estopped by graund playsaunce.

Mr Juteclaw, for the defendants, said that at the outset he wished to enter four caveats *in feodo*. His statutory declarations were registered that morning and would be available to the plaintiffs on payment of the usual stamp duty. He asked for a dismiss.

His Honour said that he observed there was no Guard in court to prove certain maps and measurements. That was a serious matter; it showed disrespect to the court.

Mr Juteclaw said there were no maps in the case; if the plaintiffs intended to produce maps, he was entitled to 18 days' clear notice and viaticum for engrossment.

Mr Faix, for the plaintiffs, said he knew of no maps; he had received no instructions as to maps.

His Honour said he would let the matter pass, but for the future it must be understood that there must be a Guard in court to prove maps; one never knew when a map would be produced, he added.

Mr Faix stated that the plaintiffs held their easements in foeff-puisaunce pursuant to a 'very old statute'; he took exception to the remarks made by learned 'counsel'. Plaintiffs' rights subsisted by sochemann in *droit à moins* and were not subject to escheat, in tail or otherwise. It was a very old principle, affirmed again and again by the Lords.

His Honour: Which Lords?

Mr Juteclaw interposed to say that he wished to utter an emphatic protest against the remarks made by Mr Faix. The defendant had fenced the land for 400 years without fee.

His Honour said that he thought the phrase was 'without fee or reward'. Counsel should be more exact in citation.

Mr Faix: It is not a legal phrase, my lord.

His Honour: Every word uttered in this court is legal.

Mr Juteclaw said he wished to make a further emphatic protest against the disgraceful remarks made by Mr Faix. Mr Faix had referred to him (Mr Juteclaw) as 'counsel'. He (Mr Juteclaw) would have him (Mr Faix) know that he (Mr Juteclaw) was fully entitled to be known by the name and style of counsel. He would take inverted commas from no man.

Mr Faix: You never in your life et a dinner above in the Inns. You were only a waiter there, I know your face.

His Honour: Many a man of ability and unimpeachable integrity followed the ancient avocation of waiter.

Mr Juteclaw said that if that was His Honour's attitude, he (Mr Juteclaw) had no alternative but to leave the court. He would not be lachessed with impunity, by squirt-attorneys or anybody else.

Mr Juteclaw then left.

Mr Faix then addressed His Honour on several knotty legal points and asked for a dismiss *in manu*.

His Honour: Here's old Jute back.

Mr Juteclaw re-appeared and said he wished to apologise for a serious solecism he had unwittingly committed. When felt compelled by the dictates of honour to quit the court, he had merely lifted his papers and left. As a lawyer of long standing, he knew that the correct and accepted thing was to *gather up* his papers and withdraw. He then renewed his apologies, gathered up his papers, and withdrew.

His Honour, addressing the court, said that he had received a signal from his tipstaff. There was a cup of tea on the hob in his room. He would adjourn the case for three days; pleadings could be re-entered and his order would be discharged.

* * *

ANOTHER interesting case was dealt with recently at the Cruiskeen Court of Voluntary Jurisduction. A man called Smoke sued a well-known Dublin surgeon for grievous bodily injuries. The defendant claimed professional privilege and counter-claimed for fees amounting to £457 12. 3.

His Honour Judge Twinfeet, mounting the bench, said 'Now, no jargon. Whoever uses jargon is for it.'

Opening the case for the plaintiff, Mr Juteclaw said that this client was a decent working man, a trade unionist and a member of the Trinity College Fabian Society.

His Honour: My heater's gone. Where's my foot-heater?

Mr Juteclaw said that he understood the apparatus had been removed by the Board of Works, possibly for repairs. He would report the matter.

His Honour: Very well, Mr Juteclaw. It must not be bruited abroad that the Irish bench is subject to 'cold feet' (Laughter).

Proceeding, Mr Juteclaw said that his client in childhood had lost two fingers during Irish at school. There had been talk of an action against the teacher. This loss had reacted somewhat against his client's ability as a wage-earner in later life . . .

His Honour: Re-acted, Mr Juteclaw? Come now. Surely the word we seek here is 'militated'?

Mr Juteclaw: I accept Your Honour's correction.

Proceeding, he said the stubs of his client's missing fingers had never properly healed. His client as a consequence was compelled frequently to have recourse to medical men. In June last year he visited the defendant.

His Honour: Gentlemen, if I may make an observation, the cold up here is fierce.

Proceeding, Mr Juteclaw said that his client's object in visiting the defendant was to seek treatment for his complaint. He received no treatment whatever and was at no time given even what is commonly known as 'the lamp'. But after an interval of inaction the defendant cut the plaintiff's hand off, when the latter was suffering from the effects of some vapour or potent drug, no doubt administered by the defendant. Mr Smoke now found himself crippled for life. He came to court seeking substantial damages.

His Honour: I am perished up here.

Mr Juteclaw repeated that his client was clearly entitled to substantial and heavy damages.

Mr Faix opening the case for the defendant traced the history of professional privilege; the origins of it could be found, he said, in so remote a document as the Hippolytus of Euripides.

His Honour: Now, Mr Faix—jargon! Counsel would do well to eschew rigorously Latinities of doubtful import.

Mr Faix: My reference is rather to the Greek (or Hellenic) era, my lord. I refer to the medico-juridical tenets of the eupatridan or the Eupatridae.

His Honour: Very well, Mr Faix. But I warn you that the case is going very much against you at the moment.

Mr Juteclaw: May I say with respect, your honour, that the plaintiff also relies upon the soothing qualities of the Bacchae of the same deceased Greek.

His Honour: The smoking mixtures favoured by non-nationals are not relevant. My toes are perished. I will adjourn unless this petty matter is hurried on by the parties.

Mr Faix then made several submissions in plain English, and asked that the court should not acquiesce in the villainous attempt to blacken—nay, to denigrate—the character of a selfless servant of the suffering poor.

His Honour, giving judgment, dismissed the action, the parties to pay their own costs. A hand, he said, must have five fingers, otherwise the English language is a 'mockery, a delusion and a snare'. Plaintiff's 'hand' had only three fingers. Therefore no action for the cutting off of a hand could succeed. If the pleadings were altered to read 'hand' rather than hand, the case could be re-entered. If counsel concerned themselves more with English rather than with Latinities primitive and barbarous of sound, of content usually licentious, the work of the court would be facilitated.

Mr Faix, thanking his honour, asked for guidance as to the meaning of the phrase 'the parties to pay their own costs'.

His Honour: It means what it says.

Mr Faix: In a lifetime at the bar I have never heard the phrase. I have frequently heard the phrase 'abide their own costs'. I respectfully ask for guidance.

His Honour: I think the tea-pot swarms with nectar in my room. I have received a wink from my tipstaff.

His Honour then left the bench. The Clerk made another entry in his books under the head of 'Held, by Twinfeet J.'

*   *   *

ONE OF THE cases called the other day at the Cruiskeen Court of Voluntary Jurisdiction concerned (of all things) immoral literature. A shopkeeper was up for 'exposing' for sale a book which, while not indecent was in its general tendency indecent.

Twinfeet J., mounting the bench, asked counsel to remember his implacable hostility to locutions tortuous of syntax, imponderable of meaning and not intelligible save by reference to 'asiatic philologies'. 'No jargon, now,' he added. 'What's on the bill to-day?'

Mr Faix: My Lord, I appear for the defendant. Although a member of the Gaelic League, a fluent speaker of Irish and a graduate of Cardinal Newman's university, he is charged with dealing in immoral literature

His Honour: Come now, Mr Faix. How could it be literature if it is immoral? Do you mean literary immorality?

Mr Faix: No doubt I do, my Lord.

Mr Lax said he appeared for the authorities 'in this sordid case' and proceeded to make several important submissions. He hoped to show, he said, that the work in question sprang from a licentious, gross and diseased mind.

His Honour: Mr Lax, the niceties of our flexible English tongue must not be permitted to lapse by reason of the haste or indifference of learned counsel. A work could not 'spring' from such a mind. It could, however, *emanate*.

Mr Lax: I accept your Lordship's correction.

Mr Faix: As to subtleties of expression (if I may say so with respect, my Lord)—De minimis non curat Lax.

His Honour: One could refer, Mr Lax, to the depravity of the author's concepts 'emanating as they do, from a diseased mind'.

Mr Lax: Thank you, my Lord, I again accept your correction and guidance.

His Honour: It is as well that we should take care, for indecencies are also possible in the sphere of Saxon grammar. One must not mate our gentle tongue with negroid importations from regions barbarous of character, of situation transalpine. Counsel jeopardise their advocacy not to say their client's guinea, by such conduct.

Mr Faix: I humbly beg your Lordship's pardon.

After Mr Lax had made several further submissions, his Honour remarked that the punctilio of judicial processes should occasionally be cast aside in order to afford the bench some small clue as to the nature of the issue it was called upon to determine. 'Gentlemen,' he added, 'is this book you have there any good? I mean, is it . . . very bad? Is it disgusting, I mean?'

Mr Lax: It is filthy, my Lord.

His Honour: Have you read it, Mr Lax?

Mr Lax: Certainly not, my Lord. I would not soil my eyes with such nefarious trash, my Lord.

His Honour: Mr Lax, I have reason to suppose that in the privacy of my room Sir Tipstaff is far from idle. He has settled a certain pot upon the hob. A potion golden of hue distends that humble vessel. Hand me that book. The court is adjourned for one hour. I will proceed with the trial solus and in chambers.

On resumption, His Honour delivered judgment.

According to the cover which clothes the work in question, he said, the title of it is Madame Bovary and is the work of one Frenchman, by name Flaubert. In addition to this explanatory printed matter, the cover also bears the likeness of a lady, executed by the lithograph process and in that pink hue which is generally held to be agreeable to the senses. The lady, while not dressed for the street, is withal attired. Her costume would appear to belong to a by-gone age, when frugality in all things was apparently the custom of the day. The picture, while tending to immodesty according to the severer standards of the present age, could not reasonably be held to be indecent, or so tending in general tendency. The work itself I have submitted to what I may claim to be a fair examination. My pronouncement upon it must be accepted as verified within the limits of human prudence. The tone throughout is elevated, urbane, even technical. It appears to be 'An Outline of Irish Grammar' and is the work of the Irish Christian Brothers. The work bears no obvious relation to the illustration I have mentioned. The case must be dismissed with costs.

THE OTHER DAY in the Court of Voluntary Jurisdiction this man Smoke again sued a well-known Dublin surgeon for malicious damage to an attaché case. It will be recalled that Smoke failed in a suit against the same man for cutting the hand off him.

Twinfeet J., mounting the bench, remarked that 'that was a hardy one'.

Mr Faix, speaking on behalf of the Dublin Bar, agreed that the day was cold.

His Lordship: How did ye all get over the Christmas.

Mr Faix: Er—suitably, my Lord.

His Lordship: Do you know what it is, there is a lot of bad stuff going around. If ever one of the criminals responsible is brought before me, I warrant you that I will make an appalling example of him. But pray let us to business. Where is the fire, Mr Faix?

Mr Faix: The fire, my Lord?

His Lordship: I observe this man Smoke in court. You cannot have Smoke without fire. (Laughter.)

Mr Juteclaw: I recall appearing for a man called Feier, a German gentleman, about ten years ago. (Laughter.)

His Lordship: Very well, Mr Juteclaw. Now, Mr Faix, Feier away with your case. (Laughter.)

Mr Faix, opening the case on behalf of the plaintiff, said he did so because the plaintiff was unable to open the case himself, owing to the fact that he was crippled.

His Lordship: Which case?

Mr Faix: The attaché case.

His Lordship: I think you'd better call it the bag.

Mr Juteclaw: Possibly your lordship might agree that it would be more appropriate to call it the *casus belli*.

His Lordship: Philologo-juridical obscurantism sits ill upon the mantle of Dame Justice and will not be permitted to besmirch the fair name of this court. (Laughter.)

Mr Juteclaw: To express your lordship's meaning in another way, one dissociates the Latin *lex* from the Greek *he lexis*, speech.

His Lordship: I do not care a rap who likes his speech, Mr Juteclaw. Mr Faix, kindly continue with your learned submissions. Come now—action! I'm perished here.

Mr Faix, re-opening the case for the plaintiff, showed the court the interior of it. The leather was extensively stained with blood. Continuing, Mr Faix said that he was instructed that this was the blood of the plaintiff. From a previous hearing he was familiar with the melancholy fate to which the plaintiff had been subjected by the defendant. On that occasion the defendant, working under cover of noxious fumes administered to the plaintiff, had cut off the latter's hand, crippling him for life. A suit for damages had failed owing to a technicality. On the occasion of this bloody-rendezvous, the plaintiff had taken the precaution of bringing with him his pyjamas in an attaché case, understandably suspecting that he might find himself in hospital as a result of the defendant's treatment. But when the plaintiff emerged from his stupor he was unceremoniously pushed into a taxi, bag and all—

His Lordship: Mr Faix, I think the word is 'bundled'. Also, I think one associates 'baggage' with 'bag' according to the correcter usage of our old tongue.

Mr Faix: I accept your lordship's correction. When the plaintiff reached home he collapsed. Many months afterwards, when he had recovered somewhat, his landlady, a most respectable widow lady, asked him when she was going on holiday, to give her a hand with the packing. He generously lent her his attaché case, I will spare the feelings of the court as to what followed, but in justice to my client I am bound to say that when the case was opened, it was found to contain the plaintiff's hand having been callously placed there by this monster the defendant. I intend to call this widowed lady and she will show—

His Lordship: May I ask is this the lady demure of aspect who sits by the side of Mr Smoke?

Mr Faix: None other, my Lord.

His Lordship: As head of this court a terrible responsibility rests upon me. Indeed, 'devolves upon me' would be a better term. I cannot run the risk of hearing irrelevant evidence. I must therefore first interview the lady in the privacy of my chamber. She will now be conducted there, and the court must be adjourned until to-morrow.

Mr Juteclaw: I protest, my Lord. This is most irregular.

His Lordship: Protest away.

Mr Juteclaw then said that in view of his lordship's attitude he had no alternative but to gather up his papers and withdraw. He then gathered up his papers and withdrew.

In his book, under the head of 'Held by Twinfeet J.,' the Clerk waggishly entered the phrase 'One plump widow'.

*   *   *

WHILE IT IS possible for our judges, by mere dint of swotting, to familiarise themselves with positive (or statute) law, there is ample evidence every day even in attenuated newspaper reports, that our jurists are weak in what is called case law. They know little or nothing about the grandiose *dicta* of decent Irishmen like Palles C.B., Bray J. or Madden J.

In the old days when it was a question of finding what was the meaning of the Malicious Damage Act of 1861, we old circuit men found ourselves in a very tortuous maze of juridical obscurantism. Take section 17. 'Whosoever shall unlawfully and maliciously set fire to any stack of corn, grain, pulse, tares, hay, straw, haulm, stubble, or of any cultivated vegetable produce, or of furze, gorse, heath, fern, turf, peat, coals, charcoal, wood or bark, or any stack of wood or bark . . . shall be liable . . . to be kept in penal servitude for life . . .' Now in *Rex v. Woodward* it was a question of setting fire to a stack of barley, produce not covered *expliciter* in the section. In the case quoted, the offence was held indictable within the section, the court taking judicial notice that 'barley is corn or grain, and that beans are pulse.' Moreover, 'a stack of the flax-plant with the seed or grain in it, is a stack of grain.' (*Reg. v. McKeever*, I.R. 5 C.L. 86; 5 I.L.T.R. 41. On the other hand 'rushes and sedge are not straw within 7 Will. 4 & 1 Vict. c. 89; *Reg. v. Baldock*, 2 Cox C.C.55.)' Furthermore, 'a quantity of straw if packed or erected on a vehicle which is capable of being moved is not a stack of straw': (*Reg. v. Price*, I.C. & P. 729). Also, a hay-cock has been held not to be a stack of hay, *per* Fitzgerald, J.

Under Section 15, which deals with malicious damage to agricultural machinery, an attempt was made to obtain compensation for damage to a plough. Held by Johnson J. that a plough is not a 'machine' or 'engine' within the meaning of the statute, a contrary decision in H.M. courts notwithstanding. Incidentally, I notice it stated in the text-books, in relation to the Shops Acts 1912, that 'the waiters who attend upon the resident guests in an hotel are not shop assistants within the Act' (*Gordon Hotels v. London C.C.*). I concur. They're just waiters.

Twinfeet J., of course, has made many strange pronouncements in the Court of Voluntary Jurisdiction. In an action brought under the Marine Hereditaments (Compensation) Act, 1901, a man who lived in an old boat located on a hill sought damages from another man who had been (as alleged) negligent in the management of a dinghy on a trolly (which he was bringing to the railway station) so as to cause the dinghy to collide with the old house-boat. The defence was that the latter structure, being rated to the poor rate, could not be a boat, vessel or ship and that the dinghy, being a land-borne wheeled article, was not a dinghy but a velocipede. Twinfeet J. inquired whether it was suggested that a small paddle-steamer was a farmcart but the defence submitted that inasmuch as a paddle-steamer could not be hauled by a horse, mule, pony, jennet, donkey or ass, it could not be a farm-cart within the meaning of the Farm-carts Act and must in fact be a paddle-steamer. The plaintiffs contended that they were the aggrieved parties in a naval collision and entitled to recover damages and compensation from the defendants, who had been negligent in the management of sea-going craft, which was their property and under their care and management. The defendants pleaded alternatively that the 'house-boat' was 'wreckage' within the meaning of the Wreckage Act.

Twinfeet, J., in the course of a long judgment, said that he could find nothing in the Act or indeed in any statute regulating matters of admiralty which made water an essential element in a collision between boats; he was satisfied that the owners of the dinghy had been negligent in the navigation of the dinghy 'Marcella' at the junction of Market Street and Dawson Hill. He assessed damages at £4 and excused the jury from service for a year on the ground that they had been at sea for four days.

* * *

THE DEBATING Society of the Clerical staffs attached to the Central Banking Corporation met last Saturday, Twinfeet J. in the chair.

Proposing the motion 'That the Pen is mightier than the Sword', *Mr Chaine* said that from time immemorial far beyond the dawn of history, the human race had evinced respect for the dignity of the human intellect. This respect had not only successfully weathered the ravages of time, but also the savage attacks of marauders, particularly in monastic times. All great human revolutions had been inspired by the pens of great thinkers, who probed into human destiny with the timeless insight of genius. He asked the house to endorse what he made bold to term 'The Primacy of the Pen' by a unanimous vote.

Mr O'Queen, opposing the motion, stated that a walk through any museum would prove that the development of the human body was the dominant characteristic of the glory that was Greece. Literature and the arts could only flourish in a civilisation which had been founded by those who wielded the sword. To admire the sword was not necessarily to endorse the principles of militarism, the doctrine of physical force, or the unprincipled maxim that might is right. The development of the body could be secured without oppressing minorities or waging war, and such development inculcated sportsmanship and manliness. The Boy Scout movement was a case in point. The House would remember the sentiments so felicitously expressed by no less a poet than William Wordsworth:

> 'To hold the fight above renown
> To hold the game above the prize,
> To honour as you strike him down
> The foe that comes with fearless eyes.'

He asked the house to endorse Aristotle's motto of mens sana in corpore sano ('a healthy mind in a healthy body') by unanimously rejecting the motion.

Miss Eiderdown said it was nothing less than a negation of democracy to suggest that the ordinary man in the street, whose interest in literature and art was of the meagerest, was inferior to so-called writers or 'Knights of the Pen' as they would no doubt dub themselves with a conceit that was typical.

Mr Tramm, supporting the motion, stated that Ireland had been a lamp of civilisation at a time when Europe was enveloped in the druidic mists and miasmic vapours of pagan materialism and owed the fame of her golden age to her life-long devotion to books and other objects of veneration and respect. It would be a sad commentary on our glorious and storied past if the house should decide that the alarums of war, which had never yet solved any problem but brought rapine, disease and death in its wake, were preferable to the things of the spirit.

Mr Snagge inquired whether Alexander, Pippin, Charlemagne, Caesar, Napoleon and other doughty warriors of the historic past—even Patrick Sarsfield earl of Lucan—were of no importance? Did they merit obliquy because of their failure to produce literary effusions?

Mr Mosse stated that only for Danish marauders Ireland to-day would have a literature second to none.

Miss Tablett said that wars were due to the fact that women were denied adequate representation on the councils of the nations. Women were home-makers but these homes were destroyed by men, who were depraved with greed and lust for power. Women, she declared, should assert their rights.

Mr Scugge said that the much-vaunted Beveridge Plan was merely a bribe to prevent social revolution; it was no panacea or nostrum for the crying social ills of the present day. What the working man wanted was work, not charity.

Twinfeet J., summing up, stated that apart from the external combustion engine, obscurantist chauvinism was the curse of the age. The human race would have to get back to first principles and reject the pernicious doctrine of *laissez faire*. He was inexorably opposed to food taxes.

The motion was carried by 44 votes to 9 and the proceedings terminated.

The District Court

IN THE Dublin Court yesterday, an elderly man who gave his name as Myles na gCopaleen was charged with begging, disorderly conduct, using bad language and with being in illegal possession of an arm-chair. He was also charged with failing to register as an alien.

A Detective Sergeant gave evidence of finding the defendant in the centre of a crowd in Capel Street. He was sitting in the chair, cursing and using bad language. He became abusive when asked to move on and threatened to 'take on' witness and 'any ten butties' witness could find. Defendant was exhibiting a card bearing the words 'Spare a copper, all must help each other in this cold world.' Defendant lay down in the gutter when witness went to arrest him; he shouted to the crowd to rescue him, that he was a republican soldier. Witness had to send for assistance.

Defendant: *Quid immerentes hospites vexas canis ignavus adversum lupos?*

Detective Sergeant: This man had no difficulty in speaking English when he was lying on the street. This sort of thing makes a farce of the language movement.

Justice: If defendant does not deign to convenience the court, we will have to get an interpreter.

Defendant (to Justice): I knew your ould one.

Detective Sergeant: Your Honour can see the type he is.

Defendant: I seen the sticks of furniture on the road in 1927, above in Heytesbury Street. Now seemingly things is changed. *Fortuna non mutat genus.* (Laughter.)

Justice: You would be well advised to behave yourself.

Defendant: Of all people.

Justice: Where did you get this chair you had?

Defendant said he got the chair from a man he met in Poolbeg Street. He did not know the man's name. The man was on his way to pawn the chair and witness agreed to take it off his hands. He bought the chair.

Justice: For how much?

Defendant: £45.

Justice: It's a pity a tallboy isn't the subject of a tall tale like that. (Laughter.)

Defendant said he was trying to go straight but the Guards were down on him. He was holding a political meeting in Capel Street when he was savagely assaulted by the Sergeant. He was discussing monetary reform and mendicancy. He had as much right to obstruct the thoroughfare as the 'Fianna Fáil crowd.' He was kicked in the ribs by the Sergeant while lying on the ground. He would settle his account with the Sergeant at another time and in another place. This much only would he say: *Cave, cave : namque in malos asperrimus parata tollo cornua.*

Detective Sergeant: This type of person gives the police a lot of trouble, Your Honour.

Justice: I can see that. (To defendant) Are you married?

Defendant: Are you?

Justice: Impertinence won't help you.

Defendant: It won't help anybody. The question you put is apparently equally offensive to both of us. I am a victim of circumstances. *Maioribus praesidiis et copiis oppugnatur res publica quam defenditur propterea quod audaces homines et perditi nutu impelluntur et ipsi etiam sponte sua contra rem publicam incitantur.*

Detective Sergeant: This is a very hardened character, Your Honour. He was convicted for loitering at Swansea in 1933.

Justice: I must convict. There is far too much of this sort of thing in Dublin and I am determined to put it down.

Defendant: What sort of thing?

Justice: The larceny of armchairs.

Defendant: It wasn't an armchair. There were no arms on it.

Justice: You will go to Mountjoy for three weeks.

Defendant asked that 6,352 other offences should be taken into consideration.

Justice: I refuse to hear you further.

Defendant: Very well, I'll appeal.

Defendant was then led below, muttering. A sequel is expected.

YESTERDAY, in the Dublin District Court, the elderly man who had given his name as Myles na gCopaleen and who had been sentenced to three weeks' imprisonment for begging, bad language, and for the larceny of an arm-chair, was again before the court in respect of offences committed, as alleged, since the date of his conviction. Defendant, on appearing, refused to remove his cap. It was removed by a Gárda.

Defendant (to Gárda): You also I know well! Woe to the wife-beater!

Non uxor salvum te vult, non filius; omnes vicini oderunt, noti, pueri, atque puellae! Not to mention yours truly!

A Detective Sergeant said the Justice would recall the circumstances of the defendant's last appearance. It was now necessary to bring further charges in respect of offences committed in custody. Defendant had damaged the window in his cell, set fire to his bed clothes, and refused to take a bath in accordance with a lawful direction given by the prison governor. He had also assaulted two warders, though not physically.

Justice: *Not physically?*

Sergeant: Well, no, your worship. He incited certain animals to attack the warders.

Justice: Animals?

Sergeant: Small ones, your worship. Fleas.

Defendant: *De minimis non curat lex.*

Justice: So you're back? What's this about the bath? What's your objection to having a wash?

Defendant: One does not have a bath in one's clothes.

Justice: Can't you take them off?

Defendant: No.

Justice: Why not?

Defendant: We won't go into that.

Justice (to Sergeant): This man is about twenty feet away from me yet I can get the smell of drink. Is he intoxicated? What on earth is going on in this court?

Defendant: *Hock erat in votis.* Surely Your Lordship has heard of the grapevine? *Dum licet, in rebus jucundis vive beatus.*

Justice: For a man who has been in Mountjoy for over a week, you surprise me.

Defendant: Joy ale.

The Sergeant said that for very good reasons defendant had not been searched before being committed. (Sergeant handed Justice a note.) It was possible that he was carrying considerable supplies of drink. When ordered to take a bath, defendant became violent. In the presence of two warders he smashed the window of his cell and threatened to 'light the bed'. The warders were reluctant to pinion and over-power the prisoner for reasons now within the knowledge of his worship. When threatened with severe disciplinary measures, defendant dragged the bedding on to the floor and set fire to it. He then took off his coat and threw it on the floor, on the warders' side of the blaze. Immediately, due to the heat, the coat was subject to certain large-scale evacuations. Apparently some of the animals had wings or at least could comport themselves with considerable agility. The warders were attacked and badly bitten. One man was still in hospital. (At this stage a number of note-takers and spectators moved from the area about the dock.)

Defendant: *De minimis non curat lex. Sunt extra judicis cura. Exponam enim hodierno die, judex, omnem rationem facti et consilii mei neque huic vestro tanto studio audiendi nec vero huic tantae multitudini, quanta mea memoria numquam ullo in iudicio fuit, deero. Multa acerba, multa turpia, multaque—*

Justice: That will do. Your turn will come.

A Warder corroborated the Sergeant's evidence and stated that he (witness) was assailed and bitten by a 'flock of animals' that flew out of the prisoner's clothes. Witness was badly stung and had to receive medical attention. 'I seen jack-fleas as big as mice barking at me,' witness added. (Laughter.)

Defendant: *Ut tigres subsidere cervis, adulteretur et columba miluo.*

The Sergeant said that other charges were pending and it would be necessary to consult the Attorney-General. In the meantime he made a strong appeal to the Justice to let the defendant out on bail.

Justice: On whose sureties?

Sergeant: My own if necessary.

The warder was understood to say that he would 'stand in' with the Sergeant.

Justice, fixing bail at £1, said defendant would do well to consider his position. It was not unknown for bailees to sojourn—permanently if necessary—*in partibus infidelibus.*

Defendant then left the court without a word.

* * *

THERE WAS another commotion in the Dublin District Court yesterday morning when the elderly man Myles na gCopaleen, who had been released on bail the previous day, was again before the Court. The Sergeant asked that the case should be taken first.

Justice: I see you are wearing bicycle clips, Sergeant. Would you have a spare pair?

Sergeant: I have, your worship.

Defendant (addressing court): Yez are all leppin' because I didn't skip. (Laughter.)

The Sergeant said that it was now necessary to charge defendant with loitering, trespass and burglary.

Defendant: *Loquitur Agamemnon.*

Continuing, the Sergeant said that defendant had been treated with great latitude by the court the previous day and allowed out on bail. When released from Mountjoy, however, he refused to quit the premises and had to be ejected.

Justice: How?

Sergeant: With a hose.

Defendant: *Pro di immortales! Quid?*

The Sergeant asked the justice to hear a warder as to defendant's condition. In the court of his evidence, the warder said: 'This man is infested be hoppers.'

Justice: *Hoppers?* What is a hopper?

Defendant (excitedly to Justice): *Habeo igitur quod ex eum quaesisti, quid esset* 'hopper'. *Non est* hopper, *non sunt* hoppers, *ut dixit: quod ego verbum agnovi. Sunt fratres minimi mei (de quibus lex non curat), numerus quorum generis late et varie diffusus est. Sunt amici, sunt fideles milites nostri qui neque nocentes sunt nec natura improbi nec furiosi nec malis domesticis impediti!* (Pointing to warder.) *Nunquam putavi—vera dicam!— tantum esse in homine sceleris, audaciae, crudelitatis!*

The Sergeant mentioned that defendant was continually conversing in this strain, leaving all as wise as if he were speaking double dutch.

Defendant: *O infelicissime!* Begob if I used the word ownshuck you might take my meaning! (Laughter.)

The Sergeant said that defendant, having been ejected from the gaol premises, was again found in his cell the following morning. He had broken into Mountjoy during the night and had filed through certain iron bars which would cost the Office of Works £9 18. 5 to replace. He was in an intoxicated condition when found and used bad language. He demanded cocoa and used certain threats.

Defendant (sarcastically): *More agni inter lupos!*

Justice (to defendant): I will hear you if you have any comprehensible remarks to make to the court.

Defendant, in the course of a long address, said that he was 'a Southern Irishman,' and as such could not accept with equanimity the suggestion that he should (by mere reason of being out on bail) reside in Belfast, 'a stern iron town of aspect unendearing of populace contumacious.' Witness had regard, however, to other principles—principles which far transcended mere expediency or what was adjudged fit in the mart of men. Had witness absconded (he thought that was the word), he would hold himself morally responsible for having provoked in that court a certain situation—a situation which he (witness) dare not contemplate.

Justice: I do not understand you.

Defendant: If I had failed to appear in this court at the time appointed, too well I knew that my bail would not be *confiscated*. Neither would it be *impounded*. (Here defendant became moved.) Neither would it be *declared forfeit*—or even *forfeited*. It would not be *attached*. It would be. . . . (Here defendant broke down and began to weep.)

Justice: You may sit down.

Defendant (sitting in dock, burying face in hands and weeping loudly): My bail would be . . . ESTREATED. I . . . I . . . could not . . . face that. Estreated! (Here defendant blubbered uncontrolledly.)

The Sergeant, having consulted with the Justice, said that he was prepared, on behalf of the State, to enter a *nolly prossy coy*. They would withdraw all charges.

The Justice said that defendant could now leave the court without a stain on his character. He would be glad to receive an undertaking from the . . . respondent that he would be prepared to leave Mountjoy and to refrain from entering the gaol at night when it was officially closed.

Defendant gave the undertaking, and the whole incident is now considered closed.

Sir Myles na gCopaleen

SIR MYLES NA GCOPALEEN (the da) was 87 yesterday. The grand old man spent the day quietly at his country place. His breakfast tray (frugal, in keeping with the times) was littered with messages of congratulation from notabilities of every rank and colour, including some of the notorious uncrowned heads of Europe. An endless stream of callers (including many a Scotch-pickled 'county' lady, horsey to the point of being horse-faced) left cards bearing scribbled felicitations. When one rather fat lady of this breed stalked up the drive, a parcel of wine-flushed stable-boys ran out, seized her with various sharp cries in horse-language, and forcibly backed her into the shafts of the landau which is kept waiting every morning to take Sir Myles for a drive round the grounds. She had been almost fully harnessed when the mistake was discovered. It is rumoured in the servants' hall that there will be hell to pay when the incident comes to the ears of Sir Myles, who cherishes for this lady his own queer brand of senile admiration—'best seat in Ireland, old boy; finest pair of hands in the county, comes down to breakfast on horseback.'

A happy function took place in the evening. Sir Myles, an imposing old-fashioned figure in his lavender waistcoat and cravat, received the tenants and villagers in the old baronial hall. Old Jem, the oldest tenant—he is said to be 113—made a suitably slavering and fawning speech, referring to certain events 'in your lordship's grandfather's time.' The magnet which drew the gathering (barrels of free beer) was then produced and the entire company partook of refreshment.

LEARN THIS BY HEART

The baronetcy, of course, is one of the oldest in the country. Sir Myles is reckoned to be the 57th of that ilk. Lady na gCopaleen is one of the Shaughrauns of Limerick, a very distinguished county family. Round after round of spontaneous applause have been won by her seat and hands at countless point-to-points. A lover of Scotch, she is reputed to be one of Europe's foremost bottle-women.

Miss Sleeveen na gCopaleen came out only last season. She is very popular with the younger set and is one of the most interesting personalities one meets at hunt balls. After a week in the saddle, she finds her relaxation in poetry, play writing, novel writing, dancing and film work. She is very popular with the younger ballet set and tells me that her hunting experience helps her considerably in this sphere. She is not in the least self-conscious when off a horse. At the moment she tells me that she is organising a Comforts Fund for the troops. 'I do definitely think that life is rather wizard, actually,' she remarked to me the other day.

I am in a position to reveal that the Sleeveen complexion, the envy of millions of women, can be had by anybody for the asking. She tells me that after a hard day in the saddle, she likes to retire to her room and rub liquid suet into her face. This is merely a 'base'. She then works in a mess that is made from flour, treacle and mashed potatoes. On top of this a liberal plaster of beaten up eggs and Scotch whisky. When all this stuff is scraped off in due course, you have the complexion that has played havoc with many a susceptible young ballet-boy.

AND THE BROTHER

Myles himself, the brilliant young journalist, will be out of town for 14 days. No letters will be forwarded. An undefatigable first-nighter, he is keenly interested in the theatre and has written several plays. Life he regards as a dialectic that evolves from aesthetic and extra-human impulses, many of them indubitably Marxian in manifestation. The greatest moment of his life (which occurred in 1924) was when he made the discovery that life is in reality an art form. Each person, he believes, is engaged on a life-long opus of grandiose expressionism, modulating and mutating the Ego according to subconscious aesthetic patterns. The world, in fact, is a vast art gallery, wherein even the curators themselves are exhibitors and exhibitionists. The horse, however, is the supreme artistic symbol—

The Editor: We can't have much more of this, space must also be found for my stuff.

Myself: All right, never hesitate to say so. I can turn off the tap at will.

The other day Sir Myles na gCopaleen (the da) was re-elected President of the Myles na gCopaleen Central Banking Corporation. The cousin, The O'Shaughraun of the Bogs, was given the vice-chair to keep him quiet. This latter office carries the right of 'operational discretion on the Number 2 Account', and is said to be equivalent to a packet—not in sterling, of course, but in consolidated credit tallies that can be re-discounted in the 'dead money' pool.

After the meeting drinks were served in the board room. A very enjoyable musical evening followed. Sir Myles gave his famous rendering of 'In Cellar Cool', and followed up with a stirring address on the ethical and philosophic basis of 'all true banking'. The O'Shaughraun was accorded an ovation for his rendering of 'Believe Me If All' and other gems from that repository of everything that is best in the national music of the old land, Moore's Melodies.

Taciturn director Theoderick O'Moyle ('Silent O'Moyle') said nothing, as usual. He just sat there.

★ ★ ★

SIR MYLES NA gCOPALEEN (the da) was standing in the conservatory in immaculate evening dress, a figure almost kingly against a riot of banksia alba, green tomatoes, and Zephirine Drouhin. The heated air was laden with the stench of paraffin emulsion, a sign that Jenkins, the head-gardener, was taking precautions against the disorder known as Cuckoo Spit. The dusk was performing its customary intransitive operation of 'gathering'. In some far tree an owl could be detected coughing.

A clink is heard. The grand old man laid a glass of scotch and soda against the gold-laced patrician teeth and is swallowing the nourishment with the calm of a man well used to it. He is lost in thought. He wishes to go to the library. He has business there. But he remembers that his is the only library (in the true old-fashioned sense) that remains in the whole country. And he knows a thing or two. He fears the worst.

He sighs, puts down the glass and passes from the conservatory. He traverses the old baronial hall, lined with dead Copaleens, each in his theatrical and anachronistic iron panoply. Sir Myles glances with affection at the last of them to be set there—the Hon. Shaughraun na gCopaleen, quondam ace-bottle-man in the southern command of the Black and Tans. Sir Myles passes on, smiling to himself with whimsical grace. He reaches the library and enters.

'I thought as much,' he sighs.

Stretched on the floor in a most ugly attitude is a corpse. Sir Myles has already taken up the telephone and asked for a number.

'That you, sergeant? Look here, those dreadful detective stories. Another corpse in the library this evening. Really, you know, too much of a good thing. Fourth this week. No doubt trouble is shortage of libraries.

What? A young man, extremely handsome. Curious scar on left cheek. Dressed? Don't be a damn fool. You ought to know he is attired in immaculate evening dress. Do not touch the corpse and leave everything as it is until you get here? What do you take me for—an ignorant fool?'

Sir Myles puts down the instrument testily and pours himself a stiff drink. He sits down sipping it and apparently listening intently for something. Soon three shots are heard some distance away, followed by a scream.

'I thought as much,' Sir Myles mutters, 'that will be the mysterious little Belgian governess who has been seen in the neighbourhood recently.'

He rises, wearily and takes a well-worn storm lantern from a cupboard. He lights it and passed with it from the library. He approaches the massive baronial stairway and mounts it. Flight after flight he traverses, the flickering light illuming portrait after portrait of deceased Copaleens. Soon he has reached the cob-webbed spiral stairs that leads to the tower. With agility that belies his advanced years, he grasps the cold iron balustrade and continues the journey upwards. Soon he is out on the platform of the old Norman tower, the icy wind playing on his old-world countenance. From a small press he has taken a telescope and his eagle eye is ranging the sea. In the gloom he can make out the shape of a small ship standing in the bay. It is exchanging mysterious light signals with some unknown party ashore.

'I thought as much,' Sir Myles sighs, 'question of some plans being thieved by international interests; obviously the agents of a foreign power are leaving no stone unturned. Well well well . . .'

The grand old man wearily descends again to the library. He has lifted the telephone and asked for a number.

'Look here, sergeant, I realise I am telling you something you must know, but the corpse has disappeared during my momentary absence from the library.'

'I expected as much, Sir Myles.'

'Also there was the usual shots and a scream and all that kind of thing.'

'Quite Sir Myles. It is a good job the body has been taken off your hands because I have changed my mind. I have no intention of going out to your place. This once we will let the mystery be solved by the private investigator who will accidentally arrive on the scene. On this occasion we will spare the police the trouble of making mistakes, following dud clues arresting innocent parties and generally complicating matters.'

'I realise how you feel, sergeant. Good night.'

Then the grand old man threw away his glass and started using the bottle.

* * *

SIR MYLES NA gCOPALEEN (the da) who has been buried in the country for some months, was exhumed last week following a dispute as to the interpretation of a clause in his will, which purported to leave certain pictures in the National Gallery to the nation. The nation in question was not named, and lawyers held that the bequest was void for uncertainty, though it is no secret that with Sir Myles, words like 'the nation', 'the Army', 'the services' mean only one thing. The grand old man was alive and well, and looked extremely fit as he stepped from the coffin. 'Never again,' he said as he jested with reporters before being driven away in a closed car.

He was later entertained to supper at the United Services Club by Ailtiri na hAiseirghe, when he was the recipient of a handsome wallet of carvers. Lady na gCopaleen, who had, on Sir Myles's passing, hastily married the wastrel cousin Sir Hosis na gCopaleen for testamentary reasons, was also present with her husband and was the recipient of a handsome six-day clock.

Returning thanks in the course of a felicitous and witty speech, the grand old man said that it was no accident that his will contained knotty and litigious provisions, such as could only be unravelled—and not necessarily to the advantage of interested appellants—by Gavan Duffy. He had taken the precaution of adding four codicils, not one of which was witnessed. He was advised that two bequests he had made were invalid inasmuch as they were contingent on the legatees 'marrying again'. The parties in question had never married and could not lawfully satisfy the repetitive requirement of the clause. Large sums were also left to certain persons if still in the testator's employment at the latter's death, but all these persons had been dismissed and had in fact been jailed for theft on the testator's uncorroborated testimony. He was also advised that four clauses in his will were repugnant to the Constitution. He had hoped that the whole document would have been impounded by the Attorney General but that little plan had evidently miscarried.

'I considered carefully,' Sir Myles said, 'the advisability of dying intestate but rejected the idea as too dangerous. Naturally I am now glad I did not adopt that course. I would like my job pursuing her nibs here and my alleged children through court after court to get them to cough up.

I would have placed upon me the onus of establishing quite novel juridical theses. For example, I would have to show that there is an alternative to testacy or intestacy, viz., extestacy, which would be the condition I would claim to be in. I would have to show that death is an essential concomitant of intestacy and this would involve lengthy legal definitions of death. I would have to show that death is not final and conclusive. This in itself would involve equally recondite definitions of life. My own 'existence' would be called in question and I would have to prove—on oath, mind you!—that I was not dead, notwithstanding my recent decease and the hasty nuptials of my dear widow. My right to review and strike out certain 'refreshment' expenses from the funeral bill charged against my alleged estate would have to be established in face of the most tortuous objections that could be devised by Costello. Even my undoubted right to participate as next-of-kin in my own estate would be called in question. The income tax authorities would challenge the inclusion of funeral charges under allowable expenses and would probably insist on sticking me for death duties. It would all be far too troublesome. I would not like it at all. Gentlemen, I would rather be dead.' (Loud applause.)

Later in the evening, the grand old man was carried into a cab. He drove to the Mansion House where he made a courtesy caul. Though the ersatz membrane was rather coarse in texture, the thing very closely resembled the genuine article and showed that the old man's fingers have lost none of their cunning.

Later the Lord Mayor returned the caul.

FOLLOWING the return to civil life of Sir Myles na gCopaleen (the da) after being exhumed, a number of interesting legal issues have arisen. The relatives bitterly regret the exhumation and now see that it would have better suited their book to leave well enough alone and risk the prodigious litigations that would be entailed in submitting the grand old man's 'will' to probate; their hope would be that at least some crumbs of the estate would ultimately reach their hands. Now they fear that any presentation of this document to the court would be successfully opposed by the testator in person, and that the court would hold with him in his submission that he was incapable of valid and effective testacy by reason of undeath.

On the other hand Sir Myles himself, though in excellent fettle and lion-spirited in his voracity for litigation, is confronted with some awkward situations. His bank has refused to honour his cheques on the ground that they have his death certificate, furnished to them anonymously, by post, and that they can release no money unless this document is quashed by the court. The Registrar-General, to whom the grand old man then had recourse, has refused to issue a fresh birth certificate on the grounds that the applicant could not be born at the age of eighty-one and that in any event he was not born but exhumed.

Sir Myles then took counsel with his attorney and it was thought that the situation could be met if Sir Myles made a fresh will leaving his entire estate to himself. This course would involve payment of death duties— a not inconsiderable sum—but a law-suit could be immediately started to compel the Revenue Commissioners to give the money back. (It was of course recognised that the danger here was that a bill would be rushed through.) It was found, however, that the legacy would not be effective in the absence of conclusive evidence of death and since ample evidence of the testator's death is what is causing all the trouble, the position is terribly obscure. The old man is reluctant to risk further obsequies because (a) his previous obsequies were not conclusive; (b) exhumation would devolve on third parties, none of whom he can trust; (c) evidence of two deaths in respect of one testator would make the legal situation, already difficult, absolutely insoluble; (d) further and more protracted obsequies might kill him. The grand old man is genuinely afraid of the incredible legal mess that would result from contingency (d), particularly if further exhumation revealed that he was neither alive nor dead, but in some sort of a trance. Sir Myles is determined that none of his relations shall get one penny but is at present in the position that the measures he has taken to that end have also deprived himself of his money.

The kernel of the legal impasse appears to be this—that life is not in law the opposite of death, nor is being born the opposite of dying. Death is *a process*, resulting usually in a serious fatality. To undo the legal consequences of death insofar as the disposal of the deceased's assets are concerned, it is apparently not sufficient merely to be demonstrably alive; it is necessary to *undie*, to the satisfaction of the court. As apparently nobody has yet performed this mysterious act, the grand old man is diffident at the prospect of being, at his age, the first to attempt it; he is in any event uncertain as to how the task should be approached.

The entire situation is one in which both sides may ultimately have to accommodate each other. The relations can get nothing owing to the suspected invalidity of the will: the testator, by mere reason of having that standing, cannot get his hands on his own money.

Sir Myles has called further attorneys into consultation, and many eminent doctors and undertakers have been called to the conferences. The other side is also taking further advice and the general situation has become very tense. An outbreak of the bloodiest warfare is expected hourly. Developments will be carefully reported in this newspaper.

THE battle of wits as between Sir Myles na gCopaleen (the da) and his greedy relatives goes on. Lady na gCopaleen, who hastily married the wastrel cousin Sir Hosis na gCopaleen on her husband's 'death' already finds herself crucified with brandy bills and has applied to the court for an annulment of the marriage and for declarations that

  i she was, prior to her marriage with Sir Hosis, *non relicta* and incapable of contracting a valid marriage with him;

  ii that, notwithstanding the foregoing, her marriage with Sir Myles was terminated on the latter's death;

  iii that she cannot be a widow in view of Sir Myles's re-appearance and that she must be a maiden lady;

  iv that Sir Myles is a person of unsound mind, having regard to his *post mortem* re-appearance in face of present taxation levels and general social instability;

  v that as next-of-kin, she is *prima facie* entitled to one third of the deceased's estate inasmuch as he died intestate (or having executed an inadmissible document purporting to be a will) and that now, notwithstanding any appearance he may enter to the present proceedings, he is incapable of lawful testacy and that he does not exist.

She also claims further and other relief. Her present husband, Sir Hosis, has so far ignored the proceedings, being incapable in a cab stabled since Friday in a lane off Fade Street. Sir Myles, however, is full of fight and has already entered 18 caveats, turned himself into a limited liability company with seal of perpetual succession, and wholly traversed this lady's claim upon him. In turn, he has applied for declarations that

  i he is immune from the jurisdiction of the court, having died;

  ii that he is not, however, dead;

  iii that he did not die intestate but made a vexatious will which the court should impound and condemn;

  iv that he is capable of making further and other wills;

  v that his obsequies were not genuine or conclusive but were in the nature of agricultural necromancy;

  vi that he is a person of sound mind, knowing only too well what he
    is about;

  vii that Lady na gCopaleen was formerly his wife, subsequently his
    widow and is again his wife and that his relative, Sir Hosis, being
    a bigamous intruder since the date of the exhumation, should be
    excluded by the court *a mensa et thoro*;

  viii alternatively, that he and Sir Hosis are jointly wedded to the lady,
    that he (Sir Myles) has precedence in all issues as senior husband
    and that he is entitled to the income tax allowance for her under the
    Finance Acts;

  ix that Sir Hosis is a dangerous maniac and is unaware of the 'marriage'
    contracted with him by Lady na gCopaleen;

  x That Sir Hosis has not been sober since June 1909, having been
    born in 1901.

The other relatives are taking their own measures to get their hands
on the estate (for such they claim Sir Myles's goods, chattels and cash
to be) and will not scruple to lay violent hands on the grand old man if
such is the only course compatible with their book. A dead pauper has
been secretly interred in the grave and in due course an attempt will be
made to prove that Sir Myles is an imposter and in fact never survived
his funeral. It is recognised, however, that this course is perilous as it
may give Sir Myles an opportunity of claiming that he never had a funeral
and that he is the victim of a diabolical conspiracy to which his wife, Sir
Hosis and the other cousins are privy.

A mysterious Colonel Coplin has appeared on the scene, claiming to be
a distant grand-uncle. This man claims to be pained at the 'unseemliness'
of trailing the family name through the courts in a fug of scandalous
vituperations and is mentioning certain 'settlements' he has in mind.
Each side assumes that he is an imposter in the pay of the other side and is
proceeding with the utmost wariness.

Any further developments will be reported.

For Steam Men

I TOOK a trip to Belfast the other day on business of a kind that cannot be discussed here or elsewhere. I was not five minutes in the train until I realised that the engine-driver belonged to the 'full regulator, short cut-off' school. In my own railway days I used to work the locomotive as a high pressure simple (indeed, the design of the steam chest made no other course feasible) with cut-off as high as 60 per cent. That was before the days of the de Glehn compound or the Walschaerts gear. (I knew Walschaerts well, he was the best of fellows and a prince among steam men.) I am not criticising the G.N.R. driver. He knows his 'car' better than I. It is true, nevertheless, that the modern low pressure cylinder is not there for nothing. Where you have 'hard steaming', short cut-off with full regulator will nearly always lead to disparity in pressure readings between boiler and steam chest. They tell me that modern research at Dundalk has shown otherwise, but that is all my eye and Betty Martin.

At Belfast I noticed that the valve rod had lost adjustment and nobody was less surprised than myself. I hate to see machinery tortured.

FURTHERMORE

One thing we must make sure of, if and when Hawlbowline gets into production, is that its 'killed' steels shall be on a controlled grain basis. This has long been a commonplace of modern steel practice in America. Carburising impairs a fine grained steel to a negligible degree because the temperature limit above which coarsening may be expected is known. Thus the use of quenches may be reduced or obviated. Your old-fashioned steel-man will guffaw if you talk of welding high-tensile steels. Nevertheless, it is possible with controlled grain sizes and let nobody tell you different. I am working on the problem at present. Watch this newspaper for an important announcement.

* * *

WHEN IT suits their book, some people do not scruple to drop hints in public places that I am opposed to poppet valves. It is, of course, a calumny. The fact is that I supported poppet valves at a time when it was neither profitable nor popular. As far back as the old Dundalk days, when the simple v. compound controversy raised questions almost of honour with the steam men of the last generation, I was an all-out doctrinaire compounder and equally an implacable opponent of the piston valve. I saw even then that the secret of a well-set poppet valve—short travel— was bound to win out against prejudice. I remember riding an old 2-8-2 job on a Cavan side-road, and my readers can believe me or not as they please, but we worked up 5392 I.H.P. with almost equal steaming in the H.P. and L.P. cylinders, a performance probably never equalled on the grandiose 'Pacific' jobs so much talked about across the water. The poppet valves ('pops' old Joe Garrigle called them—R.I.P., a prince among steam men) gave us very sharp cut-off. And we were working on a side road, remember.

There is not the same stuff in the present generation as there was in the one gone by, trite as that remark may sound. In hotels, public houses, restaurants, theatres and other places where people gather. I hear on all sides sneers and jibes at compound jobs. They eat coal and oil, they are unbalanced thermo-dynamically, they 'melt' on high cut-off, and all the rest of it. Really, it is very tiresome. Your old-time steam man understood nothing but steam, but at least he understood it thoroughly. To see some of the sprouts that are abroad nowadays and to hear their innocent gabble about matters that were thrashed out in the Dundalk shops fifty years ago is to wonder whether man is moving forward at all through the centuries.

The other day I wanted to make a trip to the south, and arrived at Kingsbridge to find the train stuffed to the luggage-racks with—well, what do you think, cliché-fan? 'Perspiring humanity,' of course. I was told there was no room for me. Perhaps it was injudicious, but I rang up the authorities and asked could I, as an old steam man, be permitted to travel on the plate, offering to fire as far as Mallow, or take over the regulator when and if required. The refusal I received was, clichély-speaking, blunt. After making this call I noticed a queer change coming over the station staff. I could hear phrases like the following being bandied around (and that's a nice occupation, bandying phrases):

Your man is here.

The boss says your man is to be watched.

Don't let your man near the engine.

Your man'll do something to this train if we aren't careful.

There'll be a desperate row if your man is let up on the engine.

Your man ought to be heaved out of here, he'll do something before he goes and get somebody sacked over it.

Don't let your man near the sheds.

I did manage to get a look at the job they had harnessed for the run. There was any amount of evidence of 'foaming'. Your men do not seem to realise that if water is carried into the cylinder with the steam, you get a sharp loss of superheat as well as damage to the piston valve liners. This, of course, is due to the use of feed water that is 'dirty' in the chemical sense. What was wanted here was a good boiler washout and the use of some modern castor oil emulsion preparation to reduce the concentration of solids and suspended matter in the f.w. I know I might as well be talking to the wall, of course.

I have received for review, by the way, a copy of *The Steam Boiler Year Book and Manual for* 1942 (London: 20s net). It contains a wealth of useful lore relating to combustion, water circulation, transmission, and so on. A copy should be in the home of every Irish boilerhouse superintendent.

* * *

DVORAK'S Humoreske is taken up by the muted first fiddles and passed to the wood-wind. The scene is the lofty richly-panelled office of an Irish Locomotive Superintendent. It is evening. From the nearby yards comes the hiss of steam and now and again the gentle susurrus of a shunter's cut-away lap valve. The Superintendent is at the window lost in thought, his hands in his trousers' pockets and his great shoulders hunched. Nearby is seated his personal secretary. She is young and gazes at the granite form of the old steam man with troubled wistful eyes. Bloom of youth's fullest peach mantles her cheeks. Ringlets of amber fall peerlessly on the white neck. Her queenly hands toy with a pencil of 18-carat gold. Her name is Bella.

There is silence. Over it steals the long hiss of a goods compound as it comes to rest far away. The gathering dusk enriches the majestic timbering of the old room. Bella speaks at last, her voice the gentle voice that is used by angels.

Bella : Penny for them, super.

Superintendent (starting slightly): O nothing, Bella. Nothing.

Bella : Something is making you sad.

Superintendent : It is nothing. I see 316 is in again. That is the second time this week. Her twin blast pipes are gone again.

Bella : But do not let that prey upon your mind, super. The Works Manager will fix her up again. The Works Manager is a clever man. He will make her as good as new.

Superintendent (turning slightly with a sad smile): It is nice of you to talk like that, Bella. You are a good kid. But we must face facts. The Works Manager will never make a job of her. I am afraid . . .

Bella (softly): Yes . . . ?

Superintendent : I am afraid old 316 will never take the road again.

(He turns back to the window to gaze at his black charges as they move about the yards, each with its white plumes of steam. A lump rises in his throat and the shade of pain crosses the strong face.)

Bella : Please do not talk like that. She will ride many thousands of road-miles yet.

Superintendent (almost gruffly): Her twin blast pipes are gone, I tell you. (He pauses.) I am sorry, Bella. I am sorry. That old job has me worried. I am not myself.

Bella : But, super, we have others.

Superintendent (bitterly): We have. And bar the two 1928 single expansion jobs, there is not a sound job in the yard. Hasn't 475 a superheat that rots her with condensation?

Bella : I know.

Superintendent : And 278 is destroyed with wiredrawing. 604's best is 14lbs. per I.H.P., and 433 has been behaving like an old tram. The Board won't give me any money. The Works Manager says he must have three new compounds by October. I tell you there is no way out, Bella. I am a broken man.

Bella (gently): But, super, there is always the Royal British Locomotive Corporation of Swindon.

Superintendent (irritably): I told you the Board won't part.

Bella : But, super, the BLC people are different. They will let us pay over twenty years.

Superintendent : What! Do you mean that?

Bella : Of course, darling. For a few hundred pounds down we can get a brand new de Glehn job with a draw-bar horse-power of 3750.

Superintendent (excitedly): And with poppet valves?

Bella : Yes, cute ones that give a wide port opening—

Superintendent: —with satisfactory mean depth and a straight steam path?

Bella : Of course!

Superintendent (rushing to embrace her): Bella, DARLING! Let us go and see them to-morrow!

Bella : Yes, super, they will give us everything we want. That is why the B.L.C. is known as the Happy House for Locomotive Superintendents. And they do not ask for references.

Superintendent (dreamily): O, darling, I feel so happy, I am a new man. (*Thinks :* Thank heaven for Bella. Now I will never have to worry any more about unsatisfactory ratio of mean horse-power to square foot of evaporative heating surface, 'foaming', 'blasting', or dirty feed water.)

From far away comes the long hoarse hoot of the night goods pulling out, working at 16 per cent of rated tractive effort. Fade out with the overture to 'Zampa'.

* * *

FEW PEOPLE will believe that I once stood on the same platform with John McCormack. Yet such is the fact. If my memory does not deceive me it was the No. 2 Departure Platform, Kingsbridge. The two men took an instant liking to one another. I invited the singer into my reserved first class compartment. Out came the Hugo Wolf scores, and for the next three hours we hummed and tapped and whistled through twenty or thirty songs, completely unaware of the world around us. That is the way with artists.

Today I cannot quite recollect precisely how this pleasant situation was in a trice completely changed. I seem to remember hearing a ticket-checker saying 'Jimmy is trying to jam her again' to the dining-car attendant whom he encountered when passing through our department. This odd remark must have penetrated through the musical anaesthetic which had sequestered my brain in a soft place hung with magic mantles: all I can say is that instantaneously I had leapt up, thrown the music sheets to the four winds and was already rushing madly up the train.

Looking back over the incident in the calmness with which the years have invested it, I think it must have been the one word 'Jimmy' which cause my sub-conscious radio to pick up the ticket-checker's remark. Steam men of the last generation—notably those who recall the stirring events of 1919 in the Inchicore shops—will be in no doubt as to whom I refer to. The man is now dead, and in charity we will give him no fuller name than 'Jimmy'. But Jimmy was the most depraved and abandoned steam man in these islands; he was worse—a sadist. Ostensibly a driver, with Grade I rating, he hated all engines. It did not matter whether they were single expansion jobs, compounds, de Glehn simples, 'street-cars' or the beautiful Manley superheats that came in about 1921 (making that year an historic date in Irish history), *he loathed them all*. His ambition in life was to do as much damage as possible to as many engines as possible. So long as he could exquisitely *hurt* the delicate organs of a locomotive, then he was happy. His logs and repair books contained a staggering catalogue of 'defects', 'breaks' etc. for each journey, no matter how new or well-conditioned the engine. He managed 531 complete breakdowns in ten years, probably sabotaged beyond repair about £500,000 worth of machinery in that time and caused endless disorganisation of traffic. Why he was not dismissed the first day he took the road is another of those mysteries one associates with the G.S.R. More than that one does not say.

To go back: I raced down the train, dealing very roughly, I fear, with any obstruction whether human or otherwise that came against me. Soon I was face to face with the locked door which separated me from the engine. It was a stout door and possibly it would have baulked me had I not heard clearly through it the poor old brute's laboured breathing: evidently the rotter had succeeded in jamming her valves. In an instant I had smashed down the door with my shoulder; one leap and I was clambering across the coal to the foot-plate. And there he was, stooped at some other villainy, the gleam of pleasure on his evil face. In one bound I had reached him, caught him by the neck and spun him round. 'Oh no, you don't!' I muttered through my teeth as my fist connected with his jaw. He went down with a thud and, thorough bully that he was, he quickly retreated up on the coal where he sat watching me with yellow baleful eyes.

I did what I could, of course. By skilfully blowing down—'to reduce priming', muryaa—he had jammed her valves wide open. To my surprise I recognised the engine. None other than she whom we called 'Cissie'. 'Cissie' was an old-fashioned 1912 simple. The funny coincidence was that she had been re-boilered under my supervision in 1917 when I was Guest Boilerhouse Supervisor at Inchicore, on loan there courtesy of the G.N.R. (for I was at that time O.C. Design Room 2, Dundalk).

Suffice it to say that I worked her up to a draw-bar horse-power of 3870 (!) before we reached Mallow. And this despite the fact that after one minute at the controls I could see that a sack of fine cinders had been emptied into the feed water.

Alas for human villainy!

* * *

I HAPPENED to take a walk round one of our railway yards recently and was struck by the fact that we are still thirty or forty years behind the times, even in the primitive science of inducing a locomotive to 'ride' properly. Your Irish technical man's attitude is a delightfully simple one: he believes that if you place a locomotive with fixed axles on the rails and then produce sufficient power, the vehicle will 'negotiate' any curve however sharp. It is of course true that any engine so managed will thump, bump, pitch, kick and scream its way round the curve, lacerating bearings, distorting flanges, racking the road and bringing replacement a net day nearer for each curve 'negotiated'. In theory it is not possible for a set of fixed wheels to do what our railway savages make them do and it is a (sad commentary) on our vaunted civilisation that violence of this order is still possible in this country, after twenty-one years of Home Rule.

In 'long' engines the problem is not an easy one to solve completely inasmuch as the central driving member consisting of two or three coupled wheels, necessarily constitutes an inflexible unit impossible to reconcile completely with a curved track, but enlightened engineers everywhere outside this island have done much research in the sphere of 'appeasement'. There is, of course, a dual problem here—one, the mere physical intractability of a mass which, according to the laws of geometry and nature, must be chord to the segment formed by the curved rails, notwithstanding the demented efforts of the engine to straighten the rails and the efforts of the rails to bend the engine; and two, the incompatibility of two wheels which are traversing a curve while fixed on the same undifferentiated axle and which are therefore travelling at disparate speeds, however minute the disparity. No engine can 'ride' properly in such circumstances. In America where curves are not so exigent because of superior national elbow room (I make no quip on the subject of women) much research has been devoted to this problem. Most people will have heard of the device of lubricating the flanges of the leading drivers, usually with water, but sometimes with a patent emulsion. But the best plan, devised by American technicians, provides for the mechanical cushioning of the drivers, permitting a minute but most valuable amount of side-play. Equally interesting is the Krauss-Hemholtz device of forming a 'flexible' bogey by coupling the fore-drivers with the leading axle. These advances give American engines great sweetness and delicacy even on the harshest curves. But your Irish 'engineer' thinks he is a very deep and subtle customer when he puts a bogey fore and aft of his locomotives, having first rivetted four articulated drivers immovably into the middle of the frame. I am damn sure that if he had his way, with no watchdogs like Glenavy to keep him in his place, he would build a 34-foot compound with eight coupled drivers and eight carriers, all locked rigid, and then hurl the whole 600 tons of it, with 4,000 horsepower on the draw-bar, at the sharpest curve in the whole country. He would afterwards regard the mass of steaming wreckage with the philosophic calm of a savant who knows he must expect reverses in the quest for perfection. Men of that calibre are at large in our shops and yards every day, giving gross rein to their sadistic talents. They do nothing to enhance our reputation for gentleness and culture, and they are not using their own money, but yours and mine, in their nefarious occupations.

I know that all this is very tiresome, but I have a responsibility in these matters and I must speak out, unpopular though my criticisms be and adversely as they may affect my purse and fair name.

'STEEL-TRACK minds'? Bah! The people who have 'opinions' on Irish railways matters make me laugh. That they have 'grievances' makes me laugh again. A third peal is occasioned by the fact that these 'grievances' are in bad condition and stuffy, making it necessary to ventilate them (a process never attempted with the third class carriages). (I sometimes leave the 'arri' out of that last word.) Dear me. Well well. I have addressed the following letter to Lord Glenavy:

'Dear Glenavy—From letters appearing over your name in the newspapers I infer that you are a steam fan. Accept my oath that I make no jocose distinction as between steam and electric fans but rather that I credit you with the wish that the Irish railway world should yet enter upon a golden era, playing a noble part in the transportation problems that await us in the new Ireland when once more the sword is sheathed and happier counsels are permitted to prevail. If in this belief I do you no injustice, will you kindly let me know why my proposal for fitting Irish locomotives with thermic syphons was scotched by a boardroom ukase in 1919. Is it because these syphons are made of copper that my proposal was not acceptable to the vested tin-trusts? Je suis, dear Glenavy, bien cordialement, à vous,

gCOPALEEN'

Cabman's Shelter,
Broadstone.

When that letter is replied to, we will be getting somewhere. Incidentally, I noticed that the anonymous writer who was discussing this question

with Lord Glenavy made some reference to *throwing good money after bad.*
Bad money, eh? Do not tell me that they have a little plant in Kingsbridge
for making the company's small change.

* * *

RAILWAY STUFF

I WAS WATCHING the goods the other evening making its way to Wexford,
rather like an old buffer of 89 en route to the post office for his pension.
Could we not erect some ironical memorial in tortured steel to the wretched
man who 'designed' the under-boilered, over-cylindered atrocity that was
yanking and bashing those trucks?

When younger and less wise I wrote to the former Dublin South-
Eastern Railway outlining a modest proposal for fitting their locomotives
with thermic syphons. This device protects the crown sheet and, of course,
considerably advances the effective heating surface. 'Dear Sir—The
General Manager directs me to state that the enclosed diagrams, which
bear your name, have been found in this office and are returned herewith.
Please note that this Company cannot accept responsibility for such
documents.'

Heigh-ho for power-operated fire-doors, mechanical stokers and a
300 lbs steam pressure. I heard of a high-up railway technician who was,
appropriately enough, killed at a level crossing by one of his own 'trains'.
He thought the train was past because he saw its tracks. Bah!

* * *

STANDING ON the platform of Donabate Station the other Saturday
morning waiting in the frost for a 'train' that was half an hour late, can you
wonder that I fell to considering once again the dreadful mess into which
our railways have been permitted to fall? When the 'train' was led in by
our old friend 493, I laughed bitterly. This engine is about 17 years old
and is suffering badly from condensation. It has been in this deplorable
state for 2 years, yet absolutely nothing has been done to remedy what
amounts to nothing more or less than a grave public scandal. Excuses
there may be, 'explanations', no doubt all very plausible. The foreman
welder is on his holidays but is expected back aMonday, when we hope
etc. etc. Meanwhile thousands of foot pounds have been lost on the draw-
bar. It is all too dreadfully typical of the dawdling mentality that has made
our name a by-word among steam-men the world over. I have written
elsewhere and in no uncertain terms about the matter of the Slieve

Gullion's valve-ports, the Kestrel's chronic 'blowing', the scandal of the Queen Maeve's piston valve lining. All very boring, no doubt, but of importance to thinking Irishmen. The Donabate engine was choked with dirty feed water and so long as there are plenty of good emulsions on the market, *there can be absolutely no excuse for this*. It is not good enough, it is not fair, and more than that I will not say.

I have noticed from the newspapers, with not a little disquiet, that Reynolds is buying horses. If this is a purely personal and private activity, well and good. But if here we have the seed of a 'brilliant' and 'resourceful' plan to have our trains drawn by cart-horses during this appalling 'emergency', *then I must enter an instant demurrer and neither the hired rough, the bribe, or the soft word will abate one tittle of the public agitation that it will be my portion to foment*. I am absolutely sick of the caprices of amateur meddlers. At no time has any personal approach been made to me in connexion with emergency engineering problems, although it is common knowledge that I have a plan that will solve—and permanently —the difficulties which arise from bad coal, duff, turf, timber and all manner of inferior fuel. A false pride prohibits this approach, while all the time the public suffers—if not in silence, at least stoically.

Will it be credited that I have had to build privately, *and from the resources of my own purse*, the proto-engine of this salvation? Will it be believed that under sacks in my back-yard stands the solution of our transportation chaos? Such, however, is the fact.

The picture of my engine, which I reproduce here, will be self-explanatory to genuine steam men, though I can imagine hurried recourse to text-books and drawings at Amiens Street and Kingsbridge. Technical details I will not enter into here but this much it is admissible to say— that the solution of the whole problem lies in the immediate erection of overhead electrical conductors throughout all our systems. This is no plan to banish steam—those who know me will have no doubt on that point. *It is a plan to banish coal*. Steam will be raised by electrical heaters and all existing locomotives can be converted to this process with hardly any expense.

Simple, eh? Perhaps. But not quite simple enough for the shameless men who to-day control our railways. Incompetence, waste, inefficiency, obsolete technique, botchery and ignorance, these are the criminal vices I assail. And it is a big day's work to tackle alone and single-handed. My other hand I lost in the Great War.

But I fight on.

* * *

RATHER CURIOUS thing happened to me (there) the other day. In a pub I happened to run across some G.N.R. chaps and we fell (I hurt the bad knee again, got the cap unscrewed Lansdowne Road 1924 when playing for Ireland) we fell to discussing the 'Gullion' as we call her. I inquired how she was, how behaving. Umm. Embarrassed pause. Come now, I said, seek not with gilded phrase to soften what may be ill news. The worst that ye may know I can with fortitude bear. The truth, I pray ye. Alas, the 'Gullion', it seems, 'blew' at Donabate on Friday week. The week before that she 'blew' at Laytown, that most curious priestless locality. Coming down from Belfast a month before she 'blew' four times in three miles, even though being worked on the low pressure cyls. only. Rafferty, it appears, had a terrible time with her, and when he got her into Amiens Street eventually, up all night with her, boiler-tubes stuffed and the whole engine absolutely crippled with 'catarrh'.

Feed water? I queried.

No no no. She gets special feed water, orders came down from Glenavy that *no expense was to be spared*. Special feed water flown every morning from Swindon, England.

I inquired whether they were using the patent emulsion I had prescribed last September.

Absolutely. Never missed a day. Man told off to look after nothing else. Piston valve liners?

No no. They are checked before and after all runs. A sample of her condensed steam was bottled and went off to Crewe for analysis. Absolutely nothing found wrong.

Mysterious, you will say. If you like. But it is not *my* fashion to call a thing 'mysterious' and leave it at that. I asked question after question, many of them surprising my interlocutors because they seemed unduly obvious and simple. Tiny clues began to emerge and soon a theory took shape in my mind. My questions now were directed towards corroboration. Yes yes. Quite. I stood up. Possibly my look was ominous, for my friends grew deathly pale as they waited for my verdict.

'Gentlemen,' I said, 'there is but one remedy. She must be re-boilered.'

You could have heard a pin drop. Then, as if by instinct, three glasses of steaming malt were raised to the thin lips and swallowed with enteric convulsion horrible to behold. Eyes looked into other eyes. At the back of the mind of all was the cold dread that never again would the 'Gullion' take the road.

Could . . . could it be done successfully? What . . . what would it cost? Would I . . . do the drawings?

How charming and child-like can man be when he trembles in the shade of fear! How engaging, how simple! And how pleasurable it is to re-assure, to pacify, to renew hope!

Yes yes, it could be done. The steam-men of yesterday did bigger things without holding themselves prodigal of talent. The cost? Well, I could promise that it would not break the Company. At that time and in that place details I did not propose to enter into. We would meet another day, not in the gilded luxury of a public house parlour, but rather in the stern environs of my lodgings. This much, however, it was admissible to say. Out of a one thousand pound note the Company must not expect much change. Nor did such rough estimate include fees or five per cent for Conditions of Employment Act. Three and a half on the drawings plus one and a half for supervision, that would be the limit of my personal demands. My interest in the 'Gullion' was frankly . . . not financial. They smiled. They were new men.

Alas, there I go. I talked earlier of a 'curious experience' and now I have not space to describe it. But to-morrow I tell all.

(*Tube Beak, Con, Tin Nude*)

* * *

TO-DAY, I continue yesterday's notes on the sick 'Gullion'. I wish to make my position absolutely clear. Ambiguity in such matters one cannot risk.

First things first. The 'Gullion' must be reboilered, and immediately. No person dares to doubt this. The fact is accepted by all. Very well. Some people will tell you, unctuous and smooth of tongue, that all is well, that the damage has been done—in a word, that all's right with the world. I disagree, I disagree profoundly. It was from a chance conversation I had with some railway chaps in a public house that it emerged that this engine was in a certain condition. Is that good enough? Is that in accord with the public conscience? Is this the world we expected to live in under Home Rule? Would it have been the British way?

All that I take leave to doubt.

My views on the Irish steam man of to-day are well known. Statements already made, not once but often, I will not re-state. Suffice it to say that your driver of to-day conceives that a social stigma attaches to a well-filled Repair Book. He simply will not notify defects in his machine. He will dissemble and hide and pass off serious things with a laugh. A knock in the bearings—what of it? Come day go day, God send Sunday. A little short in the oil system. She'll right herself, she'll be game-ball to-morrow. We'll do a little priming outside Balbriggan and then we'll see what happens. Anyway, *we* won't have her to-morrow. We'll get Rafferty blamed.

It is a fundamental weakness in the character of our people. One looks to the Churches in a matter of this kind. Single-handed I can do little. But there is one idea in my head I most earnestly commend to the consideration of Glenavy. It is simple, not very costly and *might well yield wonderful results for Steam and Ireland*. Beyond all doubt it is worth trying. We cannot in this matter afford to be timorous or conservative. We must attempt the bold remedy. If we fail, what of that? It is not shameful to fail.

In the quiet stretches behind the North Strand we must—and at once—set up a little steam clinic. There I am prepared to give my services gratis six days a week. The whole thing must be absolutely informal. Drivers must be told that half a mile up the line there is a little house, a simple structure of dressed stone, with perchance a rose bush at the door; a little haven where advice may be had on the intimate little troubles of our noble and hard-working locomotives. No scolding, no questions, no 'why-was-this-allowed-to-happen?' And no snobbery. Must a man stay away because, forsooth, his charge is an undersized, dirty 2-4-2 tank, caked with coal-dust and rattling in every bolt after a lifetime of shunting? Most certainly not. I will gladly see them all, and no disorder too trivial. A great sickness begins with a small sickness. That is the watchword of modern locomotive therapy.

I must not forget to tell you of the 'curious experience' I had (there) the other day. Went home late one night to the lodgings, put on the green eye-shade, and got to work on the new boiler drawings. Within reach was the inevitable glass of Pernod. Frankly, I got all mixed up. Drawing the boiler-tubes involved several parallel horizontal lines. Whatever I was thinking of, I found that I had inscribed on these lines the text of a rather lovely violin sonata. Nor did I realise what had happened until the following morning, when I came down to find the boiler drawings on the piano, neatly inscribed 'Slieve Gullion Boiler: Maestoso: Andante Grazioso: Presto.' And the whole, by your leave, dedicated to Kreisler! Dear me!

* * *

WHAT OF steam for 1944?

Suffice it to say that I have plans. I am writing a book on steam and it will be published in due course by that mysterious Mister Pranter who is so frequently mentioned in *The Bell*.

Readers often correspond with me on steam matters. The younger generation, I find, knows very little about the great art. Thus I am often chided, forsooth, for being 'too technical'. Bah! As well ask Einstein to provide simpler sums. *Quod scripsi scripsi.* Not one jot or tittle will I abate.

Yet ignorance can have charm. A young lady has written challenging me on the subject of railway disasters. 'Would not a plan to avoid even one be more important than a thousand thermic syphons?' But of course. Most certainly. Nobody suggested anything to the contrary. Indeed, I dealt personally with this very matter many years ago, Drawings, specifications, everything. Take, for example, my scheme for avoiding head-on collisions. It is the essence of inexpense and simplicity.

The patent apparatus I illustrate opposite tells its own ingenious story. Two trains colliding head-on do not telescope each other and kill hundreds of people. They are instantly switched off the track upon which at least one of them had no business to be and run harmlessly past each other,

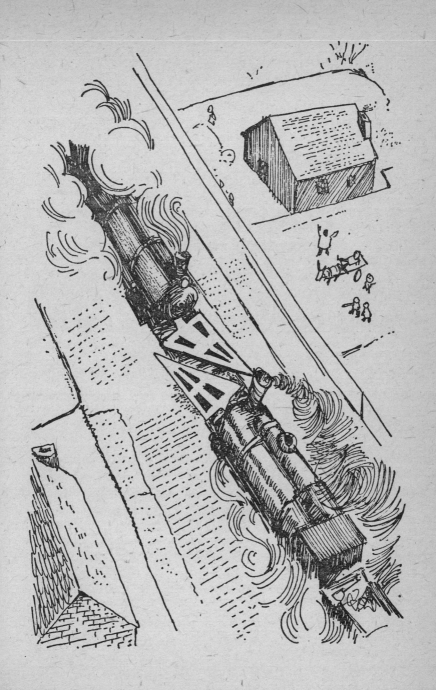

ploughing harmlessly into the earth and coming to a stand-still. Some of the ladies may be shaken, perhaps the fireman has scalded his hand . . . but the great thing is that there is absolutely no blood.

Nor in my researches did I neglect the only other sort of a collision that is possible between trains. I refer to the case where, owing to inexcusable signal-box bungling, a fast passenger train is permitted to overtake a slow local on the same track. What then?

Simple. Let the end of every slow train consist of the patent ramp-car I have illustrated. The fast train will not (as you might have imagined) run along the top of the slow train and eventually crash down on top of the slow engine. Quite no. The steepness of the ramp, allied with its motion, is sufficient to slow up the fast train and compel it to roll back again on the tracks. Thus hundreds of more lives are saved and man moves on in the coil of his dark destiny.

All these plans were shown to the old D. & S.E.R., the most ruffianly railroad concern ever to exist in any country. 'The Manager directs me to state that the Company are not interested in enclosed drawings and can take no responsibility for same.'

Do I speak bitterly? Maybe.

* * *

RECENTLY, at the Myles na gCopaleen Central Research Bureau, we were up all night with a low pressure centrifugal feed pump. Tangential acceleration of the fluid we were using caused 'blowing' in the filaments, and soon a transverse flaw developed in the automatic facing chuck. We substituted a 'cold' three-jaw chuck lined with colloidal graphite (160 c.c. per ft. lb. pressure at a temperature of 385°C.) and 'ramped back' the discharge metre, which, of course, is cast integrally and cannot be dismantled for running adjustments. At 4.30 am. it became clear that we were going to win through, and that 'Old Martha', as we call her, would survive. But what a night!

FOOTPLATE TOPICS

Coming back to the cognate subject of railway working, I should not like it to be taken from my remarks a few weeks ago that I would like to go down in railway history as a 'full regulator man'. In my railway days you would not always find me with the lever pulled right up; still more rarely would you find me yielding to the temptation to work on the 'first port' and cut off late. Sometimes, when conditions suited, you would find me blowing down to reduce priming, but never when the design left me open to the danger of having my valve jammed open. And none knew better than I when to shut off my cylinder oil feed when drifting. I could write a book on how to economise on locomotive working in the present difficult times, but our self-opinionated and pig-headed railway bosses would probably ignore it. Recently I saw shunters doing things in the Kingsbridge yards that brought a blush of richest wine-hue to my wind-scarred railwayman's cheek. Nothing but a strong informed public opinion will remedy these wasteful abuses. All up to Foster Place at 7.30 this evening, please. Fraternal delegate from the Swindon shops will attend.

Incidentally, for a fee of fifty guineas and expenses I have offered the G.N.R. Company to ride the entire road and check carefully the drivers' repair books. I have not had what is usually called the courtesy of a reply. (And by the same token there is a very bad patch out there beyond Skerries, it would need to be looked after before something happens.)

One thing that I would put down with an iron hand, G.S. as well as G.N.: and that is toping and card playing in the cabins of express trains. There is nothing so easy as to over-ride a red if you are worried by a lone jack in a misère hand. Or, indeed, exercised by the prospect of destroying your fireman with a sudden trump in the middle of his cast-iron seven hearts. There is a time and a place for everything.

Keats and Chapman

WHEN Keats and Chapman were at Greyfriars, the latter manifested a weakness for practical jokes—'practical jokes' you might call them, indeed, of the oddest kind.

One afternoon Chapman observed the headmaster quietly pacing up and down in the shade of the immemorial elms, completely submerged in Dindorf's *Poetae Scenici Graeci*. It was late summer, and the afternoon stood practically upright on the scorched lawns, weaving drunkenly in its own baked light. Sun-struck pigeons gasped happily in the trees, maggots chuckled dementedly in the grasses, and red ants grimly carried on their interminable transport undertakings. It was very, very hot. Chapman, however, had certain fish to fry and mere heat was not likely to deter him.

He wandered off to an old tool-shed and emerged very casually, carrying a small bucket of liquid glue. He took up an unobtrusive position near the pacing headmaster, and waited patiently for his chance. The headmaster approached, turned, and moved again slowly on his way. Instantly Chapman darted out, ran up noiselessly behind the pedagogue, and care - fully emptied the bucket of glue all down the back of his coat. In a flash the young joker was back again in the shadow of the elms, carefully studying the results of his work. The headmaster continued his reading, wondering vaguely at the sound of aircraft; for the shining brown mess on the back of his coat had attracted hordes of wasps, bluebottles, gnats, newts, and every manner of dungfly. Chapman from his nook decided that the operation had been successful.

But the end was not yet. Two fifth form bullies (Snoop and Stott, as it happened) had observed the incident from the distance, and thought it would be funny to turn the tables. They approached Chapman under cover, leaped on him, gagged his mouth, and lifted the little fellow in their arms. The pacing headmaster paced on. When his back was turned, the two fifth form ruffians ran up behind him, jammed Chapman on to him back to back on the gleaming glue, and were gone before the wretched headmaster had time to realise the extraordinary facts of his situation. That a howling small boy was glued to him high up on his back did not disturb him so much as the murderous punctures of the wasps, who were now angry at being disturbed.

There was hell to pay that evening. Nobody would own up, and every boy in the school was flogged with the exception of Chapman, who was regarded as a victim of the outrage.

After Keats had received his flogging like the rest, he was asked for his opinion of the whole incident, and particularly what he thought of Chapman.

'I like a man that sticks to his principals,' was all he would vouchsafe.

* * *

KEATS and Chapman once paid a visit to the Vale of Avoca, the idea being to have a good look at Moore's tree. Keats brought along his valet, a somewhat gloomy character called Monk. Irish temperament, climate, scenery, and porter did not agree with Monk, whose idea of home and beauty was the East End of London and a glass of mild. He tried to persuade Keats to go home, but the poet had fastened on a local widow and was not to be thwarted by the fads of his servant. Soon it became evident that a breach between them was imminent. Things were brought to a head by a downpour which lasted for three days and nights. Monk tendered a savage resignation, and departed for Dublin in a sodden chaise. The incident annoyed Chapman.

'I think you are well rid of that fellow,' he said. 'He was a sullen lout.'

Keats shook his head despondently.

'The last rays of feeling and life must depart,' he said sadly, 'ere the bloom of that valet shall fade from my heart.'

Chapman coughed slightly.

BRAINS AND BRAWN

Chapman's fag at Greyfriars was a boy called Fox, a weedy absent-minded article of Irish extraction. One evening, shortly before the hour when Mr Quelch was scheduled to take the Remove for prep., the young fellow was sent down the High with a jug and strict instructions to bring back a pint of mild and bitter without spilling it. The minutes lengthened and so did Chapman's face, who disliked going into class completely sober. He fumed and fretted, but still there was no sign of the returning fag. In the opposite armchair lay Keats, indolently biting his long nails. He thought he would console his friend with a witty quotation.

'Fox dimissa nescit reverti,' he murmured.

'Dimissus!' snapped Chapman, always a stickler for that kind of thing.

'Kindly leave my wife out of this,' Keats said stiffly.

THAT MAN KEATS

Once when Keats was rotting in Paris a kind old lady gave him a lump of veal and advised him to go home and cook and stuff it into himself. During a desperate attempt to grill it with a tongs over an open fire, the meat caught alight.

The poet is thought to have muttered something like 'la Veal lumière' (under breath that hinted of bountifullest barleycorn). Chapman was out at the Folies.

* * *

KEATS, when living in the country purchased an expensive chestnut gelding. This animal was very high-spirited and largely untrained and gave the novice owner a lot of trouble. First it was one thing, then another but finally he was discovered one morning to have disappeared from his stable. Foul play was not suspected nor did the poet at this stage adopt the foolish expedient of locking the stable door. On the contrary he behaved very sensibly. He examined the stable to ascertain how the escape had been effected and then travelled all over the yard on his hands and knees looking for traces of the animal's hooves. He was like a dog looking for a trail, except that he found a trail where many a good dog would have found nothing. Immediately the poet was off cross-country following the trail. It happened that Chapman was on a solitary walking-tour in the vicinity and he was agreeably surprised to encounter the poet in a remote mountainy place. Keats was walking quickly with his eyes on the ground and looked very preoccupied. He had evidently no intention of stopping to converse with Chapman. The latter, not understanding his friend's odd behaviour, halted and cried:

'What are you doing, old man?'

'Dogging a fled horse,' Keats said as he passed by.

KEATS AND ALL THAT

It is not generally known that . . .

O excuse me.

Keats and Chapman (in the old days) spent several months in the county Wicklow prospecting for ochre deposits. That was before the days of (your) modern devices for geological divination. With Keats and Chapman it was literally a question of smelling the stuff out. The pair of them sniffed their way into Glenmalure and out of it again, and then snuffled back to Woodenbridge. In a field of turnips near Avoca Keats suddenly got the pungent effluvium of a vast ochre mine and lay for hours face down in the muck delightedly permeating his nostrils with the perfume of hidden wealth. No less lucky was Chapman. He had nosed away in the direction of Newtonmountkennedy and came racing back shouting that he too had found a mine. He implored Keats to come and confirm his nasal diagnosis. Keats agreed. He accompanied Chapman to the site and lay down in the dirt to do his sniffing. Then he rose.

'Great mines stink alike,' he said.

* * *

MEMORIES OF KEATS

Keats and Chapman once climbed Vesuvius and stood looking down into the volcano, watching the bubbling lava and considering the sterile ebullience of the stony entrails of the earth. Chapman shuddered as if with cold or fear.

'Will you have a drop of the crater?' Keats said.

An ancestor of Keats (by the same token) was concerned in the dread events of the French Revolution. He was, of course, on the aristocratic side, a lonely haughty creature who ignored the ordinances of the rabblement and continued to sit in his Louis Kahn's drawing room drinking pale sherry and playing bezique. Soon, however, he found himself in the cart and was delivered to execution. He surveyed the dread engine of Monsieur Guillotine, assessing its mechanical efficiency and allowing it some small mead of admiration. Then turning to the executioner, he courteously presented his compliments and prayed that he should be granted a simple favour on the occasion of his last journey—that of being permitted to face away from the guillotine and lean back so that the blade should meet him in the throat rather than that he should adopt the usual attitude of kneeling face down with his neck on the block.

'I like to sit with my back to the engine,' he explained.

Chapman, during his biochemistry days at Munich, had spent years examining and cataloguing all the human glands. He designated each according to a letter of the alphabet, and when he had them all isolated and labelled, he settled down to write a minute medical monograph on each one of them. Gland A, gland B, gland C—Chapman's scholarly dossiers accumulated. Keats looked in to see him one day and found him apparently stumped. One of the glands would not yield to the experiment.

'What's the trouble?' Keats said.

'This gland N,' Chapman replied, 'is giving me a lot of trouble. But I'm going to keep after it. I won't let it beat me. I'll win yet.'

'That's the spirit,' Keats said. Then he began to potter about the place, whistling some tune. Chapman pricked up his ears.

'What's that your whistling?' he asked.

'Wir fahren gegen N-gland,' Keats said.

Chapman suddenly swallowed some chemical potion he had been working at.

* * *

PEOPLE WHO come to see me with their problems often wonder at the queer name I have on my house—'The Past'. Is it so queer after all? Is it not better than, say, 'The Present'? 'The Present' seems to imply that the house is the gift of some friend rather than the result of my exertions as secretary of the Gaelic League, a post which I held at a time when the language was neither profitable nor popular, at a time when the sycophant and time-server dominated the counsels of the Irish nation, at a time when our land, broken and bleeding, yielded—nay, proffered— the hand of friendship to her own exiled kith and kin resident in the distant continent of America, AT A TIME WHEN—

Excuse me.

But about this house of mine, I often hear people saying: 'Ah, that poor man. Sure that poor man is living in "The Past"!'

And so I am. The poor law valuation is fifty quid.

KEATSIANA

The 'abstract' painter Franz Huehl, son of a Dresden banker, was living in Zurich eking o. a p. l-hood (like manny a betther man) during the last European war. He was happily married, and his wife, not knowing that young Huehl's allowance had ceased many years ago (in fact when he painted a 'portrait' of his father), was pleased with their comparative prosperity; Huehl—an incorrigible gambler—had had a run of luck at the tables and had won enough to put him on velvet for eighteen months. The wife knew nothing of this. However, the money eventually ran (out) and, very worried, the young wife went to consult Keats, who at that time was supervising the construction of tramcars for the Zurich Corporation. Keats heard her (out). Sympathetic, he determined to tell her the truth.

'My dear girl,' he said, 'you have been living in F. Huehl's pair o'dice.'

When she was gone he turned to Chapman.

'F. Huehl and his Monet are soon parted,' he observed.

Chapman bought the picture next day, for one of his spare lieder.

By the way (whatever that idiot phrase means), we newspaper people often refer laughingly to Schubert as a lieder-writer.

THE medical profession, remember, wasn't always the highly organised racket that it is to-day. In your grandfather's time practically anybody could take in hand (whatever that means) to be a physician or surgeon and embark on experiments which frequently involved terminating other people's lives. Be that as it may, certain it is that Chapman in his day was as fine a surgeon as ever wore a hat. Chapman took in hand to be an ear nose and throat man and in many an obscure bedroom he performed prodigies which, if reported in the secular press, would have led to a question in the House. Keats, of course, always went along to pick up the odd guinea that was going for the anaesthetist. Chapman's school-day lessons in carpentry often saved him from making foolish mistakes.

On one occasion the two savants were summoned to perform a delicate antrum operation. This involved opening up the nasal passages and doing a lot of work in behind the forehead. The deed was done and the two men departed, leaving behind a bleeding ghost suffering severely from what is nowadays called 'postoperative debility'. But through some chance the patient lived through the night, and the following day seemed to have some slim chance of surviving. Weeks passed and there was no mention of his death in the papers. Months passed. Then Chapman got an unpleasant surprise. A letter from the patient containing several pages of abuse, obviously written with a hand that quivered with pain. It appeared that the patient after 'recovering' somewhat from the operation, developed a painful swelling at the top of his nose. This condition progressed from pain to agony and eventually the patient took to consuming drugs made by his brother, who was a blacksmith. These preparations apparently did more harm than good and the patient had now written to Chapman demanding that he should return and restore the patient's health and retrieve the damage that had been done; otherwise that the brother would call to know the reason why.

'I think I know what is wrong with this person,' Chapman said. 'I missed one of the needles I was using. Perhaps we had better go and see him.' Keats nodded.

When they arrived the patient could barely speak, but he summoned his remaining strength to utter a terrible flood of bad language at the selfless men who had come a long journey to relieve pain. A glance by the practised eye of Chapman revealed that one of the tiny instruments had, indeed, been sewn up (inadvertently) in the wound, subsequently causing grandiose suppurations. Chapman got to work again, and soon retrieved his property. When the patient was re-sewn and given two grains, the blacksmith brother arrived and kindly offered to drive the two men home in his trap. The offer was gratefully accepted. At a particularly filthy part of the road, the blacksmith deliberately upset the trap, flinging all the occupants into a morass of muck. This, of course, by way of revenge, accidentally on purpose.

That evening Chapman wore an expression of sadness and depression. He neglected even to do his twenty lines of Homer, a nightly chore from which he had never shrunk in five years.

'To think of the fuss that fellow made over a mere needle, to think of his ingratitude,' he brooded. 'Abusive letters, streams of foul language, and finally arranging to have us fired into a pond full of filth! And all for a tiny needle! Did you ever hear of such vindictiveness!'

'He had it up his nose for you for a long time,' Keats said.

* * *

CHAPMAN thought a lot of Keats's girl, Fanny Brawne, and often said so.

'Do you know,' he remarked one day, 'that girl of yours is a sight for sore eyes.'

'She stupes to conquer, you mean,' Keats said.

A MEMOIR OF KEATS

Keats and Chapman once lived near a church. There was a heavy debt on it. The pastor made many efforts to clear the debt by promoting whist drives and raffles and the like, but was making little headway. He then heard of the popularity of these carnivals where you have swing-boats and roundabouts and fruit-machines and la boule and shooting-galleries and every modern convenience. He thought to entertain the town with a week of this and hoped to make some money to reduce the debt. He hired one of these outfits but with his diminutive financial status he could only induce a very third-rate company to come. All their machinery was old and broken. On the opening day, as the steam-organ blared forth, the heavens opened and disgorged sheets of icy rain. The scene, with its drenched and tawdry trappings, assumed the gaiety of a morgue. Keats and Chapman waded from stall to stall, soaked and disconsolate. Chapman (unwisely, perhaps) asked the poet what he thought of the fiesta.

'A fête worse than debt,' Keats said.

Chapman collapsed into a trough of mud.

* * *

LITERARY CORNER

Chapman was once complaining to Keats about the eccentric behaviour of a third party who had rented a desolate stretch of coast and engaged an architect to build a fantastic castle on it. Chapman said that no sane person could think of living in so forsaken a spot, but Keats was more inclined to criticise the rich man on the score of the architect he had chosen, a young man of 'advanced' ideas and negligible experience. Chapman persisted that the site was impossible, and that this third party was a fool.

'His B.Arch. is worse than his bight,' Keats said.

A GLIMPSE OF KEATS

Keats and Chapman were conversing one day on the street, and what they were conversing about I could not tell you. But anyway there passed a certain character who was renowned far and wide for his piety, and who was reputed to have already made his own coffin, erected it on trestles, and slept in it every night.

'Did you see our friend?' Keats said.

'Yes,' said Chapman, wondering what was coming.

'A terrible man for his bier,' the poet said.

* * *

KEATS (in his day) had a friend named Byrne. Byrne was a rather decent Irish person, but he was frightfully temperamental, politically unstable and difficult to get on with, particularly if the running board of the tram was already crowded with fat women. He frightened (the life) out of his wife with his odd Marxist ideas.

'What shall I do?' she implored Keats. 'Politics mean nothing to me; his love means much.'

Keats said nothing, but wrote to her that night—'Please Byrne when Red.'

KEATS once bought a small pub in London and one day he was visited by Dr Watson, confrère of the famous Baker Street sleuth. Watson came late in the evening accompanied by a friend and the pair of them took to hard drinking in the back snug. When closing time came, Keats shouted out the usual slogans of urgent valediction such as 'Time now please!', 'Time gents!', 'The Licence gents!' 'Fresh air now gents!' and 'Come on now all together!' But Dr Watson and his friend took no notice. Eventually Keats put his head into the snug and roared 'Come on now gents, have yez no Holmes to go to!'

The two topers then left in that lofty vehicle, high dudgeon.

* * *

A MEMOIR of Keats. Number eighty four. Copyright in all civilised countries, also in 'Eire' and in the Sick Counties of Northern Ireland. Pat. Appd. For. The public is warned that copyright subsists in these epexegetic biographic addenda under warrant issued by the Ulster King of Farms (*nach maireann*) and persons assailing, invading or otherwise violating such rights of copy, which are in-alienable and indefeasible, will be liable to summary disintitulement *in feodo* without remembrances and petty sochemaunce pendent graund plaisaunce du roi.

A Memoir of Keats. No. 84. Copyright.

Keats once rented a trout-stream and managed to kill a sackful of fish every day. Transport was poor and he had no means of marketing the surplus, which, however, was not large. Chapman, hearing of this, presented his friend with a small mobile canning plant. (He managed to pick up (rather than buy) this machine for that odd mercantile cantata, a song.) Calling to see the poet some months later, he was astonished at his robust and girthy physique.

'You must be eating a lot,' Chapman said. 'I suppose you are making money out of the canned trout?'

'I eat what I can,' Keats said.

* * *

CHAPMAN had a small cousin whom he wished to put to a trade and he approached Keats for advice. The poet had an old relative who was a tailor and for a consideration this tailor agreed to accept the young man as an apprentice. For the first year, however, he declined to let him do any cutting, insisting that he should first master the art of making garments up.

One day Chapman accidentally spilled some boiling porridge over his only suit, ruining it completely. The same evening he had an appointment with a wealthy widow and was at his wits' end to know how he could get another suit in time. Keats suggested that the young apprentice should be called upon in the emergency. Chapman thought this a good idea and sent the apprentice an urgent message. Afterwards he had some misgivings as to the ability of a mere apprentice to produce a wearable suit in a few hours.

'He'll certainly want to spare no effort to have it finished by six o'clock,' he said gloomily.

'He'll have his work cut out,' Keats said reassuringly.

* * *

CHAPMAN once fell in love and had not been long plying his timid attentions when it was brought to his notice that he had a rival. This rival, a ferocious and burly character, surprised Chapman in the middle of a tender conversation with the lady and immediately challenged him to a duel, being, as he said, prohibited from breaking him into pieces there and then merely by the presence of the lady.

Chapman, who was no duellist, went home and explained what had happened to Keats.

'And I think he means business,' he added. 'I fear it is a case of "pistols for two, coffee for one". Will you be my second?'

'Certainly,' Keats said, 'and since you have the choice of weapons I think you should choose swords rather than pistols.'

Chapman agreed. The rendezvous was duly made and one morning at dawn Keats and Chapman drove in a cab to the dread spot. The poet had taken the 'coffee for one' remark rather too literally and had brought along a small quantity of coffee, sugar, milk, a coffee-pot, a cup, saucer and spoon, together with a small stove and some paraffin.

After the usual formalities, Chapman and the rival fell to sword-play. The two men fought fiercely, edging hither and thither about the sward. Keats, kneeling and priming the stove, was watching anxiously and saw that his friend was weakening. Suddenly, Chapman's guard fell and his opponent drew back to plunge his weapon home. Keats, with a lightning flick of his arm took up the stove and hurled it at the blade that was poised to kill! With such force and aim so deadly was the stove hurled that it smashed the blade in three places. Chapman was saved!

The affair ended in bloodless recriminations. Chapman was warm in his thanks to Keats.

'You saved my life,' he said, 'by hurling the stove between our blades. You're tops!'

'Primus inter parries,' Keats said.

* * *

KEATS AND CHAPMAN once called to see a titled friend and after the host had hospitably produced a bottle of whiskey, the two visitors were called into consultation regarding the son of the house, who had been exhibiting a disquieting redness of face and boisterousness of manner at the age of twelve. The father was worried, suspecting some dread disease. The youngster was produced but the two visitors, glass in hand, declined to make any diagnosis. When leaving the big house, Chapman rubbed his hands briskly and remarked on the cold.

'I think it must be freezing and I'm glad of that drink,' he said. 'By the way, did you think what I thought about that youngster?'

'There's a nip in the heir,' Keats said.

* * *

CHAPMAN was much given to dreaming and often related to Keats the strange things he saw when in bed asleep. On one occasion he dreamt that he had died and gone to heaven. He was surprised and rather disappointed at what he saw for although the surroundings were most pleasant, there seemed to be nobody about. The place seemed to be completely empty and Chapman saw himself wandering disconsolately about looking for somebody to talk to. He suddenly woke up without solving this curious puzzle.

'It was very strange,' he told Keats. 'I looked everywhere but there wasn't a soul to be seen.'

Keats nodded understandingly.

'There wasn't a sinner in the place,' he said.

* * *

KEATS AND CHAPMAN met one Christmas Eve and fell to comparing notes on the Christmas present each had bought himself. Keats had bought himself a ten glass bottle of whiskey and paid thirty shillings for it in the black market.

'That is far too dear,' Chapman said. 'Eighteen shillings is plenty to pay for a ten glass bottle.'

Chapman then explained that he had bought a valuable Irish manu-script, one of the oldest copies of the Battle of Ventry, or *Cath Fionntragha*. He explained that the value of the document was much enhanced by certain interlineal Latin equivalents of obscure Irish words.

'How many such interlineal comments are there?' Keats asked.

'Ten,' Chapman said.

'And how much did you pay for this thing?' Keats asked.

'Forty-five shillings,' Chapman said defiantly.

'Eighteen shillings is plenty to pay for a ten gloss battle,' Keats said crankily.

* * *

KEATS once tried to collar the Christmas card trade in pretty mottoes. He bought a quantity of small white boards and got to work burning philosophical quotations on them with a tiny poker. *Festina Lente*, *Carpe Diem* and *Dum Spiro Spero*, were produced in great numbers. Becoming more ambitious, the poet showed Chapman a board bearing the words *Proximus Ardet Ucalegon*.

'One does not like to be captious,' Chapman said, 'but I'm afraid there's a word left out there.'

Keats looked at the board again.

'You want *Jam* on it,' he said.

* * *

WHILE KEATS and Chapman were at Heidelberg arranging for the purchase of cheap doctorates, the latter conceived a violent, wholly mysterious attachment for a practically supernumerary lecturer in Materia Med., by name Jakob Arnim-Woelkus, an incredible bore and a man wanting in the meanest of personal accomplishments. Chapman never wearied of this person's company and in his absence, was for ever retailing the 'pleasantries' and sophisms of the deplorable bore. Keats, who could not bear this, kept out of his compatriot's way as much as possible. Late in term, however, Keats, to heal the scars he had received in a duel, went walking into the mountains and persuaded Chapman to accompany him, fearing less the devil he knew than any foreigner. The two walked for hours, Keats gloomy, Chapman meditative. Not a word was exchanged till eventually they came to the brow of a hill whence a fine landscape was to be seen. Chapman, moved, spoke, student-wise, in dog-Latin: Ah, Keats! Hic utinam nunc sit Jacobus Arnim-Woelkus, doctor praeclarissimus noster! Keats snarled, *Odi*, he roared, *odi Prof. Arnim-Woelkus!*

* * *

KEATS had a nephew who evinced, even in early childhood, an unusual talent for manufacturing spurious coins. At the age of twelve he was already in the habit of making his own pocket money. His parents were poor and could not procure for him the tuition that would enable him to proceed from the science of penny-making to the more intricate and remunerative medium of work in silver. The boy's attempts at making half-crowns were very poor indeed and on one occasion resulted in the father being presented with six months hard labour by a local magistrate. Keats, who was in reduced circumstances and could not offer any help himself, put the problem before Chapman, who was in tow with a wealthy widow. The widow was induced to give £100 to have the boy educated. Six months after the money had been given over and a tutor found, Keats and Chapman visited the boy's home to see what progress was being made. They found the boy in his workshop engrossed in the production of a very colourable half-crown, working with meticulous industry on what was a very life-like representation of his late majesty, King Edward. To Keats, Chapman expressed satisfaction at the improvement in the boy's skill.

'I think he is making excellent progress,' he said.

'He is forging ahead,' Keats said.

* * *

ONCE CHAPMAN, in his tireless quest for a way to get rich quick, entered into a contract with a London firm for the supply of ten tons of swansdown. At the time he had no idea where he could get this substance, but on the advice of Keats went to live with the latter in a hut on a certain river estuary where the rather odd local inhabitants cultivated tame swans for the purposes of their somewhat coarsely-grained eggs. Chapman erected several notices in the locality inviting swan-owners to attend at his hut for the purpose of having their fowls combed and offering 'a substantial price' per ounce for the down so obtained, Soon the hut was ssurounded by gaggles of unsavoury-looking natives, each accompanied by four or five disreputable swans on dog-leads. The uproar was enormous and vastly annoyed Keats, who was in bed with toothache. Chapman went out and addressed the multitude and then fell to bargaining with individual owners. After an hour in the pouring rain he came in to Keats, having apparently failed to do business. He was in a vile temper.

'Those appalling louts!' he exploded. 'Why should I go out and humiliate myself before them, beg to be allowed to comb their filthy swans, get soaked to the skin bargaining with them?'

'It'll get you down sooner or later,' Keats mumbled.

* * *

A MILLIONAIRE collector (whose name was ever associated with that old-time Irish swordsman of France, O'Shea d'Ar) once invited Chapman and Keats to dinner. The invitation came quite at the wrong time for Keats, who was crippled with stomach trouble. Chapman insisted, however, that the poet should come along and endeavour to disguise his malady, holding that millionaires were necessarily personable folk whose friendship could be very beautiful. Keats was too ill to oppose Chapman's proposal and in due course found himself in a cab bound for the rich man's bounteous apartments. On arrival Chapman covered up his friend's incapacity by engaging the host in loud non-stop conversations and also managed to have Keats placed at an obscure corner of the table where little notice would be taken of him. Slumped in his chair, the unfortunate poet saw flunkeys deposit course after course of the richest fare before him but beyond raking his knife and fork through the food in desultory attempts to make a show of eating, he did not touch it. When the main course was served—a sight entirely disgusting to the eye of Keats—Chapman and the host were in the middle of a discussion on rare china. The host directed that a valuable vase on the mantelpiece should be passed round to the guests for inspection. Chapman gave a most enthusiastic dissertation on it, identifying it as a piece of the Ming dynasty. He then passed it to Keats, who was still slumped over his untouched platter of grub. The poet had not been following the conversation and apparently assumed that Chapman was trying to aid him in his extremity. He muttered something about the vase being 'a godsend' and after a moment handed it to the flunkey to be replaced on the mantelpiece. On the way home that evening Chapman violently reproached his friend for not making a fuss about the vase and pleasing the host.

'I saw nothing very special about it,' Keats said.

'Good heavens man,' Chapman expostulated, 'it was a priceless Ming vase, worth thousands of pounds! Why didn't you at least say nothing if you couldn't say something suitable?'

'I'm afraid I put my food in it,' Keats said.

* * *

CHAPMAN once called upon Keats seeking advice on a delicate matter. It appears that he had accompanied his eldest son to a school cricket match. In the course of the day, Chapman found himself without cigarettes, and was told that the nearest shop was ten miles away. He took the obvious course of making his way to the visitors' cloakroom, which was then deserted, and carefully went through the pockets of the guests' overcoats. His haul amounted to about seven packets and contentedly he went back to watch the play. A rather ironical thing happened the following day. The Headmaster wrote to Chapman to say that Chapman's son was strongly suspected of having pilfered from guests' overcoats on the day of the match and that the question of expulsion was under consideration. What was Chapman to do? That was the question he posed Keats.

Keats advised that Chapman should reply saying that he had personally witnessed another boy going through the coats; that he did not care to reveal this boy's identity but that in view of his own carelessness in not reporting the matter, he for his part would penalise himself to the extent of replacing all the missing property.

Chapman accepted this suggestion.

'I hope it will work,' he said. 'I believe there is a very bad atmosphere in the school since this happened.'

'It will clear the heir,' Keats said.

* * *

KEATSIANA

Keats was once presented with an Irish terrier, which he humorously named Byrne. One day the beast strayed from the house and failed to return at night. Everybody was distressed, save Keats himself. He reached reflectively for his violin, a fairly passable timber of the Stradivarius feciture, and was soon at work with chin and jaw.

Chapman, looking in for an after-supper pipe, was astonished at the poet's composure, and did not hesitate to say so. Keats smiled (in a way that was rather lovely).

'And why should I not fiddle,' he asked, 'while Byrne roams?'

* * *

CHAPMAN once became immersed in the study of dialectical materialism, particularly insofar as economic and sociological planning could be demonstrated to condition eugenics, birth-rates and anthropology. His wrangles with Keats lasted far into the night. He was particularly obsessed by the fact that in the animal kingdom, where there was no self-evident plan of ordered Society and where connubial relations were casual and polygamous, the breed prospered and disease remained of modest dimensions. Where there was any attempt at the imposition from without—and he instanced the scientific breeding of race-horses by humans—the breed prospered even more remarkably. He was not slow to point out that philosophers of the school of Marx and Engels had ignored the apparent necessity for ordered breeding on the part of humans as a concomitant to planning in the social and economic spheres. Was this, he once asked Keats, to be taken as evidence of superior reproductive selection on the part of, say, horses—or was it to be taken that a man of the stamp of Engels deliberately shirked an issue too imponderable for rationative evaluation?

The poet found this sort of thing boring, and frowned.

'Foals rush in where Engels feared to tread,' he said morosely.

* * *

(READERS ARE warned that this is extra special; if you don't get it, you probably have a permanent cold in the head—high up.)

Keats and Chapman were entrusted by the British Government with a secret mission which involved a trip to India. A man-of-war awaited them at a British port. Leaving their lodgings at dawn, they were driven at a furious pace to the point of embarkation. When about to rush on board, they encountered at the dockside a mutual friend, one Mr Childs, who chanced to be there on business connected with his calling of wine-importer. Perfunctory and very hasty courtesies were exchanged; Keats and Chapman then rushed on board the man-of-war, which instantly weighed anchor. The trip to India was made in the fastest time then heard of, and as soon as the ship had come to anchor in Bombay harbour, the two friends were whisked to land in a wherry. Knowing that time was of the essence of their mission, they hastened from the docks into the neighbouring streets and on turning a corner, whom should they see only—

Mr Childs? No.

Just a lot of Indians, complete strangers.

'Big world,' Keats remarked.

* * *

IN THEIR LEANER days Keats and Chapman were reduced to making a living in the halls. Chapman had invented a fortune-telling device operated by a 1 h.p. electric motor. He called this machine 'The X-Ray Eye'. It was —as were most baffling gadgets in those days—worked with mirrors. Inside the 'electric eye' was set a very strong electric bulb which cast, through the lenses of the 'eye' a penetrating shaft of light through the darkened auditorium. Inside the eye and opposite the machine was a little screen upon which various character-reading words such as 'GENEROUS', 'WARM-HEARTED', 'BRAINY' could be made to appear one at a time by the mere turn of a handle. By manipulating the handle and turning the universally-jointed eye hither and thither about the auditorium, Chapman could make the magnified reflection of these mottoes appear in blazing letters on the chests of members of the audience. Naturally the words were altered to suit the taste of local audiences. It was Keats' task to attend to this but on one occasion he neglected to make the change with the result that the unsuspecting Chapman appeared one night before a refined London audience with mottoes which had been in use in Lancashire. First time the 'eye' fixed on a most respectable captain of industry, who saw—to a horror that was no less than Chapman's— that the word 'DRUNKARD' was engraved by the 'eye' on his boiled shirt. The outraged citizen leaped to his feet, shook his fist at Chapman, pro-tested furiously, and began to call for the manager. The situation was saved by Keats.

'He's casting no reflections on you,' he called out from a box.

CHAPMAN once laid out the entire savings of himself and his friend Keats on a pedigree bull. He also beggared nine weak-minded relatives on the purchase of a vast farm for the grazing of this animal, who was expected to repay all the money laid out on him within a year and with such addi-tional profit as would enable Keats and Chapman to emigrate to America. After nine months Keats was incarcerated in respect of unpaid fodder bills and Chapman had gone into hiding for similar reasons. The bull merely ate everything before him, gored several yardmen and did not bring in one penny towards his keep. Chapman at length contrived to visit the jailed Keats in disguise in order to discuss the disastrous pass to which things had come. He found the poet in a vile temper.

'I think,' Chapman said lamely, 'that that animal will have to be extirpated.'

'You had better eradicate the whole wretched project,' Keats said acidly, 'brute and ranch.'

Chapman bit his lip.

* * *

CHAPMAN on one occasion was commissioned by an enormously wealthy business man to advise on wall-papers for the state-rooms of a yacht then building. The millionaire was however unbelievably busy and could talk to Chapman only in his luxurious car on the ten-minute journey between mansion and office. At first Chapman, being well paid for his pains, did not mind this exiguous procedure but as time passed a number of unknown advisers on other matters were picked up at various corners so that on some mornings the car was packed with up to eight people simultaneously giving the fur-coated boss very expensive advice. This amazed Chapman enormously, as he was failing completely to make himself heard on wall-paper schemes. The last straw was provided one morning when the car, packed to the roof with babbling experts, was joined by a mysterious lawyer, who stood outside on the running board of the racing vehicle pouring advice in through the window. This happened several mornings in succession, and Chapman eventually complained bitterly to Keats.

'That solicitor should be struck off the Rolls,' Keats said.

* * *

ONE EVENING Keats, working quietly at his books, was devastated by an inundation of Chapman. The poet's friend was distended with passion, inarticulate, a man driven mad by jealousy. When given a drink and pacified, he related the events which led to his condition. To a lady of the most ravishing beauty he had lost his heart; his sentiment was warmly reciprocated, and an early marriage was all that remained to perfect his bliss. Quite suddenly, however, a lout of an artist who specialised in ladies' portraits arrived upon the scene, begged to be permitted to paint the lady, and was granted this boon by the unthinking lover. His chagrin and rage may be guessed when it is revealed that the rascally artist forthwith laid siege to the lady's heart—with not inconsiderable results. After a time she ceased to be in when Chapman called with flowers; on two occasions she had been seen boating with this artist.

'I am beside myself,' Chapman cried, beating his head, 'and so far as I can see only two courses are open to me. I must either take my razor and slit that wretched fellow's throat from ear to ear—that or terminate completely my association with this woman, break off utterly and irrevocably my association with her!'

Keats considered the problem in silence for a considerable time. Finally he spoke:

'If I were you,' he said, 'I'd cut the painter.'

* * *

ONE WINTER'S evening Keats looked up to find Chapman regarding him closely. He naturally inquired the reason for this scrutiny.

'I was thinking about those warts on your face,' Chapman said.

'What about them?' the poet said testily.

'Oh, nothing,' Chapman said. 'It just occurred to me that you might like to have them removed . . .'

'They are there for years,' Keats said, 'and I don't see any particular reason for getting worried about them now.'

'But they are rather a blemish,' Chapman persisted. 'I wouldn't mind one—but four fairly close together, that's rather—'

'Four?' Keats cried. 'There were only three there this morning!'

'There are four there now,' Chapman said.

'That's a new one on me,' Keats said.

* * *

KEATS AND CHAPMAN were invited to view the wonders of a steel rolling mill and gratefully accepted the invitation. They watched with awe the giant hammers and rollers moulding crude steel into hawsers, plates and bars. The poet was so fascinated by this that he did not notice that a travelling overhead head had caught Chapman by the coat and yanked him away through a sinister aperture in the brickwork; nor did he perceive, either, the subsequent crash and sound of muffled screams. He was thus astounded to be shown Chapman later seated in the firm's first aid station, a bloody spectacle whose anatomical attitude suggested broken bones.

'What on earth happened you?' Keats demanded.

The injured man made some attempt to reply but his jaws were smashed and his words could not be heard. His effort to speak, however, was a serious strain and he instantly fainted.

'He looks as if he has been through the mill,' Keats remarked to a frightened bystander.

* * *

KEATS AND CHAPMAN, in funds for once, decided to take a two-day trip to Ostend, having in mind the not uncharacteristic belief that there was, for a modest initial stake, a fortune to be made on the tables. The steamer was new and large, the channel like glass. A few hours out, Keats suggested a few bowls of nourishing bouillon, and to his surprise noticed that Chapman's face, which was deadly pale, became green. He collapsed on a seat and covered his face with his hands. Keats, having reflected on the oddity of Chapman's condition against the background of happy holidaymakers, all in the most jovial spirits, repaired to the bar and consumed some cognacs. Returning later in search of his friend, he found him now putty-coloured, moaning dreadfully and staring at his lifeless hands. His condition was not enhanced by the titters of passers-by, chiefly women who should in justice be far sicker than he.

'You will be all right when we land,' Keats said helpfully. 'It is only four hours.'

'I don't mind sea-sickness so much,' Chapman wailed, '—it's the ignominy of being the one person on board who is sick. If everybody was the same, the thing would be at least bearable . . .'

Keats studied his friend with compassion.

'*O si sic omnes*,' he murmured.

* * *

CHAPMAN, ever in search of new enthusiasms, joined a body known as the Society for the Defence of Civil Liberties. The Society financed the grandiose legal battles which individuals undertook in order to secure some primitive right, such as the right to put cats out at night, to place dust-bins on public streets, play musical instruments in congested residential districts, and so forth. An important permanent activity of the Society was the review of the propriety, legality and fairness of taxation, both in substance and in incidence. Its Council found that there was ample ground for assailing all taxes and did so with great ferocity. The President of the Society, in particular, impressed Chapman. He was unremitting in his denunciation of taxation and had single-handed addressed tens of thousands of letters and telegrams of protest to Government Departments. After a rise in Income Tax rates had been announced one year, he solemnly declared that the new taxes would utterly beggar people of his own class, even to the extent of depriving them of essentials such as food and clothing. He bitterly challenged his own assessment and appealed to the Special Commissioners. Time after time he obtained postponements of the hearing on the ground that he had no clothes in which he could appear to make his case. The Commissioners began to lose patience and announced a final date beyond which they would agree to no further postponement. The President of the Society on this occasion duly appeared—but attired in a paper suit which he had contrived by taking the offending Finance Act apart and sewing the pages together in the semblance of a jacket and trousers. The appeal was disallowed but the President's ingenious gesture delighted Chapman, who gave a very long and enthusiastic account of the incident to Keats. The President was, Chapman said, the greatest champion of liberty since Napoleon.

'That fellow's always putting on an Act,' Keats said, drily.

* * *

KEATS AND CHAPMAN once went into a very expensive restaurant and ordered roes of tunny or some such delicacy. The manager explained apologetically that this dish had just gone out of season. Keats, however, insisted and the manager promised 'to see what he could do'. We do not know whether he called in the aid of some other restaurant, but the desired dishes were eventually produced. The two diners gorged themselves delightedly. Then Keats began to hum a tune.

'What's that you're humming,' Chapman asked.

'The last roes of summer,' Keats said pleasantly.

The Myles na gCopaleen Catechism
of Cliche

It is about time certain things were said and if they won't be said in the leader columns they will be said here. We have had about enough of this thing that the Germans call *unmaessigkreisenheit*. A certain thing happened the other day but not a word about it in the papers. I have now made up my mind to shoot my mouth off, whatever the consequences may be. Listen to this, for example—

The Editor : You will keep the fun clean like the rest of us.

Myself : O is that so, who said I will, you and who else?

The Editor : Your man will be down on us if we are not careful.

Myself : But surely we are prepared to suffer for our principles?

The Editor : Yes, yes, yes. Come out and have a cup of tea, I want to talk to you about Sibelius.

Myself (muttering): O all right but don't think I've forgotten about this, I will be back to it another time. 'Gone with the Wind' picture banned, all my books banned, now this, I will not stand for it do you hear me.

Mr Patrick Kavanagh was recently reported as having declared that 'there is no such thing as Gaelic literature'. This is hard luck on the Institute of Advanced Studies, who are supposed to be looking into the thing. I attended the Book Fair in the Mansion House the other evening in the hope of overhearing other similar pronouncements from the writing persons who infest such a place. I heard plenty, and have recorded it in my note-books under 'Stuff To Be Used If Certain People Put Their Heads Out.'

The Fair was fine. Bright, rearing stands; melodious loud speakers, women beautiful, long and smooth as the strand at Tramore, dazzling big print, colour standing on colour in every pattern, bright bland books of fine worth, exquisite arrangements of everything that is nice. Yet it was not that Nature had cast o'er the scene, Her purest of crystal and brightest of green, It was not sweet magic of streamlet or hill, O no, it was something more exquisite still oh ho no, it was something more exqueeseet steel. 'Twas that Friends of the Academy of Letters were near, Who made every dear scene of enchantment more dear, And one felt how the best charms of Nature improve, When we see them reflected in books that we love.

The Myles na gCopaleen Catechism of Cliché. In 356 tri-weekly parts. A unique compendium of all that is nauseating in contemporary writing. Compiled without regard to expense or the feelings of the public. A harrowing survey of sub-literature and all that is pseudo, mal-dicted and calloused in the underworld of print. Given free with the *Irish Times*. Must not be sold separately or exported without a licence. Copyright, Printed on re-pulped sutmonger's aprons. Irish labour, Irish ink. Part one. Section one. Let her out, Mike! Lights! O.K., Sullivan, let her ride!

Is man ever hurt in a motor smash?

No. He sustains an injury.

Does such a man ever die from his injuries?

No. He succumbs to them.

Correct. But supposing an ambulance is sent for. He is put into the ambulance and *rushed* to hospital. Is he dead when he gets there, assuming he is not alive?

No, he is not dead. Life is found to be extinct.

Correct again. A final question. Did he go into the hospital, or enter it, or be brought to it?

He did not. He was admitted to it.

Good. That will do for today.

MORE OF IT

The Myles na gCopaleen Catechism of Cliché, part two. Copyright of course. What's more, all rights reserved. Reproduction in whole or part, etc., etc.

Is treatment, particularly bad treatment, ever given to a person?

No. It is always meted out.

Is anything else ever meted out?

No. The only thing that is ever meted out is treatment.

And what does the meting out of treatment evoke?

The strongest protest against the treatment meted out.

Correct. Mention another particularly revolting locution.

'The matter will fall to be dealt with by so-and-so.'

Good. Are you sufficiently astute to invent a sentence where this absurd jargon will be admissible?

Yes. 'The incendiary bombs will fall to be dealt with by fire fighting squads.'

Very good indeed. Is that enough for wan day?

It is, be the japers.

THEY'LL SAY IT ABOUT YOU

The Myles na gCopaleen Catechism of Cliché. An invaluable compendium of all that is etc., etc. Part three.

Of what was any deceased citizen you like to mention typical?

Of all that is best in Irish life.

Correct. With what qualities did he endear himself to all who knew him?

His charm of manner and unfailing kindness.

Yes. But with what particularly did he impress all those he came in contact with?

His sterling qualities of mind, loftiness of intellect and unswerving devotion to the national cause.

What article of his was always at the disposal of the national language?

His purse.

And what more abstract assistance was readily offered to those who sought it?

The fruit of his wide reading and profound erudition.

At what time did he speak Irish?

At a time when it was neither profitable nor popular.

With what cause did he never disguise the fact that his sympathies lay?

The cause of national independence.

And at what time?

At a time when lesser men were content with the rôle of time-server and sycophant.

What was he in his declining years?

Though frail of health, indefatigable in his exertions on behalf of his less fortunate fellow men.

Whom did he marry in 1879?

A Leitrim Lady.

And at what literary labour was he engaged at the time of his death?

His monumental work on the Oghams of Tipperary.

And of what nature is his loss?

Well-nigh irreparable.

MORE OF IT

The Myles na gCopaleen Catechism of Cliché. Part Four and no wonder. Hold your nose, boys.

What is Mr Blank made after 109 years' of faithful service with the firm?

The recipient of a clock and handsome set of carvers.

By whom?

His friends and colleagues.

And as what?

A small token of their esteem.

What, according to the person making the presentation, does Mr Blank carry with him and where?

The best wishes of the firm and staff; into his well-earned retirement.

In what are these wishes expressed by the person making the presentation?

In the course of a witty and felicitous speech.

How does Mr Blank reply?

Suitably.

What does he declare himself to have received and from whom?

Nothing but kindness from all those he was privileged to come in contact with.

What did the proceedings then do?

Terminate.

ANOTHER LUMP

The Myles na gCopaleen Catechism of Cliché. Part Five Dedicated to the Bar Library in affectionate recognition of the fact that it contains all that is best in Irish life.

What physical qualities have all barristers in common?

Keenness of face and hawkiness of eye.

Their arguments are—

Trenchant.

Their books?

Dusty tomes; but occasionally musty old legal tomes.

In what do they indulge?

Flights of oratory.

If they are women, what is their description?

They are Fair Portias.

In their obituary notices, on which circuit is it invariably said they first went?

The western.

Where they—?

Quickly built up a lucrative practice.

What did they never make?

An enemy.

And never lose?

A friend.

Their wit was—?

Dry. They sometimes indulged in *sallies* of it.

What phenomenon in brackets did such sallies evoke?

(Laughter.)

Quote a suitable obituary extract.

Never too robust, his health of late years had given anxiety to his friends, but physical frailty did not abate one jot his great qualities of courage or deter him from breaking a lance with the bench in the service of his client. He was a fearless advocate.

Good. To what was he an ornament?

The profession he adorned.

What prize did he win in the late eighties?

The President's Gold Medal for Oratory.

In what had he shone?

In many famous cases before the Master of the Rolls.

And in what manner did he address the Judge?

As M'Lud.

CATECHISM OF CLICHÉ

Of what nature is the newspaper in which one craves the courtesy of its space?

Invaluable and widely read.

For what purpose does one crave the courtesy of its space?

Saying a few words *anent* the gas supply.

In criticising the Gas Company, what does one wish to make it clear one holds for the Electricity Supply Board?

No brief.

Of what nature is the attitude of the Gas Company to say the least of it?

High-handed and dictatorial in the extreme.
In what hands should such service not be and why?
Private; because it is a public utility service.
What would the situation be were it not so tragic?
Humorous.
Why is it necessary for the Government to take immediate steps to safeguard children from the injuries to health that may be caused by gas rationing?
Because the children are the men and women of tomorrow.
And what does one hope one's letter will catch?
The eye of the powers that be.

FOR YOUR CLICHÉ ALBUM

In what can no man tell the future has for us?
Store.
With what do certain belligerents make their military dispositions?
Typical Teutonic thoroughness.
In what manner do wishful thinkers imagine that the war will be over this year?
Fondly.
Take the word, 'relegate'. To what must a person be relegated?
That obscurity from which he should never have been permitted to emerge.
What may one do with a guess, provided one is permitted?
Hazard.
And what is comment?
Superfluous.

CÚINNE NA gCLICHÉ

Cad fé isé ár nguidhe go mbeidh Nodlaig agat?
Shéan.
Agus aithbhliain?
Fé mhaise.
Cé nach mbíonn gan locht?
Saoi.
Agus cad nach go cur le chéi'e?
Neart.

IN MY recent pronouncements on clichés I must apologise for having overlooked until this late day that awful swine, the Clerk of the Weather. All stand and uncover, please. 'Thanks to the benevolence of the Clerk of the Weather, large crowds availed themselves of the opportunity to spend the day by the seaside. From an early hour there was an exodus by 'bus, tram and rail . . .' Yes. And please do not forget his butty, King Sol, the monarch who is always 'genial' and 'beams on the occasion'. What's the matter? Why are you biting your nails? Can you not take it?

Faith, avic, I could hurt you more than that. Take drinking. It is lawful for a group of citizens to enter a tavern and order drinks. But according as they swallow their golden thimblefuls, they deem it desirable for some reason to invent pretexts for having one more. These reasons are always somewhat tenuous and to set them out in the frigid medium known as 'cold print' brings us once again back into the underworld of cliché. Let us treat the matter catechistically.

What is it that a final drink will not do us?

Harm.

What is the condition which, by reason of the long time we will be subject to it, supports the theory that it would be safe to have one more?

The condition of being dead.

For what service maintained by the rating authority is it permissible to have still another final drink?

The road.

And upon what did a bird never fly?

Wan wing.

THERE IS AN INTERVAL HERE

An interval is right. What we all want is a good long walk in the country, plenty of fresh air and good wholesome food. This murder of my beloved English language is getting in under my nails. There are, of course, other branches of charnel-house fun into which I have not yet had the courage to lead my readers. Not quite clichés but things that smell the same and worse. Far worse. Things like this, I mean:

Of course, gin is a very depressing drink.

The air in Bundoran is very bracing.

You'll see the whole lot of us travelling by air before you're much older.

Your man is an extraordinary genius.

Of course, the most depressing drink of the lot is gin.

Did you get what I'm driving at? Can you visualise the list of dirty pale goading phrases with which I may—yes—'regale' you next week? What?

I beg your pardon?

Well that isn't my fault. I merely record what goes on around me. I just write down what goes on.

SOCIAL INTELLIGENCE

(All musical Dublin) (is agog) (with expectation) of the new symphony by Milesius Chapaline which will form the main item in next Thursday's concert at the Antient Concert Rooms. The new work, the 1st (today) in Ut Majeur (owner H.H. The Aga Khan) is in three movements, red, green and ambergris and will be performed by the Dublin Waamaphony Orchestra, leader Charles Stewart Parnell, conductor 3429, car No. 4, outward bound for Booterstown and points south.

If you don't think that's funny, write and tell me why.

* * *

CATECHISM OF CLICHÉ

WHAT, as to the quality of solidity, imperviousness, and firmness, are facts?

Hard.

And as to temperature?

Cold.

With what do facts share this quality of frigidity?

Print.

To what do hard facts belong?

The situation.

And to what does a cold fact belong?

The matter.

What must we do to the hard facts of the situation?

Face up to the hard facts of the situation.

What does a cold fact frequently still do?

Remain.

And what is notoriously useless as a means of altering the hard facts of the situation?

All the talk in the world.

Is this killing you?
It certainly is.

CLUICHE NA gCLICHÉ

Do what I do. Carry a small grey American automatic and make sure that it is always stuffed with bullets. Then when some bleating fish-gilled bags opens up and says—

'Of course, backing horses is a mug's game.'

—just empty the gun into his low-grade jungle forehead and explain what you have done to the police. The whole thing will be hushed up and you will never hear another word about it. To try you for murder after such provocation would be to make lobster salad out of the courts of justice. If you did not kill him, he would probably go on and tell you that gin is a very depressing drink, or that September is the best month of the lot for holidays, And then it would simply have to be your life or his.

While you are here, please answer me this. In relation to any problem, what commodity of apparently fluid nature is it necessary to hammer out?
A solution.
What obscure and unhelpful act is often done with a problem?
That of only tinkering.
And to what degree is a problem sometimes insoluble?
Well-nigh.

* * *

CATECHISM OF CLICHÉ

What is a bad thing worse than?
Useless.
What can one do with fierce resistance, especially in Russia?
Offer it.
But if one puts fierce resistance, in what direction does one put it?
Up.
In which hood is a person who expects money to fall out of the sky?
Second child.
If a thing is fraught, with what is it fraught?
The gravest consequences.
What does one sometimes have it on?
The most unimpeachable authority.

What is the only thing one can wax?
Eloquent.
By what criterion is the value of a game assessed.
The candle.
What action is usually taken by people with respect to delusions and what is their relative physical situation to these states?
They labour under them.
On what article manufactured in Switzerland are hypochondriacs, paranoiacs and the like continually to be found?
The watch.
In what is it better to give over before we all go mad?
The circumstances.

Do you know any notorious yachtsmen? ('Make fast the main-sheet there, you . . . , what the . . . do you . . . think you're here for?') Well, picture him, get him into your mind, pale blue eyes and all. Now answer me this:
What remark may justly be made about him, assuming he bites off the ear of an inoffensive landlubber in a tavern brawl and then sets off across Dublin bay in his old leaky smack, which forthwith capsizes?
That his bark is worse than his bite.
And what does a good game of solo put in?
The night.
Like whom did our friend go out under article ten?
Like a good many more who were too . . . patriotic to work for a native government.
What is that?
About the size of it.
What considerations of indeterminate value are some people most parsimonius with, steadfastly refusing to give them?
Continental damns.
With what may the continental damn be equated?
A haymaker's spit.
What are some people if they will do what you ask?
Jiggered.
In what curious shape is it usual to find a drunk man?
Crooked.
What is a particularly presumptuous performance?
The limit altogether.

What nourishing confection for which the city of Dublin is famous the world over does it take?

The biscuit.

With what laudable epidermis is it customary to identify our friend?

A decent skin.

An imaginary decent skin?

No, a real decent skin.

What is he as good an Irishman?

As ever wore a hat.

What downward cooking operation does it engage in when coming to the same thing?

It boils down.

When?

In the end.

* * *

[THIS is the first time a newspaper article was started in brackets. Innovation, you see. The homeric tasks of creation. Bringing into being a thing hitherto not here, much more exhausting than building pyramids in Egypt. Please remind me to close the bracket at the end of the article. We must be neat, have some system. Otherwise we will merit the doubtful epithet 'slovenly' and the finger of scorn will be pointed at us. Only last night it occurred to me that a good name for a skin specialist's motor vehicle would be 'acne-car'. And to-day that impeccable little lumpeen of wit is on your breakfast table. Speed, efficiency, see? At lunch time you can pass it off as your own. Now please stop biting your nails and listen to me.

What inexpensive unrationed commodity is often said to exceed the man possessing it in value?

His salt.

What action is never taken with regard to alcohol?

Touching it.

What ruined many a man?

The same horses.

Where was our friend in 1916?

Under the b— bed like a lot more.

What would our friend do to you or me?

Take us out and lose us.

When was our friend born?

Not to-day nor yesterday.

When did he not come down?

In the last shower.

What are on our friend?

No flies.

In what capacity would he be trusted at a crossroads?

Mindin' mice.

Quod tempus omnibus est vitae?

Breve et irreparabile.

Quo in gurgite saepe volvuntur Aeneas et Co.?

Vasto.

Quo saepe Aeneas vox haeret?

Faucibus.

Quid faciunt omnes?

Stant.

Quo est facilis descensus?

Averno.

Quod autemest opus, quae labor?

Revocare gradum, superasque evadere ad auras.

De quibus non curat lex?

Minimis.

Quideat emptor?

Cave.

Quae regio in terris nostri non plena laboris?

Westminster.

What is one's reaction to all this?

Mens immota manet; lacrimae volvuntur inanes.

That apocryphal juridical personality, the reasonable and prudent man, will probably agree with me that that is enough and plenty for wan good day. Goodbye to yez all now.

The Plain People of Ireland : Whot abouit thon brocket, d'ye ontherstawnd?

Myself : Sorry].

* * *

WHAT IS the only thing you have which you can plight?

Your troth.

What (I ask in astonishment) do you do at the same time as you tell me so?

Mean to stand there.

What sort of cheek had your man to stand there and tell me so?

Brazen.

What are climes?

Sundrenched.

What is a bike now in?

Valuable.

By whom is your man out?

Himself.

And on what obscure thing belonging to himself is he out?

His own.

What article, which one would not expect to find in him, would a catastrophic occurrence not take out of him?

A feather.

How are heights?

Great. (How's yourself)?

How are great heights reached?

Pardon me. ATTAINED, old man. By soaring, of course.

Whom may we expect (with proper coaching) to soar to great heights?

Certain promising youngsters.

Where?

In the world of sport.

Into what must all the facts be taken?

Consideration.

What is it usual to swing?

The lead.

What would you recommend for a person who is too incredibly lazy to swing the lead for himself?

The machine overleaf, which will do it for him.

What party usually works with all?

Sundry.

What relatives (often given in its stead) does a puck in the wind have?

The father and mother.

What member, deed and physical region did one not have in it?

Hand, act or part.

What things point to a prolonged war?

All the indications.

What two substances are generally held to be dissimilar?

Chalk and cheese.

What is a sweet and fair land, a rich and rare land?
This native land of ours.
Unde illae lacrimae?
Hinc.
Quae mens in corpore sano sit?
Sana.
Per arquod ad astra?
Dua.
Usque ad quideam?
Naus.
Quid inducit nauseam?
Usque baugh.

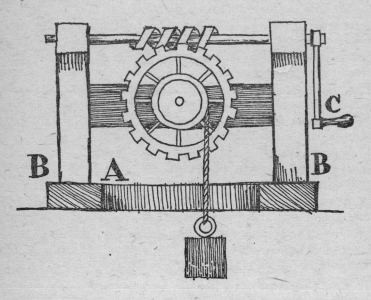

* * *

CLIS É. A CHARA!

Of what colour is that horse?
Another.
To what should you put your shoulder?
The wheel.
What will your man some day come into?
His own.

Quando timeo Danaos?
Et dona ferentes.
Dum spiro?
Spero.
Si vis pacem?
Para bellum.
Quid est dulce et decorum?
Pro patria mori.
Quo est dulce disipere?
In loco parentis.

*   *   *

MEASURE FOR MEASURE

In what is abundant space (in the sense of 'room') measured?
Bags.
And abundant time (as when catching a train)?
Bags.
Name two units of measurement of money when it is plentiful.
(a) Bags. (b) Tons.
But how is money measured when there are enormous quantities of it in question?
In relation to the surplus available for incineration.
In what are cigarettes and small articles measured when one has them in unlimited quantities?
Pucks.
What is the unit of measurement applied generally to commodities or articles which are available in gigantic quantities?
The oodle.
When stout is available in large quantities at a party, what are the usual links of measurement?
Lashins.
But where the quantity available is unprecedentedly large, what additional units of measurement must be resorted to in order adequately to describe the quantity?
Layvins.

*   *   *

Q. & A.

For what occasions does one have a boring and displeasing topic of conversation?

For breakfast dinner and tea.
From what aryan prototype do I not know you, sir?
Adam.
What is the nature of the objection which you have?
It is rooted.
On what is it usual to have one's hours of waiting?
End.
In what opulent manner does one deserve a thrashing?
Richly.
With whom is one prepared to take one's chance?
The next man.
Whom is one every bit as good as?
The next man.
To what does one think one will rise as well as the next man?
The occasion.
Like what fire does the news spread?
Wild.
How are quarters usually informed?
Well.
Quid Sap?
Verb.

* * *

OF WHAT HUE is a stranger?
Black.
What can I not stay out of any longer?
My money.
How does a person of frugal habits eat?
Sparingly.
Amicus Plato, amicus Socrates, sed quid est mihi veritas?
Magis amicus.
Bene qui latuit quomodo vixit?
Bene (Goodman).
Quis palmam ferat?
Qui meruit.
Ubi nemo me lacessit (inquit Ghandi)?
In Poona.
Noli me quidere?
Tang.

Quid dicerent Censorship Board?

Mega biblion, mega kakon maxima debetur puero reverentia.

Et quid dicerent Irish Academy of Letters?

Vita sine litteris mors est.*

Qualis virginibus pue—?

Risqué.

Quid est beneficium accipere?

Libertatem vendere.

Quid dicerent Dublin Transport Company?

Falsus in uno, falsus in omnibus.

Quid est femina?

Varium et mutabile semper. (And simper).

Quis custodiet ipsos custodes?

Mulieres eorum.

Quid tetigit quod non ornavit?

Nihil.

Quis?

Ego.

See, man, you meant him.

Circumspice.

Which omnibus line is best augured?

Fortuna favet 40 Bus.

Quem deus perdere vult, prius quid facit?

Prius dementat.

Quae pereunt et imputantur?

Hip, hip— Horae!

Quid non habet legem?

Necessitas.

Quid dixit Virgilius?

'Exegi monumentum aere per Aeneas.'†

Quid et sapere ipsi Jovi non datur?

Simul amare.

Quando bonus dormitat Homerus?

Ali—

---

* Meaning, no doubt, that life without the guidance of books is a riddle, a closed book, a mors code.

† Which shows that his grammar wasn't (everything that it might be) (everything you would expect) (everything it's cracked up to be).

Subpopulus Hiberniae: Hoc dixit Horatius Flaccus!

Ego: Favete linguis, canes!

LAST WEEK I had a long (almost, indeed, a protracted) conversation with an important foreign personality who was passing through Ireland on his way elsewhere. The conversation performed that curious act known as ranging over a wide field. Perfect agreement was reached on many points and it was felt that the relationship between the two countries had (much to gain) (from this frank exchange of views). It had been intended also to exchange notes but owing (to pressure of time) it was only found possible to exchange views. Afterwards a short visit was paid to the Zoological Gardens.

Who this person was and what we talked about, of course, I am (not in a position to disclose). A (prominent spokesman) would probably call what we were doing (intense diplomatic activity). It is necessary to emphasise, however, that the whole thing was entirely unofficial. It is unlikely that any announcement will be made.

Farther than this I regret I cannot go. I know better than to shoot (off) my mouth when tipped (off) to keep it shut. Remember that lovely thing by Goethe?

'Kommst du in des Königs Haus
Geh blind hinein und stumm heraus.'

Not that it was that particular party, of course.

LOCK, STOCK AND BARREL

From what small two-letter word may the whole thing be said to have been a wash-out?

The word go.

From what sort of time does a custom date?

Time immemorial.

To what serious things does an epidemic sometimes attain?

Proportions.

De gustibus quid est non faciendum?

This pew, Tandem (if you don't mind old boy).

Wo jetzt ist meine Geduld?

Zu Ende.

What may you talk yourself in the face before I give in to you?

Black.

What completely non-existent thing is frequently stated to be still there?

The nothing more that often remains to be said.

Till what great dairy-farm re-union may you sit and talk there?
Till the cows come home.
With what two cognate effects do I invite you to clear out of my house?
Bag and baggage.
Quis quoque?
Tu.
Quis est faber fortunae suae?
—que.

* * *

THERE IS NO END TO THIS

What does it behove us to proclaim?
Our faith.
In what does it behove us to proclaim our faith?
Democracy.
From what vertiginous eyrie does it behove us to proclaim our faith in democracy?
From the house-tops.
At what time should we proclaim our faith in democracy from the house-tops?
Now, more than ever.
What action must be taken in relation to our energies?
They must be directed.
In what unique manner?
Wholeheartedly.
In what direction?
Towards the solution of the pressing post-war problems which the armistice will bring.
How will the armistice bring these problems?
In its train.
By what is the train hauled?
A 2–4–2 compound job with poppet valves and Pacific-style steam chest.

* * *

YES, MORE OF IT

What happens to blows at a council meeting?

It looks as if they might be exchanged.

What does pandemonium do?

It breaks loose.

Describe its subsequent dominion.

It reigns.

How are allegations dealt with?

They are denied.

Yes, but then you are weakening, Sir. Come now, how are they denied?

Hotly.

What is the mean temperature of an altercation, therefore?

Heated.

What is the behaviour of a heated altercation?

It follows.

What happens to order?

It is restored.

Alternatively, in what does the meeting break up?

Disorder.

What does the meeting do in disorder?

Breaks up.

In what direction does the meeting break in disorder?

Up.

In what direction should I shut?

Up.

* * *

WHAT WOULD do him but to march me into the nearest public house and stand me a glass of malt?

Nothing.

Under what did I think I might as well have it?

The circumstances.

Nevertheless, assuming there were relations between us, in what state inevitably must such relations have been?

Strained.

And owing to what being beyond my control did I accept the drink?

Circumstances.

Under what archaic conditions of military (and indeed piecemeal) sale did this same party sell out my mother's property years before?

Lock stock and barrel.

But in all what plural and surrounding abstractions did I pretend to have forgotten that episode?

The circumstances.

What bound literary work did my pretended forgetfulness suit?

My book.

What pathetic articles belonging to my mother's furniture did he formerly put out on the side-walk?

The sticks.

And under what tragic things did this eviction take place?

Circumstances.

What did this eviction take under tragic circumstances?

It took place.

Whose fool was I when I decided to accept hospitality from this person?

Nobody's.

What transparent recreation could I see through?

His game.

From what person to what other person did he think he could send me?

From Billy to Jack.

With what three commonplace gentlemen did this attempt of his suggest he was confusing me?

Tom, Dick and Harry.

Where did he think he could send the fool?

Farther.

But what act did I perform in relation to him with long lengths of narrow fabric?

I had him taped.

What thing belonging to him did I have?

His measure.

Where precisely did I have him?

Precisely where I wanted him.

What abundant essential, firm and durable thing did I take from under his feet?

The ground.

What useful articles of furniture did I invert?

The tables.

What abstract thing did I inform him he was beneath?

Contempt.

In what peregrination of at least twelve hours' duration would you not meet a more despicable specimen?

A day's walk.

What visceral mess did I inform him he was not fit to bring to what Arctic mammal?

Guts to a bear.

What furthermore did I inform him he was not worth?

Hitting.

What temporal interval did I inform him he was not worth hitting?

My while.

What sort of respect for me did this veiled threat of violence induce in him?

A healthy.

When departing, what obscure thing belonging to him was fallen?

His crest.

* * *

MORE DEAD WORDS

Here's a quare one. What will we not feel now till Christmas?

It.

What is the nature of a certain sort of shame?

It cries.

What rich nourishing liquid is associated with a joke?

Cream.

What thing of eschatological aspect will you acquire if you don't come offa that wet grass?

Your end.

What metal container is associated with the acting of certain people?

The cannister.

What is your misfortune the price of?

You.

What monetary evaluation of you is your misfortune?

The price.

In what dexterous and thorough manner does it serve you?

Right.

* * *

DEAD ENGLISH

Life can be bitter. Did you ever notice how easily the amateur can eclipse the industrious professional like myself in the (sphere) (of cliché)?

I take this wonderful thing from the current issue of the Journal of the Irish Medical Association.

'The returns show that the outbreak was by no means confined to the Dublin area as rumour had suggested and prove, if proof were needed, that Dame Rumour continues to justify her reputation as a lying jade.'

Now let me follow up with a few poor efforts of my own. When things are few, what also are they?

Far between.

What are stocks of fuel doing when they are low?

Running.

How low are they running?

Dangerously.

What does one do with a suggestion?

One throws it out.

For what does one throw a suggestion out?

For what it may be worth.

What else can be thrown out?

A hint.

In addition to hurling a hint on such lateral trajectory, what other not unviolent action can be taken with it?

It can be dropped.

What else is sometimes dropped?

The subject.

Quid humani a te alienum putes?

Nihil. (Et quid obstat? Nihil.)

*   *   *

TURNING ASIDE (stick your hand out there Joe) from this cliché stuff of which you are not half so heartily sick as I—it occurs to me that I should record (for the benefit) (of posterity) those appalling attempts at adult chat which (invariably) follows certain set introductory formulae. I mean, a phrase such as 'In my humble opinion . . .' Clearly, no decent person could (bring himself) to start talking with such a despicable preamble. But consider the sort of thing that always follows these further phrases I have listed below. If you do so conscientiously I will have you excused from jury service for the next seven years.

'Unaccustomed as I am to public speaking . . .'

'I rise . . .'

'We are all g. t. h. to-n. . . .'

'You all know why we are all g. t. h. to-n. . . .'

'It needs no words of mine to introduce the next speaker . . .'

'Needless to say . . .'

'I may be old-fashioned, but . . .'

'Your headmaster has asked me to speak to you this evening . . .'

'I don't know much about art, but . . .'

'The donor of this banquet is a very shy man; he has asked me to come among you to-night and let you know how much he . . .'

'I have to speak to you boys this morning about a very painful matter . . .'

'I yield to none in my admiration for . . .'

'I crave the courtesy of your columns . . .'

'At the risk of boring my listeners . . .'

'In this connexion I recall an anecdote . . .'

'After all . . .'

'Double You Bee Yeats once said to me . . .'

'I remember your poor father saying . . .'

'I must say it always has been a mystery to me . . .'

And lashed but not lost, that great trumpet of epileptic perfidy:

'WHEREAS . . .'

I regret all this. Bitterly.

IN view of the vogue of this drug (which takes care of everything from pneumonia to what your uncle Joe had), why not revise the primary medical degrees to read M. & B., B.Ch., B.A.O.

You don't think that's funny? Well let's hear one of your own. Tell a funny story. Kill us, strangle the life out of us with lethal gurgles. Sad affair at Sidney Parade. Strange man collapses after hearing joke from *Irish Times* reader. An unknown man, respectably dressed and of middle age, collapsed and died yesterday after listening to a humorous anecdote related by a reader of a Dublin newspaper. With the deceased man passes the last link with Parnell. A man who spoke the Irish language at a time when it was neither profitable nor popular, he had a large circle of friends. (And tell me, pray, why do friends always adopt this irrectangular information?) A popular figure in Irish dancing circles, he was a firm believer in the immutable principles laid down by the Manchester school.

THIS LICENSING BILL

I read a newspaper article on this subject recently. To what congregation of beasts and humans did it bring me? The fair. It was stated that the bill would give rise ('give rise', mind you) to what? (Controversy.) Private controversy, that eminent member of the defence forces? No, public. What about the inevitable fate of the sponsor's purpose? Efforts would be made to thwart it. Efforts? I beg your pardon—'determined efforts'. By what engrossing imponderables would these efforts be made? By interests. Come, now, what sort of interests? Powerful, of course.

Later on in the article we see young men and women (in hostelries) drinking their heads off without what two inseparable abstractions? (Let or hindrance.) We are shown (the whole business) as a (nefarious traffic).

Did you ever hear of 'farious traffic'? Faith then I did, plenty of it goes on of an Easter Monday night after Fairyhouse, I once seen an Oxford B.Litt. on the broad of his back in Little Liffey street, trying (for all he was worth) to claw the bedclothes over his much-plastered chest with the Tote double and a small Scotch the cabman gave him inside in his stomach.

Later on in this (self-same) article we get a picture of whole parties which were (turned out) of a city publichouse at ten o'clock at night ('at night', mark you) going to some 'way-side lounge bar' to ens—

Come now, to what themselves?

To ensc—?

Do make an effort, darling. PLEASE.

To ENSCONCE themselves, of course.

This much I will say myself and in that total state of gravity known as 'all seriousness'. When the minor recourses of civilisation become a matter of minute legalistic regulation, when one has to drive the traditional coach-and-four not through an act of parliament, but five miles along the border of it to get a bottle of stout (and a small sherry for her nibs), the civilisation that can produce such an absurdity would merit the word decadent were it not for the fact that it never reached any eminence from which it could be said to recede.

* * *

WHEN AND AGAIN have I asked you not to do that?

Time.

Time out of what enumeration have I asked you not to do it?

Number.

What is our civilisation much?

Vaunted.

What is the public?
Gullible.
What are interests?
Vested.
Haud non loquor?
Expertus.
Quis post equitem sedet?
Atra cura.
To what medieval engine does your property go on the way to ruin?
Rack.

★　★　★

BEARLA MARBH

To what solitary personality are all the family Gaelic-speakers?
To a man.
Like what diverse superior personalities was I when I gave my services to Ireland (when the call came) (without thought of fee) (or reward)?
Like many a better man.
With what cardiac phenomenon, increased by fifty per cent, will I lend you ten pounds?
A heart and a $\frac{1}{2}$.
To what obscure cardiac shellfish is heat imparted by the sight of the national flag flying over the Old House in College Green?
It warrums the cockles of me heart.
What negative ossification does a dacent man make about doing a pal a good turn?
No bones.
What bisected cerebral phenomenon have I to shut up? Come on, that's an easy one.
You don't know?
$\frac{1}{2}$ a mind.
In what non-downward condition of being tapped am I sometimes to be found?
I am knocked up.
What mysterious cipher am I not up to on such occasions?
The mark (God save it).

★　★　★

A CLICHÉ is a phrase that has become fossilised, its component words deprived of their intrinsic light and meaning by incessant usage. Thus it appears that clichés reflect somewhat the frequency of the incidence of the same situations in life. If this be so, a sociological commentary could be compiled from these items of mortified language.

Is not the gun-history of modern Ireland to be verified by the inflexible terminology attaching to it? A man may be shot dead but if he survives a shot, he is not shot but sustains gun-shot wounds. The man who fires the shot is always his assailant, never his attacker or merely the gun-man. The injured party is never taken to hospital but is removed there (in a critical condition). The gun-man does not escape, even if he is not caught; he makes good his escape.

Oddly enough—unnecessary phrase—a plurality of lawbreakers behave differently; they are never assailants but armed men. When they are not caught, they do not make good their escape; they decamp. If there be defenders on the scene, shots are *exchanged*. And the whole affair is, of course, a shooting affray. You see, there is no other kind of affray. If it is not a shooting affray, it is not an affray at all. But it might be a fracas.

Criticism, Art, Letters

YOU KNOW the limited edition ramp. If you write very obscure verse (and why shouldn't you, pray?) for which there is little or no market, you pretend that there is an enormous demand, and that the stuff has to be rationed. Only 300 copies will be printed, you say, and then the type will be broken up for ever. Let the connoisseurs and bibliophiles savage each other for the honour and glory of snatching a copy. Positively no reprint. Reproduction in whole or in part forbidden. Three hundred copies of which this is Number 4,312. Hand-monkeyed oklamon paper, indigo boards in interpulped squirrel-toe, not to mention twelve point Campile Perpetua cast specially for the occasion. Complete, unabridged, and positively unexpurgated. Thirty-five bob a knock and a gory livid bleeding bargain at the price.

Well, I have decided to carry this thing a bit farther. I beg to announce respectfully my coming volume of verse entitled 'Scorn for Taurus'. We have decided to do it in eight point Caslon on turkey-shutter paper with covers in purple corduroy. But look out for the catch. When the type has been set up, it will be instantly destroyed and NO COPY WHATEVER WILL BE PRINTED. *In no circumstances will the company's servants be permitted to carry away even a rough printer's proof.* The edition will be so utterly limited that a thousand pounds will not buy even one copy. This is my idea of being exclusive.

The charge will be five shillings. Please do not make an exhibition of yourself by asking me what you get for your money. You get nothing you can see or feel, not even a receipt. But you do yourself the honour of participating in one of the most far-reaching experiments ever carried out in my literary work-shop.

MY REGRETS

Owing to circumstances outside my control, the same picture appeared in this column a short time ago two days running. Of course, the pictures should have been different. I understand, however, that this mistake provoked domestic rows all over Ireland. Thus:

Where's the paper, Maggie?

There.

Where?

There.

That's yesterday's.

It's not. That's to-day's.

I tell you it's yesterday's, woman.

IT'S TO-DAY'S. Can't you look at the date.

I don't have to look at the date, I know very well it's yesterday's. I'm not a fool. I distinctly remember that picture in yesterday's paper, every single day that passes I have to turn the house upside-down to get my own newspaper. I spend half my life going round my own house like a lost fool, I ask a civil question about my own newspaper that I purchased for tuppence and I am practically called a liar to my face . . .

SOCIAL AND PERSONAL

I overheard a curious snatch of conversation at one of the weekly socials that are run at the Club Cruiskeen. A pretty golden little baggage was talking to her lover.

'D'you know, Godfrey, only last night I learnt many interesting things about my family. D'you know that my great-grandfather was killed at Waterloo?'

'Rayully, sweetness, which platform?'

The golden head was tossed in disdain.

'How ridiculous you are, Godfrey. As if it mattered which platform.'

Naturally, I cannot guarantee that this couple said these words or even opened their beaks at all. The room was full of my Escorts.*

* * *

THE FIRST TIME I woke up to Disney's 'Fantasia' was when I noticed a film writer in the *Irish Press* saying that Disney fans were now known as 'Fantasians'. When I read this I flew into a temper. Immediately I demanded to know from all the hacks who write this stuff for me why we had not thought of this first. Memo from the Boss. Please furnish written explanation. What is the reason? WHAT IS THE REASON? (Your man is in a fierce temper, walking up the walls above in his office, chawin the face of everybody that puts his head in.) A disused National Teacher that works

* See WAAMA

for me—as a matter of fact he wrote that Escort Service stuff we had some months ago, the stuff that had to be taken off because it smelt—well, this man had the cheek to say that he had thought of it all right but decided not to use it because it was not up to 'our standard'. I didn't quite know what to say to this because maybe he wasn't far wrong.

Anyhow, this 'Fantasia'. Listen to what a writer in this very newspaper said recently:

' "Fantasia", in my humble opinion the highest form of cinemato-graphic art imaginable—make no mistake about that—is no feast for children.'

Make no mistake about what? This adult's humility?

'Fantasia' is (in my snivelling, fawning, obsequious, cringing opinion) quite the last crippling feat of virtuosity in the art of sub-vulgarity. It will induce in decent people a feeling of shame and humiliation.

Take it this way. Charlie Chaplin was once a great clown. In the 'twenties I was laughing myself (sic) at his jerky funniness. He was good. He was a terrible hard case—but the lower-cases ('film art: an international review of advance guard cinema') found him out. One day some toad—some velveteened work-shy 'marxist' toad—sternly reproved people for laughing at Mister Cheplin. Do you not see, old boy, thet in Cheplin we hev an expression on the highest artistic plain of all our pathetic human striving. I mean the pursuit of heppiness and all thet, our poor frustrated human nature. The little tremp, I mean, is you and I. Cheplin is a great artist, I mean. You mustn't loff, you now. Such pure, such exquisite sensibility!

And poor Chaplin, a simple soul if ever there was one, gets to hear this chat and makes 'The Great Dictator'. The end of 'The Great Dictator' is also the end of what is possible in the sphere of human degradation. I remember blushing.

Now take a gander (or a donalduck) at Disney. This man (milord) would mind mickeymice. He was the best man in the world for clever honest fun, for sneering at bores, buffs and bowsies, the best man for drawing, invention, imagination and vituperation. He was one of the smartest boys that ever came out of Beverley Hills. (There's Goldwyn, by the way, in them thar hills.) And then Mr Stokes, who for years has been selling 'Music' to miniature American snobs (on a bach market) hears about Mr D., whose sensibility and purity of sentiment have by now been freely commented upon by the high-browed hybrids. So with the assistance of the philadelphian eu-phonies and the Canadian North

West Montage, Mr Michael Mouse becomes part of the material of art. He becomes, as *The Bell* would say, something taut, alert, an intimate thing in aesthetic experience. And his father, poor Mr Disney, begins to neglect his dress, try to look a bit wild-eyed and go for long walks in the rain. Next thing you know will be an agitation for little shaded lights so that every cod that walks can arrive to 'Fantasia' with a miniature score (to be held carefully up-side-down). I mean, a synthesis, old man, of artistic apprehension in terms of line, colour and sound. Quite definitely the highest form of cinematographic art imaginable. A multi-plane spiritual anabasis in the filmic métier, UNITING FOR THE FIRST TIME ON ANY SCREEN all that is best in Beethoven, George Raft, Diaghilev and Tom Mix. With an orchestra of 800 blonde cuties and thousands of trombone players.

The Editor : Have you seen this picture?

Myself : No.

The Editor : Why?

Myself : Because the free list is suspended.

The Editor : But why condemn something you have not seen?

Myself : Why suspend the free list?

The Editor : Then is all this an exhibition of spite because you are not admitted free?

Myself : Not necessarily. It is something taut, elegant, alert.

* * *

FLASH! When the roof leaks and the piano needs tuning, when the geyser explodes and the brother (home on leave) slips quietly into the jigs, what do I do? I send for the expert, the trained man, and leave the solution of my problem to him. And when the day of reckoning comes I fix up according to the standard rates hallowed by a couple of centuries of collective bargaining. When I want to read anything, however, I usually write it meself.

But recently on the newsstands I have noticed PUCK FARE printed regardless on white paper fully glazed and fashioned and dedicated to the nice whimsy that the writer—*the writer*, do you know—is a professional man, a *craft*sman, a highly trained party who should never be paid less than five bar for a good job. (I could do it for four and a kick, Mr O'Faoláin, *but it wouldn't be a job.*)

Since this magazine is offered as evidence of the spontaneous adoption by a whole nondescript gang of professional status and since the contributions of these ex-waamateurs may be considered as perfect *technica* jobs at least ('Art, finally, is not measurable by (sic) a footrule') the layman may be permitted to check admiringly over the shining machinery. Grammar and spelling, I mean—we know it's all right but we'd like to look. The emptor is entitled to demand that his hired literary man be literate at least.

Page 19 is devoted to the ballet but the author found it necessary to refer twice to a foreign gentleman by the name of Jooss, economically cropping an 's' from his name each time and thus saving paper. Ten pages later the head pen-waama presents a piece beginning 'Seano Carissimo' and lashes on at a pressure of five hundred pounds per square inch to 'What did I hear but a piano, behind one of those lighted yellow blinds, flinging out the grand ripe, thunderstorm drops of the Concerto in G Major!' Anybody that can play a concerto on a piano deserves more than five bar *anny* day of the week. Two more foreign gentlemen appear and the writer imagines that they are called Breughel and Bocaccio. The curious phrase, too, 'cario mio' which appears towards the end of this work does certainly suggest *some* romance language. (And what's more, 'cyclops' is singular.)*

On page 35 we catch a glimpse of 'Robert Emmett', but there is no mention of 'John Mitchell' or 'Arthur Griffiths'. Two pages later we are introduced to the Gaelic novelty. 'Ni thagaim geilleadh do'n chúirt seo Guvóradeeaurinn!

Page 41 brings us to an exquisite *divertissement* (or what they would certainly call a divertisement)—an interview with The Bellman. The literary tone is higher even here, even if 'Dinneen' gets a total of only two 'n's' and atrocities like Faoileánn, Faoileánnda and Faoileánndacht are gratuitously attributed to the great lexicographer. Here also appears for the only time in literature the word tournédos.† (We have them all right but not with that accent old boy.) On page 42 we view from below our arched eyebrows the sentence 'Night after night I'd fill up my pal with these horrific stories of Jean-Jacque's' (absolutely sic).

All this reads like petty quibbling; I'll agree with you there, it certainly does. But the point is this: if these uppish highly trained writing savants who are sure they are worth more than five bob insist on dragging in foreign words by the scruff of the fair hair, why not do it accurately and

---

* But all this may be deliberate remember.

† I just can't help this sort of thing—considerable sums were spent on my education. Clongowes, Oxford, Sorbonne, Leipzig, Harvard and so on. Fáinne at the age of four.

thus show that the use of these words is perfectly natural and the result of long sojourns abroad?

Get back to the bucket. On page 55 a work of Mr Joyce is referred to as 'Finnegan's Wake'. That poor writer's end was hastened by that same intrusive apostrophe. On page 63 there is an allusion to Homer's 'Illiad'; on this page too the word *Primevera* follows the article *Le*, the word Pièta appears where apparently Pietà is intended, triptych is rendered tryptich and Miss Jellett's name lack a 't', a thing that doesn't suit her to a

Any professional hack would be sacked overnight if he were guilty of the things I have mentioned. The parties responsible may be worth one and six in the writing world but certainly not five bob.

* * *

A WORD ABOUT MUSIC

The 'guest conductor' act is a good one. Bring over to this country some silvery-haired gentleman that is supposed to understand about bands and the theatre will be stuffed while you wait. Did you ever notice that he never needs a score? Did you ever notice that if the cor anglais is .0000013 of a tone out in the second movement of the Franck D Minor he has to have injections to bring him round? O yes, took the orchestra through the whole thing without a note of music in front of him. As if 'a note of music' would have helped.

It's a fake act, of course. Look at it this way. Take a list of the boys starting anywhere. The actual symphony concert range is a strictly ding-dong limited list for a kick-off: Beethoven, Brahms, Bach, Berlioz, Schubert, Haydn, Mozart, Mahler, Handel (let us say)—then a couple of fellows with slav-minds, Rimsky-K., Tschaik., Prokoviev, Straw., Dvorak and this new bags, Shostakovich. Then a few 'modern' buffs and how often do you hear them—Schönberg, Bloch, Bartok, Honegger, Satie, Hindemith, an dochtúir O Dubhthaigh, and folky persons like Gus Holst. Throw in a dozen operas (and the man that does Wagner won't be asked to do Verdi) and there you are. Of each of these composers only a limited number of pieces is listed. Say the whole works is twenty symphonies, ten concertos and a few miscellaneous suites and overtures. Sure anybody with a sound national school education could master that much in no time and if you compare it with the versatility that's expected from myself, an actor, a chef or a civil servant, what have you got?

* * *

LITERARY CRITICISM

My grasp of what he wrote and meant
Was only five or six %.
The rest was only words and sound—
My reference is to Ezra £.

*　*　*

A LIFETIME of cogitation has convinced me that in this Anglo–Irish
literature of ours (which for the most part is neither Anglo, Irish, nor
literature) (as the man said) nothing in the whole galaxy of fake is comparable with Synge. That comic ghoul with his wakes and mugs of porter
should be destroyed finally and forever by having a drama festival at which
all his plays should be revived for the benefit of the younger people of
to-day. The younger generation should be shown what their fathers and
grand-daddies went through for Ireland, and at a time when it was
neither profitable nor popular.

We in this country had a bad time through the centuries when England
did not like us. But words choke in the pen when one comes to describe
what happened to us when the English discovered that we were rawther
interesting peepul ek'tully, that we were nice, witty, brave, fearfully seltic
and fiery, lovable, strong, lazy, boozy, impulsive, hospitable, decent, and
so on till you weaken. From that day the mouth-corners of our smaller
intellectuals (of whom we have more per thousand births than any country in
the world) began to betray the pale froth of literary epilepsy. Our writers,
fascinated by the snake-like eye of London publishers, have developed
exhibitionism to the sphere of acrobatics. Convulsions and contortions
foul and masochistic have been passing for literature in this country for
too long. Playing up to the foreigner, putting up the witty celtic act,
doing the erratic but lovable playboy, pretending to be morose and
obsessed and thoughtful—all that is wearing so thin that we must put it
aside soon in shame as one puts aside a threadbare suit. Even the customers who have been coming to the shop man and boy for fifty years are
fed up. Listen in the next time there is some bought-and-paid-for Paddy
broadcasting from the BBC and you will understand me better.

This trouble probably began with Lever and Lover. But I always think
that in Synge we have the virus isolated and recognisable. Here is stuff
that anybody who knows the Ireland referred to simply will not have. It
is not that Synge made people less worthy or nastier, or even better than

they are, but he brought forward with the utmost solemnity amusing clowns talking a sub-language of their own and bade us take them very seriously. There was no harm done there, because we have long had the name of having heads on us. But when the counterfeit bauble began to be admired outside Ireland by reason of its oddity and 'charm', it soon became part of the literary credo here that Synge was a poet and a wild celtic god, a bit of a genius, indeed, like the brother. We, who knew the whole inside-outs of it, preferred to accept the ignorant valuations of outsiders on things Irish. And now the curse has come upon us, because I have personally met in the streets of Ireland persons who are clearly out of Synge's plays. They talk and dress like that, and damn the drink they'll swally but the mug of porter in the long nights after Samhain.

The Plain People of Ireland : Any relation between that man and Synge Street in Dublin where Bernard Shaw was born?

Myself : I don't think so, because Bernard Shaw was born before Synge.

The Plain People of Ireland : The Brothers run a very good school there—manys a good Irishman got his learnin there. They do get a very high place in the Intermediate and the Senior Grade every year.

Myself : Faith you're right.

The Plain People of Ireland : But of course your man Shaw digs with the other foot.

Myself : Aye.

* * *

SINCE THE controversy over the Rouault picture raises important issues in the sphere of aesthetics and public morality. I know that many readers will look to me for an authoritative pronouncement.

The picture was bought for £400 by the Friends of the National Collections and offered as a gift to the Municipal Gallery. (Here let me digress to reiterate once more my demand that that narrow thoroughfare in Parnell Square where the Gallery stands should be re-named Hugh Lane.) The Board of the Gallery, presumably composed of members of the Corporation, rejected the picture. The ex-Lord Mayor, Mrs Clarke, is quoted as having said that the picture is 'a travesty' and 'offensive to Christian sentiment'. Mr Keating says it is 'childish, naive and unintelligible'. On the other hand, a foreign nobleman is cited as praising the work. M. Rouault himself preserves silence.

The picture is executed in the modern manner, and could not be expected to please persons whose knowledge of sacred art is derived from the shiny chromo-lithograph bon-dieuiserie of the Boulevard Saint Sulpice, examples of which are to be found in every decent Irishman's bedroom. Such persons, however, never enter picture galleries, and there is no obvious reason why their opinion should be considered at all. What is important is the attitude of the 'intelligent' person. Many forms of modern art are devoid of rules. The artist makes his own. However formless or chaotic the manifestation, it is art if it expresses something, possibly something bad and negative. Even our own pathetic and untidy advance guards who have never learnt to draw are artists because they express artistically (and convincingly) the fact that they can't draw. But inasmuch as the modern artist makes his own rules, the onlooker must also be permitted to fix his own standards of appraisal. In other words, the faculty of appreciating a 'modern' painting is just as personal and individual as that exercised by the artist. A 'representational' portrait of a bishop (such as is carried out so embarrassingly often) can be assessed by merely mechanical standards. The best judge of such a picture would be a child of three who could say authoritatively whether 'it is like him'. But what different dual parts of a garment is the 'modern' picture?

Pair of sleeves.

It is safe to say that, while the bishop's portrait strikes everybody in the same simple way, it is scarcely possible that the reaction of any two individuals to Rouault's work could be identical. Indeed, how divergent they may be has been demonstrated. His picture has been stated to be 'blasphemous' and 'charged with deep religious significance'.

It will be seen, then, that the charm and value of such work lies in the diversity of the communications achieved by the artist. The attitude of each individual to the picture is personal, and is not necessarily related to any conventional artistic criteria. For that reason it is an impertinence for Mr Keating to say that the picture is 'childish'. Nobody wants to be bothered with Mr Keating's opinion. We can form our own. Equally inadmissible is the attitude of other commentators who have assured us that Rouault was taken a high view of by the stained-glass man Healy, and that a bunch of Frenchmen (who alone in the world understand good taste) thought so much of him that they devoted a whole room to a display of his work. What has that got to do with it? Must we 'like' whatever some individual or coterie has pronounced to be good?

Impertinent as the expression of individual opinions must be in such a situation, it is a gross outrage that this Board of the Municipal Gallery, having apparently formed opinions desperate and dark of hue, should decide that the citizens of Ireland should not be permitted to form any opinion at all. By what authority does this bunch take custody of the community's aesthetic conscience?

The members of the Corporation are elected to discharge somewhat more physical tasks, such as arranging for slum clearance and the disposal of sewerage. Here there is scope for valuable public service, a vast field of opportunity confronts the eye. Why must the members trespass in other spheres where their intellectual equipment cannot be other than inadequate?

* * *

WHAT ONE might call the pathology of literature is a subject that a person with education and intelligence should examine. What prompts a sane inoffensive man to write? Assuming that to 'write' is mechanically to multiply communication (sometimes a very strong assumption, particularly when one writes a book about peasants in Irish) what vast yeasty eructation of egotism drives a man to address simultaneously a mass of people he has never met and who may resent being pestered with his 'thoughts'? They don't have to read what he writes, you say. But they do. That is, indeed, the more vicious neurosis that calls for investigation. The blind urge to read, the craving for print—that is an infirmity so deeply seated in the mind of today that it is (well–nigh) ineradicable. People blame compulsory education and Lord Northcliffe. The writer can be systematically discouraged, his 'work' can be derided and if all else fails we can (have recourse) to the modern remedy known as 'liquidating the intellectuals'. But what can you do with the passive print addict? Absolutely nothing.

Consider the average day of the average man who is averagely educated. The moment he opens his eyes he reads that extremely distasteful and tragic story that is to be found morning after morning on the face of his watch. Late again. He is barely downstairs when he has thrown open (with what is surely the pathetic abandon of a person who knows he is lost) that grey tablet of lies, his newspaper. He assimilates his literary narcotic in silence, giving 5 per cent of his attention to the business of eating. His wife has ruined her sight from trying for years to read the same paper from the other side of the table and he must therefore leave it behind him as he departs for his work. Our subject is nervous on his way, his movements are undecided; he is momentarily parted from his drug. Notice how advertisements he has been looking at for twenty years are

frenziedly scrutinised, the books and papers of neighbours on the bus
are carefully scanned, the bus ticket is perused with interest, a fearful
attempt is made to read what is printed on the tab of a glove held in the
hand of a clergyman two seats up. Clocks are read and resented.

At last the office is reached. Hurrah! Thousands of documents—books,
papers, letters, calendars, diaries, threats to sue, bailiffs' writs. Writing,
typescript, PRINT! An orgy of myopic indulgence! Consider the countless
millions who sit all day in offices throughout the world endlessly reading
each other's writings! Ink-wells falling and falling in level as words are
extracted from them by the hundred thousand! Tape-machines, typewriters, printing-presses wearing out their metal hearts to feed this
monstrous lust for unspoken words!

And now consider that rare and delightful soul (admittedly he lives
mostly in the Balkans)—the illiterate. Think of his quiet personal world,
so untroubled by catastrophes, cures for heart disease, the fact that it is
high-water at Galway at 2.31 p.m. or even the lamented death of a person
who spoke Irish at a time when it was neither profitable nor popular!
Recall the paragraph of a brother scribe of mine who saw a countryman
'reading' the morning paper upside down and remarking that there was
another big one sunk as he gazed at an inverted battle-ship! Think of
the illiterate's acute observation of the real world as distinct from the pale
print-interpreted thing that means life for most of us!

If you know such a person, leave him to his happiness. If you even hint
he is unusual and has a 'story' he will probably start going to the tech.
and eventually write a book, second 20th thousand now printing, the most
naïf spiritual document of our times!

* * *

PEDANTIC old gentleman that I am, I received a lot of annoyance a few
weeks ago and it is only now that I have stopped fuming that I can sit
(down) and write about it (in cold blood). I look into that alien print,
'The Sunday Times', and see that my friend Desmond MacCarthy is
discussing Mr Eliot's latest thing, 'Little Gidding'. Explaining the title
of the book, Mr MacCarthy writes as follows:—

'Little Gidding is, of course, the name of a lonely spot not far from
Peterborough, where Nicholas Ferrar and his few followers in the reign
of Charles I built a small plain chapel in which to worship undisturbed . . .'

Now in the whole underworld of print there is surely no more gratuitous
or insulting phrase than that 'of course'. Why 'of course'? Probably there

aren't in the whole world more than a thousand people who had ever heard of Little Gidding and I resent, on my own behalf and on behalf of the civilised circle to which I belong, the suggestion that everybody is aware of this unimportant statistic. It's like saying 'Mr T S Eliot, of course, wears his boots when taking a bath.'

Then I throw away this foreign newspaper and take up something decent and native. In this month's 'Bell' I am asked to accept as authoritative and penetrating an article on James Joyce. Throughout the piece the master's last work is consistently referred to as 'Finnegan's Wake'. That apostrophe (I happen to know) hastened Mr Joyce's end. To be insensitive to what is integral is, I fear, not among the first qualifications for writing an article on Mr Joyce.

Let there be no more of this nonsense.

*   *   *

HAVING CONSIDERED the matter in—of course—all its aspects, I have decided that there is no excuse for poetry. Poetry gives no adequate return in money, is expensive to print by reason of the waste of space occasioned by its form, and nearly always promulgates illusory concepts of life. But a better case for the banning of all poetry is the simple fact that most of it is bad. Nobody is going to manufacture a thousand tons of jam in the expectation that five tons may be eatable. Furthermore, poetry has the effect on the negligible handful who read it of stimulating them to write poetry themselves. One poem, if widely disseminated, will breed perhaps a thousand inferior copies. The same objection cannot be made in the case of painting or sculpture, because these occupations afford employment for artisans who produce the materials. Moreover, poets are usually unpleasant people who are poor and who insist forever on discussing that incredibly boring subject, 'books'. You will notice above that I used the phrase 'illusory concepts of life'. If you examine it carefully you will find that it is quite meaningless but since when did such a trifle matter? Poets don't matter and an odd senseless bit of talk matters little either. What is important is food, money, and opportunities for scoring off one's enemies. Give a man those three things and you won't hear much squawking out of him.

In a violent article in a contemporary, Mr P. S. O'Hegarty assails the 'philosophy' behind the Beveridge Plan. He sees in it a plan to maintain the dissolute, the lazy and the work-shy at the expense of the industrious. He denounces such a term as 'the right to work' as jargon, and says that what it meant is 'the necessity for working'. There is much sense in this view. In the present century we have amassed a formidable list of 'rights' never heard of before. I think it is true to say that only an inferior person has rights. When you hear a person talking about his rights, you may be sure he is trying to gain by dint of shouting something which he lacks (or had and lost) by reason of some culpable deficiency in himself. You never hear successful men talking about their rights.

* * *

LAST SUNDAY evening I pulled over a chair and took from the top of the wardrobe the old cardboard box, opened it and pulled out the claw-hammer, complete with ball-buttoned black waistcoat as worn at the Vice-regal Ball in nineteen O seven. How my old ball-dancing days surged back through the fug of lavender and mothballs. I tried one of the pockets. An old programme, Gaiety Theatre, 18th June, 1911, Martin Harvey in 'Proserpine's Folly'. I cannot remember the play or the man. The theatre, I'm told, is still there. One recalls that debased French drug addict of bygone revolution days, 'Neiges' Dantan.

In no time I had stuffed myself into the 'suit' and was speeding down-town in a taxi, clutching my miniature scores. (I don't know why—I nearly wrote 'miniature sores' there.) Into the large, crowded hall to hear our Gaelic radio orchestra being thoroughly well conducted by Mr Constant Lambert, distinguished visitor. Interesting programme, the usual sweetbreads relieved by the Tchaikovsky Symphony No 5 and a piece by Glazunoff. Relieved in the wrong way, however, because I dislike both works, and cannot see what Mr Lambert admires in them. Back in my library a bit depressed, I administer simultaneous enteric and mental stimuli by drinking French brandy and reading bits from Mr Lambert's well-known book, 'Music Ho'. Seems he agrees with me about Tchai-kovsky:

'But for the typical nineteenth-century symphony as represented by Tchaikovsky No 5 . . . there is frankly nothing to be said; the mingling of academic procedure with undigested nationalism or maudlin sentiment, or both, produces a chimerical monster, a musical Minotaur that fortunately has had no progeny . . .'

As to Glazunoff, 'Glazunoff . . . relapsed into premature middle age, producing a series of well-wrought symphonies whose (*sic*) occasional touches of national colour only throw into greater prominence the conservatoire qualities of the rest of the work.'

It is interesting to have a conductor certifying in writing that his programme is largely trash, but I am not so sure that any notice will be taken by this nation of befuddled paddies, whose sole musical tradition is bound up with blind harpers, tramps with home-made fiddles, Handel in Fish-handel street, John McCormack praising our airport, and no street in the whole capital named after John Field.

From music, one passes to musical criticism and criticism generally. At present, one of the Dublin newspapers sends a young countryman to review plays, with results that may be imagined—and even read from time to time. Here is a true story arising from a comparable situation obtaining in the days of the *Freeman's Journal*. Some poor old man who was good at funerals, police courts and the like was sent by accident to review a recital by Paderewski. When he was seen in the theatre, the management became alarmed. After considering the problem, they invited him into a back room, gave him a few drinks, explained that music was rather a bore and promised to let him have a reasoned and technical review of the whole programme, nicely typed out, to save his time and trouble. The reporter was very thankful, and in due course went back to his office with one of the best-informed notices ever written in his pocket. He was about to send it in when he felt that some little comment of his own was called for to make the thing look genuine. He added the following as a last paragraph:

'Mr Paderewski gave a musicianly rendition of the above items, and was observed to play with equal facility on the black notes as the white.'

* * *

THE WRITING crowd, it is well known, are only a parcel of dud czechs and bohemian gulls and if I am seen in that notorious ultimate rigour it will not be in their company, though I can predict that on that day there will be wailed throughout the length (not to say breadth) of this rich and rare land loud cries of 'Wisha, he wasn't the worst!' (Bah, if I may say so, omnia post obitum fingit maiora vetustas or if I have not made myself Cleary—maius ab exsequiis nomen in ora venit.)

It was the very same with the other crowd. That fellow la Fontaine that made a stack out of translating Father Peter's *Aesoip A Tháinic go hEirinn*, do you know that that chancer was never in his life known to have asked a pal if he had a mouth on him. (And that would be a nice remark to make to a man that was afflicted with vampires, eh?) O yes, that's known— that's well-known. And do you remember that other party that put French on a lot of Lady Gregory's stuff—Francis Villyan? Villyan was a narky character. He once spent a day out with la Fontaine. Then straight home in a rage and wrote the piece beginning, je meurs de seuf aupres de la Fontaine chault comme feu, et tremble dent a dent . . .

Now here is an astonishing thing that will please a certain type of reader never mind what type. Consider these four words, which convey between them the whole picture of the last war.

KAISER
SERBIA
JOFFRE
FRENCH

Now take out your pen (a pencil will do also, of course) and draw a vertical line through the middle of the words. Now if you read down each half, you will get precisely the same words that you get across. Get it?

And now, back to our eternal French. Somebody 'reviewing' something here some Saturdays ago wrote as follows: 'A misinterpretation of a passage (cited) from Valéry's "Ebauche d'un Serpent", a misquotation . . . and Laforgue's name twice mis-spelt are some of the minor pleasures which this work will afford the pedant . . .'

I haven't any of Mr V's poems by me as I write, chiefly because it looks so damn silly hauling a bookcase into a pub, but unless I am Miss Teaken, the Ebauche kicks off like this:

> Parmi l'arbre la brise berce
> La vipère que je vêtis;
> Un sourire, que la dent perce,
> Et qu'elle éclaire d'appétits,
> Sur le jardin se risque et rode,
> Et mon triangle d'émeraude
> Tire sa langue à double fil.

And that's only the first verse. Can you imagine the sneering dare-devils who despise each other for not 'understanding' grey incomprehen-sibilities like this? As for Laforgue, I believe the correct way to spell his name is E-L-I-O-T. Give me at all times the stern logicacity of the German muse (lately polluted, I am told, by a wretch called Rilke) which won't stand for any nonsense or 'difficulty' and can be read even by those who have only B.A. German.

> Hat alles seine Zeit.
> Das Nähe wird weit,

Das Wärme wird kalt,
Der Junge wird alt,
Das Kälte wird warm,
Der Reiche wird arm,
Der Narre gescheit,
Alles zu seiner Zeit.

Not to mention, of course, that der Myles wird müde, if I may make a personal observation in my chaste Göthe syntax.

* * *

I AM, of course, intensely interested in education. I have every reason to be because I was disabled for life at the age of fifteen by a zealous master (although I had the laugh on him afterwards when I came back from hospital with my two hands amputated). When I was taking a bath last night (fearful job disconnecting the taps and getting the thing out through the window) I found some bits of paper, blue and gamgee coloured, lying about the floor. They were examination papers—indeed, they probably still are. They told me clearly that my suspicions were correct—my father, secretly rather a social climber, I fear, is doing the Leaving. He, poor fellow, is a rich man and believes (a) that 'education' is something rather pleasant and (b) that it can be acquired by doing the Leaving. Neither of these propositions, of course, is tenable, never mind what Tierney says.

Education—greedy eggs pair toe—is (using the term in its real sense) what has unfitted me for the drapery trade, what makes me sneer at money, reject the physical 'beauty' of the world as meretricious and seek the community of quiet minds in disputation on the Greek style of this or that departed heresiarch—knowing well that terrestrial time cannot be better spent. It is not, I protest, the cynical arrangement which contemplates timely regurgitation in the summer examination hall of gargantuan scholastic gluttonies supervised in winter by men with whips and clubs, even if this process guarantees that one will emerge a Boy Messenger Grade III, increasing by annual increments to £95 at the age of 70. I have looked at these examination papers and the beliefs implied by them are genuinely embarrassing, even to my equable lordship.

Perhaps the English Honours Paper best illustrates what I am trying to say, and saying (in my own way). It is not so much that the student is expected to be familiar with the works of very many inferior persons, for after all what else is literature but just this? What is disquieting and cannot be borne is that one is expected to admire or decry these things and that one will obtain marks and consequently be considered educated only in so far as one's admiration and contempt corresponds with those of the person who sets the paper (who is of course entitled to his opinions but not necessarily to those of other people).

Listen to this, will you: *Describe with quotation, the famous long simile at the end of 'The Scholar Gypsy'. What do you see to admire in it?* The question is not asked ironically and you'll never be a Subordinate Writing Clerk, Grade 5b, if you answer it in that spirit. *What do you see to admire in it?* Elsewhere in the same paper I see the phrase *Say more particularly what you find to admire in it.* An eccentric student who admires rather than finding or seeing to admire would probably be expelled from the examination hall (with ignominy). I suppose it's too much reading of the French that causes English like that to be written.

Appreciate Ruskin as a describer of the richly splendid and the desolate. Leave aside the tautology of 'richly splendid' and tell me why any educated person should know anything whatever of this awful little blue-nosed schoolboy whose smugness and ignorance were so appalling that he would be admitted to nowhere except girls' schools for the delivery of his 'lectures'. Why should young people who have done no harm be compelled to 'appreciate' this unthinkable alien with the elastic-sided boots and the stomach full of home-made custard?

Later on, in the pathology section, we get this: *Why does the poet pray to be made one with the West Wind?* For that matter why do I take damn good care not to walk on the cracks in the pavement? Why does my wife fall out of the bed four times every night every July? Really, who wants to know the answers to these essentially Viennese questions?

I shall say nothing of the remaining questions. They are concerned with names which, being a modern person, I have never heard before—Wardsworth, Milltone, Bruening, William Bleck—I quote from memory. It amuses me to think that any schoolboy who shares my lordship's perfectly reasonable ignorance of these people will fail the examination and go through life as a person who is not 'educated'. Excuse me while I blow my nose.

FUTILE, FUTILE

I see (where) Sir Bernard Shaw has been writing letters to the papers in reply to a meaningless controversy as to where 'St Joan' was written.

He explains that there is no foundation for 'the belief that a dramatic poet, when he writes a play, sits down on a particular spot on the earth's surface and does not rise until, in a frenzy of inspiration, he has dashed off the play, the process taking, say, two hours or less'.

In My Lordship's view that statement is memorable merely for the creaky defective English: If a man sits down, he necessarily sits down on a 'particular' spot and the spot (I hold) must necessarily be on the earth's surface (unless he is a miner as well as a 'dramatic poet'). Phrases like 'frenzy of inspiration' and 'dashed off' are not admissible in any context, though heaven knows what is regarded as English in Synge Street. Moreover it is sheer nonsense to say that a play cannot be written in two hours. What is much more stern a task is to spend two hours looking at a play. Above all, it is of no consequence at all where 'St Joan' was written and it is the height of damn nonsense to suggest that admirable Glengarrif is to be admired because some play was written there. (Not that Shaw and I have quarrelled: far from it. We remain the best of friends. It is merely that in some issues we go two ways.)

I LIVE in Warrenpoint and the paper reaches me nearly a month late. Hence it is only now that I come to deal with a remark made by our Cinema Critic in respect of *General Suvarov*, shown in the old 'Empire' by the Royal Irish Film Society. 'Made two years ago,' I appear to read, 'and directed by the renowned Pudovkin, this historical epic has little about it to distinguish it from a Hollywood picture of the same type . . .

I see. (Fearful frown gathering on the 'brow'.) *I see.*

I don't seem to have any free nights these times and it happens to be true that I haven't been to the pictures for near on thirty odd years last time I tried to crash a show was in the old Electric there in Mary street. Jimmy Joyce back from Paris gives me the cold shoulder doesn't know annyone it wouldn't have been old Simon's way.

But don't think that because of that I know nothing of this business. Nothing, is it? Pish! Who stood behind Lumière and held his hand? Who coached Schufftan? Who put the Warner brothers on their feet? Who put their feet on Warner brothers? Pathé Frères? Who suggested to Griffith to move the camera in a bit nearer (one night there above in the Bailey)? Who discovered Miss Gustafsson? Pabst, Périnal, Lang, Metzner, Tisse? Who stood up to the Wall-street boys? Not Zanuck, not Joe Meyer nor the brother Kuno, not Thalberg., not Schenck—ME. Me. Kaplan.

But don't get me wrong, don't think I haven't been around, don't think that time and time again I haven't had to watch Duvivier, Epstein, Feyder, aye and Renoir too, and Cavalcanti, making fairhaired fools of theirselves and then come along grovelling and flattering me with their eh bien, Myles, mon vieux, tu veux nous aider encore une petite fois, n'est-ce pas?

Aw, bah!

And do you know what I'm going to tell you, the crowd beyond in St Pethersburgh is every bit as bad, for all the long words and scratched sepia negatives they are a lot of small boys if you compare them with the men on the coast and that's what they are a lot of small boys. *The renowned Pudovkin* . . . if you don't mind. Oho, I could tell you a few things there. That's a man didn't know a threatment from a continuity when I took him in hand. I seen him there one night in the projection room checking a few rushes and do you know what I'm going to tell you the operator ran the spool through the machineupsidedown and your man never knew. Never knew. And as for Dovjhenko, Alexandrov, Dvertov, Timoshenko, yes, there *was* a Timoshenko in the game—and . . . ho-ho . . . Misther Sergei Eisenstein don't be talking how far do you think he'd have got with his *overtonal montage* and his theory of the '*dynamic square*' if there hadn't been a certain modest Dublin man with nothing but a sound Synge Street education no names no pack drill at his side night and morning dinning it into him and writing it all out for him in black and white in the heel of the hunt. The Russian man . . . is a very nice man . . . a very dacent man . . . and can handle a hurley with anny man . . . (pause, eyes dropped demurely, then a frightful roar) BUT DON'T FOR THE LOVE OF HEAVEN LET HIM NEAR A CAMERA BECAUSE DO YOU KNOW WHAT I'M GOING TO TELL YOU HE'LL WRECK IT HE'LL WRECK IT. (Don't interrupt now or you're ruined). DE MILLE? DE MILLE, IS IT? CECIL WOULD TAKE THE WHOLE BLOOMING SHOOTING MATCH OUT AND LOSE EVERY MAN JACK OF THEM AT THAT GAME!

Phew . . . !

* * *

I HAVE NOT, of course, seen Mr Carroll's new play. 'The Wives Have Not Spoken'. But the title is good. Take myself. Had a fearful row with the wife about a fortnight ago—over Picasso, of course. Any word uttered in my house since then was uttered by the BBC announcer.

But this play, I am told—how reliably I cannot say—that all the characters in it go mad one by one. That, of course, is fine. It is not European, but it is fine. It gives me a thrill. One after another, they all go mad. At the end, everybody's crazy and you have . . . tragedy. (But have you? Surely, I mean . . . for . . . tragedy, you must have somebody there sane enough to experience pity . . . and terror . . .? Surely . . . the Greeks . . . still mean something . . . in this old Georgian Athens of the West . . .?)

I may, of course, be misinformed about 'The Wives Have Not Spoken' but what I heard gives me an idea for a fine play, three bangs of the gong up with the curtain and on the stage twelve characters sunk in a frightfully celtic condition of rural lunacy. Then one by one they all get better. Doctor chap comes in, cerebral electrolysis, occupational therapy, most modern drugs and they all respond, soon the house is happy, everybody has a healthy mind. They all become registered readers of *The Standard*, develop 'a healthy outlook' on life and one by one, they go up to Dublin and become fully-fledged Knights.

If Mr Carroll's theme is tragedy, is mine comedy? I don't think so. Mine's rather tragic, too, you know.

CAN WE awful Irish louts (leaving aside for the moment our red faces, high cheek bones and gnarled hands) ever be made into little jintlemen? One may wittily reply that where there's a will there's a way.

The current report of the Friends of the National Collections says: 'Anyone who has the future welfare of Ireland at heart cannot fail to be deeply touched by Mrs Shaw's wish that graciousness should flourish in our land, and the fine gesture by which she has pointed the way to its fulfilment.' It is true to say that this is a deplorable little piece of English, pocked with clichés; it must be sighed out rather than spoken to get the delicate custard-coloured winsomeness of 'our land' and 'graciousness'. It is entirely odious.

How wonderful to be told by these 'Friends' that we must be 'gracious'! This word, according to my dictionary, means 'agreeable, pleasing (archaic); kindly, benevolent, courteous (chiefly poet.); condescending, indulgent & beneficent to inferiors . . .' Its present connotation in Ireland is rather different. If you would be gracious in Dublin, for instance, number wan is the little shelf with nothing on it bar the paper-covered novels, all written in the French. Next, the drop of red wine and the pot of French mustard. Next (and all the time breakfast dinner and tea) the monstrous crippling chat about 'art' and 'pictures' and Cossa and Tintoretto and Piombo (by yer honour's lave), not forgetting Filippino Lippi, that poor man with the trench mouth. (One does not . . . talk . . . about the moderns any more. Nao. One goes back. Fundamentals, I mean. These . . . strange times.)

'Art' surely is a laugh. It is not, of course, distinguished as such among a people to whom an artistic perception is traditional and natural. In the great gombeen metropolis of 'our land', it is the one thing that your newly-emancipated peasant finds irresistible; even after two generations he is still flabbergasted at the idea of seeing books that are not almanacs, pictures that are not given away with Christmas numbers of religious periodicals, and 'drink' that is not lethal two year-old Irish. Selfconsciousness about 'Art', then, is the stamp of the gombeen-bourgeoisie. Myself, children and wives *have always known about art* and we were always absolutely saturated with graciousness. Nor do we talk about Money or 'the price of things nowadays'. We *always* had money. Neither do we ask you to hear us on the subject of our 'rights'. You see, we have no 'rights'. Only serfs or ex-serfs find it necessary to draw up a statement of their 'rights'.

But what one finds really disquieting in 'our land' is the vast number of individuals and organisations who are profoundly dissatisfied with the people here and who issue instructions to them as to how they should behave. For example, these 'Friends' tell us that we should be gracious. By what authority do they issue this impudent admonition? Who are *they* to talk? One passes by a street corner to hear oneself being told by a brat standing on a stool that one should be ashamed of oneself, that one has betrayed Emmet and Lord Edward and Tone, that an Ireland without Gaelic is no Ireland at all. The speaker can hardly speak English himself and is evidently uneducated. An Anti-Vivisection group forbids me to cut the head off my dog, even though he has bitten the leg off myself. Muintir na Tire takes a very poor view. The Monetary Reform Association takes a very poor view. *The Standard* takes a very poor view. *The Leader* is very unhappy. The GAA will not allow that one is Irish at all. Dear one! Dear me, I mean.

How frightfully eccentric to behave precisely as one thinks fit, without taking orders or advice from any self-appointed pedagogue! Yet how frightfully ungracious, how unFriendly!

* * *

OCCASIONALLY I have hard words to say here about aesthetes. For sensibility, paranoiac reception and all the sublunar paraphernalia of infra-psychic recordings I have not, it is true, concealed my contempt. For appreciation, discrimination and good taste I have nothing to say. These matters do not concern me or any adult. They are the things of childhood and together with the Meccano jersey in purest jaeger, the cogged ekkers and the consumption of neat lemonade, I have cast them behind me.

Search any old lukewarm bath and you will find one of these aesthetical technicians enjoying himself. He is having a luke-warm bath, it is rather good, it is something real, something that has its roots in the soil, a tangible, valid, unique, complete, integrating, vertical experience, a diatonic spatio-temporal cognition in terms of realistic harmonic spacing, differential intervals and vector (emmanuel) analysis, of those passional orphic inferences which must be proto-morphously lodged in writing with the Manager on or before the latest closing date. Hmmmm. All round this person in the bath life is going on, nothing is ever lost, over in Harlem Einstein is testing a diminished seventh for over-stimulated thyroid, in Milan Buonaparte is writing the letter that ends *Ah, Joséphine! Joséphine! Toi! Toi!*, in the Bank of Ireland Silken Thomas has laid his sword on the counter what will they allow him on it, in Bohemia they are throwing the Emperor's ambassadors out of the window while always waddling comically into the polyphonic aureole of the sunset recedes the tragic figure of Charlie Chaplin. This is life, and stuffed contentedly in the china bath sits the boy it was invented for, morbidly aware of the structure of history, geography, parsing, algebra, chemistry and woodwork; he is up to his chin in the carpediurnal present, and simultaneously, in transcendant sense-immediacy, sensible that without *him*, without *his* feeling, *his* observation, *his* diapassional apprehension on all planes, *his* non-pensionable function as catalyst, the whole filmy edifice would crumble into dust. He likes the lukewarm water. He likes himself liking the lukewarm water. He likes himself liking himself liking the lukewarm water. Aesthetics, in other words, is a mental ailment, the perversion whereby the sufferer believes that to be consistently ... *passive* is the prime bacon, the *summum bonham*. The perfect aesthete logically feels that the artist is strictly a turkish bath attendant. This is true nearly always but ... consider my own case. Suppose I write a symphony. No, that is a crude way of putting it. Suppose that contained in my cranium is a work of dimension so vast, of nature so autonomous, supreme, trismegistous in its modes, that it cannot be noted down on paper. Suffice it that it ... explores, discovers, dismantles, inaugurates ... stuns! Its composition was achieved not without a succession of cosmopathic agonies in my heart. This effort was, of course, in itself a complete artistic event. Now it seems superfluous to say this, but

I did not . . . could not . . . would not perform the *moyen age* crudity of . . . of . . . *scoring* this work. Why should I ? How to orchestrate something the instruments for the performance of which are incapable of being constructed by ham-like contemporary machine-hands? Why note an opus, all the virtuosi being dead or as yet unborn? How to convey the sense of a work when the very notation I had to invent for it would be incomprehensible to my contemporaries? But, most blindingly significant of all, why or to whom should I wish to convey . . . *anything*? What is added to the grandeur, the immensity of my art by . . . *expressing it*? I should expose it to—Swede Evans, this were folly!—the . . . appreciation . . . of . . . persons of sensibility? I should stand by and watch these people founding the Royal Irish Academy of Myles-ian Art? The Rt. Honble. The Friends of the Nagcoplian Collections? The National Society for the Prevention of Cruelty to Cruiskeens and the Fiends of the O'Kaddemagh of Lettuce? Never! Better far better that I should elect to become that oddly speechless mouth-wash, a mute Englorious Milton! They can't take that away from me.

In this book I mentioned yesterday—'Irish Art'—there is a shampoo-sium entitled 'What is a Portrait?' and there are some damn fine things in it. 'It must be admitted,' one savant says, 'that the standard of achievement is conditioned to a great extent by the subject matter which the artist has to work upon, and so many portraits are of those people whose highest aim in life or the summit of whose ambition is merely to be captain of the golf club, president of some trade association, chairman of a commercial enterprise, or the wife of one of these.'

I do not know what the wife of a commercial enterprise is, nor does heaven vouchsafe me the wit to understand the distinction that is made between the summit of ambition and the highest aim in life. But this much I do know—(face gets very red and neck bulges) this much I do know—that there is nothing contemptible about being the captain of a golf club or owning a jam factory that makes a lot of money and if the eldest girl now in Eccles Street manages to become the wife of a jam factory, there certainly will be no complaints from yours truly; it will be a little bit more satisfactory than having her mess up bits of canvas as well as her face with 'paints'. Or is it suggested, forsooth, that it is 'easy' to succeed in business? (I can't off-hand think of anything easier than to be an 'artist' in Ireland today—if it be not to be a newspaper funny man.)

'Let artists once free themselves,' this writer continues, 'from the influence of those women whose worldliness they must always resent— and seek their inspiration elsewhere and we shall see a fresh flowering of an art which in its delineation of creation at its highest point and deepest significance comes nearest to depicting the meaning of life.'

The first thing I must make clear is that women are part of the creation. It cannot too often be pointed out that women are people. The creation has no 'highest point' (apart from the top of Mount Everest) nor is its significance distinguished as between deep, deeper and deepest. The creation is the creation. Art has nothing to do with the 'delineation of creation', whatever about the creation of delineations. And it is news to me that there are still people in the world who are still brooding on that tawdry old conundrum, 'the meaning of life'. Would readers who are troubled in this regard write to me in confidence, enclosing a stamped addressed envelope?

Another man writes: 'It was not until the time of Donatello in sculpture and Botticelli, Mantegna, Dürer and Van Eyck in painting that men and women were portrayed as the artist saw them. This has gone on ever since.'

I beg this man's pardon. Gone on ever since it certainly has not. Even getting the 'likeness'—most rudimentary of studio chores when I was a student—is entirely beyond not a few of your present-day 'artists'. As for drawing hands . . .

The only other thing I have space to notice today is a curious misprint in a fine article by Mr Sean O'Sullivan R.H.A.:

'The dullness of many portraits,' he is made to say, 'may often be traced to the timidity of the painter who fatally allows himself to be intimidated by his sitter . . .'

It is clear that 'sitter' is wrong in that context, but which should it be— 'sister' or 'setter'?

(Reminds me that I must feed that bone-setter of mine.)

* * *

READING, not with distaste, Mr Raymond McGrath's article in 'Irish Art' on the prefabricated house, it occurs to me to point out that houses traditionally rise from ground-level to the sky only because our primal forbears were not interested in excavation. Yet there is no good reason why a house should be built up rather than sunk. The advantages the conventional house is supposed to have in respect of light and fresh air can be largely discounted in these days of air-conditioning and ubiquitous E.S.B. Here are a few things in favour of the downward house.

1. Most of the animals live underground and apparently find the situation healthy, warm and hygienic.

2. At least three-quarters of the over-ground house is not used during daylight hours and might as well be underground so far as light is concerned; and the entire first floor of the underground house, being glass-roofed, will be day-lit.

3. Indoor heating will only be a fraction of present costs as the loss of heat by radiation from over-ground wallsteads will be eliminated.

4. Construction costs will be only a fraction of present costs because the 'house' will have no outside and the householder will no longer have to submit to acute interior discomforts because his home is designed primarily to present a pleasing exterior to the eye of a lot of strangers who pass in the street.

5. There will be no 'streets'.

6. Valuable sub-soils will be made available for agriculture.

In fairness, however, I must set down a few of the drawbacks that must be considered:

1. No back-door.

2. Danger of flooding.

3. Danger of astronomy becoming an obsession with all householders.

4. Danger to inebriates in manipulating a horizontal hall-door.

And add to those, if you want to be funny, the danger of people dropping in on you at all hours.

If you reflect, however, you will see that most of the disadvantages of the underground house are bound up with the householder's persistence in the old habit of going 'out'—that is, up, and out along the crust of the earth. His pretexts for this are rarely very sound and if the time is about nine o'clock at night, they are indefensible. Consider a clerk living in a small basement flat on the outskirts of London. He gets up so early that he does so in darkness nearly all the year round. He rushes up and out and after a few seconds on the surface, he has disappeared into the bowels of the earth to get a train to town. His office, even if not a basement, will be dark and sepulchral. He goes home by tube and is soon asleep in his underground bed. He has never really been up or out at all, and if private subterranean accommodation roads could be built from underground houses to tubes and underground traffic arteries of one kind and another, an entire city could be permanently submerged, with no worse effects than an owl-eyed and untanned citizenry.

A lot of nonsense is talked about the sun. Get plenty of fresh air and sunlight, a doctor will tell you. Observe the effect of fresh air and sunlight on flowers. Almost under your eyes they are forced to precocious bloom, now they are already withered and crumbling to dust. The sun blasts the tender slow cycle of growth, forces the human plant as it will rhubarb under glass. The sun kills because its direct energy, undiluted and untransformed cannot indefinitely be sustained by any form of life. The corrosive light that comes from radium abounds also in sunlight. Avoid the sun, reader. Better the genial battery that has ever digested and stored the sunlight—the earth. Go into the earth, burrow into your progenitrix, live among your travelled and returned predecessors, lie on top of your descendants.

We who are Irish come from the earth of Ireland and to it we will one day return. I am not so sure that we have not taken a grave risk by coming up at all. (And think of the convenience of getting rid forever of this dreary mess known as 'the weather'.)

* * *

YOU MUST KEEP this strictly under your hat but I received an invitation to be in attendance at 86 St Stephen's Green last Thursday evening to hear a 'paper' on . . . guess ? . . . 'The Function and Scope of Criticism'. It interests me as a scientist that there is to be found today in this humble island a young man who is anxious to explain this matter to me and it will be a regret to me, always, that a malignant destiny decreed that on that evening I should be elsewhere. I feel rather tired but surely if one explains concisely the function of criticism, one has also defined its scope; if it be the function of the Slieve Gullion to draw passengers train to Belfast, is it necessary to add that this engine should not sell race-cards in Dublin on Baldoyle days ?

Again, I must ask you to regard what I say as private and confidential. The document I have received says *No Press References* and one must not (if only out of deference to the distinguished Knight who is among the signatories) outrage this most understandable desire for secrecy. You see, these bodies are about something far more hush-hush than jet-propulsion. They are (this is quite incredible but I swear it so help me) they are interested in . . . Art! (!!!!!!)

Well well. Wasn't it a shame, Paud, that they kept it all from you until now, that they didn't tell you about it, that you have to fly into back rooms in your hundreds to have it explained to you! Poor poor Paud.

These people, disdaining extraordinary water, call themselves 'Common Ground'. With gigantic presumption they begin by calling me 'Dear Sir' and then continue as follows:

'As you are probably already aware, some few years ago a group of persons interested in literature decided to meet about once a month to hear a paper read by one of their numbers. A discussion followed each paper and much benefit and enjoyment was derived by those present.'

'As you are probably already aware' is surely effrontery of an unusual order. As well say, 'as you are probably already aware, my sister had a pimple on her nose four months ago'. Why should it be assumed that a schoolgirl's pimple is a matter necessarily within the public's knowledge? Why should anybody know about the rebel back-room conclaves of 'a group of persons interested in literature'—least of all My Most Equitable Gaelic Palatinity? (????) And if they are so interested in literature, why don't they learn to be literate? How could one be aware of something without being already aware of it? Could this 'group' be otherwise than a group 'of persons'? Could a group of black-faced mountain sheep be interested in literature? Could . . . could a group of asses be interested in literature? Could the benefit and enjoyment (sic) that was derived (very eclectic word 'derived' in that context) be derived by those not present? 'Literature' how are you!

'Arising out of the experience of those concerned with 'Common Ground' in its early stage, it was thought advisable recently to widen its scope. Henceforth 'Common Ground' will be designed primarily to be of help to Catholics interested in literature, art, learning, and in social and political theory . . .'

Don't go away—keep reading. The English alone is marvellous. (I feel awful.)

'A series of lectures have been planned for the coming twelve months. Widely different topics have been tentatively chosen for treatment. (*M. & B?*) The Function and Scope of Criticism; Political Thought in Ireland—Past and Future; The Irish Social Order; The Scope and Content of Irish Culture. It was thought advisable to have three papers at successive meetings from different lecturers on each of these subjects, each dealing with a particular aspect of the matter. The views put forward by the lecturers, together with the opinions expressed by the subsequent speakers, should prove stimulating and beneficial to all concerned.'

Wouldn't it be terrible if a (subsequent) speaker put forward views instead of expressing opinions? 'To all concerned' is superb.

I cannot recall in recent months a more virulent eruption of paddyism.

* * *

THERE IS a funny idea abroad (by which I mean, of course, in Ireland) that if you scream loudly enough against 'censorship' you are therefore a litherary man and an 'intellectual'. You are 'advanced' and 'read books'. It is a handier resort than the beard act, though the two together are formidable. Against a dull day I cut (out) some weeks ago the following bit from our awful Litherary Page—you know the poem made of rhubarb in the middle and the surround of bubonic marzipan:

'. . . The censorship mind is not loosening its grip on Ireland. At the bottom of it is a belief that man is unable to choose and to criticise for himself—that he must be guarded, like an infant in the nursery, in case he should fall into the fire. It might be argued that this is something very like a negation of freewill; it is certainly a negation of the basic principle of democracy—the principle that man is an adult, who has the right to make up his own mind. We concede every grown man and woman the right to choose their own rulers—can we not concede them the right to choose their books and their films?'

I am not acquainted with the Daddy Christmas who wrote the foregoing matter but it interests me as a scientist. I like the idea of the mind with a bottom in which reclines the belief that Mahon is unable etc. Also the bit lower down where we concede every grown man and woman the right to choose 'their' (sic, ho-ho!) *own* rulers. A terrible drop for school-going chislers, who have to buy theirs. And Democracy? I never touch it but if it means a Saturday paper full of articles by persons who 'write' about the doctrine of free-will', 'the basic principle of democracy' and 'belief', I think it is time we all changed over to the *Nietzsche Nietzsche Shinbum*.

Though I am a weary, lovable old person, I can see that this young gentleman-writer wishes to imply that . . . all is not well here in Ireland, that something closely resembling a grim show is getting a continuous performance, that too many . . . negeishas are going round negating the doct. of f-w., and (b) the basic prin. of democ. quote amid laughter the principle that man is an adult unquote. I . . . I . . . I know nothing of this democracy (—though as an Irishman I can discourse learnedly on the only systems we have tried here, Tanistry and Black-and-Tanistry—) but I am anxious to learn. It has been tried, presumably, and has been found satisfactory, or this precocious literary youngster would not thus praise it. Emmmm . . . *where*? Do please drop me a card. I mean if one admits that life here is not too smart, unlike what does that make us? And where—to change the conversation—is the evidence that man is unable to choose and criticise for himself, of all people? How has this paragon of animals shown that he must not be guarded like an infant? Is his faculty for falling into the fire not embarrassingly perennial? How has he benefited by his . . . adult status, his 'right' to make up his *own* mind, to 'choose'—delicate euphemism!—his own rulers. Where is he at the present moment—or have I said the wrong thing?

As for this poor 'adult' boob choosing his own films . . .! Even the poor cinema owners are not conceded that right.

* * *

ONE DOES NOT like opening old sewers but a rather interesting issue arose in connexion with Mr Patrick Kavanagh's review of the Exhibition of Modern Art. He found the presentation 'middle-class', favoured one or two works and contrasted the cautious awe that 'difficult' pictures evoke in Dublin as compared with the treatment—come, what is the word?—the treatment . . . *meted* out to 'writers'.

As regards writers, let it be said at once that there is no major personality in Irish letters today. In the last century, Joyce and Yeats were the only two who were men of genius. For the rest, we have had an infestation of literary vermin, an eruption of literary scabies for which all the patience of scientists notwithstanding, no cure has yet been found. Call it, if you will, 'type-phoid'. We all know them, they are very serious 'young' men, their 'work' is important. But there let severe judgment end. It is very doubtful if they are as bad as our 'painters' (one means the 95 per cent awfully bad ones) and the writers do not have an annual orgy comparable with the Academy Exhibition. No no no! (Wards off protests with yellow wax-like hands.) Earnestness, honesty, good purpose—these are not enough. *You must learn to draw.* If, after many a summer, you find you cannot draw, then . . . then . . . be a writer. And there is not a terrible lot wrong with earning one's living behind the counter of a drapery shop. 'Art' is so *terribly* often no more than vocational malfunction.

Miss Norah McGuinness, who is in nowise to be classed with the duds, quotes Mr Kavanagh as saying 'I know nothing about painting but I do know that with the exception of four pictures the rest of the exhibits should be at the bottom of the Liffey.' Now among artists Mr Kavanagh's image should evoke interest and meditation rather than anger. For if this remark proves anything, it proves that Mr Kavanagh is a raging post-

post-impressionist, far more impatient with out-moded 'academic' forms than Miss McGuinness. Take for instance that serene and charming picture 'The Seine at Argenteuil' by Sisley. How would that look at the bottom of the Liffey, the French blue slow water enlivened by our green own? Who will say that true art is not materially and majestically implicated in that flux of dissident modes and morphologies the impact of the real on the 'interpreted', the live Dublin pinkeen nosing for grub in the soil of the Gallic bank? It would be a difficult thing to achieve physically in a manner that would permit of adequate inspection but the idea is far less fantastic than those of the French surrealist brethren, who probably dislike Sisley far more than does Mr Kavanagh and who had frequently implored people who attend their exhibitions to bring hatchets and hammers so that they may demolish anything they dislike—even boxes of paints so that they may 'improve' exhibits that seem to stand in need of such treatment!

The promoters of the present Exhibition talk with awe of the 'fauves'— the wild beasts who shattered with pitiless talons whatever remained of the academic in impressionism, the boys who took nothing for granted, made their own rules and certainly took nobody's word that any given picture was 'good'. Did they know about art, any more than Mr Kavanagh? The rather embarrassing fact is that Mr Kavanagh is himself, according to any known method of artistic mensuration a 'fauve', and it seems extraordinary that he should be attacked for exhibiting this prepossessing attribute. Art, remember, does not vary intrinsically as between different media or techniques. Mr Kavanagh's *saeva indignatio* seems to be what the promoters of the Exhibition are anxious to propagate. Why then write bitter letters to the paper about him? And why—above all—pretend that artistic appreciation and patronage is not middle class?

LET US LOOK further into this 'Loan Exhibition of Modern Continental Art'. A glance at somebody's else's catalogue—I will not immolate my third boy's Allowance for such a purpose—made me note with relief that the paper shortage is over. *Sixty* pages, fifteen of them blank. And do you know, reader, the date of the exhibition? No, you'd never guess. This—

'AUGUST MCMXLIV'

'M' for *mile*, 'C' for céad—go on, work it out for yourself. Do you mind the dainty, sherry-sodden coyness of it? Are you much of a man—or a wumman—for the Latin? Ever do the History of Rome by 54y at school?

Sorry—I mean Livy. O, well I know the kind you were, no interest in the buicks at all but spending every available moment in the picture palaces, lapping up the cowboy stuff, Tom 1,009, his lariat, his long nose, his black hair and his white horse! And 'The Perils of Pauline'! O tempora! (O Grace Moore!)

' But this exhibition. It is commonplace enough in all sooth (I assume all present are educated) but it brought into my own mind an old theme that I haven't seen around the place for years. We are not all agreed on either the nature or function of art—how could we, it is years since I lectured on the subject. But a comprehensive and consecutive inspection of the work of the modern French masters—where you get imagination, great technical resource and certain intuitive . . . occurrences—impresses one again and again with the inadequacy and limitation of painting as a medium of adult expression. Primitive painting, passing from the merely explanatory to the decorative, could be said to have been *a trade*. Certain branches of present-day Dublin painting might be described as an episcopalian diversion. (But forget that.) My point is that succeeding generations of painters, becoming more and more neurotic, more obsessed with their 'messages' and with the self-evident task of 'interpreting' decadence and decay, sought to charge their mundane visual media with psychic . . . (waves white hand in air) . . . with . . . infra-human implications . . . even with horror, distortion, ugliness. There is, of course, a great difficulty here. (Frowns, glances at watch, compares watch with large clock at end of hall.) A sensual picture can appeal immediately to the heart, for here there is an instantaneous emotional contagion. A picture charged with what one may call . . . intellectual evocatives, however, is always a great risk—if only by reason of the diversity of human receptivity. The result is that serious painters become more and more desperate or keep experimenting laboriously like a woman trying on new hats. Thus Rouault, in the picture refused by the foreign Dublin Corporation, rejects the reverence and formalism that are traditional in treating sacred themes and (while our back is turned, so to speak) tries to pulverise our minds into acceptance of his view by a terrible paroxysm of brutality. Whether he succeeds depends on the customer's taste, education and upbringing. Thus modern art tends to surround itself with 'difficulties'. You must know about it, be told about it, go to lectures in freezing halls. To a large extent, this is also true of music —although in music the artist cannot escape from the discipline of what is equivalent to line in the plastic job. (Puts on chilblain mittens, class shuffles uncomfortably.) But the main thing to bear in mind is the unimportance of all art. It is very much a minority activity. Mr Patrick Kavanagh is stated to have declared, while visiting the Exhibition with a view to criticising it in print, that he 'knew nothing about art'. This evoked reprimands. I fear I must deal with this whole matter at great length tomorrow. (Suddenly rings bell for morning period; class look at each other, mooch out shifty-eyed.)

* * *

MY NOTES of last week have brought me some very boring letters about art and the like. ('And the like' is good.) Some people simply cannot get this thing straight. Look at it this way—you are (yourself) a great artist, that is to say you arrived in Paris before the last war and lived in Zürich and Lausanne for its duration, Later, you did some work for Diaghilev; and the dealers (those cagey card-players) in London and New York became your agents. After a while Berlin and Munich lost interest in you. But you no longer starved. Christmas 1939 you were in Lisbon: now you are in New York, the great rebel, the great outcast, the enemy of society. Only the rich understand you, sympathise with you, are terribly eager that you should postpone that suicide . . . at least until you have finished this magistral composition 'Homunculus Sapienticulissimus', the finest thing you have ever done. You are very rich, very tired; with you painting is not simply a talent—it's a disease. Eighteen hours a day—always to create and always that morbid horror of . . . copying yourself. Sometimes critics do not understand, but no matter—the dealers always do. You have said that your work is *not* experiment, you are *not* a laboratory worker.

'I do not seek,' you say, '—I find.' That is all. 'What I find is not always what is beautiful. *But what is beauty?* If you make something that is . . . new, then must it be ugly? Look at Stephenson's "Rocket", the Wright Brothers' first plane, or that wonderful film The Great Train Robbery! Yet once these things have been thought of and translated into reality— how easy then to improve them, to make people see how fine they are! Who now wishes to deny the qualities of grace, harmony and clarity to a Boeing, a Sikorski, a Curtiss-Wright?'

A fine speech—but who pays attention to it? Nobody. It is not news. The herculean convulsion of innovation, discovery, creation, is incomprehensible to all save the connoisseur. Nowhere does one find sane standards of appraisal and judgment. No one criticises a sea-plane for not flapping its wings when taking off. No one sneers at automobiles for not being able to win the Grand National. No one despises traffic lights because you can't quench them with your cap. But when *I*, an artist, paint something and send it down to the dealers (always paint it first—much safer) the 'public' come in and laugh. I am approached by infants of twenty, thirty, fifty years of age and they say to me: These pictures are no good, we have never seen pictures like them before, a child could paint them.

I do not reply to these lackeys, a glance shows that they are not properly dressed (and this latter statistic is important only because they are trying to be): their blindness is shown in the allusion to children. Who has the intelligence of a child? You? Or *you*?

If I paint you a still life (—remember, you are no longer the patron, I am now the one with the money and the 'taste'—) if I do you this favour, you must understand that this canvas can be placed *beside* any similar 'natural' object, a flower, a shell, a leaf, in *competition*, not in imitation. A shell, in its accidents, is the phenomenal expression of a design the meaning of which is not accessible to us but which is rigid, logical, co-ordinated, formed according to a morphology that transcends our understanding of these terms. In the human scale, my painting must inevitably exhibit the same characteristics—under my own control and use of light, pigment, canvas, form, texture, colour, chroma, value, sense, line, impasto and chiaroscuro. These . . . events are . . . organised to produce not merely a symbol, a *décor*, but a . . . sort of legendary organism which is to be appreciated and can only be judged in terms of itself.

That is really all I can say.

* * *

EXAMINATIONS are in the air again. The papers once more demonstrate the curious immutability of examination marks. Nobody denies that the £ is now about half its pre-war value and that all other values have altered *pari passu*. Yet the examination marks are exactly the same as they were ten years ago. Take this example from the current Leaving Certificate paper in Arithmetic.

'A person holds a Bill of Exchange for £1,450 payable in six months and hence. He gets the Bill discounted in a bank at 4% per annum and invests the proceeds in a 10% Stock at 245. What will be his half-yearly dividend? (30 marks).'

You see? Only 30 marks. Leave aside the fact that the first sentence has no meaning, forget even the indelicate reference to G.S.R. Surely it is ridiculous to offer a paltry 30 marks, at present market levels, for calculations so laborious and recondite as those implied in the question?

Another consideration arises. The whole theory of awarding marks is misconceived psychologically. Walk into a pub and take a look at one of those electric pin-tables. You can shoot six balls for a penny and your score will depend on whether you have the skill to direct your ball into certain channels more highly valued than others. But suppose you know nothing about the game and with your first ball score the absolute minimum. To your delight, you will find that you have scored 1,000. Thus encouraged, you keep on and make possibly 5,000. Even if you are aware that the total score possible is 48,000, you think you have done very creditably for a beginner. After all, 5,000 is a lot of points. You insert another penny.

Students should be encouraged in the same way. I know of no reason why the question given above should not carry 3,000 marks. And if there is a reason, does it not also apply to 30? Why not 3?

(No answer, of course.)

These examination papers in general would repay a closer study. There are mistakes in them, of course. One notes in passing that while English-speaking students may obtain mathematical tables from the Superintendent, Irish-speaking students may obtain them from 'the waiter'. Dinneen says that the word they have for 'waiter' also means 'heir'.

The English paper is still—in 1944—the same stuff your poor father had to put up with in his day. You are expected to be familiar with the 'works' of alleged poets like Wordsworth (who wore elastic-sided boots), Shelley, Tennyson (who called 'lotus' 'lotos' to show off the Greek), Hazlitt, Polonius and Gougane Barry. Dear me.

Also—and this is worse—you are expected to 'like' these essentially Saxon windbags. You are to 'write an appreciation' of this or that. 'Write out your three favourite stanzas from Shelley's *Ode to a Skylark*.' Conceive the loutishness of a student who simply hasn't got three favourite stanzas from that base, effeminate, affected nonsense. 'Recall that portion of Belloc's *Landfall* that gave you the most pleasure.' Never heard of Belloc or his landfall; but supposing one *has* heard of the landfall and can't stand it—what then? Failure in the exam. and a row with the da?

In one question the examiner writes: 'By examining his lines on France, *or* those on Italy, show that these words help us fittingly to understand the poem.' What he really means is 'help us to fittingly understand the poem.' Why then does he not say so?

In a day or two I hope to present my own ideas of what an examination paper should be.

Irish and Related Matters

l n-Éirinn l n-Allód.

Loc: Caisleán Átha Cliath.
Am: An t-am go raibh Gaoidhil i n-Éirinn beo.
Pearsain: EAMON A'CHNUIC, SHEAN O DUIBHIR A' GHLEANNA, FEAR NA MNA
Ruaidhe, Sheán Buidhe, agus lucht Coimhdeachta an duine—uasail iar
ráidhte

Sheán Buidhe: Iú, Éadhbard Hill fbhait acsplainéisin cean iú gibh for
  thabhaing des seidisius dochúmaints in iúr poisiéisiun?
Eamonn a' Chnuic: Níl ann acht athchuinge go dtabharfí dúinn cead
  aighnis.
Sheán O Duibhir: agus radharc ar an gcoróin.
Sheán Buidhe: Fbhait ár iúr méin traighing thú sae, Sairdint?
Sairdint Tharbhaigh: Aigh tink dae ár tócuing abamht a bhuman cóld
  Agnes, a biútiful accomplas eigh supós.
Sheán Buidhe: Méic amht a bharant for thur airéist. Namh deintilmein—
Sheán Ó Duibhir: níor dhubairt mé fhaic i dtaobh Agnes.

Sheán Buidhe: Tabh iú famhnd ánaigh mór seidisius dochúmaints bitheighnd deir Teairlí.

Poiléismeán Bairlí: Bucats obh dem Sur.

Poileismeán Deonson: ond thiar ár mór sur.

Éamhon a' Chnuic: bhéarfainn mo lámh dheas acht fáill a' fhagháil an fear gránna buídhe seo do réabadh mar réabfainn sean-bhróg.

Fear na mná ruaidhe: Bheil dá mbeadh sean-bhróg agam-sa geallaim duit nach í réabadh dhéanfainn. Chaithfinn ar mo chois í agus bheinn lán-bhuídheach.

Shean O Duibhir: Namh deintilmein díos docúmaints ár bhéarigh sióruigheas, iú hav nó reispeict for ló and óirdiur—

Fear na mná Ruaidhe: God séabh dé Cbhín.

Sheán O Duíbhir: iu sbheign;

Sheán Buidhe: Aigheam glad tú saoí dat bhun obh iú ios loigheal.

Reilís thim and loch de odars up, só dat dé mé leirn tú bí gúid and loigheal suibdeicts obh thur mós gréisius maidistigh. Díos tú ár a disgréis tú thur aighrís suibdeicts.

* * *

Aigh nó a mean thú ios só léasaigh dat thí slíps in this clós, bhears a bíord, and dos not smóc bíocós obh de trobal obh straigeing a meaits. It is só long sins thi did an anasth dea's bhorc dat thí thincs 'manuil leabear' is de neim obh a Portuguis arditeitear.

[Lamhd láftar]

TALES FROM CORKADORKY

Sa tsean-aimsir bhí fear 'na chonuí insa tír seo a dtoirfí Síomus air. Cha robh áit mhaith ige agus is air éigin abhí se abulta e hín a chothú. Siocair fíor-bheagan bídh bheith ige, bhí se i dtólamh corthaí agus cha robh se abulta a chuid graithe a gheanamh.

Bhí se ag goil air gcúl sa chíos agus bhi dóigh bhócht air uilig.

Ach an t-acras an rud ba mheasa abhí ag goilstin air.

'Mura bhfuighe me hoult ar ghíota *bread* go luath,' adubhairt sé leis hín lá, 'creidim go bhfuighe me bás'. Cé bhéadh ag goil a'bhealaigh a' lá sin acht a'diabhal. Chuala idh an lad dubh goidé bhí ráidhte ag Síomus agus rinn se *delay* beag ar a bhealach "Goidé seo tá cearr leat a Shíomuis?" arsa diabhal, adeirse. 'Tá acras air mo *belly*' arsa Síomus 'agus chan fhuair me hoult air giota *bread* le fada an *day*' air seisean, adeirse.

'O bhal', arsa diabhal, adeirse, 'gluais liomsa go dtí a leithid seo d'áit agus gheobha me *feed* mór duid'.

'Creidim go bhfuil a' ceart agad', arsa Síomus, adeirse, agus d'imigh siad frid a' tír, miles agus miles soir agus go leor miles eile siar. Fuaidh siad leofa go dtí gur *reach* síad a leithid seo d'áit. Bhí cró beag ionn agus dubhairt a' díabhal le Síomus gur honuí se sa chró leis hín.

'Tar isteach, a Shíomuis', arsa diabhal, adeirse.

'Creidim go rachaidh', arsa Síomus.

Fuaidh an dís isteach agus leag a' diabhal *feed* mór amach air a tábla.

'Anois a Shíomuis', adeirse, 'tá an oiread nourishment sa *feed* seo,' air seisean, 'nach mbeidh *feed* a dhíth ort go bráth má chaitheann tú é. Bhéara mé duid é air a leithid seo de luach.'

'Creidim go bhfuil a' ceart agad,' arsa Síomus.

Shuidh Síomus síos agus chaith se a' *feed*. N'áir abhi a' *feed* caithte fuair se bás nó bhi nimh curtha ionn ag a' diabhail, Cha robh *feed* eile a dhith air Síomus go bráth agus thug a' diabhal leis go h-Ifreann é. Char chúalaidh mé goidé mar bhí sé ag teanamh ó shoin.

A Péid obh éinsint Thistirí.

O chlé go deis: Séairdint Deoinstin, Sheán O Duíbhir a' Ghleanna, Eamon a' Chnuic, an Spailpín Fánach agus Tadhg a' dá Thaobh.

An obair seo atá breachta sa pictúir, tháinig sí i gcúrsa ins an am go raibh Goidhil in Éirinn beagnach marbh.

Fuarthas scéala go raibh Sur Sheán Buídhe le cuaird do tabhairt ar chríochaibh Fodhla agus le cur faoí i gcaisleán Átha Clíath.

Bhí fhios ag na Gaoidhil gurbé an gnás imeasc daoine úaisle a gcuid bagaiste do chur lá nó mar sin rómpa le giolla i dtreo is go mbeadh gach nidh ár foghnamh fa na gcoinne ar shriochtan dóibh a gceann scríbe.

Lá fuarthas scéala go raibh an bagáiste tagaithe agus bhris an dream beag thuas isteach sa Chaisleán an oidhche sin. Fuaireadar Séardint Deoinstin i gcúl-tseomra ann agus na málaí ina chúram. Chuireadar in-iúl dó go raibh sé i bpeiriceal a scriosta acht 'bhun píp' do leigint as.

Annsin d'ionnsuigheadar na málaí. Cuaidh Sheán ag cuartú agus ag tóraíocht ar a dhícheall.

'Ní fheicim í', ar sé fá dheireadh. 'Nil sí ann.'

'Bí cinnte, bí cinnte,' arsa Eamon a' Chnuic go deifreach.

'Doirt amach an t-iomlán'.

'Níl sí ann,' adeirim.

'Bféidir go gcaitheann sé i gcómhnuidhe í in ionad hata,' arsan Spailpín, 'agus go mbeidh sí leis ar a cheann i mbárach.'

'Maighgod,' ars Sheán Ó Duibhir go scáthmhar, 'ná h-abair liom nach mbeidh radharc ar an gcoróin againn anocht taréis ár ndicheall, taréis a bhfuil déanta againn de chreich agus de bhriscadh tighe.'

'Cluinim duine éigin ag teacht.' arsan Spailpín. 'Iú bhil pae for dios, iú reibeal sbhaighn,' arsa Séirdint Deoínstin.

'Iú siut iúr durtaigh trap,' arsa Tadhg a' dá Taobh. Annsin ós íseal leis féin:

'Geobhaidh mé pighinn maith i mbárach nuair dhórtim na pónairí seo i gcluais Sur Sheáin. Dis ios a béaraigh profitibil géam seiling dé peas'.

'Leits go,' arsa Shean Ó Duibhir. 'Nil coróin na fiú leath-choróin ins na málaí seo.'

Seirdint Deoinstin: Durtaigh disloigheal Reibeal aighris dogs.

(Ecseunt).

POEM in five spenderian stanzas. By Myles na gCopaleen, M.R.I.A. Limited edition of 90,000 copies (of which this is Number 64,284) printed on hand-scuffed antique barley-grained vellum. Each copy signed by author and artist. Entered as second class matter at the Post Office of St Louis. As read and recited by prominent Verse Speakers. 'Here we have something that is alert, sensitive, taut.'—*The Bell.*

My song is concernin'
Three sons of great learnin'
　Binchy and Bergin and Best,
They worked out that riddle
Old Irish and Middle,
　Binchy and Bergin and Best,
They studied far higher
Than ould Kuno Meyer
And fanned up the glimmer
Bequeathéd by Zimmer,
　Binchy and Bergin and Best.

They rose in their night-shift
To write for the Zeitschrift,
　Binchy and Bergin and Best,
They proved they were bosses
At wrastling with glosses,
　Binchy and Bergin and Best,
They made good recensions
Of ancient declensions,
And careful redactions
To their three satisfactions,
　Binchy and Bergin and Best.

They went for a dander
With Charlie Marstrander
Binchy and Bergin and Best,
They added their voices
(Though younger) to Zeuss's,
　Binchy and Bergin and Best.
Stout chase the three gave
Through the Táin for Queen Maeve
And played 'Find the Lady'
With Standish O'Grady,
　Binchy and Bergin and Best.

They sang in the choir
Of the Institute (Higher)
Binchy and Bergin and Best,

And when they saw fit
The former two quit,
   Binchy and Bergin and Best
But the third will remain
To try to regain
At whatever cost
Our paradigms lost,
   Binchy and Bergin and Best.

So, forte con brio
Three cheers for the trio,
   Binchy and Bergin and Best,
These friends of Pokorni
Let's toast in Grand Marnier,
   Binchy and Bergin and Best—
These justly high-rated,
Advanced, educated,
And far from facetious
Three sons of Melesius,
   Binchy and Bergin and Best.

Páipear beag dána iseadh 'AN GLÓR' Ní choshnuigheann sé acnt pighin ruadh agus bíonn sé ar fáil dhá uair sa mhí. Cuir an dhá phighin chaitheann tú air sa mhi i gcompráid leis an scilling glan airgid agus an raol trom luaidhe a iarrtar uait ar 'THE BELL' agus ní fheadar an mbeidh tú sásta.

Ní fheadar nach bhfuighidh tú níos mó adhbhar léightheoireachta (atá inléighte) sa 'GLÓR' ar do dhá phinghin. Ní bhionn an stuif is fearr i gcómhnuí sa chulaith éadaigh atá daor mar adeir Muireadh Ó Buirtín.

I n-eagrán déannach don 'Glór' chuir mé suim agus sonnadh i bpíosa dár teideal 'ERSATZ IRISH LITERATURE'.

Sean-chnámh atá á chognadh ag an údar ann. Ní aontuigheann sé gur ceaduithe 'IRISH LITERATURE' do thabhairt ar aon saothar nach bhfuil i nGaedhilg.

Ní 'IRISH LITERATURE' a bhfuil scríobhtha ag James Joyce adeir-sé, acht tá an teideal sin ion-luaidhte aige i dtaobh 'SÉADHNA' leis an Athair Ó Laoghaire. Ní bhainfidh an té a léigh an dá leabhar tathneamh as an ráiteas sin. Gan bacadh leis an focal 'IRISH', is litríocht den chéad aicme 'ULYSSES' agus ní litríocht ar chor ar bith, olc nó maith, aon líne a scríobh an t-Athair Peadar. Is féidir leat (má tá an léigheann agat rud nach bhfuil) 'ULYSSES' a léigheamh i Seapanais acht ní féidir 'SÉADHNA' a léigheamh fiú i mBéarla.

Gan amhras bhí tábhacht ag baint le 'SÉADHNA' lá den tsaol ar an ghaedhilg atá ann agus bhi glaodhach mór ar an leabhar ag macaibh léighinn. Acht ní chun sochair do macaoimh ná maighdeana a ceaptar fíor-litríocht. Is bocht an dríodar 'SÉADHNA' má mheastar mar litríocht é; mar an gcéadna do beagnach gach leabhar eile a luadhann an scríobhnóir seo sa 'GHLÓR'. Ní thuilleann siad an t-ainm litríocht. Tá a lán aca 'ar an gcúrsa', dí-mholadh nach féidir a sharú.

RUD EILE

Acht i litríocht, cuir i gcás 'AN t-OILEÁNACH', níl aon leabhar (againn-ne nó ag aon treibh eile) i mBéarla ata ion-churtha leis.

Agus ní an 'Chainnt na ndaoine' nó na 'cora deasa cainnte' atá ann a bhronnann uaisleacht litríochta air. Níl aon bhaint ag liteardhachas an leabhair leis an nGaédhilg. Tá an fíor-stuif udarásach daonna ann, tá sé ealadhanta, bogan se an léightheóir chun cumhtha nó áthais do réir mar is rogha leis an údar. Ní h-amhlaidh, faroar le 'SÉADHNA'. Nó le 'NIAMH'.

Más náir dúinn 'ULYSSES' go bhfóiridh Dia orainn. Léirigheann an leabhar san Baile Áth Cliath agus a Mhuintir go h-iomlán agus go h-iongantach agus láthair an t-Saoil mhóir. Minigheann sé eagna, meon agus dearcadh na ndaoine, ath-chruithuigheann sé a saol, a ngrádh, a ndrúis agus fiú a smaointeacha mar bhíodar aca triocha bliain ó shion. Ní raibh príomh-cathair na h-Éireann Gaelach ó togadh í. Ní fhéadfaí 'ULYSSES' a scríobhadh i nGaedhilg ná aon líne de.

Bhéadh leagan Gaedhilge ar 'ULYSSES' comh bréagach le fáilte lucht gaimbín.

Acht 'na dhiaidh sin, deirtear linn nach 'IRISH LITERATURE' an leabhar is luachmhaire a tháinig as Éirinn leis na cianta.

RUD EILE FÓS

Is den tír seo go smior gach siolla dár scríobh an Seóigheach riamh. Tá an blas agus boladh go h-údarásach ar a shaothar tríd síos. Níl an

mothú céadna Gaelach ná blúire de ar shaothar Phádraig Uí Chonaire.
Ní h-amhlaidh go raibh an Seoigheach 'níos Gaelaí' ná an fear eile acht gur
thuig sé a cheárd ó bhun go bárr, go raibh d'éirim agus d'acfuinn agus
d'ealadhain ann a raibh aige ina cheann do chuir i dtuigsint don léightheóir
agus ni beag sin.

Agus féach an 'CROCK OF GOLD' le James Stephens. Níor scríobhadh
riamh (agus ní scríobhfar ní dóigh liom) aon leabhar i nGaedhilg atá
leath comh Gaedhleach leis. Tá Gaelachas sa leabhar san atá níos Gaelaí
'ná an Ghaedhlig.féin.

Agus tá greann thar na beartaibh ann, rud nach bhfuil le faghail
thoir ná thiar i 'Litríocht na Gaedhilge'.

Acht ní 'IRISH LITERATURE' an leabhar aoibhinn seo. Bféidir gur 'ENGLISH
LITERATURE' é.

FOCAL SCUIR

Tuigtear an méid seo. Ní chumann ná ní chruthuigheann litríocht an
saol acht leanann sí é. Beidh litríocht náisiúnta na h-Éireann i nGaedhilg
amháin ní h-eadh an lá ar a bhfuil an Ghaedhilg á labhairt airís go
forleathan ar fúd na tíre, acht céad bliain, bféidir, taréis an lae sin. Ní ar
indiú, ná amáireach, atá an deaghúdar ag féachaint, acht indé. An fhad
go mbíonn Gaedhilg agus Béarla in Éirinn againn is dual dúinn litríocht
sa dá theangaidh.

Ní fiú mórán go fóill litríocht na nua-Gaedhilge. Ghoid Sasana a lán
neithe maithe uainn—an Ghaedhilg féin.

Faire nach dtabharfamuid anois mar féirin do Shasana an rud beag
amháin ealadhna atá nua-dhéanta againn, ár litríocht ghall-Ghaelach. Is
beag atá againn in a h-éaghmuis.

Tugann 'An Glór' 'Ersatz Irish Literature' ar ár saothar liteardha i
mBéarla cuid den 'Nua—Litríocht ata againn i Gaedhilg ba mhaith an
teideal di 'Erse-atz Irish Literature' dar liomsa.

Do réir an fhoclóra 'PIARÓID' an Deaghghaoidhilg ar 'parrot' acht mise
nár ghéill riamh do dhaoine nach aithnid dhom i gcúrsaí gramadaighe ná
briathrachais, ní ghlacfaidh mé le 'Piaróid'. Is fearr liom pearat. Tráth i
n-Éirinn bhí Teach Mór i gceanntar áirithe agus bhí buic uaisle gallda 'na
gcomhnuide ann. Bhí mná caola buidhe aca ann agus iad amuigh ag
iascaireacht, ag ridireacht ar muin capaill, ag seilg, ag lámhach agus ag
déanamh gach ní is dual do bhean uasal atá 'Conndae'. Bhí na fir uaisle ar
an déanamh céadhna acht amháin gur chaitheadar a lán ama i bhfeighil

agus i mbun Snúcoir. Bhíodar go léir eadar fearaibh agus peatai go galánta thoití-toití agus bhí na tuaithe urramach dóibh.

Bhí pearat uasal as an t-Sín ag na daoine móra so sa Teach Mhór agus bhí deis urlabhra bronnta ag Dia ar an bpearat. Ní nach ró-iongnadh, labhair sé le guth a mhaighistir. Lá amhán, d'eírig leis an bpearat ealodh as a bhosca. Bhí fuinneóg an t-seomra ar oscailt agus amach leis an chréatúr Síneach ag folamhain go ciotach cigilteach i measg na gcraobh amuigh.

DARA LEATH AN SCÉIL

Taréis tamaill don éan ag taisteal san aer uachtarach, tháinig sé ar bhothán shuarach abhí i seilbh sliocht Éremon agus Éber—Padaí bocht éigin a bhí mar sclábhuidhe ar Thailte an Tighe Mhóir ar phighin sa lá.

Tháinig an pearat anuas ar dhíon an bhotháin agus shuidh annsin i n-áirde agus é ag leigint an tuirse as taréis a thurais.

Tháinig an fear fiadhain Padaí amach le na dreancaidi a chraitheadh dá chuid 'éadaigh' agus bhraith sé an créatúr allmhordha eadrocht ar mhullach a thíghe, sómpla iongantach i bfuirm éin le dathanna go léir na gréine 'na ruball.

Ghlac an scológ bocht íontas dá leithéid seo agus ghlaodh ar a theaglach eadar bean agus fiche paiste teacht ag breathnú an tsamhla neamhshaolta. Annsin smaoinigh sé go raibh tairbhe aige le fáil acht breith ar an rud agus b'fhéidir é dhiol le lucht an tíghe mhóir.

Ní túisce an obair sin beartuithe aige ná é 'na bun go dioghrasach. Le mórán duaidh chuaidh se in áirde ar mhullach a thighe agus bhog go faichilleach i dtreo an phearait.

Níor chorruigh an t-éan iar-ráidhte seo. Go h-obann rug Padaí greim ar an gcois bhig bhuidhe agus gan mhoill fuair sé sruth cainnte i gcanamhain uasal an Tighe Mhóir.

'How daeh you, Sir: How daeh you?

'Oi big yer pardon sor' arsa Padaí go scannruithe 'Oi tought you was a burd. Ackscoos me, Sor, yer honour'.

SMAOINTE

Tá litríocht na Gaedhilge agus gach litríocht eile ar a bhfuil eolas ar bith agam lán de stuif molta croidhiúil i dtaobh éanacha an aeir. Ní féidir go leor a rádh ar mhaithe leis na créathúirí beaga clúmhacha abhíonn ag cantain agus ag ceileabhar agus ag píobarnaigh i measg na gcraobh.

Ní cuala, a luin Doire an Chairn, ceol ba bhinne ná do cheol is tú fa
bhun do nid.

Fáilte do éan is binne ar chraoibh; A Bhunnáin bhuidhe, sé mo leán do
luighe agus mar sin de go bruinne an bhrátha.

Aoinne a mheabhruigheas an cogadh so atá ar siubhal agus an scrios
fuilteach atá a dheanamh gach lá tuigfidh sé gur na h-éanacha atá cionntach
80 sa chéad ann.

Gan amhras, is dual achrann don duine. Bíodh na h-éanacha ann nó as,
bheadh cogadh de chineal éigin ar siubhal againn-ne na daoine. Acht ní
bheadh an t-ár uathbhásach agus an léirscrios millteanach is aithnid comh
maith dúinn indiu indéanta ar chaoi ar bith meireach na h-eitileáin. Agus
ni bheadh eitileán againn go deo meireach na h-éanacha.

An chéad fear riamh a bhraith éan ag sciordadh go glan glic tríd an
aer, ag treasnú gach baic agus toirmisc tíre, thainic éad air. Is le neamhf-
honn taréis an lae sin a thaisteal sé an domhan ar a chosa troma toirseacha
do-bogtha. Bhí an síol curtha. Leis na mílte bliain bheadh an gam daonna
ag tnúth le caoi éigin gluaiste ar fud na spéire agus bheadh na h-éanacha
go deo á ghriogadh leis an ghaois aerdha a bhí aca féin ó dhúthchas.

Orainne na linne seo ata an mí-ádh go bhfuil maighstreacht fálta againn
ar an aer níos fearr ná mar bhí riamh ag na gobadáin. Beidh cnumha á ithe
againn fós!

*   *   *

Seadh, 'ROSS' iseadh an ghearmáinis ar 'capall' Féach an t-seanfhocal
úd—'Ní dhéanfaidh an saol capall (Ross) d'asal. 'cé soir du mois de ianbh-
hier, 1882 le promenoir des Foilies Bergere regorgeait de monde 'Il était
dies heures et demie lá premiere partie du programme bhenait de finir sur
un chatoiant ballet . . .'

Slánabhaile Eh? Kod ay soh?

Mise: Saothar beag stairiúil. An chéad uair riamh ó cruthuigheadh an
domhan a cuireadh Frainncis sa chló Ghaelach.

Slánabhaile: Ock Kunahayv?

Mise: Dochum neartuighthe clú Mhílis ar ghliocas agus dochum onóra
na h-Éireann agus na Frainnce, dhá thír atá gaolta agus comhchairdiúil
maidir le suim sa bhantracht, spéis i ndigh, clisteacht cainnte, fallsacht,
bitheamhnachas agus ansmacht.

Slánabaile: Tigim. Guramahagut.

Ceist: Conus mar d'éirigh le James Joyce le linn dó comhnuidhe agus
buan-mhaireachtaint do dhéanamh i ríocht na Frainnce?

Freagra: D'éirigh le Séamus go Seoighe.

Ceist: Agus conus mar saothraig sé a choid?

Freagra: Le Uilís a mhallacha.

Ceist: Cad a d'ól sé?

Freagra: Chartreuse.

Ceist: Agus cad a bhí uime mar éadach ar na balaidh iochtaracha?

Freagra: Sár-triubhais.

Ceist: An raibh vie mhaith aige sa Fhrainnc taréis clú do bheith buaidhte aige?

Freagra: Vie.

Ceist: An raibh sé seal i Vichy?

Freagra: Vichy.

Seadh, Seadh, Seadh.

Amannai léighim filíocht. Caitheann sí aimsear agus níl sí comh costasach le pórtar, pictuirí potaiocht, cúl-chainnt, ithe-feola, suibaloidhche, cúl-éisteacht Radio, curadóireacht, gabháil-muisice, bainisteoireacht bainnce, teachtachas Dála, lon-éisteacht, dochtúireacht, pósadh, nó pé gairm-bheatha nó caitheamh-aimsire eile atá ar domhan.

An dán úd ar an Impire Alacsandar atá fágtha againn ag an láimh anaithnid, tá an rann so ann:

'Do bí', arsan treas ughdar glic,

'An bith indé ag mac Philip;

Indiu aige nochan fhuil.

Acht seacht dtroigthe do thalmhain'

Nuair léigheas sin, smaoinigheas ar Landless Men na linne seo. An t-órdú contráilte atá ortha go fíor. Le linn a mbeo bíonn seacht dtroighthe de talmhain aca—oiread is dheanfas ionad tighe. Teacht lá a mbás agus a n-adhlactha, is leo an domhan uile. Táid rann-pháirteach sá chré go léir. Is mar an gcéadna domhan agus duine. Roinn na Talmhan is teideal don aireacht rialtais atá freagarthach agus 'roinn' an focal oparataibh i dtuairim na Landless Men. Feirmeóir ar bith a chastar ort, níl ag teastáil uaidh acht feirm mhór.

AN FHIRINNE SHEARBH

Le na thaisbeáint an rian gheár atá fágtha ag na Scannáin Aimeiriceanacha ar inntin ar nDaoine, éist le seo. Bhíos ar tram an lá fa dheireadh agus chúamair thar teach an Árd-Aighne (nó Attorney General).

Bhí beirt fhear oilte deas-labhartha ar mo chúl. 'Do you see that house' arsa fhearr amháin 'that's where the District Attorney lives."

* * *

AN SCÉAL

Ag seo síos fáisnéis shuimiúil atá fálta agam ón Mhean-oirthear, mar a bhfuiltear na Tomáis, agus na Gearoidíní ag cogaint agus ag cogaíocht (le fada an lá) (mar deirtear ins na clísí). Acht ar dtús tuig go soiléir nach mbeadh a leithéid seo ceaduithe i mBéarla.

Bhí saighdiuir airithe ann darb ainim Peadar agus gidh go raibh an t-éadach Sacsanach ar a dhruim, bhí sé fior-ghaelach 'na chroidhe istig agus is i gCorchaig a chonnaic sé solus an lae i dtosach.

Bhí Peadar agus a chomraidí ar a gcomh-chosaint i gcampa i lár an fhásaigh gainnmhe agus ní raibh faic le déanamh aca acht fuireach ann go foighdeach go dtí go gcuirfí tús ar fuilteachas agus achrann.

Acht bhí an Peadar so mí-cheádfach; niorbh ghnás aige bheith díomhaoin agus níor thaithnig an saol socair suaimhneach so leis (in-aochor) (ná ar chor ar bith).

Bhí nós aige dá bhrigh sin ceamal a fháil agus ealodh amach i ndorchadas na h-oidhche as an gcampa agus lá nó dhó a chaitheamh ag fánaíocht ar fud an fhásaigh ag faire ar na h-éanacha, an aimsir nó aon ní eile abhí ion-fhairithe.

Cúis agallmha agus magaidh ag na saighduirí eile an nós eagsúil seo a bhí ag Peadar agus nuair tháinic an scéal ar eolas lucht ceannais an champa, dubhradar go neamh-bhalbh le Peadar nach raibh an seachrán-oidhche seo ceaduithe agus go raibh air fanacht sa champa agus a dhualgaisí míleata do chóm-líonadh mar bhí a dhéanamh ag cách eile.

TUILLEAMH

Acht ní fhéadfadh Peadar an mian mire seo do smachtú. Amach leis airís ar an gceamal an chéad oidhche eile. D'éirigh leis teacht arais airís slán acht an chéad uair eile a chuaidh sé amach, bhí sé seachtain as baile. Ar bhfilleadh do gabhadh é ag geata an champa, tugadh é i láthair na cúirte míleata agus fuair sé mí sa charcair.

Acht taréis tamaillín tionoladh dáil-chómhairle ag lucht ceannais an airm agus shocruigheadar fear do chur amach le spideoireacht do dheanamh ar an tír agus eolas do bhailiú ar suidhe agus ordú na nGearmánach.

Chuimnigh Oifigeach éigin ar Pheadar agus d' aontuigheadar go léir nach raibh éinne eile sa champa comh h-oilte ar a leithéid sin d'obair. Tugadh i láthair na cómhairle é agus mínígheadh a dhualgaisí dhó. Annsin cuireadh ar mhuin cheamail mhaith é, tugadh gléas mors-radio dhó le na chuid teachtaireachtaí do chur abaile agus scaoileadh amach an geata é. Cailleadh Peadar as amharc ar imeall na spéire.

TUILLEAMH EILE

Bhí súil ag lucht an champa go gcluinfeadh siad scéala ón bhfánaí taréis trí lá nó mar sin acht ní raibh faic acht fíorchiúnas le clos ar an radio. D'imthigh lá agus lá eile.

D'imtigh seachtain gan aon scéala.

D'imtigh dhá lá eile agus fágadh lucht an champa beagnach briste.

Acht go mall trathóna, núair is lugha bhí coinne leis, bhíog an radio agus tháinic da fhocal Beárla uaidh: -

'ROMAL CEAPTUIRD'

Rith an nuaidheacht iongantach timpeall an champa le luas teinntrighe. Thuit na buic mhóra beagnach i laige.

Annsain cuireadh na gunnaí móra agus na h-innil cogaidh i dtreo agus i n-ordú a ngluaiseachta. Dubhradh le gach fear bheith ollamh le mairseáil leis an gníomh mhór so do dhaingniú agus do chur i gcrích agus cromadh ar bheith ag éisteacht oidhche agus lá ag dúil go dtiochfadh sceála eile ón Radio. Acht ní tháinig. D'fhan an maisín balbh. Chuaidh lá tart agus lá eile. D'imthigh seachtain, bhí na h-oifigí anois beagnach ag rinnce le neart feirge agus cíocrais. Annsin go h-obann, labhair an Radió airís:

'Last . . . mesids . . . siúd thábh . . . red 'ceamal ruptiúrd'.

*　*　*

SEAM ÓLD DEÓC

Loc: Bothán ar Bhán-chnuic Éireann ó.

Am: An t-am go raibh Gaoidhil i nÉirinn beo.

Pearsain i láthair: Sur Tharbhaigh Baigineal, an óifisear obh de Cbhín, in ful réidiméinteals; Tadhg agus Taidhgín; Éamon a' Chnuic; Seán Ó Duibhir a' Ghleanna; Séadna; agus Bran.

Sur Tharbhaigh: Aigh airéist iú, Éadbhart Hill, in de néam obh de Cbhín! Aigh bhas reidhding baigh—

Bran: Bhuf, bhuf!

Sur Tharbhaigh: Damhn, iú réibeal cur! Aigh bhas reidhding baigh ond théard iú méic fbhait samhndad leidhc a seidisius spíts. Thú ios dios péarson iú méintiond Shawn Brogue?

Seán Ó Duibhir: Cad é seo atá á rádh aige inonimadeel?

Éamon a' Chnuic: Is follus gur chualaidh an phiast mise ag aithris mo chuid filíochta. "Sasanaigh do réabfainn mar do réabfainn sean-bhróg."

Taidhgín: Thí bhas tócuing abamht boots, Sur.

Sur Tharbhaigh: Iú cean téil dat tú de Diuids. Éabharaighbodaigh thiar ios undar airéist. Aigh bhil títs iú tú bí dioslóigheal. Cbhuic meairts! (Ecseunt go dubhach.)

LITERALLY FROM THE IRISH

I was a day in Dingle and Paddy James, my sister's man, in company with me and us in the direction of each other in the running of the day. A man he was that would not have a glass of whiskey long between the hands, or a pint of black porter either, without shooting them backwards; but he got no sweet taste ever on the one he would buy himself, and great would be the pleasure with him that another man should nudge him in the back to ask him to have one with him.

*   *   *

A time after that my brother Paddy moved towards me from being over there in Ameriky. There was great surprise on me he is coming from being over there the second time, because the two sons who were at him were strong hefty ones at that time; and my opinion was that they were on the pig's back to be over there at all. On my seeing my brother on his arrival, there was no get-up on him—as would appear to any person who threw an opinion with him—save that it was in the woods he had spent his years yonder. There was no cloth on him, there was no shape on his person itself, there was not a dun-coloured penny in his pocket, and it was two sisters to him yonder who had sent him across at their own expense.

*   *   *

We had easy times then for a while, and the year that was in it, she was a fine quiet one. A lot of fish were being brought in by the big boats. The three boats were full to the tops, a day. Owing to the force of two men— my father and Patrick—being at us, there was a fine sight of it in the cabin. That was the first day of mine, I think, completely separated from being a mollycoddle, because a hard straining was taken out of my sides pulling the fish to the house with me in a bag down beyant on my back. A thousand fish had each single man on that particular day. That left two thousand to us. My father said that I had brought a thousand and more of them home.

—From 'An tOileánach', by Tomas Ó Criomhthain.

*   *   *

THE IRISH lexicographer Dinneen, considered *in vacuo* is, heaven knows, funny enough. He just keeps standing on his head, denying stoutly that *piléar* means bullet and asserting that it means 'an inert thing or person'. Nothing stumps him. He will promise the sun moon and stars to anybody who will catch him out. And well he may. Just *take* the sun, moon and stars for a moment. Sun, you say, is *grian*. Not at all. Dinneen shouts that *grian* means 'the bottom (of a lake, well)'. You are a bit nettled and mutter that, anyway, *gealach* means moon. Wrong again. *Gealach* means 'the white circle in a slice of a half-boiled potato, turnip, etc.' In a bored voice he adds that *réalta* (of course) means 'a mark on the forehead of a beast'. Most remarkable man. Eclectic I think is the word.

That, of course, is why I no longer write Irish. No damn fear. I didn't come down in the last shower. Call me a bit fastidious if you like but I like to have some idea of what I'm writing. Libel, you know. One must be careful. If I write in Irish what I conceive to be 'Last Tuesday was very wet,' I like to feel reasonably sure that what I've written does not in fact mean 'Mr So-and-So is a thief and a drunkard.'

Do I exaggerate? Not at all. For fun let's look for a moment at a bit of somebody else's Irish. One picks up that little print *An Glór* dated the 22nd January. (*Glór*, of course, just means 'noise'—they are hinting there at the funny word 'noisepaper', I'll go bail.) They have a few pars on the back page about the concert that was got up in the Capitol a few Sundays ago. Here's how they open up:

Is rud nuadh ar fad cuirm cheoil siansach (symphony) a bheith ar siubhal in éinfheacht le cór Gaedhealach . . .

Note first of all the cautious gloss 'symphony'. They half suspect the danger. But too late. Dinneen is already roaring at us. Let's see just what all that Irish really means.

First, *rud. Rud* means 'concern, sympathy, anxiety, sorrow'. *Nuadh* means 'act of strengthening, intensifying'. It also means 'strength'. '*Fad*' just means 'longitude'. Then we come to *cuirm*. The lexicographer is only warming up now. In his frightfully superior voice he explains that *cuirm* means 'a kind of ale formerly used by the Irish; drink in general; a feast or banquet'. He assigns absolutely no other meaning to the word. *Ceol* means 'activity, vigour, sprightliness'. *Siansach* (despite the gloss) means 'wise, sensible'. The next word is *siubhal* and the crafty master messes up everything with vindictive skill when he announces that this word means 'a measure in music between fast and slow (*moderato*)'. The cuteness of this move is beyond belief. He won't allow that *ceol* has anything to do with music, but insists that *siubhal* has. '*In éinfheacht*' means 'at once' and '*cór Gaedhealach*' means 'an unsophisticated troop'.

Now let's see what we have. Dinneen says the passage quoted has the following meaning:

'It is longitudinally a strong anxiety that a wise and vigorous ancient Irish ale should be in *moderato* time at once with an unsophisticated troop.'

I infer that the writer (I know the type well) meant to say this:

'It is entirely a new thing that a symphony concert should be held in conjunction with a Gaelic choir.'

Mr Charles Lynch is announced as giving *dreas ceoil*, 'a sprightly bramble'. He is described as a *pianadóir*, Dinneen says *pianadóir* means (exclusively) 'a punisher, a tormentor'. Granted that we're not all fond of music, isn't that a bit . . . hard? And brambles!

What a man.

* * *

THE GAELIC

A LADY lecturing recently on the Irish language drew attention to the fact (I mentioned it myself as long ago as 1925) that, while the average English speaker gets along with a mere 400 words, the Irish-speaking peasant uses 4,000. Considering what most English speakers can achieve with their tiny fund of noises, it is a nice speculation to what extremity one would be reduced if one were locked up for a day with an Irish-speaking bore and bereft of all means of committing murder or suicide.

My point, however, is this. The 400/4,000 ration is fallacious; 400/400,000 would be more like it. There is scarcely a single word in the Irish (barring, possibly, *Sasanach*) that is simple and explicit. Apart from words with endless shades of cognate meaning, there are many with so complete a spectrum of graduated ambiguity that each of them can be made to express two directly contrary meanings, as well as a plethora of intermediate concepts that have no bearing on either. And all this strictly within the linguistic field. Superimpose on all that the miasma of ironic usage, poetic licence, oxymoron, plamás, Celtic evasion, Irish bullery and Paddy Whackery, and it a safe bet that you will find yourself very far from home. Here is an example copied from Dinneen and from more authentic sources known only to my little self:

Cur, g. *curtha* and cuirthe, m.—act of putting, sending, sowing, raining, discussing, burying, vomiting, hammering into the ground, throwing through the air, rejecting, shooting, the setting or clamp in a rick of turf, selling, addressing, the crown of cast-iron buttons which have been made bright by contact with cliff-faces, the stench of congealing badger's suet, the luminance of glue-lice, a noise made in an empty house by an un-authorised person, a heron's boil, a leprachaun's denture, a sheep-biscuit, the act of inflating hare's offal with a bicycle pump, a leak in a spirit level, the whine of a sewage farm windmill, a corncrake's clapper, the scum on the eye of a senile ram, a dustman's dumpling, a beetle's faggot, the act of loading every rift with ore, a dumb man's curse, a blasket, a 'kur', a fiddler's occupational disease, a fairy godmother's father, a hawk's vertigo, the art of predicting past events, a wooden coat, a custard-mincer, a blue-bottle's 'farm', a gravy flask, a timber-mine, a toy craw, a porridge-mill, a fair-day donnybrook with nothing barred, a stoat's stomach-pump, a broken—

But what is the use? One could go on and on without reaching anywhere in particular.

Your paltry English speaker apprehends sea-going craft through the infantile cognition which merely distinguishes the small from the big. If it's small, it's a boat, and if it's big it's a ship. In his great book *An tOileánach*, however, the uneducated Tomás Ó Criomhthain uses, perhaps, a dozen words to convey the concept of varying super-marinity—*árthrach long*, *soitheach*, *bád*, *naomhóg*, *bád raice*, *galbhád*, *púcán* and whatever you are having yourself.

The plight of the English speaker with his wretched box of 400 vocal beads may be imagined when I say that a really good Irish speaker would blurt out the whole 400 in one cosmic grunt. In Donegal there are native speakers who know so many million words that it is a matter of pride with them never to use the same word twice in a life-time. Their life (not to say their language) becomes very complex at the century mark; but there you are.

SLIGHE AN ALLUIS

Tá litir fághalta agam o Muilte Farannáin adeir gur mithid go gcuirfí ar fagháil don lucht léighte, blúire eile den eolus atá in mo fhoclóir príobháideach féin (agus nách bhfuil in-aon foclóir eile). Seo thíos a bhfuil le leigheamh ar leathnach a 115.

Buachaill báire—a follower of Shels, a ball-faced youth, a moulder of suet balls.

Buachaill cúinne—a corner boy, a local boy who has turned the corner, a tool used by an unscrupulous wheat cartel.

Buachaill árd—a tallboy, one who tells tall stories, a youth addicted to looking over walls.

Buachaill Mara—a buoy, a sea scout.

Buachaill anbhruithe—a broth of a boy, a whey-face, a gruel complexioned wastling.

Buachaill Oidhche—an owl.

Buachaill Maidne—a peep o'day boy, a milkman's nark, a hangover (facetious).

Buachaill Gunna—a garage 'MEXICAN' or greaser, a rowdy, a 'Son of a gun', a card, a terrible man.

Buachaill Siamsa—a play-boy, a waster, a tap-dancer, a jazzer, a George Raft.

Buachaill Soic—a nosey parker, a muzzle faced meddler, a van driver's butty who has custody of the horse's nosebag.

Buachaill Mála—a young Commercial Traveller, a young bag-eyed inebriate, a convict, a cat keeper, a 'spook' who stands on the fringe of strangers' billiard games and retrieves the balls from the pockets, *a 'malley-boy'*, a bag snatcher, a wearer of plus-fours, a porter, a 'bags'.

* * *

FEACHTAR leat go beacht, a anam a liquoiuor, dánta grádha et corpus gean-fhilíocht fear Erenn (sraith moron nach maireann, farrier) et taréis infhiúchta, measta agus meaidhte na binnbhairdne sin duit, fíor go mbeidh deirhbiú agaibh, a léathóir, ar ar bhaineadar ár amateurs sinnseardha de thaithneamh, de shult et de chaitheamh—(cailín)—aimsire as an mbantracht. *Binn a mbriathra, gasta a nglór, aicme narab mór mo bháidh; a gcáineadh is mairg nár loc; mairg adeir olc ris na mnáibh!* Ita cecinit Gearóid Iarla, acht go deimhin is 6 baramhail an Mhíleasa úi cCopúláin gur ag faithbheadh ocus ag dénamh fonamhaide do bhí fitz fileata ngearailt an tan do grafadh ris an dréacht neaphróis odpertomor. Thamhéibhir bí deat as iot mé, iot ios ab-bhíos deait hí bheais neat iondifirint tú de féar séacs agus dearbhaimíd-ne (aos gCoupling) gurbh é a dhála-sa dála gacha bhaird có-aimseardha leis (et dála gacha bháird & beard & bird & bored & buyer & byre & Board & Bart & Bert & bear & Baer & beered & Byron noch aut olim in Ierne vixit). Ciodh trácht, a liuqcgrwthóir a anamchara, nach iongantach (ar fad) a annamhaighe is ainmnítear nó a sloinntear i rannaibh riartha rachtmhara roscacha ár sinnsear (rogers) adhbhar a suime teinntrighe? Or let me put it this way (I pray you): whereas we angle-irons, pardon me anglo-irish cry woo is Sylvier wot is she, or Lesbia hat a beaming i or Oh my poor Nellie Grey, níorbh'in gnás an tsein-fhile ghaedhealaigh: fear cúramach cigilteach discréideach abhi ann a thuig gur ró-mhaith an dídean an dorchadas agus nach mbíonn an ráth acht mar a mbíonn an rún. Ba leisg leis dá bhrigh sin ainm, sloinneadh nó seoladh (nó fiú uimhir telefón—) a sheirce do scéitheadh nó do nochtadh—agus an tan dar leis go raibh sé riachtanach lideadh a thabhairt cé in Eirinn í agus gan aon dul-as aige, é sin do dhein sé sa chaoi go mbeadh sé deacair ag an gcoitchiantacht a h-aithint nec possint curiosi fascinare mala lingua. Agus é seo go léir fá ndear a leithéid seo d'fhilíocht, mairg an díol:

> Coll is nion go nua-ghloine,
> Is dá choll ar n-a gceangal,
> Ruis is coll go cruadhshnigthe,
> Ainm na mná so dam mealladh.

Seadh faith. Nó an amhlaidh go raibh an beautiful blonde spy beo in Eirinn sa tsean-aimsir (nó sa blackandtan-aimsir). Agent XP2. Please contact WR6, await instructions Ballyhickey. YSAKBN-576 will contact you Friday, please dress as bishop.

> Cuid do dheireadh báid ós tuinn
> Is seacht gcuill ar nach bid cna,
> An t-ainm fá bhfuilim i mbroid;
> Is aon do sgoil bheanfas as.
> Smólach bheag agus lon dubh,
> Agus naoi gcoill 'na gcruth féin,
> Ainm na mná dá dtugas grádh,
> Tré bhfuilim do ghnáth i bpéin.

Agus mar sin de. Acht cheana, tá teoiric agam féin maidir leis an ngean-fhilíocht seo go léir agus nílim ró-chinnte an raib cur-sios agam uirthi cheana. A leithéid seo—go bhfuil de dheacracht is de chastacht ins na meadarachtaí Gaedhilge gur cabhair ó Dhia don fhile an focal *bean* toisc go bhfuil fuaimeanna éagsúla aige do réir mar is tuiseal de .i. *bean, mná, mnaoi, ban*; agus dá bhrí sin go gcuireann na fili síos comh minic ar na mnáibh toisc an triall ceapadóireachta bheith níos fusa.

Mo chuidse den adhbhar, measaim gur chóir frainncis agus gaedhilg a mheascadh agus fille-eacht a thabhairt ar an obair seo go léir.

LAST WEEK we had a rather stern address over here ———→* regarding the inadmissibility of the Irish language and although it is almost a *gaffe* for anybody who is qualified to speak on this subject to express opinions on it in the public prints, I feel I must speak out; otherwise there is the danger that the lying rumour will be spread by my enemies that I am silent

* i.e., in the editorial columns of the *Irish Times*.

because once again money has changed hands. (It cannot be too often repeated that I am not for sale. I was bought in 1921 and the transaction was final and conclusive.)

In my lordship's view the movement to revive the Irish language should be persisted in. I hold that it is fallacious to offer the Irish people a simple choice between slums and Gaelic. (Indeed, it is hardly an adult attitude and is known in hibernian philosophy as the *Ignoratio Mac Glinchy*.) If this doctrine of bread alone were followed, we would have (for one thing) to divert the revenues of Trinity College to slum clearance, and Alton and I simply will not have this. The horrible charge is made that Mr de Valera is spending half a million a year on reviving Irish. I may be a wild paddy but I take the view that the free expenditure of public money on a cultural pursuit is one of the few boasts this country can make. Whether we get value for all the money spent on Irish, higher learning and on our university establishments is one question but that we spend liberally on these things is to our credit and when the great nations of the earth (whose civilisations we are so often asked to admire) are spending up to £100,000,000 (roughly) per day on destruction, it is surely no shame for our humble community of peasants to spend about £2,000 per day on trying to revive a language. It is the more urbane occupation. And what is half a million in relation to slum clearance? Faith now, could we be honest enough (for one moment) to admit to ourselves (in our heart of hearts) that there is another sort of Irish, and forced down people's throats, too, and that we spend enough on it every year to re-build all Dublin.

Irish has an intrinsic significance which (naturally enough) must be unknown to those who condemn the language. It provides through its literature and dialects a great field for the pursuit of problems philological, historical and ethnological, an activity agreeable to all men of education and good-will. Moreover, the language itself is ingratiating by reason of its remoteness from European tongues and moulds of thought, its precision, elegance and capacity for the subtler literary nuances; it attracts even by its surpassing difficulty, for scarcely anybody living today can write or speak Irish correctly and exactly in the fashion of 300 years ago (and it may have been noticed that the one person qualified to attempt the feat has been too tired to try for the past two or three weeks). True Irish prose has a steely latinistic line that does not exist in the fragmented English patois. Here is a literal translation of a letter addressed by Hugh O'Neill to a hostile captain:—

'Our blessing to ye, O Mac Coghlin: we received your letter and what we understand from her is that what you are at the doing of is but sweetness of word and spinning out of time. For our part of the subject, whatever person is not with us and will not wear himself out in the interest of justice, that person we understand to be a person against us. For that reason, in each place in which ye do your own good, pray do also our ill to the fullest extent ye can and we will do your ill to the absolute utmost of our ability, with God's will. We being at Knockdoney Hill, 6 februarii, 1600.'

That seems to me to be an exceptional achievement in the sphere of written nastiness and the original exudes the charm attaching to all instances of complete precision in the use of words.

There is probably no basis at all for the theory that a people cannot preserve a separate national entity without a distinct language but it is beyond dispute that Irish enshrines the national ethos and in a subtle way Irish persists very vigorously in English. In advocating the preservation of Irish culture, it is not to be inferred *that this culture* is superior to the English or any other but simply that certain Irish modes are *more comfortable and suitable* for Irish people; otherwise these modes simply would not exist. It is therefore dangerous to discourage the use of Irish because the revival movement, even if completely ineffective, is a valuable preservative of certain native virtues and it is worth remembering that if Irish were to die completely, the standard of English here, both in the spoken and written word, would sink to a level probably as low as that obtaining in England and it would stop there only because it could go no lower. Not even the Editor of the *Irish Times* is an authority on the hidden wells which sustain the ageless western Irishman, and cannot have considered the vast ethnogenic problems inherent in a proposal to deprive him of one of his essential chattels. I admire Liverpool but if Cork is to become another Liverpool by reason of stupid admiration for the least worthy things in the English civilisation, then I can only say that the Corkmen will not live there any more, the mysterious language they speak, which is not Irish and certainly not English will be heard no more, and a race of harmless, charming and amusing people will have been extirpated.

There is another aspect to this question. Even if Irish had no value at all, the whole bustle of reviving it, the rows, the antagonisms, and the clashes surrounding the revival are interesting and amusing. There is a profusion of unconscious humour on both sides. The solemn humbugs who pronounce weightily on the Irish language while knowing absolutely nothing about it I hold to be no less valuable than monetary reformers in the business of entertaining the nation. The lads who believe that in slip-jigs we have a national prophylaxis make life less stark. And the public-spirited parties who write letters to the papers in illiterate English expressing concern at the harm the revival movement is doing to the standard of education generally are also of clownish significance. They all combine to make colour and to amuse.

To one and all I would say this, my hand upon my heart: Go your ways build and take down, capture and set free, gather in conclave and debate ... but ... do not tamper with the Irishman, touch not his sacred belongings, be solicitous that thy tongue contemneth not the smallest thing he may prize or the least thing he may love. For he is unique; if you kill him he cannot be replaced, and the world is poorer.

* * *

THE OLD BONE!

Sooner or later one comes back to this question of 'compulsory Irish' and from it that is not a long way off to the other question of teaching through the medium of Irish. It has been held that the teaching of 'subjects' other than fishing not through Irish but through the medium of Irish leads to a generation 'illiterate in two languages' and this venerable joke is expected to make us smile bitterly. Upon all this I claim to have an objective view inasmuch as I am an old Westminster man and I still prize the old battered Greek grammar that was placed in my infant hands in the old school. It was rather different with us English, I mean. One's parent—persons, when one was 'born' entered one for the old school—the idea being that one should learn to fight that odd angular hereditament, one's corner. Incidentally, as it were, one became educated—viz., one 'learnt' Greek. This grammar of mine has an amusing preface beginning: *ALTERVM jam faeculum ad finem vergit, cum vir pietate et doctrina praestans, Edwardus Grantus* ... and then, anti-climax ... *scholae regiae Weftmonafterienfis moderator* ... *Graecam grammaticam in ufam scholae ejufdem publicavit* ... (Terrible men for lifping in those days!) But anyway this old boy (I think he must have been one of the first University Grants before the County Councils came along) goes on to say *Graecae linguae fpicilegium prae modeftia appellare ipfi placuit* ... (*Prae modeftia*, eh?) I admit I never got beyond the first page of that grammar—

Graecae grammaticae, I remember it said, *quattuor funt partes: orthographia, etymologia, fyntaxis et profodia* . . .

No doubt you see what I'm getting at. It's not so much that you have to be got out of your mother's way for a few years before you go up to Oxford; the point is that education means H.M. Humanities, i.e. one learns Greek and the grammar is in Latin because, of course, one already knows Latin. Our Irish educationalists, in reviving Irish, are therefore proceeding in a well-tried classical tradition.

Bores

CHRISTMAS come and gone, eh? Let's associate for the moment a few banalities and bores associated with the season.

Easily first is the person, usually a woman, who says: 'Christmas? Do you know I wish it was over.'

Next possibly is the person who says:

'Christmas? Do you know, I do always think it is a sad time.'

Next:

'Well well. Another Christmas! The way time flies is somethin' shockin'.' And next?

'Do you know, the best Christmas I ever had was in Morocco. There was a crowd of us on the boat—I hadn't been married more than a week at the time—and we dropped anchor at Algiers. The first thing we see is . . .'

Then there is the gambit:

'Do you know the hardest day in the year to get through?'

'I don't. What?'

'Christmas Day.'

Then there are the alternative commentaries, each proffered with the utmost earnestness:

'Do you know what it is, I never seen a quieter Christmas.'

'I'll tell you wan thing about this Christmas. It was the fiercest Christmas I ever seen.'

Then there is this terrible thing:

'Do you know what I do of a Christmas Day?' (Looks of interest.)

'No. What?'

'Bed.'

'Bed?' (Looks of incredulity, stepped up to please the moron.)

'Off up to bed after dinner. Never put a leg out of bed until 4 o'clock Stephen's Day. Fair enough if there's a game of cards fixed up after that. But get me up *before four*? (Fearful faces are made.) No—fear.'

Finally, this portrait of undead human decomposition, not peculiar to Christmas but most frequently encountered about that time.

(Enters public house on St Stephen's Day, obviously shattered with alcohol. Lowers self into seat with great care, grips table to arrest devastating shake in hands. Calls for glass of malt. Spills water all over table. Swallows drink with great clatter of teeth against glass. Shakily lights cigarette. Exhales. Begins to look around. Fixes on adjacent acquaintance. Begins peroration.)

'Bedam but you know, people talk a lot about drink, Whiskey and all the rest of it. There's always a story, the whiskey was bad, the stomach was out of order and so on. Do you know what *I'm* going to tell you . . . ?

(Pauses impressively. The eye-pupils, almost dissolved in their watery lake, rove about with sickly inquiry. Accepts silence as evidence of intense interest.)

'Do you know what it is?'

(Changes cigarette from normal inter-digital position, holds it aloft vertical; taps it solemnly with index finger of free hand.)

'Do you see that? That thing there? Cigarettes. Them lads. Do you know what I'm going to tell you . . . ?'

(Is suddenly overcome by paroxysm of coughing; roots benightedly for handkerchief as tears of pure alcohol course down the ruby cheeks. Recovers.)

'Them fellas there. *Them fellas has me destroyed* . . .'

(Collapses into fresh paroxysm. Emerges again):

'I wouldn't mind *that* at all (indicates glass). I *know* what I have there. There's eatin' an' drinkin' in that. Damn the harm *that* done annywan, bar been taken to excess. But *this* . . .'

(Again points to cigarette, looks of sorrow and horror mingling on 'face'.)

'Them lads has me destroyed.'

* * *

MY NOTES of some days ago on the man who, shattered by whiskey-drinking, swears he is 'desthroyed be the cigarettes', prompts me to record a few other bores who have standard lines of chat. For instance—

THE MAN WITH THE WATCH

Somebody remarks that his watch, solid gold, 98 jewels, cost £50, wears it swimming, has broken down after only five years' service. The Man smiles primly at this, produces a turnip-watch, and puts it solemnly on the table. The harsh tick silences further talk. Those present perceive that the thing was once nickel-plated, but is now a dull brass colour at the edges.

'Do you know what that cost me?' the Man asks.

Everybody knows that the answer is five bob or thereabouts, that it was bought eighteen years ago, that it never lost a minute, and was never even cleaned. But nobody is brutal enough to spill that out. People are weak, and tend to play up to bores.

'I suppose about two quid,' somebody says innocently.

'Five bob,' the Man says.

Fake surprise all round.

'Know how long I have it?' the Man asks.

'Five or six years, I suppose.'

'I bought that watch in Leeds in September 1925. That's nearly twenty years ago. Since then it has never stopped, never lost a minute *and wasn't even cleaned once!*'

Phoney astonishment on every face.

'A grand little time-keeper,' the Man says, replacing the turnip in his pocket with considerable satisfaction.

(This particular type of pest also owns incredible cars, fifty-year-old fountain pens, gloves bought in 1915 and never lost or worn-out, makes his own cigarettes with home-made filter-wads at the ends, reckons that they cost him roughly (always this 'roughly') a farthing each, and is convinced that 'people are mad' to pay more. Let me present one further bore):

THE MAN WITH THE BLADE

Somebody says: 'It's very hard to get decent blades these days,' and in explanation, grimaces and rubs jaw. 'I haven't had a decent shave for weeks,' he adds.

The Man is present and looks puzzled.

'You don't mean to say you *buy* razor blades?' he says.

Various people confess they do.

'Well I don't,' the Man says. 'I admit I *have* bought one, but that was two years ago . . .'

Again dutiful surprise is registered.

Everybody has heard of patent blade-sharpeners, the various sharpenings that can be attempted with mirrors, strops and tumblers, but nobody has any guts and nothing is said.

'It's quite simple,' the Man says, thoroughly delighted with himself.

'Get a good tumbler and keep it by you. Smear the inside with vaseline. Every morning before you shave, give both sides of the blade three or four rubs along the inside of the tumbler, keeping strong pressure on the centre of it with your finger. That's all.'

Pauses to accept gratefully the due looks of incredulity.

'You'll get the best shave you ever got in your life, man. And a tuppenny blade'll last you five years.'

(On your life don't show this article to anybody. Nearly everybody belongs to one or other of these two classes in some capacity; you'll get black looks for your pains. Ever meet the man whose petrol lighter always works, explains why? 'It's quite simple, the whole secret is . . .')

* * *

I'M AFRAID I have some more bores here today. (I am sorry, but the function of the historian is to record completely, not selectively.)

Have you met—look, this hurts me as much as it hurts you—have you met *The Man Who Buys Wholesale*? (You're in for it this time.)

You have asked this gargoyle to 'dinner' because he has put some business in your way during the year, and there may be more where that came from. The clown comes into your room rubbing his deformed, calloused hands, looks round, checks up on fittings, decoration, etc. Walks over to your radio. It is a year old—1947 should see it paid for. He examines it closely, taps it, disconnects it, turns it upside down, shakes it, breaks one of the leads, leaves it on its side, takes out handkerchief and wipes hands. Infuriated, you manage to say:

'What do you think of the radio?'

'Hah? The radio? Aw, yeh. Aw, with a bit of adjustment it'd be a nice job. I'll get you a nice one. Them nine pound ones wears out in no time . . .'

By now you are practically rigid with hatred and disgust. This figure of £9 is, of course, a trap—and you are going deliberately to fall into it. You thoroughly despise yourself. You say:

'But look here—*nine pounds*! That set is costing me eighty-seven pounds . . .'

The foul mountebank springs from the chair, comes over, puts both hands on your shoulders:

'Are you mad, Mac? Are you in your right mind man?'

'It's a perfectly good set,' you stammer, now loathing yourself utterly, 'it . . . it . . . works quite well and eighty-seven pounds is the recognised retail price. I thought *you'd* know that!'

The claws are now taken off your shoulders. The monster elaborately averts the face and, addressing the far wall, says: Th'unfortunate man must be mad! Makes a show of walking away sadly, suddenly whips round and shouts, showering you with saliva:

'*Are you crackers?* Have you taken leave of your wits? I wouldn't have believed it of you, that's all I can say. *Of course* I know it's the *retail* price. But shure, man alive, *no one* is supposed to buy stuff retail! Shure that went out years ago. Now I've two sets at home . . .'

Is that enough for today? Could you take a little more?

The Man Who Is His Own Lawyer?

Is it fork out me good-lookin' money to them hooky solicitors? Them fellas, that has th'office on a weekly tenancy and a season ticket to Belfast, ready to skip the minit they get their claws on some unfortunate orphan's dough? Ah no, thanks all the same. I think I'll just carry on a little bit longer the way I am. And I'll tell you this much: I know more law nor anny ten of them put together. I didn't want the help of anny solicitor back in nineteen and thirty-four when I made the landlord take down and rebuild back wall and replace gutters, *and* pull out the joyces in the front drawin' room and put in new wans. Oh Gob no bloody fear, I know me rights. I took out the probate single-handed after the mother went and I got ten pounds nine for Christy the time he was humped offa the bike be a lurry. I know me law and I know me rights.

The foregoing samples, of course, represent *attitudes*. There are, however, troglodytic specimens who can get their effects by a single and unvarying remark which, injected into thousands of conversations in the course of their lifetime, enables them to take leave of humanity knowing that they have done something important to it. Have you ever heard this:

Of course Dan O'Connell Was A Freemason Of Course You Knew That?

IN TRYING to arrive at a proper conspectus of every-day bores, it is important not to overlook (merely because he has been mentioned so often and so casually before) the head-bore: I mean The Man Who Spoke Irish At A Time When It Was Neither Profitable Nor Popular. (Don't forget that lad.)

And here is another: The Man Who Never Gives Pennies To Beggars.

This fearful know-all is walking with you, a beggar approaches; by accident you let slip into his hat a few coppers you were toying with in your pocket. As you walk on, you notice the 'friend' in a frightful state of agitation, the face growing redder, the shoulders heaving, the little eyes dancing in their puffy pig-skin pouches.

'What's wrong, man,' you cry, alarmed, 'Are you ill?'

A crackling 'laugh' is heard; he is very angry now.

'Gob I thought you knew better than that,' he says, 'a man of your age . . .'

'What are you talking about?' you ask.

'Shelling out a wing to that lad back there. You must be bats. Easy seen you were on the beer last night . . .'

'I am not ashamed of such trivial eleemosynary acts, let me tell you. Charity . . .'

'Charity? *Charity?* Oh-ho, that's a good wan! I oney wish, listen here to me. I oney wish you were earning *in the year* what he pays in income tax *in wan week*! Yes! Your man has a house out in Carrickmines would take the sight out of your eyes. Ever see his wife?'

'I can't say that I did . . .'

'Ah well you wouldn't, of course, you don't get asked to them Legation doos.'

'But—'

No, reader; all the buts in the world won't do you any good. You must not attempt to argue with this person. Just dial O and ask for the police.

Incidentally, if his talk is not as in the foregoing, it will inevitably be as follows:

Your arm is twitched. Eyes that are almost frightened peer into yours:

'Look,' the monster babbles, 'you don't mean to say you gave that person . . . *money?*'

'I donated the sum of tuppence sterling,' you reply facetiously. You are not yet aware that you are in the presence of a terrible disease. Your banal remark has a terrible effect. The shoulders are hunched, arms shoved down vertical into coat pockets, the eyes stare straight ahead, on the 'face' a black frown wherein disgust with you and a loathsome compassion for your failings and weaknesses struggle for dominance.

'I say,' you stammer, 'what's wrong with giving that poor old man a copper? Did you see his boots . . .?'

(You speak bravely, no doubt, but you know you are lost.)

'What's *wrong* with it? My God, man, have you no sense at all?'

The wretch has you now by the arm and is severely hurting some small muscle near your elbow, so fanatical the grip.

'Do you know what that fellow will do with the money you have given him?'

'No.'

'Straight into a public house and drink it.'

'But surely . . . tuppence, I mean . . .'

'Tuppence, is it? That man makes a fiver a day on the touch and drinks every penny of it. It so happens that I know what I'm talking about. And it's people like you that are responsible for every act and word of that unfortunate man. Offer him a day's work in your garden and see what happens. O, I'm up to them, believe you me.'

'But—'

No, reader, it's no use.

* * *

I HOPE I am not . . . a . . . a bore but there is one other character I would like to speak to you about privately. You probably know him. He was just leaving the Brothers beyond in Richmond Street the year your poor grandfather first came to school. Grandfather unfortunately is no longer to be seen due to the highly technical business of interment (1908 R.I.P.), but this other person is still in town, the button-less camel-hair overcoat worn slightly off the shoulders, the snap-brimmed green felt nestling in a nest of curls formerly worn by a certain foreign horse, present whereabouts unknown. To your certain knowledge this man is one hundred and four years of age (if he's a day). Through a calamitous neglect of keeping your eyes skinned—I admit the skin *does* grow rather quickly, but what are surgeons for?—you meet this person. Then it starts. You are dragged into a public cottage, sorry public house, and drinks are poured into you while you listen to this person's account of his life. The horse out on Merrion Strand before breakfast, after that a couple of brisk sets of squash (still before breakfast). Then out with the dumb-bells (they would need to be) and then a little toast and a glass of limejuice. After that, into the running shorts and round and round the lawn until the *petit déjeuner*: then, of course, the fencing class until lunch; after lunch brings togs down to Lansdowne Road on the off-chance and always gets a game, plays on the wing but is rather a useful back. A shower and home to dinner but not without a few sets on the hard courts. After dinner takes out the gloves and up to the SCR for a couple of bouts with the boys. On slack nights, you suspect, he goes down to Shelbourne Park and runs round the thrack in front of the electhric hare to show it the way. You assimilate all this without a word and then to your horror you hear yourself saying: .

'Begob you know you'll want to go easy—you can't do that forever. You'll have to give a lot cf that up, you know, when you pass thirty-five. Because . . .'

He is delighted. God forgive you—he stands there with the embalmed profile up to the light, he has raised the hand to stop you and then says:

'*How old would you say I am?*'

You look at him steadily, unsmiling: you know that you are worse than he is and that the whole thing is the price of you.

'Well,' you say, 'Well, Jack, I'm not going by your *appearance*—you certainly don't *look* your age, never seen a man wearing so well. But from what I know of you around the town, knocking around and so forth, I'd say you must be a man of thirty-two, indeed I suppose you'd be a man that's goin' on for thirty-three. I'd say you're pushin' thirty-three, Jack . . .'

The vile clown is by now beside himself with delight. Observe him— the sphinx-like smile, the slow shaking of the 'head', the pause, the holding of the glass to the light, the slow draining of it—revealing the pure lines of chin and jaw. Slowly the face is turned to you and now you perceive at close quarters the deathly meshed mask apparently clogged with baking powder, the breaking fissures in it that denote a half-smile of deprecation:

'*Mac, I was born in 1908.*'

Suddenly your own face is blanched with horror; you tremble; you mutter some inarticulate excuse and stumble out into the cold, cursing bitterly. You *know* it was 1808.

Is there, you may ask, any remedy, any way out for weaklings like you, is there any hope for the man who is too cowardly to insult such 'people'? Well, *don't go out at all* is the only thing I can think of. Stay at home in bed, windows closed, blinds drawn, electric fire going full blast. Only the really tough bores will follow you there—and after all they're your relatives, aren't they? You can't get away from them, can you?

A DUBLIN READER has kindly written to inform me of a bore (petrol lighter species) who infests a local public house. Apparently the lighter is used as an instrument for gaining admittance to parties of drinkers not known to the bore personally; naturally, this means free drink. I am terribly sorry but this type of person is not a bore within my terms of reference. The sort of bore I have been attempting to define in recent notes is a born and outright bore; boring other people is his sole occupation, enjoyment, recreation. No thought of gain would he permit to sully his 'art'; indeed, many of them are prepared to lose money—to *stand* drinks—if they see a good opportunity of pursuing their nefarious vocation. Let me give a few further examples. Have you met The Man Who Has Read It In Manuscript? Let me explain.

You are a literary man, you never go out, all you ask is to be left alone with your beloved books. But the Man calls. A desultory conversation starts. The Man is peering and poking about your private apartments. You are interested in a book you read recently, would like to get other people's opinion on it, innocently enough, you ask:

'By the way, have you read *Victorian Doctor*?'

'Never heard of it,' the blight says.

'Most interesting book,' you say. 'All about Oscar Wilde's father, gives a very good picture of Dublin life in those days . . .'

'Oh, *that*?' the bore says, his back turned in a very casual way as he interferes with some personal documents on your desk. 'Ah, yes, I read that. Actually he meant to give the book another name, I hadn't heard it was published under that title. I read it in manuscript as a matter of fact.'

Thus you are vouchsafed a glimpse of the anonymous adviser, critic, confessor and daddy christmas of literary men.

'Ever read *Warren Peace* by T. Allstoy?' you inquire.

'Ah, yes, I read that thing in the manuscript years ago. Is it published yet?'

See? Grrrhhhhhh!

Indeed, it is all too easy to think of other types of this baneful presence, this monstrous cretin. You have, of course—some time or other since 1939—encountered The Man Who Always Burned Turf? If not, please accept my solemn oath that he exists. Here is his line of chat:

'Coal, is it? That . . . dirt! Shure what are you talking about man, what's wrong with turf? Isn't it the natural fuel for this country, hah? I got married in nineteen O five and since that good day to this one solitary lump of coal I haven't let into me house. Know why? Because a turf fire, *properly built in a proper grate*, is the best—fire in the world. Don't let anybody tell you different. I know what I'm talking about. I used to get turf—good black turf—off the canal-boats at fifteen bob a ton—*delivered*, mind. Ah yes . . . (an alcoholic frown, black but sad, is hoisted in memory of the good old days: the waste-pipe voice continues). At a time when

plenty more was planking down thirty and forty . . . and . . . forty-five
bob for the rakings and the muck of the British coal fields, dirt and smuts
everywhere, blowing and puffing and poking for a half an hour in the
morning to get the thing going, shure is it anny wondher the country's
half rotten with TB? Oh, say what you like, you can't beat th' old-
fashioned turf fire. The whole secret of the thing, of course, is how you
place the sods. End up—like this, look . . .'

Empty match-boxes are used in illustration. There is one thing about
that Man—you can always be certain that in his concrete garage resides
(even today, 1945) at least three tons of peerless pre-war Orrel nuts,
fifty bob a ton.

* * *

IT'S QUITE a little time, I think, since I wrote on the subject of bores.
I come back to this problem only because I have since encountered a
pretty bad specimen. He is a monster to be avoided like the pledge, a
colossal imposition who will make you very angry and cause your heart
to beat like a sludge-hammer (*stet*). I refer to The Man Who Does His
Own Carpentry And Talks About It.

This savage lives in a little red brick box four by two, basically a one-
room cell. Inside you have himself, the missis and the eight girls. Next
week the eldest Anny is to get a job as a typist at eight-and-six a week in a
solicitor's office. This man has the place got out beautiful. And regardless.
Suppose you happened to live a in telephone box—like the fourteen
blonde women in the one under Moore's statue any time I went to ring
up. Well, I assume you would accept the thing and try to make the best of
it. Not so, however, The Man Who Does His Own Carpentry; *he* makes it
hard for himself—*he builds partitions*. He subdivides the sentry's home
and erects shelving, window-seats, cupboards, hot presses, built-in
wardrobes. And anything in the way of circulation—I mean walking
about—in that house takes the form and rhythm of a Cuban rhumba;
your feet stay where they are, though your hips and knees move somewhat.

The partitions this Man has made are exceptional manifestations in
the sphere of Home Crafts. He is so handy with his hands (round the
house in brackets), he has Vol. IV of somebody's Building Encyclopedia.
He makes this . . . thing, this 'wall', by laying a couple of sticks along the
sagging unjoisted floor. Next, he introduces a long horizontal member
into the room and raises it into the position of Mahomet's coffin, strutting
both walls and threatening to bulge out the gable. This, reader, is the

'framework'. In between go the bits of paper. *Yes*, the bits of newspaper well wetted and rolled into soft balls. And there you are—you only wait for the thing to harden!

Come into this prodigy's signal-box some evening—it will be the first time you ever used a tin-opener to enter a friend's house. He will rub his hands, grin, look obliquely at his 'handiwork' and without doubt you will find yourself, craven lout that you are, saying this:

'Gob, you've laid out a lot of money on the ancestral home since I was last here, Mac. Who did you have on the job?'

You are a friend, you have said the right thing. Now he can put on his act. Surprise, beating of the breast, walking backwards like a crab, letting the mouth hang open pointing at himself:

'Who? *Me?* Is it me employ a contractor? Me, is it—*me* hand out me good money to your men when I have two hands God gave me and the chisel, hammer and hack-saw I picked up in Pauls's of Aungier street? Is it hand out the money that's put by for me old age to hooks and fly-be-nights that wouldn't know a screw-driver from a bradawl, have the house for months occupied be lads makin' tay and smokin' cigarettes—*in my time*—ME . . .?'

'But surely . . . surely you didn't do all this yourself?' (You are afraid to lean against the partition in case you suddenly find yourself in the 'bathroom'—but you are saying the right thing still, you hypocritical dog!)

'And why not? Shure there's nothing to it man. There's not a damn thing to it. Shure anywan shure even yourself could do that much. But come up till I show you the wee chest of drawers I put in the nursery . . .'

Come 'up', mind you, and the 'nursery' . . . ! And all the time you have to pretend not to see the wife and eight children asleep under the 'bookcase'.

This man also makes all his own coffins. The bought ones aren't a job, he avers.

* * *

THERE IS one other awful man I feel it my duty to describe; I mean the one who is mortally curious to know 'how is it done?' This monstrous clown never looks at you when he is talking and never mentions names; he is a very wealthy; he says:

'I went out to Leopardstown on the bike on Saturday. Lost a packet, of course . . .'

You shrivel slightly at this humility of going to a race meeting on a bike, in order to lose the price of fifty taxis. You know this man is insane and cravenly await what you know is coming. He continues:

'Who do you think I seen there?'

'Who?'

'Our friend.'

'Our friend? Who?'

'A certain particular party that you know and that I know.'

What makes you choke with rage here is the realisation that you know perfectly well whom he is talking about and thus that you are yourself embroiled in his paranoia. The voice goes on:

'*On the inside*, of course, chatting jockeys and owners, getting the card marked all over the show. And the big heifer of a wife standing about in the fur coat. Know what I'm going to tell you?'

'What?'

'That man put fifty notes on a thing that was rode be a certain jockey that wouldn't be third home if he was on a V2. But did that take a feather out of our friend ...?'

Charnel-house chuckles follow, hinting that no feathers were taken out of this speculator. Your tormentor goes on:

'Back in town at half six. I feel like an egg and a bit of toast and I walk into the counter of a certain place that you know and that I know. Who do I see there with two dames?

'Our friend?' (O wretched man! You have *answered* the fiend, and correctly!)

'Sitting up there as large as life. Bowl of soup first, of course, but not without a drop of madeira in it. Know what he fancies next?'

The monster has produced a penknife and goes through the wrist motions associated with the opening of oyster shells.

'A dozen each for all hands. Know what they had next?'

You would dearly love to say something outrageously exaggerated, like 'roast peacock's breast' but you lack the courage to stand up to this torturer. You say:

'No. What?'

'A whole turkey between the three. They were working away there for two hours' chattin' the heads off each other, with all classes of liqueurs being fired back thirteen to the dozen. *And* a taxi ticking away outside ...!'

There is a pause here. The fiend is getting ready for the finale, you can nearly hear him flexing his madhouse nerves. When the voice comes again, it is changed and earnest:

'Now to my certain knowledge, that man is in a certain department of a certain store and he is paid the munificent subvention of three pounds fifteen per week. *Three pounds fifteen shillings per week!*'

You know the sad watery eyes are looking vacantly upwards in mute puzzledom. You know that he is now about to enunciate his supreme interrogatory formula. You dread the impact of the end of this inevitable predestined 'conversation'. But you are powerless. The voice says:

'What I want to know is this . . .'

Yes, there is a pause here. You knew there would be. Then:

'*How is it done?*'

You are a bit dazed. You notice his fingers go through the motions of pressing the keys of cash registers. You have received a pat on the back —this ogre's only form of farewell—and he is gone.

And you are lucky to be alive, so you are.

* * *

OR HOW ABOUT a few *brief* notes on notorious practitioners of boredom? For example—

The Man Who Can Pack. This monster watches you trying to stuff the contents of two wardrobes into a small attaché case. You succeed, of course, but you find you have forgotten to put in your golf clubs. You curse grimly but your 'friend' is delighted. He knew this would happen. He approaches, offers consolation and advises you to go downstairs and take things easy while he 'puts things right'. Some days later, when you unpack your things in Glengariff, you find that he has not only got your golf clubs in but has included also your bedroom carpet, the kit of a Gas Company man who had been working in your room, two ornamental vases, and a folding card-table. Everything in view, in fact, except your razor. You have to wire £7 to Cork to get a new leather bag (made of cardboard) in order to get all this junk home. *And* offer outrageous bribes to the boots for the loan of his razor. Or—

The Man Who Soles His Own Shoes. Quite innocently you complain about the quality of present-day footwear. You wryly exhibit a broken sole. 'Must leave them in tomorrow,' you say vaguely. The monster is flabbergasted at this passive attitude, has already forced you into an armchair, pulled your shoes off and vanished with them into the scullery. He is back in an incredibly short space of time and restored your property to you announcing that the shoes are now 'as good as new'. You notice his own for the first time and instantly understand why his feet are deformed. You hobble home, apparently on stilts. Nailed to each shoe is an inch-thick slab of synthetic 'leather' made from Shellac, saw-dust and cement. Being much taller than usual, you nearly kill yourself getting into a bus. By the time you get home you have lost two pints of blood and the wound in your forehead looks as if it will turn septic. Or—

But no—it is too painful to describe some of these fiends in detail. You have met *The Man Who Can Carve*? No matter if the dish be a solitary roast pigeon, the coat is taken off, two square yards of table cleared, several inoffensive diners compelled to leave the room to give the ruffian 'a bit of freedom'. By some miracle everything carved by this person is transformed into scrag-ends, so that *nobody* gets anything that is eatable.

Or *The Man Who 'Believes'* (or *Does Not 'Believe'*) in this or that commonplace thing. One wretch does not 'believe' in electric radiators. He is horrified if you turn one on, pretends he is choking, makes motions of removing collar and tie. They 'dry up the atmosphere' of course. Just like the other oaf who does not 'believe' in real fires. Nothing for him but the electric fire. He has five or six in every room, and one or two on the stairs. A coal fire 'only makes dirt'. It also 'makes work' and you have to be 'always stoking it'. Whereas the electric fire (here he makes plugging-in motions) you just push it in and there you are! Four times cheaper than coal, gives twice as much heat, and so forth. The only thing you can do with this beast is to provide him with an electric chair, as a present for himself.

Or *The Man Who Wouldn't Let A Radio Into The House*?

Or *The Man Who Doesn't Believe In Fresh Air*? ('Do you know what it is, there's more people killed be that fad . . .')

Who then is the supreme demon? Would it be that not unfamiliar person who confesses that he never 'sees' the *Irish Times*?

BORES is it?

Faith now there is one monster I have overlooked and I know I have only to drop a hint and you will recognise him instantly. He professes to love his fartherland (*stet*) by reason of its sheer oddity; this endearing quality, he thinks, is enhanced by the brilliance of the indigenous autocthons and by every citizen's mastery of wit, repartee, humour and paradox. Everything that happens 'proves' this man's point.

He is standing on the kerb, let us say, talking away ($21 = 1$ doz.) and one of the Cleansing Dept's immense sludge waggons inadvertently backs into him and tips up smelly contents of hold so that he is deluged by it. You might think that should annoy him, might shut him up. Not at all.

Two seconds later, a large section of the putresence begins to move, it crawls along the path *and stands up*! It is our friend of course—he is hurrying back to you; an aperture high up in the column of slime lets us know that he is grinning. He hobbles towards you badly injured in body but clearly filled with an immense happiness. He waves a plastered arm at you.

'Where else,' you hear the muffled voice saying, 'where else could that happen but in Ireland!'

That's his supreme and universal apothegm. It embraces, defines and explains the whole of Ireland, all Irishry, everything Irish. More particularly it covers the following occasions:

Late arrival and departure of trains, buses, etc.

Non-repair of watches, shoes, etc., by appointed dates.

Election of well-known illiterate, venal, criminal, or otherwise inadequate persons to Parliament or to high public office.

Consumption of drink in police headquarters after hours.

Discovery that beggar speaks Greek.

Discovery that university professor cannot speak English, Irish, etc.

Use of fake producer plants on motor vehicles propelled by petrol.

Discovery that bin-man's brother is Field Marshal in army forces of a Great Power unnamed.

Incompatibility of mutually adjacent public timepieces.

Pensionability of entire local populations in respect of military service, notwithstanding international convention as to non-combatancy of juveniles, children and women.

Discovery that various ex-military personnel, decorated by an imperial personality for bravery in a past war, are unfriendly to imperial ideals.

Banning as obscene of literary works advocating chastity, continence, honesty, etc.

Participating by ecclesiastical authorities in real estate, financial and speculative enterprises.

Philanthropic projects of distilling and brewing families.

Distaste of *Irish Times* for organisation of government departments, etc., according to systems devised by non-nationals no longer resident here.

Discovery that famous novelist is a peasant.

Ready cashing of cheques in public house containing large notices stating this activity is not pursued.

Unreliable nature of similar notices certifying the complete absence of rationed commodities.

And so forth. This man's crowning and abiding comfort is the conviction—gleaned from a life-time of incidents and remarks in the most unexpected places—that the Irish, though fiercely rebellious at heart, cherish a warm clean frank *love* for the Royal Family of an adjacent monarchy. With the concomitant phenomenon involving hatred of a certain imperial organisation as such and, simultaneously, a devouring affection for the individual Englishman!

(Do you also, reader, feel you're suffocating?)

THERE IS still another monster I would like to warn you about. (To be warned is to be four-armed.) You have, very indiscreetly, complained about the price of clothes: worse, you have commented adversely on the quality of much of what is available. You see a light dawning in the monster's eye and to your alarm you realise that you are for it. Fascinated, you observe him primly take a garment he is wearing between finger and thumb. (Too late to correct the absurd ambiguity of that last sentence.) He savours the fabric appreciatively, then courteously invites you to do the same. Your fingers, hypnotised by him, obey against your own strict orders. He appears to be wearing sandpaper but your cowardice does not permit you to say this. You withdraw your hand, covertly explore your fingers for splinters, and cravenly murmur some noises of approval.

How old would you say this suit is?

You are blushing furiously now—it may be shame or anger or both—but you still dare not protest.

Would you believe me if I told you that I've that coat on me back for ten years. Know what I paid for it?

You keep on making polite noises, sorrier than ever that you were born at all.

Fifty bob!

More muttering, swallowed curses, tears.

And I'll get another ten years out of it too, you can't, do you know what it is, you can't wear stuff like that out.

Let me add that this gent has a brother wants to know How Much He's Making In The Year, Go On, Tell Him, How Much Would You Say He's Making Now.

I AM HUMILIATED and astounded to find that in all my writings—and it goes without Synge that many of my writings are very fine indeed—I have so far made no reference to the P.S. maniac. Some people are absolutely incapable of writing a letter without a postscript and the postscript must go in even if the writer has nothing whatever to add. Where the postscript does make sense, the disease lies in making it a postscript at all instead of embodying it in the letter.

> 'Dear Tom: Thanks very much for the books which arrived safely. I am going to Cork on Tuesday for two days and will give you a ring when I get back.
>
> > Yours, Jack.
>
> P.S. I saw your brother at the races on Saturday, but I didn't get talking to him. J.'

That is one kind of futility and you are as familiar with it as I am. Or how often have you seen this:

> 'Dear Tom: The books arrived safely and I am obliged to you for sending them. I will return them as soon as possible.
>
> > Yours sincerely, Jack.
>
> P.S. I hope all at Number 8 have escaped the flu D.V. May was complaining on Saturday but she's fine today. J.'

Please note that the ridiculous addendum is always initialled and thus authenticated. As if anybody could doubt the authorship of it. Ladies often use the P.S. as a coy and rather (?) charming sally.

> 'Dear Tom: I will be only too happy to go to the dance with you on Tuesday.
>
> > "Betty".
>
> P.S. Thanks for ignoring me when we met yesterday in Dame Street —B.'

Yah!

The P.S., however, can occasionally have a legitimate office in the craft of literary nastiness.

A civil servant once received a letter from his superiors somewhat as follows:

> 'A Chara: It is noted that in submitting your account for travelling expenses you have entered a sum of £7 10s in respect of car-hire between Ballymick and Ballypat. The distance between these two points as the crow flies is 2½ miles. I am to request an immediate explanation of the entry referred to.'

Your man writes back:

'A Chara: In reply to your minute (ref. No. XZ 86231/Zb/600/7/43) of the 4th instant, I desire to inform you that a deep and unnavigable river separates the towns of Ballymick and Ballypat and travellers are compelled to take a car fifteen miles upstream to the only bridge which affords a crossing.

> 'Mise, le meas,
> Seán O'Pinion.

P.S.—I am not a crow—S.O'P.

If I had any weakness in this direction, I would devise a mysterious literary embellishment to be known as the antescript.

'A.S. How about that fiver I lent you in 1917?—M. na gC.
'Dear Tom—The books which you were kind enough to send me do not appear to be approved by H.M. Board of Censors and I cannot therefore peruse them. Believe me, my dear Tom,

> Yours very sincerely,
> M. na gC.'

That sort of thing.
Or go the other hog—start off with the briefest letter in the world—

'Dear Tom—Thanks. Yours, M. na gC—' and then a P.S. running into 20 pages both sides of the paper and coming back to the top of page one—Hegel, Nietzsche, Emerson, Gide, Beethoven, Suarez—all the boys trotted out in reams of pretentious blather.

What can one say, I wonder, of the dreadful creatures who are addicted to the P.P.S.? Say in a family newspaper, I mean?
'P.S. Hoping all at Number 8 are A.1.—J.
'P.P.S. May sends her regards to Bella and hopes to call on Tuesday D.V.—J.'
The Plain People of Ireland: We'll write what we like.
Myself: Eh?
The Plain People of Ireland: We'll write what we like in our own pairsonal letthers.
I make no reply to that, I do not wish to offend anybody, plain or coloured, but I do hope my remarks will be taken to Harte, marked, noted, pondered and committed to the manuscript of memory.
P.S. hoping this reaches you as it leaves me, in the pink. M. na gC

* * *

'ON THE OTHER hand', one noticed the somewhat didactic Editor saying on Saturday last: 'Mr de Valera is asking for *carte blanche* to give effect to his preposterous policy of a Gaelic-speaking, potato-digging Republic.'

In my capacity as scientist, I am terribly interested in that sort of writing. The *carte*, of course, would have to be *blanche*. (The war.) There hasn't been a *carte noire* come into this country for near on four year; they're not making them now. What I want to know is—what is the opposite of a Gaelic-speaking potato-digging Republic? Granted that the opposite of Gaelic-speaking is English-speaking and that the opposite of republic is monarchy—what is the opposite of potato-digging?

No answer.

Very well. Are we then to be an English-speaking potato-digging monarchy? What king would dream of presiding over a confraternity of harsh-voiced peasants eternally engaged in exhuming spuds? Or forsooth, would our new rulers be a dynasty of British Queens?

I hold that potatoes are terribly important. They make admirable feeding for man and beast. You remember what happened nearly a hundred years ago? We were largely Gaelic-speaking then but owing to circumstances over which we had no control, the potato-digging had to be discontinued for a year or two. The result was catastrophic. The firm was, of course, under different management then.

Can this distaste for potato-digging be due to the foot with which the digging is done?

LOOK OUT

Talking of potatoes, here's a gambit that you must look out for. Murder is justified in the circumstances.

Two men go into a restaurant. One of them picks up the menu idly and says *Oh good! There are new potatoes on the card today!*

The other man doesn't seem to understand and says *I beg your pardon? New potatoes*, the first man says, *only a shilling extra.*

The other now looks genuinely puzzled. He searches his friend's face. *I'm afraid I don't quite get you*, he says. *Exactly what do you mean? New potatoes?*

Naturally this leads to some exasperation. *I see there are new potatoes on the card today, that's all*, the first man says rather shortly.

New . . . potatoes?

The second man has now built up a pucker of frowns on his face to show that he is completely at sea. He stares, lost. Then slowly . . . very slowly . . . light is seen to break. He has a clue. He grasps at it. Soon the meaning of his friend's remark is flooding out upon him. His face becomes smooth. He smiles.

Oh . . . I get you. Of course. New potatoes . . .

Here there is a carefully-nursed pause.

We have had them at home, of course, for the last three months. St Patrick's Day, I think, we had the first.

Another brief pause.

They were a bit late this year, of course. Last year it was about the first of March we had them, I think . . .

(It's at the second pause you use the gun.)

Miscellaneous

THE NEWS that my name appeared in Stubbs last week will come as a pleasant surprise to my enemies. A green satisfaction will fill their souls.

The Plain People of Ireland : Your enemies? What enemies?

Myself : I can mention no names. Be assured, however, that there are hordes of them in every walk of life. They ask nothing better than to do me an ill turn. They are working and scheming against me night and day. They pursue me with infinite venom and cunning. Slander and calumny, whispers in the ear. The unseen hand, backstairs influence, I believe our friend was up in court last week, but had it kept out of the papers. Is that so? On what charge? O you'll laugh when you hear. Listen (whisper-whisper-whisper). WHAT! Are you serious? O it's a true bill, had it from the Guard. And another thing, I believe the unfortunate wife gets a hammering every night. In at ten past ten full of prunes and porter. Where's the cigarette-butt I left on the mantelpiece this morning? You don't know? Don't you? Well, take *that*!

Any mud is good enough so long as it sticks. Back-slandering and poison-pen letters. Get him one way if you can't get him another. False friends everywhere. The small corrosive word half-uttered in the right place. He's no good I'm telling you, *he's no good*. No matter where I go my traducers have been there before me. Sorry, sir, you can't come in here, sir. Them's my orders, sir, Sorry, sir.

No explanation. If our friend puts his nose in tonight, slam the door in his face. Never mind, do as you're told. No, don't say I said so. Just slam the door. And see that you make no mistake about it. We don't want that particular customer in here.

Even my young sons, my innocent little lads of twelve. Hello, sonny, I believe your poor father is locked up again. He's not? He's laid up? In bed? Ah, the poor man. Well, he didn't sound very ill at three in the morning last Saturday night when he nearly pulled my door down and smashed four bottles on the step. The poor man is laid up, is he? Dear, dear, dear.

Of course, if they think that this campaign will deflect me from my course or abate by one tittle my advocacy of the far-reaching reforms to which I have dedicated my life, they are vastly mistaken.

Further comment is superfluous. The whole thing would be humorous were it not so tragic.

* * *

THE MYLES na gCopaleen Banking Corporation is experimenting with a new kind of cheque book. The whole thing would be laughable were it not so tragic. Each cheque looks perfectly ordinary, but when it is drawn, cashed and returned to the Bank, strange things happen behind closed doors. The Bank's officials get to work on it, and if you could only see them at it, you would observe that each cheque is in reality two cheques cleverly stuck together and separated by a sheet of fine carbon. Thus, when you draw a cheque in favour of 'Self' for ten pounds, you get that much money, but the Bank gets *two* cheques for ten pounds. Furthermore, since the genuine endorsement is on the back of the second cheque and the drawer's genuine hand-writing on the face of the first, both can readily be established, in a court of law or elsewhere, to be genuine documents, notwithstanding any minor pretexts for suspicion; it is a simple matter to forge a colourable endorsement on the back of the 'genuine' top cheque.

All this means, of course, that our clients are unwittingly spending their substance twice as fast as they think they are and qualifying speedily for a permanent abode in that populous thoroughfare, Queer St. And the Bank gets more and more dough.

* * *

I WILL TELL you a good one. It was tried on us recently at the Myles na gCopaleen Central Banking Corporation (all stand and uncover, please), and we were not the slowest to learn our lesson and take the recipe for our very own. It is a new dodge and one that will save you hundreds of pounds a year if it is used intelligently. Cross that out and say thousands. It is a secret weapon that will close the doors of our fancy competitors in College Green if you see fit to use it against them. (And why shouldn't you, pray, what about the £31 10. 0, is that forgotten already?)

It is a new sort of ink. It looks no different from the sort you use every day. It is blue-black, bright, thin, clean, and runs like sweet fancy through your fountain pen. It has this great virtue, though. *Six hours after you write something with it, the writing has completely disappeared.* The paper is again restored to its virgin white. Not a speck of 'ink' remains. Just think about that for a minute.

You walk into your bank, take out your cheque-book and special pen and write out a 'Pay Self £20'. You get your money, three fives and five singles and thanks very much, it's a bit cold today but sure what can you expect in the month of March? Out you go. That evening the poor banker is puzzled to find a completely blank cheque among the bundle marked 'paid'

In the meantime you have not been idle. The fifty publicans to whom you are all too well known are called upon. Tobacconists, grocers, bookies and solicitors are whipped in. Just a little bit short, old man, could you let me have a fiver, will I make it out to yourself or the firm? Thanks very much. The following morning a hundred dupes are holding a clean blank cheque between finger and thumb, gazing at it with a wild surmise. By the way, you owe me £35, I've got your I.O.U. here. Have you? Show me it. That's not an I.O.U. man, where's my signature? Don't try to pull any quick ones like that, old boy, I owe you nothing.

Write to me at this office for a small bottle of the stuff. Twenty-five shillings a time and no cheques taken in payment.

The last of the Mohicans.

Sure I knew them well, man, used to live beyond in Dartry, the eldest girl was very delicate and the son turned out to be a very bad bit of work, sold all the furniture to buy drink when the dacent ould couple were having their three days in the Isle of Man and then skipped it to America, a wild no-good waster with a whiskey nose on him before he was in long trousers, he was never seen or heard of from that good day to this. A fierce disappointment to his father, ould Shaun Mohican, the dacentest man that ever stood in shoe-leather, an out and out Parnellite that follyed the Chief to the very end, never wavered like so manny more. The Mohicans were always there when Ireland called, I knew the uncle that was in the Connaught Rangers, in a day's walk you wouldn't meet a dacenter man than the Star Mohican, the family came from Meath originally and were very big people down there in the days gone by. Ah yes. Of course you'll find one bad egg in the biggest basket. It takes all classes to make a world. Who? Me? Oh, another bottle of stout, I suppose.

WILL OLD Ireland survive? Not unless we *work*. We will survive if we deserve survival. Our destiny is in our own hands. *Quisque est faber fortunae suae*. We must pull together, sink our differences and behave with dignity and decorum. And above all, *work*. Work for Ireland. How queer that sounds. Not die, mind you. Work. Work for the old land. And at evening time, when reclining at our frugal fireside, saturated by the noble tiredness that is conferred by honest toil, in the left hand let there be no alien printed trash but the first book of O'Growney. There, then, is an ideal for you, something that you can do for Ireland. 'I will let no evening pass without an hour at O'Growney.' The old tongue. The old tongue that was spoken by our forefathers. Learning Irish and all working together—for Ireland. Let us do that and we will surely survive. Erin go bragh! Unfurl the old flag, three crowns on a blue field, the old flag of Erin. Our hearts are sound and our arms are strong. And what is our watchword? 'Work.' Let our watchword henceforth be that small word of four letters—w-o-r-k. WORK!

Next speech, next speech, please. Clapping. Old slow senile chairman. An hour standing up and another hour sitting down again. That cold whipping wind, you could get your death here, I was lost without that glass of malt, it's always safer to have something warm under the belt when you're above on the platform. Thin sullen crowd. Here only because there's no pictures on Sunday. Next speech.

Yields to no man in his respect for last speaker. While the integrity of his outlook, his fine national record, the lucidity of his thought and his ability to marshal facts must needs command respect, nevertheless, ventures with all due humility, to voice some small doubts as to the ultimate expediency of many of his more radical proposals. Turn to question of Irish language. Always made it a point to keep an open mind. Not out of place to remark spoke it at a time when it was neither profitable nor popular. (Cheers.) But cultural movements dwarfed by present world events. Considered opinion that we are witnessing titanic struggle between forces of good and evil, the end of which no man can foresee and few could be so foolhardy as to predict. Young men, aye, and young women leaving the country in ever-increasing numbers, drain on our national resources. Behoves us to move with caution. Something must be done; words not enough; promises not enough. Country calls for action on part of Government. Only most drastic curtailment essential services, elimination unnecessary luxuries, cutting our organisation to bone, reduce overheads, stringent regulations, mobilise country's resources, paramount importance of agricultural industry, community must stand shoulder to shoulder in hour of peril.

Next speech. Hurry please. Get this thing over. A drunk on our left trying to heckle. A rossiner wouldn't be bad, have a double one after this. Next please.

Much pleasure rise speak today this distinguished gathering; particularly on same platform last speaker. Last time we spoke together great Longford Rally 1829; doubtless he's forgotten. We've gone our different ways since then. Suppose no two men in this country more representative divergent poles political thought. Not what came here to say. Came say few words present crisis dark clouds lowering over fair face this country poverty unemployment transport problems turf hunger; country never greater danger. But spirit Irish people will prevail as ever, come to top. Only solution to problems before us is serious interest revival tongue our fathers spoke. Great revival work must go on. National heritage, nothing worth having left if not saved, receding rapidly in west. Save ere it is too late, only badge of true nationhood.

(Loud mad frenzied cheering.)

* * *

OUR AIM, by the way, is to give complete satisfaction. If this column is not in good condition when you receive it, return it to this office and your money will be refunded. In addition, you will receive six stouts in a handsome presentation cooper. When the column is written, it weighs exactly 0.03 grammes. Due to heat, evaporation or damp, the contents may become impaired or discoloured. In case of complaint, return it to this office with the rest of the newspaper and we will gladly replace it, or, at your option, return your money in full. Our aim is to make every customer a friend for life. We wish to give you complete satisfaction. We are your obsequious handwashing servants. We are very meek and humble. One frown from you and we feel that we have made a mess of our whole lives.

As the man said.

MY CLAIM

Recently, in mixed company, when boasts and brags of every kind were flying in and out through the hot murk of words, I ventured to make the claim (not without some show of humility and modesty) that I was the greatest living swine. Instantly sharp cries of dissent rang out on every side. How could I say such a thing, I was asked, when we have so-and-so and so-and-so in the country? The names mentioned were those of public and semi-public personalities that you know and that I know. What an exquisite pleasure it would be to print them here! But look, draw up your own list. Spend half-an-hour pondering our unique national assortment of cods and humbugs. Indeed, there is one so obvious that his name will leap to everybody's mind—none other than—

The Editor : Hey, stop! Have you gone off your head?

Myself : I was only going to give one name. Just a small one. One that you know and that I know. Sure what harm would that be? Everybody knows it. It would only mean £800 and costs. And think of the reputation we would win for outspokenness, courage, fearlessness, honesty, and so on. 'The Paper That Cannot Be Gagged.' Indeed, damages might only be a nominal farthing. It was held by Pallas C.B. that—

The Editor : For heaven's sake, man, have a little sense. If you attempt to put any name down I will scratch it out again.

Myself : O all right, you're the boss.

* * *

IN DUBLIN'S College Green (Excuse me. In Dublin's bus-humming pedestrian-jostling grey-colonnaded College Green) I met a poor man who was a stranger to these parts and who asked me to direct him somewhere. I did so with pleasure or at least with something that was meant to look like it. Then he pointed to a big building and said what's that. I said that's the Bank of Ireland. He said what do they be doing in there. Well, I said, banks lend money, you know. He looked wistfully at the Old House and said I wonder would they lend me ten bob. Why not try I said. Begor I think I will, he answered, a yellowish suffusion of worthless diluted blood mounting through his second-hand face, a symbol that the last thing to die in each of us is hope. Grey carrion soul-mincing hope, the one quality above all others that makes the human creature ridiculous and pathetic.

I left him, hoping he would drop dead. 'Yesterday, an unknown man
. . .'

* * *

ERWOOD STANDARD TYPEWR. Reason that out. It's before me on my
desk as I write. (That's a phrase you often see in travel books—the jewelled
and beaded purse of Stevenson, picked up for a few *dhraksi* in a junk
shop in Samoa, if you could believe the boastful swine; before him on his
desk as he writes. Can anybody write at anything but a desk?) But get
back to this ERWOOD STANDARD TYPEWR. It's all along the top of my
machine in golden letters. Do you get it? My flying thumb, sweeping up a
million times a year to whip back the carriage, has erased the last four
letters of TYPEWR. The equally active other thumb, darting and re-darting
to click the roller round, has wiped out the UND. There's an explanation
for everything old boy.

It's fairly obvious I haven't much to say today. Sow what? Sow wheat.
Ah-ha, the old sow-faced cod, the funny man, clicking out his dreary
blob of mirthless trash. The crude grub-glutted muck-shuffler slumped
on his hack-chair, lolling his dead syrup eyes through other people's
books to lift some lousy joke. English today, have to be a bit careful, can't
get away with murder so easily in English. Observe the grey pudgy hand
faltering upon the type-keys. That is clearly the hand of a man that puts
the gut number one. Not much self-sacrifice there. Yes but he has a
conscience, remember. He has a conscience. He does not feel too well
today. He casts bleared cataractic (Gk. katarrhaktes) sub-glances over his
past self. Why am I here? I want a straight answer that can be subjected
to intellectual criteria. No, I know what you were going to say, you won't
put me off with that. Why is this man here? What for? Eats four fat
meals a day, Wears clothes. Sleeps at night. Overpaid for incompetent
work. Kept on out of pity for wife. Is worried. Ho ho. Feels dissatisfied
with himself. Feels ought to be doing something. Feels . . . wrong. Not
fulfilling duties of station in life. How often is the little finger raised per
diem? Feels . . . dirty. Incapable of writing short bright well-constructed
newspaper article, notwithstanding fact editors only too anxious print
and pay for suitable articles, know man who took course Birmingham
School of Journalism now earns 12,000 pounds in spare time. If you can
write a letter you can write articles for newspapers. Editors waiting.
Payment at the rate of one guinea per thousand words. Always enclose
stamped envelope for return if unsuitable. Importance of neat typing.
ERWOOD STANDARD TYPEWR. Editors have not time to study decipher

puzzle out illegible scrawls on both sides of paper. Covering note not essential. But if desired brief courteous note saying take liberty of submitting for consideration literary article on how spent summer holidays. Or the humours of stamp collecting.

Remember once being stuffed in hot German train (before present war, of course), O a long time ago, forget what year it was, maybe '33 or '34. Courteous offizier present rauching long cheroot. Me, pointing out window: Bitte, ist das der Donau? Kolonel-major mit merry gold-dented smile: Nein, nein, das ist die Donau. Then the red hot bubbly blush.*

*

Print is one extreme of typographical development, the other being mathematical notation. It consists, in the occident anyway, of the representation of sounds by purely arbitrary shapes, and arranging them so that those in the know can reproduce the spoken words intended. This process is known as Reading, and is very uncommon in adults. It is uncommon because, firstly, it is in many cases frankly impossible, the number of phonetic symbols being inadequate; secondly, because of the extreme familiarity of the word-shapes to a population whose experience is necessarily derived in the main from marks printed on paper. It is in this second circumstances, familiarity with the word or phrase shapes, that has led to the unpremeditated birth of a visual language.

Now, you (yes, YOU) before you tear this paper into little bits, kindly tell me whether that last paragraph was written by me as part of my satanic campaign against decency and reason or whether it is taken from a book written in all seriousness by some other person. On your answer to that query will depend more than I would care to say in public.

Mister Quidnunc is even more stimulating today than usual. Turn to his little corner and have the time of your life.

*

THERE IS a lot of talk nowadays about repatriating our foreign acids. The agitation has my heartiest support. I have a tank of citric acid standing in Lisbon for the past two years, but so far I have been denied shipping space. The tank is on the quays, and is being depleted seriously by the inroads of marmalade-loving lascars, who loot oranges and sugar from other sources and then must have some of my citric acid to complete their yellow palate-corroding brew.

Lavoisier, incidentally, took the view that acids were binary oxygenated compounds, and that the associated water was an extraneous passive

* Not my own joke, however.

'element', which served merely as a solvent. He was really the daddy of the absurd theory that *all* acids are monobasic. An ancestor of my own (who landed at Killala when Ireland called and at a time when it was neither profitable nor popular) was all for the theory of polybasicity, and proved his point in the teeth of scurrilous opposition from Lavoisier and butties like Guy-Lussac and Gmelin, who were no better. That was a long time ago, of course.

I read that Ireland's acids in England are valued at £300,000,000. They are mostly organic acids of the carboxyl group, but we have several tanks of malonic and succinic acids and many thousands of cans of miscellaneous acids where the intrusion of carbon atoms (no doubt the work of persons who have no love for Ireland) makes classification according to empirical molecular formulae out of the question. How this vast accumulation of bitterness can be transported to this country after the war, or what possible use we would have for it, I cannot imagine.

The Plain People of Ireland : You're right there, we have enough bitterness in this country.

Myself : We have bedad.

The Plain People of Ireland : But of course the sulphuric is very handy for the batteries.

Myself : Aye indeed.

ME AND MY SOUL

This dripped off my assembly belt the other night (when I could have sworn I had the machines turned off for the night). Print it on barley-fudged crême-primed Hungarian sub-paper in good, old 12-point Gracatia Sancta and next thing you know I will have hair on my face and I will perceive indubitably Marxian strata in the subconscious, suggesting that all irrational impulses etc. etc. etc.

> the antic soul
> rides the wry, red brain;
> horses know horses know
> what they're thinking about
> (you might say curse that alien corn),
>
> the bloody heart
> lusts in its foul tenement
> o blow, viaticum pump, blow
> on your last glazed fruit-valves.

RECIPE

Stuff the breast of the chicken with some of the sausage meat. Place the sugar thermometer in the syrup while it is boiling. Withdraw the pan from the burner as soon as the correct temperature has been reached. Wash the sago. Mix the cornflour into a paste with some of the cold milk. Fill with prepared paste, using either a hot knife or a forcing pipe. Transfer to a tin lined with greased paper and bake for 1 hr. 45 minutes with the Regulo at Mark 4. Mix and turn out on a floured board, shape into cutlets, coat with the egg and bread crumbs and fry in hot fat for the rest of your natural.

*   *   *

WALKING the other day through Dublin's motorcar-denuded pinknailed-damsel-crowded O'Connell street (the broadest thoroughfare in Europe remember) I noticed with a start that the Bank of Ireland's office is surmounted by the motto BONA FIDES REIPUBLICAE STABILITAS. In plain English, this means, 'Bona fides* are the standby of the State'. Mark that. Not merely are those nocturnal beerswillers and liquorslobberers worthy people, valuable citizens, delightful souls that one likes to know: they are the backbone and the be-all of all we mean by 'Ireland'. By their existence they make possible our existence as an independent state. They are a sort of elated élite, a hiccup-shaken Herrenvolk. That's what the Bank of Ireland says.

What then is the reason for this? Most of us pay the State a lot of money in direct taxation in the course of our daily struggle to preserve life and reach our beds once more intact—threepence on this and twopence on that. But your bona-fide, who also does the same, is only starting out on his grandiose tasks of tax-paying when the rest of us are going to bed. He will journey into the wilds on the bitterest night, spend the still watches far from the snug company of wife and child and journey back in the dawn bereft of speech and money but gloriously distended with all that is best and excisable in Irish life. Sixty tax-bearing cigarettes have made the wind rattle in his scorched neck like a crow caught in a chimney; the dry barren husk of old disused drink loiters loathsomely through his haggard entrails; he has lost his cheque-book and a button has been wrenched from his coat: but he is happy, he has made a daring bid to maintain the Supply

* i.e. licensed drinkers (publisher's note).

Services and has not scrupled to face poverty, ill-health and dishonour that the Central Fund might be saved.

Yes, life is like that. You never know who is saving your bacon behind your back, you never *think*. Who will send me subscriptions for the erection of a statue in O'Connell street to The Unknown Traveller? Let his back be turned politely to Father Mathew and brave unflinching eyes turned towards the Swords Road and all the havens of sweet snug-bound far-niente which that way lie.

MARGINAL COMMENT

And talking of the Bank of Ireland, I came across the other day a copy of the Report of the Banking Commission. The Majority Report was annotated here and there marginally by an unknown hand in the following terms:

> Paragraph 25 is tendentious rubbish.
> Paragraph 21 is muck.
> Nó.
> Senile decay.
> What about the advances to farmers in the years 1920–21?
> Where???
> 'Normal times' have no relevance to 'the problem of liquidity', even if it be granted that the problem exists at all.
> Ye Gods!
> Oh Yeah!
> Blah!
> Tautology.
> All very simple.
> What about the deposits created by the banks to be lent to people in whose names they are created?

CATECLICHM

(At a time when) (our ever-dwindling fuel supplies) (bid fair) (to write finis) (to the most valiant efforts) (of the powers that be) (to maintain efficient transport services) (no words that I can say seem strong enough) (to express my abhorrence) (of ignorant fuel-wasting full-regulator men).

THIS IS AWFUL, I MEAN

I am having serious trouble in the management of my slum property. Penal legislation has made us landlords responsible for major repairs and sanitation, even if our tenants spend their spare time deliberately tearing our tenements to bits and trying to burn the bits in our own grates (and very expensive modern Hammond Lane jobs some of them are, installed in 1936 regardless of expense). My point is this. Supposing one of my gables develops a bulge. My tenant (who does not know his prayers but could recite the entire Landlord and Tenant Act for you without once drawing breath) flies off to the Corporation and makes his due statutory whine. Next thing I know I have a notice slapped in on me, whereas and unless, I send for my handyman and tell him to square up this bulge and see about doing some plastering and pointing and so forth. Then after a day or two an inspector from the Corporation turns up when I happen to be having a look at what my handyman has done—a perfect job, as a matter of fact, as good as new. The inspector picks his teeth and squints up at the gable. Then he puts his nail on the plaster and begins to scrape. Then he begins to tap here and there with his cheap folding pocket rule. Then scarcely without a glance at me he says:

ALL THAT'LL HAVE TO COME DOWN.

I get as pale as a ghost and tell him to listen here, that the job cost me twenty-five pounds and that I can produce the contractor's bill. The inspector is in the middle of a new slit-eyed squint and without turning his head says:

THAT'LL ALL HAVE TO COME DOWN THAT'S ALL THERE'S TO IT IT'LL ALL HAVE TO COME DOWN THE WHOLE LOT'LL HAVE TO BE TAKEN DOWN.

I stutter some thing about seeing further about it and having no intention of being robbed and bested by any inspector after landing out twenty-five good-looking pounds to a well-known and respected firm of building contractors. But the voice comes again:

THE WHOLE LOT'LL HAVE TO COME DOWN I'M SORRY BUT THAT IS ALL THERE IS TO IT THAT'LL ALL HAVE TO BE TAKEN DOWN.

I ask you.

* * *

TWO THINGS are required remember for a tryst, rendezvous or appointment. It is necessary to specify (a) time, and (b) place. Let me make my meaning clear. I want to avoid all ambiguity. Supposing I tell some girl or other that I will meet her at 8.30 p.m., thus specifying (a) but not (b). What happens? She turns up promptly enough at, say, the house where Dean Swift was born in Hoey's Court. But in the meantime I am waiting patiently in the Bull Ring, Wexford, listlessly inhaling fag after fag. Result: we fail to meet and letters of passionate recrimination are on their way in the next post.

Now let us turn from that and take the opposite case. I tell the lady to meet me outside the picture house in Skerries. Please note that in this case we are ignoring (a). She turns up at 1.18 p.m., waits for an hour and flounces off in a huff. I, however, (connoisseur of clichés that I am) put in that odd thing—an appearance—at 4.53 p.m. Again I produce the box of fags and embark on another of my lengthy incinerations. People passing say: I wonder who your man is waiting for. Your man has been standing there for an hour. Your man is up to something, that's a certainty.

See my point? The appointment is again broken, simply because we neglected to provide for both (a) and (b). Next time your girl fails to turn up, ask yourself whether you have followed the simple rule I have outlined.

The Royal M. na G. Institute of Archaeology

WE LIVE in strange times. It can now be revealed that there has been in existence for the past year (notwithstanding anything that may be contained in the Offences against the State Act) a body known as the Royal Myles na gCopaleen Institute of Archaeology (and you can bet your life that the latter term embraces Palaeontology, Eolithic, Palaeolithic and Neolithic Anthropology). Some months ago this body sent an expedition to *Corca Dorcha* (or Corkadorky), the most remote Gaeltacht area in Ireland or anywhere else. Violent excavations have been in progress since, and preliminary reports which are reaching Dublin from the explorers indicate that discoveries are being made which may mean the end of civilisation as we know it; and the end, too, of all our conventional concepts of human, social, artistic, geological and vegetable evolution. If these messages are to be believed, the Corkadorky researches will throw again into the melting pot the whole sad mess of Tertiary Man, Sir Joseph Prestwich's theory of the essentially pleistocene palaeolithic character of the Kent 'plateau-gravels', Stonehenge, the glacier theories, the 'proofs' of European neolithic eskimo stratigraphs, and even show that the gigantic mammalian skeletons which are honourably housed in our museums are fakes of the first order, perpetrated by 'Irish' Iberian flint-snouted morons (c. 6,000 B.C.) who practised the queer inverted craft of devising posterity's antiquities.

Local observers are hourly awaiting the emergence of the Corkadorky Man, who is expected to prove himself the daddy of every other Man ever pupped by scholarly dirt-shovellers. Unlicensed short-wave radio transmitters are standing by to flash the news to the learned societies of the world. Herr Hoernes, the famous author of *Der diluviale Mensch in Europa*, is maintaining a 24-hour watch at the earphones in Stockholm with M. Mortillet, whose *Le Préhistorique* is still read.

A word about this Royal Myles na gCopaleen Institute of Archaeology. There is some mystery about the 'Royal', many commentators holding that the term has reference to the bar of a certain theatre where it is alleged the first meeting was held and the learned objects of the Institute defined. Be that as it may, it would be rash to suppose that the Institute is just a gatherum of clay-minded prodnoses. Every branch of research has a sub-institute of its own and the heavily documented reports of each sub-institute are appraised, co-ordinated, catalogued, sifted, indexed, cross-referenced, revised, checked and digested by the 'Royal Institute', which is essentially an assessive, deductive and archivistic body. Within the 'Royal Institute' you have, for instance, the institute of Comparative Bronzes. This body is concerned only with time-bronze progressions (mostly based on millennial variations in the obliquity of the earth's orbit) and has already disproved practically every thing that has appeared in *L'Anthropologie: Materiaux pour l'histoire primitive de l'homme*, the somewhat inexact French publication. Then again you have the Association of Superior Muck. This body is composed of chemists who spend their time surveying the testing samples of alluvial muck and all manner of water-borne ordure. All this goes to show that the researches now in progress have no relation to scare journalism, 'all that is best in Irish life', 'progress', or any other shibboleth. It is an exercise in scientific discovery and deduction. There is no margin for emotion, conjecture or error. That is why Herr Hoernes stays up all night in Stockholm.

I have no intention of entering into the contents of the perturbing preliminary reports I have mentioned, or describing the larger objects stated to have been dug up. I illustrate here, however, a few of the smaller and less disturbing relics which were unearthed. The figures shown over are carved in stone. As a laymen I do not know what to make of them. The lower stone seems to be a representation of primitive greyhound racing, with every chance that our friend in front will clock 30.15. The upper stone may mean that we once had a national sport of fish-racing.

An observer on the spot, and who assisted in some of the excavations, has given me a somewhat far-fetched story which I pass on for what it is worth (and not, mark you, for what it is not worth). According to him the primeval human remains unearthed were fossilised, and bore on the legs certain serrated markings that suggested corduroy. Various other aspects of hair remains, neckwear remains and whatnot provided an impressive accumulation of evidence that the Corkadorky Man was an Ice Age

fly-boy and the progenitor of the present indefeasible Irish nation. It will be a nice cup of tea for the G.A.A. if this is proved to be the case.

I will have more to say on this subject.

A SPECIAL despatch from the explorers sent to Corkadorky by the Royal Myles na gCopaleen Institute of Archaeology states that large masses of diorite rock have been unearthed. The rocks look like adamellite and contain orthoclase, plagioclase felspar, micropegmanite starch, igneous hornblende, baking soda, gangrene-pale pyroxene, not to mention andesine strata tinged with accessory deposits such as zircan and apatite.

The Plain People of Ireland : Begob appetite is right, you'd need a square meal and a pint of stout after that mouthful of chat. What book did you cog all them jawbreakers out of?

Myself : The Encyclopaedia Britannica.

The Plain People of Ireland : And a fine man he is when he's at home, God bless him.

* * *

IN CORKADORKY

The savants sent to Corkadorky by the Royal Myles na gCopaleen Institute of Archaeology continue to send back curious despatches. The latest says that the Corkadorky Man is at last a reality. It appears that he is streets ahead of the famous Monmouthshire Man, nor has he anything to fear from Iceland's renowned Stelvik Man. He is one of the most interesting men ever discovered, and while an account of his more singular characteristics must be postponed to a future article, I may say here that one remarkable feature about him is the right index finger. Beyond yea or nay, it is the longest finger ever encountered by anthropologists. The Long Finger of the Corkadorky Man has, in fact, fascinated the explorers, and keeps continually cropping up in their somewhat incoherent messages. There is a long indentation or sign of wear on the top of it and the archaeologists argue that this must be proof of the Man's practice of putting things on the Finger and keeping them there for lengthy periods. 'Lengthy periods' in this context would, of course, mean centuries. This corroboration of the well-known folk idiom about putting things on the long finger is curious and may mean that the Corkadorky Man may explain for us at last why our record in the world as men of affairs has always been so miserable.

From inquiries I have made, I am glad to say that no traces of old fossilised meal have been found in the Man's mouth and that the hands bear no traces of cheese or of the despised cheese-paring tool. That is something to be thankful for and something to be going on with.

A ROVING PARTY from the Myles na gCopaleen Institute of Archaeology have arrived in Killarney and have chosen to start excavating at the bottom of the lakes. It is a safe bet that nobody else in the world would have thought of doing that or anything like it. As usual, the operations have resulted in a flood of wild rumours. Preliminary messages arriving in Dublin say that the explorers have found that the bottom of the lake consists, not of the usual mess of muck and weeds one might expect, but first-grade waterproof concrete. The Institute contends that this (with other proofs they have) goes to show that Killarney is not a divine accident of nature or 'heaven's reflex', but the personal handiwork of our crafty ancestors. If the Institute is correct, the whole hash of lake and mountain with its wealth of sublimely inconsequent *nuance* was carried out with hod, trowel, plumb-line and muck-bucket. It seems also that the whole place is a network of hot pipes and that it is thus that the sub-tropical vegetation effects were got. The pipes are buried at varying depths and are said to be connected with hot subterranean spas in Clare and places even more distant. Apparently what the Institute is getting at is that the whole of Ireland is a vast construction job and that we have nobody but ourselves to thank for our peerless scenery. Sea shells have been found on top of the Devil's Mountain, proving that sea-level soil was heaped up by human agency to make the mountain. It is thought that the Firbolgs (or 'Bagmen') were the slave-artisans who did the carrying work in primitive times. The large hollow left by the excavation necessary to construct even a small mountain was always carefully concreted and filled with water.

The savants who are in Kerry hope to produce a Killarney Man in due course. What they intend to do with him we can only guess.

CLOVING

A MAN I know got wind last week that cloves were going to be rationed. He was cute and set about buying up every vestige of this commodity that was on offer. Carts, vans and boys on bicycles began to arrive in an endless stream at his modest suburban house. Soon the place was packed out from floor to ceiling with barrels, boxes and sacks full of cloves. He had managed to corner about half the nation's supply, and possibly could be excused the chilly Shylock smile that had begun to creep about his well-kept clock. He got a nice let-down, with parsley on it, when he learnt later that it was clothes—not cloves—the people had been talking about.

Of course there's a moral in this. Be careful lest you inadvertently season your hot whiskies and pies with old clothes.

> *Waiter, what's this?*
> *That's a bit of an old shirt, sir.*
> *What—in a pie?*
> *Yessir. We couldn't get cloves, sir, so we had to use an old shirt, sir.*
> The result would be no tip, of course.

ANOTHER MATTER

Talking of the general question of supplies, could not our foodstuffs be augmented by doing something about the many thousands of mealy-mouthed persons we have in this country? The meal could be extracted from their mouths, sterilised and packed away in sacks. (And please don't blather to me about the legal snags in such a matter or the 'liberty of the subject'—you can do anything from frying onions to squirting old chocolate on a fly boy's yellow shirt under the Emergency Powers Act).

And then what about all the cheese-paring types we have also? Why can't we collect all the cheese-parings, melt them down into 1lb lumps and add them to our dwindling stock of vitaminous eatables? All we want is a little bit of organisation and energy.

YOUR GRANDMOTHER'S EGGS

All right, you don't like your eggs hard. Very well. But stay. Do you feel hot and angry when some unspeakable hack writes: 'This book is like the curate's egg—good in parts'? Does that hideous cliché make you close your fist in murderous resolve? Does it kill you? Very well. Look at my machine.

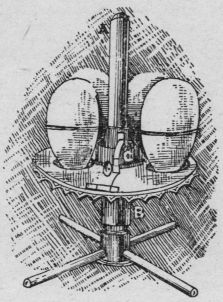

The hollow central cylinder A slides over the other cylinder B, containing a notch in which the trigger C will catch when the upper cylinder is pressed down. Put the whole shooting gallery into a saucepan of cold water, press down A until the eggs are immersed, lock all doors, pull down the blinds, hang some crêpe on the hall door and then light the forbidden gas. As soon as the eggs are cooked, the pressure of steam will release the trigger and the spring in the central cylinder will yank up the eggs clear of the water and at the same time raise the lid of the saucepan.

By a screw attachment to the trigger the time of cooking may be regulated. The machines are thirty shillings each, direct from this office.

The idea came to me in 1893, when I was firing the Dublin–Drogheda run.

SOCIAL AND PERSONAL

Myles na gCopaleen has left 31 Westmoreland street, and will be away for twenty-nine years.

WE ALL MAKE his praise: William Shakespeare. Governs a nice quiet land: Victoria, England's queen. Do you get it? Anagrams. Not everybody can make good anagrams and hardly anybody can do the smart job I've done above—make another phrase appropriate to the phrase worked upon.

Now in your father's day making anagrams was a polite occupation and was encouraged in girls' schools. But, of course, all that is changed, old boy. If you were found nowadays sitting in an old rose garden making anagrams, people would ask you to run messages for them, or keep nix while the new lodger's letters are being steamed. Indeed now, faith, times change. Well do I remember taking my seat on the first train ever run on the old Kingstown Atmospheric Railway, using a pass kindly given to me by my old friend, Sir Albert Hall. Your mother, child, was the engine driver. How we met is another story, and one not entirely without charm. Hand me my old album there till I show you my 1876 sprig of fern.

To come back for a moment, the Northern Premier said recently that 'Sir Dawson Bates enjoyes my implicit confidence.' The Oxford Dictionary says that the word implicit means 'entangled, entwined . . . : implied though not plainly expressed . . . : resting on the authority of another, as 'implicit faith, belief', etc. *Hence erroneously*, absolute, unmitigated.'

It is a nice thing to find that the King's English is as weak in Belfast as elsewhere. What must these people's Irish be like?

* * *

OFTEN I SIT here remembering, the eye glazed and meditative, beautiful in reverie despite the old trachoma scars. I often wonder does anybody remember as much as I. The great Irish Language Procession of 1903, yes, we all remember that. I wheeled the first Irish-built bicycle in it. But do you remember the Tottenham Court road in that terrible winter of 1876, the dark slime on the road, the slow clip-clop of walking horses, the foul icy fog punctured for a second by a drab lighting a cigarette with a pale lucifer match? Shaw and I often look back on those days, but there's no nostalgia nonsense about us. Neuralgia, if anything.

OBVIOUSLY GENUINE

I am continually overhearing chat like this, and I (make you a present of it) (for what it is worth).

Do I know the Bottle-o'-Bass Quinn? Do I kn—? Do I—? (*Here there is simulated incoherence and inarticulateness to convey that the question is almost comically unnecessary.*)

Do I KNOW him? Sure didn't we go to school together man.

But do you know what it is. I wouldn't know him now if I saw him.

You would boy you would then, he's always the same.

Is that a fact?

The Bottle-o'-Bass didn't grow older . . . and he didn't grow younger in the last twenty years.

Well is that a fact now. Do you know what it is, the Bottle-o'-Bass was a topper. A topper.

What's that you said? (*This is the fiction of deafness, which conveys that the statement made is so obviously true that it is an abuse of speech to make it at all.*)

I said he was a topper.

A topper . . .? (*A pause here and a lowering of pitch.*) Do you know what it is Bottle-o'-Bass was too good that's what he was he was too good.

You might well say it sure he was a cousin of me own.

Many's the time I'd go down there selling fish and no matter what hour of the morning it was you had to go in and there was a big mug of tea planted down in front of you.

I believe you, I believe you.

And if you wouldn't take it . . .

I know, there'd be a sour . . .

And if you were there about lunch time begob in you'd have to go there like the rest of them.

I can believe it of him.

And if you went along there around tea-time . . .

If you didn't go in you were the worst in the world.

Ah yes, the Bottle-o'-Bass . . .

HERE IS SOMETHING I bet you did not know—that your second finger (beside the little finger) is longer than the other one beside it, all appear-

ances and preconceived notions to the contrary. Lay your hand palm down
on the table and measure both fingers carefully along the left edge.

Some days ago, when Caucasian Armavir was captured, I was thinking
of trying to link the event with prophetic Virgil. (qui ce-cinit ca-casum
Troiae). But my restless wasplike mind moved away from Troy to Troytown, from that to Shawn Spadah and thence to noble Orby that sleeps
under the great rock at Boss Crokers in Glencairn. You are too young
to remember them but they were kingly animals, each of them carried
enough real nobility in one fetlock to blast skyhigh all the egalitarian
spoof ever mouthed by your unkempt work-shy Marxists. I had five
shillings on Troytown (borrowed from one of our gardeners) and that night,
with no warning at all, I asked that pink empire of flesh which I own to deal
with its first bottle of Guinness's stout, brewed within a stone's throw of
the little house where first I saw the light of day. I was fourteen, I think,
on the day when Troytown showed them all what an Irish horse was, and
I remember being afraid to go home while carrying internally my tup-
pence-worth of infantile inebriation. But the grandfather, with whom I
was staying, had also known a thing or two that day and was above in
the bedroom being undressed by the gardeners. To this day I hear his
frenzied screams of 'Up the Boers!'

Troytown. Troy. As yes. How time flies! How the bird wingeth! How
fast the great black oxen trample us down, in a wild phantom mess of
Disney technicolour! Why do we wonder at war today and blame poor
Baldwin when the earliest surviving flights of the human intellect could
deal with nothing else? Arma virumque cano.

There is some Hungarian Count Kano concerned in the present Krieg,
on one side or another. Arma virumque Kano?

Or what about Armagh virumque cano?

Remember my old one? You can't have your Caucasus and eat it.

When is a sign refreshing?
When it is of the times.
When does it boil down to the same thing?
When all is said and done.
What does a thing suffer through the centuries?
Many vicissitudes.
In what is the origin of the Irish round towers shrouded?
The mists of antiquity.

You have discovered by now, I suppose, that the statement made at the beginning of this article is a lie. Do you realise that I have thieved several seconds of your life from you without a hope of recompense? Your little store of time is smaller. The bird, etc. And good enough it is for you, sticking your beak into the papers when you should be working.

If you are a lady, please overlook the asperity of my tone. Sit down and on mauve note-paper of rarest fragrance write me a letter that reeks with passion, with the warm travail of the heart. That will keep me quiet for a while.

* * *

THE POST OFFICE has asked me to explain in detail how to make a 'Personal' Trunk Call. (Is that your personal trunk, Miss Garbo, or is it only a lay figure?)

The particulars of the call should be given to the Trunk Operator (who, being an elephant, will remember them), as follows:—

(a) Assuming that Mr Kelly (Killanne 12345) wants to speak to Mr Doyle (Erin 9876), or, failing him, Mr Burke (of Messrs Kelly Burke and Shea, Solicitors, Commissioners for Oaths, Parliamentary Agents and Registered Undertakers); Mr Kelly should say: 'Erin 9876, Mr Doyle or Mr Burke (of Kelly, Burke and Shea) wanted by Dublin 12345, Mr Kelly.'

(b) If Mr Kelly wants to speak only to Mr Doyle, Erin, who may be at another telephone station in the same local fee area, he should give this other telephone number as a second choice. If Mr Doyle (or, indeed, Mr Burke) cannot be found, or will not be available until later, Mr Kelly will be so informed, and it will be 'open to him' (as civil service cliché-mouthers would have it) to slip down to the local public house for a pint (unless it is closed to him).

That is how the telephone book has it, and I suppose it is all simple enough. But I wonder is it? Suppose you can't (for the life of you) remember Doyle's name? Supposing you've forgotten your own name— a situation not uncommon with professional debtors? Supposing your humping name isn't Kelly—this last is my own problem? The G.P.O. seems to think that Dublin is Baile Atha Kelly be the look of things. Supposing you ring up Myles na gCopaleen and a lady answers, what then? Supposing you could swear it was your wife's voice? Supposing the whole telephone installation falls out of the wall and crushes your feet? Supposing you cut the finger off yourself trying to get your pennies back? Supposing you smash your nail, break it right across the middle after accidentally bending it back until it—

The Plain People of Ireland : Thop that! Thop!

Myself : All right, squeamish.

There is another thing about the telephone. At least once in a life-time one's telephone call happens to be answered by a person who had never used the telephone before, a young maid, possibly, or an imbecile gardener. You say 'Hello'. Back comes an answering hello. Then you say:

'This is Mr Doyle Erin speaking. Could I speak to Mr Burke of Kelly, Burke and Shea ?'

'Hello.'

That is the sole reply. Then you say loudly:

'Hello. This is Mr Doyle Erin. Could I speak to Mr Burke ?'

'Hello.'

'Hello! This is Mr Doyle Erin. Will you please listen to what I am saying, this is most important and urgent. I arranged with Mr Burke yesterday that I should ring him today at this hour to confirm a tentative business arrangement. Is he there, please ?'

'Hello.'

Then you drop the overheated supercharged tone and drop to the steely 'conversational' voice in which an American gangster says Listen, Bugs, just turn your back and walk over there, I'm not going to do a thing to you. Thanks Bugs. Bang!

'Listen,' you say, 'will you please tell me is Mr Burke there ?'

'Hello.'

'I said will you please tell me is Mr Burke there ?'

'Hello.'

'Is Mr Burke there ?'

'Hello.'

'Is Mr Burke there, damn you ?'

'Hello.'

The illiterate stupid . . . clodbrained . . . half-witted . . . platter-faced . . . cuckoo. Hello. Hello. Yah! Yah. Yah!

Recently I had a word to say about a certain literary man's 'laurels' and the advice he received to 'look' to them. The other day I was passing the house of another literary man and it occurred to me to call to see how his laurels were (faring) and what he was doing with them. I found him resting on them. Squatting there with his gross carcase on a heap of the decayed vegetation, he looked (for all the world) like a clucking buzzard perched on some jungle eyrie trying to digest some unspeakable feed while hatching its own evil eggs.

We talked for four hours, and the entire conversation (I may say) was in French. And never once (let me add) did he ask me whether I had a mouth on me. He is one of the old crowd.

*   *   *

THE FUTURE

I read somewhere the other day (by mistake, I was looking for something else) that the great motor car manufacturers are continuing for the duration of the war to design 'phantom' models of their vehicles, one new one every year, each improving on its predecessor, but that the public is to be kept in ignorance of all this. After the war (if that means anything) the first model to be (launched) will be as much an improvement on 1939's model as 1939 was on 1910, the year I bought the old De Dion from your uncle Joe. This is awful nonsense. By 1978—not that I suppose your men will have laid off their scrapping by then—I'll certainly have forgotten how to drive the 1939 car (first, down, second up and across and so on —I ask you, how could a poor blind rheumatic old man like me be expected to (turn round) (all over again) and learn how to drive these divilish new-fangled injins of 1978?). Sure 'tis nonsense, boy, nonsense.

And wait. Supposing this strictly private progress is also carried on in (other spheres)? What then? Suppose Montague Burton in his secret laboratory turns out each year a phantom lounge suit, gradually streamlining it, knocking off a pocket here, a lapel there, changing the trousers, taking them off, turning the waistcoat back to front, sewing the buttons on inside, coming out with two spare sleeves as well as the usual two, eventually throwing aside all accepted dress theories in favour of some mad invention (in shark-skin probably) buttoning down the back with a pair of stainless steel elastic breeches, hollow glass-tiled shoes and a hat with a periscope and a radiogram that turns records over and plays them upside-down and pours out drink for you and your pals every time you press the button on the zip fastener at the back of your neck. What decent Irishman would be seen in that rig-out matther a damn what year is in it? Sure it's nonsense, nonsense, Jack, do you see. You can't believe all the stuff you read in the papers, boy, no, sir, not by—

Not by what extended calcinated writing tool?

THE OTHER DAY I was reading that man down there on the right—£nunc*—and I caught him saying this:

* i.e. *Quid*nunc, the name used by the *Irish Times* columnist.

'If you have the bones of a typewriter lying in an attic they are worth money today.'

This seems reasonable enough until we bring (to bear) upon it our whole fatuous battery of professional paranoia, perversion and catachresis, rushing out with our precast vaudeville clown-routine of quotation, misinterpretation and drivelling comment. Does the result please anyone, bring the most faded polite laugh, the most tenuous giggle, the most bilious sneer?

Well, all I can say is this: if I have the bones of a typewriter, £nunc can do nothing for me, Harry Meade can do nothing for me, Barniville can do nothing for me, and it's a sure thing I won't be lying in an attic reading this newspaper's advice on how to make money. I'll be stuffed into some circus and billed above the Bearded Lady. On payment of sixpence you will be permitted to view my unique bones through some X-ray gadget.

Remington I knew well. He had the whole of his insides taken out of him, bones and all, when he was a lad—he was suffering from diffused chrythomelalgia—and had new bones made for him out of old typewriters. And, mark this, when he grew up, he was as fine a looking man as you'd meet in a dazed walk. (No, no, no, put away that pencil, I didn't mean you to mark it that way. I meant you to read, mark, and inwardly digest, that's all.)

In middle life Remington discovered that he had a weak chest and (what would do him), (only) have a complete brand-new typewriter built into the upper part of his metal torso. Occasionally he would accidentally tap down a key or two when leaning against counters or bridge-parapets. People said that mysterious tips for horse races were often found on his internal roller; (be that as it may) (certain it is) that he never went out without a sheet of paper stuck in his 'carriage'.

I well remember an embarrassing incident that occurred—I think it was the year of the split—the last time I was talking to him. (What would do me) (only) get into a political argument with him. I kept (on) tapping him on the chest to bring home all my points. Only when I heard the tinkle of a little muffled bell did I remember that I was talking to no ordinary man. Did he take offence? Not old Bill Remington. With exquisite refinement he excused himself, turned away, and inserting a hand under his waistcoat, drew back the carriage. I often wonder what stupid motto I typed out during that encounter. 'Up the Prince of Wales' or something, I suppose.

Poor old Underwood and that astute statesman, Smith Premier, were also men who had the typewriter in their bones. I knew them well. Decenter men never stood in that substance one associates with hot feet—shoe lather.

Towards the end of Premier Smith's life he was a sick man. And at what was he a very sick man?

At that.

But old George Underwood was a bright soul, always up to practical jokes and harmless rascality, you couldn't have a party without him. What shrill acoustical phenomenon was he?

A scream.

* * *

I FIND IT very hard to conquer this neurotic weakness of mine, reading newspapers. In this (very) paper the other day I read the following:

> 'The Department of Defence announces that persons who are not in receipt of a military service pension, or in possession of a military service certificate entitling such persons to a pension, must apply for a medal to the Secretary, Department of Defence. Such application will not be necessary from persons in receipt of a military service pension or in possession of a certificate.'

I'm not very sure about this. Suppose the population of this country is three millions and suppose that 5,000 citizens have these pensions or certificates. That leaves a total of 2,995,000 persons who must apply for a medal. For that proprietary fraction, my own part, I have no objection (in the world) to applying for this medal, providing reasonable arrangements are made to deal with the vast hordes of people who will be converging on the Department of Defence. But I have one serious doubt. Is there not an important principal at stake here? Is it wise to *compel* so many people to apply for a medal? Is it judicious to introduce into our democratic civilisation the ugly word 'must'? If I concede the right of a state department to compel me to apply for a medal today, how do I know that tomorrow I will not be compelled to call to some dispensary and swallow a bar of chemical chocolate? And the day after to have all my teeth extracted in the public interest? *Do réir a chéile seadh tuitid na caisleáin.*

Conceiving my liberty to be threatened, therefore, I have decided after the fullest consideration of all the relevant facts (funny how nobody bothers considering the irrelevant facts) to refuse to apply for this medal, and if need be to suffer jail or any other punishment that may be (visited) upon my head. (I digress again to remark that I am thankful that punishment is always confined to the head, which is a thickly-boned eminence and well able to endure it.)

Of course, I realise the awful futility of all this. I make a noble gesture in the cause of human liberty. I will not apply for or accept a medal. I sacrifice myself. I go to jail. I suffer. I lose weight. It is whispered that I am ill, nay, dying. People pray for me. Meetings are held. The public conscience is moved. A protest comes from the Galway County Council. There is a strike in Portarlington. Milk churns are upset at Athlone railway station. From my lone cell I issue an appeal to the people of Ireland to remain calm. High political personalities are closely guarded. Anonymous ballad-mongers sanctify my cause. The public temper mounts. Sligo County Council makes its voice heard (in no uncertain manner). The Banner County is next with a sternly-worded resolution. The Gaelic League comes into the open, calling me a martyr. Muintir na Tire dissolves itself as a token of mourning. The sea-divided Gael, meeting in solemn conclave, at Chicago, pledges its 'inalienable community of feeling with the people of Ireland in their devotion to the glorious martyr now lodged in the citadel of Mountjoy.'

And it all works. I am released. Cheering crowds bear me from the grim fortress. It is 8.15 of a winter's night. Grotesque torchlights enflame the city. I am wheeled away in Parnell's coach. Massed piper's play 'A Nation Once Again'. Where are we going? Dorset Street, O'Connell Street, Nassau Street. The Mansion House! Doyle is there and all the boys. The wan emaciated figure is assisted to the platform. Speeches. Different people keep standing up and sitting down. Speeches speeches speeches. Then I find that some very distinguished person has walked over to myself and is talking to me. What's this? I struggle to my feet. What has he there? A little black box. More talk. Then he opens it. A medal!

Then the crowd goes mad, but they don't feel half as mad as I do.

HERE'S ANOTHER THING I read in this paper recently:—

'When your unlocked bicycle disappears from the kerb of some unfrequented side-street, you can have no grouse coming—it happens every day of the week—but when the office stair carpet vanishes from under your eyes it is time to get perturbed. At that stage you unhook the nearest phone and communicate with the law.'

I don't get it. Look. There you are, miraculously enough, in an *unfrequented* side-street, your bike propped at the kerb, and behind you a hired thug in tweeds, clutching a shotgun. Suddenly the bike is gone. What I want to know is—why must it be assumed that there is no possibility whatever of the chance appearance of those dun-feathered fowl? That a carpet should magically disappear from under our feet may be surprising, but surely it is far more astounding that there should, in fact, ever have been a *stair* carpet under the feet of myself and my gunman when we are standing in an 'unfrequented' side-street waiting for a bicycle to vanish and for grouse *not* to appear. I mean. And worse, more complicated still, the carpet has also to vanish from under our eyes. The truth is very few people wear carpets under their eyes—though little bags knitted by Seán Jameson, yes.

And when this mysterious carpet vanishes, 'at that stage you unhook the nearest phone and communicate with the law'. A tramcar stage, I suppose, although we are told it is an unfrequented side-street. And 'unhook'? Alexandre Dumas Père? Period stuff. Unhooking phones, electric broughams, call me a hansom, you're a hansom, Yellow Book, Wilde, Harris, Marie Lloyd, murder in gaslight.

Now let us consider the thing on another plane as the pilot said to the rear gunner. Your carpet is stolen by what this anonymous writer calls 'light-fingered gentry'. Listen that's nothing. I left the office here in Westmoreland street the other day for a drop of lunch at five o'clock, locked the front door so that none of the crowd could get out and spread lies about me when my back was turned. Back to the office punctually at a quarter to eleven. No office, no great newspaper building. Westmoreland street, yes, but no sign of the archaic *buzantion* facade behind which. Stolen, Locke, Stack and Birrell (three best backs Ireland ever had, Ernie Crawford was only trotting after them). What did I do? I unhooked the nearest telephone box and asked for Commissionaire Guard Sheehan Daniel Depoe Finished Pork. Look, I want to report a robbery. My offices at 31 Westmoreland street have been stolen. Could you help? Last seen wearing a handsome old-world front of no particular (recognisable) period, wears a brownstone moustache and speaks Greek fluently. Certainly sir, not at all sir, a pleasure sir. I went back to a certain place greatly relieved that (the matter) had been taken out of my hands (though not by a doctor). Cycling home at five I noticed that the building had been put back again. But in their hurry the light-fingered gentry had replaced it back to front. It looked very queer I can tell you.

We are now having the thing chained.

* * *

I CANNOT stand or understand the sort of typographical shouting that goes on in that hierofrantic sheet, my income tax form, and it would not surprise me in the least to learn that yours is the same. This sort of thing: 'If you are a MARRIED MAN and your wife is living with you . . .' I think it is very bad taste using those heavy black caps, as the convict said to the trial judges (*pace* Hanna J. and this thoughtful letter to Ireland's premier finest most tunisian-minded newspaper, the *Irish Times*, all uncover, please). 'If you are a MARRIED MAN.' Undoubtedly there is some dreadful sneer intended here, some recondite official indecency that could be understood only in the underworld of please attach file, have you papers please, please speak, can you discharge file please, I am directed to say that the matter is under consideration.

'If you are a MARRIED MAN and your wife is living with you.' These hidden baroque-rats have the cool cheek (warm cheek for some reason is considered rare) to suggest that it is the exceptional thing in Ireland for a married man to have his wife living with him. One expects the formula to go on like this: 'If, however, you are a MARRIED MAN and have your wife parked out in Shankill so that you will not be embarrassed by her fearful appearance, ludicrous "conversation" and appalling clothes, give her address and telephone number.' Yes. But read the thing again. 'If you are a MARRIED MAN and your wife is living with you . . .' Supposing your wife is living with and you are not a married man (or even a MARRIED MAN), what then? What subtle poor oak rat's distinction is being made here?

If I understand English, a wife is what a woman becomes after she is married and no account of equivocal chat can convince me that anybody other than a married man can have a wife. (I am assuming all the time that cab-horses, cows and cats are not regarded as being in receipt of (mark that lovely phrase, 'in receipt of') a taxable income. Why then the 'if you are a MARRIED MAN' when the word 'wife' follows on at once? Why not say 'if you have a wife living with you . . .'? It would be too simple, I suppose. Incidentally, what is the legal meaning of 'living'? Supposing I am a MARRIED MAN and my wife is dying with me? Yes, I see it. The cold official brain thinks of everything. They must insist on this word 'living'. Leave it out, they will say, or even to change it to 'if you are living with your wife' and you will have all sorts of unprincipled persons claiming relief in respect of a wife who is (sure enough) sitting in the drawing room, very well preserved woman considering she died in 1924. Can you beat that for ghoulish circumspection? (It just occurs to me that there must have been a lot of official jargon in our jails in the oul days, have you file please, please attach file, is file with you please. Why this eternal tender supplication 'please')?

On the next page of the form I see CLAIM IN RESPECT OF PERSONAL ALLOWANCE (TO A MARRIED MAN), 'HOUSEKEEPER', CHILDREN, DEPENDENT RELATIVES, AND LIFE ASSURANCE PREMIUMS. Why this sneering sophistication of putting my housekeeper into inverted commas? The woman has a blameless character and makes that indigenous culinary complication, an Irish stew, that you would get up out off yoor bad en tha maddle off tha neight fur tay eet a wee bet off ut, d'yeh ondherstond me. Is a dependent relative what happens when you are unwise enough to say: I seen you with the man that you were speaking to whom? And why cannot I get relief in respect of dependent absolutes? The wife's mother, for instance?

I will not harrow you with the dreadful mess that this form assumes you to be in 'if you are an UNMARRIED PERSON'. Earlier it was a question of ? MARRIED MAN; if you happen to be unmarried, you are only a PERSON, which I consider insulting and sinister. Furthermore, I see no provision for the situation where you are a MARRIED WOMAN and (decently enough) support your husband. Listen to this: 'If you are an UNMARRIED PERSON having living with you . . . your mother.' What gaucherie! Unmarried persons in Ireland do not have their mothers living with them, they live with their mothers.

Small wonder faith that nobody likes this wretched form. Small wonder every bank, insurance office and big business firm in the country is tearing down and building up its walls rather than pay. Please speak. Bah!

* * *

YEARS AGO when I was living in Islington a cub reporter in the service of Tay Pay, founder of that modern scourge, the 'gossip column', I had great trouble with my landlord. The man was a vulgar low bowler-hatted plumber who tortured me exquisitely by his vulgarity of dress, talk and aspect. The situation rapidly became Russian. Evenings in the yellow gaslight, myself immersed in a letter to George Harris or painfully compiling my first novel, the gross plumber audibly eating tripe in an armchair behind me. The succession—the crescendo of 'Greek' emotion—irritation—anger—loathing—then hatred. And then the quiet grey thought —I will do this creature in. I will do for him, gorblimey, if I have to swing for it!

It is funny how small things irk far beyond their own intrinsic significance. The way he sucked at his dirty pipe, too lazy or stupid to light it. The trick of never lacing his boots up completely. And his low boasting about his drinking. Forty-eight pints of cider in a Maidenhead inn. Mild and bitter by the gallon. I remember retorting savagely on one occasion that I would drink him under the table. Immediately came the challenge to do so. 'Not now,' I remember saying, 'but sooner than you think, my good friend.' That is the way we talked in those days. Possibly it was just then that I first formed my murderous resolution. But I digress.

When I had finally decided to murder this insufferable plumber, I naturally occupied my mind for some days with the mechanics of sudden death. I was familiar with the practice of homicide fashionable in the eighties, and I laid my plans with some care. I took to locking my bedroom so that the paraphernalia of execution could be amassed without arousing the suspicions of the patient. The chopper was duly purchased, together with a spare hatchet in case the plumber's skull should withstand the chopper. I attended a physical culture class to improve my muscles. Alcohol and tobacco were discontinued. I took long walks on Sunday afternoons and slept with the window wide open. But most important of all—remember that I speak of the gaslit eighties—I purchased a large bath and the customary drums of acid.

I was then ready. The precise moment of execution did not matter so much. It would coincide with some supreme extremity of irritation. And it did. One evening re-opening the manuscript of my novel I discovered traces of tripe on the clean copper-plate pages. The wretched plumber had been perusing my private documents. I went upstairs whistling 'The Girl in the Hansom Cab', came down cheerfully with the chopper behind my back, and opened the ruffian's skull from crown to neck with a haymaker of a wallop that nearly broke my own arm. The rest was simple. I carried the body up to my room and put it in the bath of acid. Nothing more remained but to put things in order for my departure next day for a week's holiday with my old parents in Goraghwood, my native place.

When I returned to London, I went up to the bedroom with some curiosity. There was nothing to be seen save the bath of acid, I carried the bath down to the sitting room and got a glass. I filled the glass with what was in the bath, crept in under the table and swallowed the burning liquid. Glass after glass I swallowed till all was gone. It was with grim joy that I accomplished my threat that I would drink this plumber under the table. It was the sort of thing one did at the turn of the century.

WHEN A RESPECTABLE lady was up in court recently for removing not clothing but articles of clothing from a crowded shop when she thought nobody was looking, the District Justice remarked that there was far too much shop-lifting in Dublin, and then imposed (well, what can you impose?) a heavy sentence of imprisonment.

I suppose he was right when he said there was far too much shop-lifting in Dublin but I am not clear how one calculates what is the right amount of shop-lifting for Dublin. Would we be in a worse mess if there was too little shop-lifting? I think a small committee of D.J.'s should be convened to determine the optimum incidence of shop-lifting for Dublin and other urban centres and sentence only ladies who exceed their quota.

Another thing. God be with the days when I was in business meself. I opted for a gratuity when I left the Black and Tans and bought two small shops. I think it was groceries I was selling. I did very well and in no time had bought five others. Soon I was a chain-store king (although I'm going to be honest and admit that chains was the one thing we never stocked). But I'll tell you what happened. I ran into a frightful epidemic of shop-lifting. First my Stoneybatter house was lifted, then the Inchicore one. The loss of the shops was bad enough but as well as that I got into trouble with the Corporation over the gaping empty sites. PLEASE RE-INSTATE MISSING PREMISES WITHIN TEN DAYS FAILING WHICH. Red ink.

Then in one week six other shops were lifted, including the head office, which contained a personable typist. One of the shop-lifters got qualms of (surely I needn't say of what) and put the shop he had taken back but of course on the wrong site, it looked like a small boy in man's clothes, it didn't fit anywhere. Whereafter, of course, there was only one thing to do. We had to chain all the chain-stores. People thought this was odd and custom declined. Worse, my enemies started to taunt me about my 'tied houses'. The only customers who did not desert me were the chain-smokers, who came to my chain-stores in the hope of getting chains, despite the fact that we never stocked the things. Ineffective custom of this kind was no use to me and I sold out to a wealthy Stater the year of the split. That was my only venture as an entrepreneur, which is a much nicer word than middle-man.

And now I have a letter here I want to answer. A correspondent (and he's fairly substantial. I looked him up in Thom's, PLV £38) asks me what is the meaning of the Dublin word 'moppy'. He had overheard somebody saying that so-and-so was moppy. What did moppy mean? Well, here are a few synonyms.

Moppy; drunk; jarred; fluthered; canned; rotten; plasthered; elephants; fluthery-eyed; spiflicated; screwed; tight; mouldy; maggoty; full to the brim; footless; blind; spaychless; blotto; scattered; merry; well on; shook; inebriated; tanked up; oiled; well-oiled; cock-eyed; cross-eyed; crooked; boozed; muzzy; sozzled; bat-eyed; pie-eyed; having quantum sufficio; and under the influence of intoxicating liquor.

Curiously enough, the latter rather prim phrase is the only one used by the Gárda Siochána; they use it even when it emerges in the evidence that the defendant had only two small sherries in Swords, that he never takes drink, and that on the present occasion he was offered the sherry by his brother-in-law, who was celebrating a happy event.

Alas, the poor human.

* * *

TWO ATTITUDES are admissible in relation to roads: one, that there are not enough roads in this country and that more should be provided; two, that all existing roads should be ploughed up and wheat sown.

In relation to proposal No. 1, competent engineers have informed me that new roads could be most economically provided side by side with existing roads; this for the reason that road-making machinery can be readily and cheaply transported and operated on the existing roads. It must be borne in mind, however, that once a duplicate road has been constructed beside an existing road, the second road can itself be used as the 'base' for the construction of a third road; thus there is no considerable engineering difficulty in constructing an indefinite number of new roads provided they are located parallel and together. Hollows in the terrain can, of course be filled in with cement and eminences removed by mechanical excavators. It must be added, however—and I have the authority of an agricultural expert for saying this—that the construction of a large number of new roads in the manner suggested would tend to diminish tillage activities. Generally speaking, then, the proposal is feasible but open to objection by sectional interests.

Very well. Now as to proposal number two. The cultivation of wheat on roadways is not, I am advised, impossible; it would be, however, difficult and a successful crop could not be expected save at the cost of great skill and diligence in husbandry. Roadways of some centuries standing could not, of course, be dug or ploughed in the ordinary way. Excavation whether by mechanical means or with pick and shovel would be necessary.

Arable soil would scarcely be reached at a lesser depth than 3 feet and thus a considerable quantity of material would have to be excavated to secure an arable trench of even moderate width. The disposal of this material presents a problem. Assuming that a stretch of roadway fifty miles long is to be prepared for wheat, it would be necessary to remove the material by motor lorry, starting from the remote extremity; this for the reason that since the roadway is disappearing, traffic must be confined to the portion still intact at any moment. Fleets of fast horse carts could, of course, be used for less ambitious undertakings but mechanical transport is essential for long hauls.

There is, however, another alternative. The excavated material could be stacked on the roadside at both sides of the trench. It is true that this plan would curtail the area available for cultivation to a strip two or three feet in width, but this cannot be avoided without permitting the excavated material to *encroach upon the adjoining fields*, thus diminishing what is called the agricultural potential. Since this is (for obvious reasons) to be avoided at all costs, it is possible that on a very narrow road, where abnormally deep excavation would be called for, the excavated material would have to be erected in the nature of a wall on each side of the trench, and the trench would only be of diminutive lateral dimension—possibly as little as six inches. These crude rubble walls would, of course, obstruct sunlight and even rain, and to that extent growth in the trench-bed would be retarded. Moreover, where excavation had to be brought in such a trench to a depth of four or five feet, the side-walls would be a corresponding height above ground level, so that the wheat, even if it attained normal height, would be about three feet below the level of the walls. In a trench six inches wide it would be impossible to save such wheat unless special machinery could be devised for the purpose. Whether such machinery could be devised and economically manufactured and marketed would depend on the number of very narrow wheat trenches in the country having high side-walls.

All these considerations must be weighed by every thoughtful Irishman.

★   ★   ★

IT ONLY OCCURRED to me the other day that I will have biographers. Probably Hone will do me first and then there will be all sorts of English persons writing books 'interpreting' me, describing the beautiful women who influenced my 'life', trying to put my work in its true and prominent place against the general background of mankind, and no doubt seeking to romanticise what is essentially an austere and chastened character, saddened as it has been by the contemplation of human folly.

One moment. Where is Con? Con! Here he is. Con, do you like sole bonne femme? A very stylish dish. Con, fashion is good for the sole.

Here is my confession, which I address to Hone. Call it a solemn warning if you like. *Believe nothing that you see in my cheque-book stubs.* The entries therein might well have been made by that historic protolouse, the father of lice. Let me confess. At the beginning of the month when I get my wages from across the way ——→ (often paid by mistake in mysterious Russian and Tunisian currencies, frightful row every now and again trying to get Caffey to change them into humble Irish uncomplicated agricultural notes) I naturally put five pounds in my pocket (not my mouth) and stick the remaining £145 into the bank. A day passes. On the evening of the second day I am in the usual place giving out about the Labour Party; I have ordered 4 at elevenpence each, two at sixpence halfpenny plus eightpence halfpenny for ten cigarettes slipped in under my coat-tails and to my surprise I find I have no money to meet this commonplace mercantile obligation. Out comes the cheque-book and a docket is written out for five pounds. Do I enter 'Self, £5' in the stub? I certainly do not.

I am ashamed to do that because these payments to myself are so embarrassingly frequent. I have no desire to have Hone making me out as a sore hedonist. Hence the appearance in my life of a mysterious character called Hickey. I always write 'Hickey, £5' or 'Hickey, £6', or 'Hickey, £3' whatever it may be. I have a cheque book stub before me as I write. In the space of a fortnight the following payments are recorded against Hickey: £5, £5, £3, £4, £2, £2. But let me be perfectly honest, let me make of it that immaculate pectoral phenomenon, a clean breast. I have not told all. Apparently my shame in writing 'Self' begot a counterfeit secondary shame at the frequency and consecutiveness of these windfalls to Hickey and—pray bear with a weak character in the agony of confession—I notice that between the £4 and the £2 towards the end, there is a payment of £2 to 'Hodge'. Later on in the book, both Hickey and Hodge get £5 apiece within three days of each other. Later again, Hickey alone benefits to the tune of £2, £2 and £4. So far as I can ascertain, Hodge has received only four cheques totalling £21 10s od in a space of eighteen months but Hickey has received hundreds of pounds.

Consider the ass Hone would have made of himself had I not chosen to make this revelation in the interests of history. Some terrible drama would be invented. Blackmail. 'It is scarcely to be credited that while engaged in giving masterpiece after masterpiece to the world, the master was in the toils of a blackmailing ruffian called Hickey, who, with a confederate called Hodge, extracted from him practically every penny he earned.'

Or would he insist on Mrs Hickey, a mysterious widow? A sordid entanglement, straightened out eventually with money to make her keep away? Would the public believe in the existence of a woman so rapacious?

But do you mind the cuteness of me.

* * *

I HAVE A NEW BOOK in Hands (the name of the family I'm in digs with) and I have been slaving away in connexion with it night after night above in the National Library. (Drop in there some day if you want a laugh— watch many a forthcoming 'novel', 'play' or 'biography' being copied straight out of the nation's books—and all under the auspices of that handsome soldier, 'Buck' Shea!) This book of mine will be all about the Wild Geese, you know the crowd that were concerned with putting absurd counterfeit pennies in the sea, grey wing upon the tide and so on. Of all the men that fled with that quaint letter heading, RESHAYMUS, perhaps none was so glamorous, none so handsome, none so romantic as Brigadier Remus O'Gorman. Though born in Cookstown and a fine broth of a boy, he is sometimes referred to as an Irish Swords-man; this is nonsense, he never set foot in a bona fide in his life. Be that as it may certain it is that here we have perhaps the most successful Wild Goose that ever laid a golden ague. He founded (by marriage) a family that shed that cheap old-fashioned cloth, lustre, on the country of his origin and gave to the country of his adoption a Marquis, two Marshals including a traffic marshal, a King (under the Empire), three Presidents, four Princes (under the second empire) and the imperishable poet and racketeer, excuse me, raconteur, Rémy de Gourmont *nach maireann*. (Some of the boys were a bit wild—do you remember that reproach to a certain party for the reason that nunc in quadriviis et angiportis glubit magnanimos Remi nepotes?) You must order a copy of this book (all orders will be dealt with not so much in rotation as in strict rotation)—it will be fully documented and will have a handsome appendix presented to me by Barniville in memory of the old days in Cecilia street. The price will be a quid.

ADVICE TO PARENTS

One thing you'll have to make sure about if you're a father—never permit your son to consort with anybody in the building trade. Take my own boy. I can only conclude that he spends practically all his time in the company of some plasterer because, do you know what it is, that fellow comes home thoroughly plastered every night. Frightful business. And then all this talk about shortage of supplies.

It worries me, I may tell you. I sit at home every night thinking about it and smoking endless cigarettes. If you call to my place any evening after seven I will show you one of them. Quite circular, like a hoop. My endless cigarettes are made specially for me by Carrolls of Dundalk, that hateful centre of everything that spells reaction in the steam world. G.N.R.(I.). Bah! Why not put the whole show into the brackets while they're at it? G.N.R.(I.) looks like a man lying naked in bed with a hat on him.

And why this (I) at all. One thing that is to be admired about the English is their superb conceit. Thus they call their papers 'The Times', 'The Daily Telegraph' and so on, scorning to mention their nationality. But our Irish newspapers, railways, natives and stews always bear an explicit statement that they are *Irish*—as if anybody in any part of the world could be in any doubt about it.

A MEMOIR OF KEATS

Of course there is no drink can compare with a bottle of stout. It is *sui guinnessis*. Keats once called a cab and was disgusted to find the beautiful upholstery ruined with milk spilt by some previous reveller who had been going home with it. Instead of crying over the spilt milk, Keats said to the cabman:

'What's this? A cabri-au-lait?'

ANY TIME you happen to visit the kingdom of the blind, you will find the one-eyed Manus King.

Excuse me. I have been glancing over an old newspaper and I read that on the 21st May the City Council will meet for the purpose of 'striking this year's rat'. This is probably one of these medieval ceremonies, like the one where the Lord Major fires a dart into the Liffey estuary to proclaim the borough's dominion over the port. Where is this rat caught?

What is it struck with and how hard are the blows? It may be the N.S.P.C.A. in me but I think it's damn silly for a crowd of grown-up men to gather in the City Hall to beat up one defenceless rat, matteradamn what the excuse is. It's not so much that I'm friendly with rats but I could think of creatures that deserve a hiding far more. I regret we cannot print their names here. We're afraid of libel but there's also the difficulty of space remember.

* * *

You know that thing of Yeats beginning When you are old, Dan Grey, and full of sleep? Well, I have translated it into rather fine French. Write to me enclosing a damped stressed envelope and I will send you a copy printed on black glazed buckram with a handful of parsley and two hard-boiled eggs. My version begins Quand vous serez bien vieille, au soir, à la chandelle, assise auprès du feu . . . and ends with this really pukka sob: Cueillez des aujourd'hui les roses de la vie. The thing doesn't need a frame and can be bent, screwed or nailed just like a piece of steak.

I am also doing a German version, into what mercantile contract?

> Upstairs in his empty room
> Gaspard plays his violin
> And the embarrassed corpses whom
> He asks to dance, just grin.

> So he calls his sister Cissie
> (Whose surname now is Derham)
> And asks would she pepulisse
> Ter pede terram.

I like to give a domestic tip now and again because I have reason to think that a few ladies read my notes here. A good way to prevent blood from curdling is to make sure that only the purest ingredients are used. Secondly, pour the blood in very slowly, a spoonful at a time, and thin it out with a few drops of vinegar when the mixture threatens to become too turgid.

I think some of our government departments should see about getting themselves more appropriate names. Our military ministry, seeing we are neutral, should be called the Department of the Fence. And surely the Department of Agriculture is a poor title—would it not be better to call it the Department of Yokel Government?

Really, stuff like this should not appear in a respectable newspaper like the *Irish Times*. It should refuse to print it. Or else change its name to the *Irish Mess*.

Enough.

IT IS FASHIONABLE for you women to jeer at us men and pretend that we spend our lives in the sheerest self-indulgence without a thought for anybody else. This is quite wrong, as I have reason to know from something that happened the other day. I was approached by two friends who were very worried about a third party, a great friend of us all. This man (a frightfully decent sort) was making a fool of himself. Question of running around with a married woman. There was talk. The whole thing was most unsuitable. My two visitors thought it was up to the three of us to do something. They thought that I knew the erring man best of all and would I think of seeing him and having a talk as between men of the world? I immediately saw that it was my duty to do so. However unpleasant the interview might be—and some men are inclined to resent advice on personal matters—I saw that I owed it to my fellow-man at least to reason with him and to try to make him see that he was transgressing the rules of good conduct. Accordingly I went. I called to my friend's rooms at 3 p.m. on Sunday and according to my watch it was 3.6 p.m. when I emerged. My other companions, who were nervously waiting for me round the corner, remarked that my face was red. I explained to them what had happened. Yes, it was quite true that he was carrying on with a married woman. He was married to her, of course. Detestable business. We haven't spoken since.

WASTED TIME

I was passing the *Irish Times* office the other day, and, realising how dreadfully dull newspapers are nowadays, I suddenly dived down on all fours and bit a passing dog in the leg. The creature squealed. I immediately went into the *Irish Times* office and reported the occurrence. Here was genuine news at last, a scoop. But no, they wouldn't use it. Sorry sir but the public would not be interested sir. Times have changed sir. Very sorry sir. And so forth. I ask you.

I went and hung my head in Shame, that well-known suburb of Canossa.

ABSINTHE MAKES THE HEART GROW WARMER

WAITER, what was in that glass?

Arsenic, sir.

Arsenic. I asked you to bring me absinthe.

I thought you said arsenic. I beg your pardon, sir.

Do you realise what you've done, you clumsy fool? I'm dying.

I am extremely sorry, Sir.

I DISTINCTLY SAID ABSINTHE.

I realise that I owe you an apology, sir. I am extremely sorry.

EVERY NOW AND AGAIN my friend Quidnunc down here on my left (your right) sees Fitt (best tailor in Dublin) to make mysteriously incomprehensible and far-from-called-for observations. (I digress to remark that uncalled for drinks are rarely served in Irish dram-shops.) A few weeks ago I caught him saying in that charming high-pitched voice (there is nothing better than one coat of pitch and tar applied evenly with a mop for preserving timbre) the following:

I hope that the church and monastery of San Niccolà, the most interesting buildings in Catania, have survived the recent fighting.

To this I make one unanswerable query: Why?

If you are going to make observations like this on Sicily, why pick on the one thing we know to be a piece of unthinkable theatrical shoddy, so ruthlessly 're-built' in the last century as to be completely unrecognisable, even to those of us who measured it in the sixties. I have the drawings above in a drawer to this day together with a prayer book belonging to Father Johnson and a silver calipers once the property of Cooley R.I.P.

Look at me, I hope that nothing happens to the temple of Zeus at Agrigento, to temples 'C' and 'D' at Selinus, to that long pseudo-peripteral hexastyle agglomeration of architectures at Segesta, comprising the styles of ten centuries on one site, and presenting, through century-slow fragmentation, the artistic erasures of Time, which is cunningly enough removing the more recent, leaving the oldest to the last. I know a fair amount about this subject but do not shout about it, unlike a certain other person.

Look at me again. I have a passion for the Moslem work that was there before the Normans came and which Roger and the bishops he brought with him from Provence were broadminded enough to admire. (I knew the Guiscards well—all excepting the brother of Pope Urban.) Yet do I talk of all this?

I hope to heavens nothing happens to the Church of the Martorana that the Admiral George of Antioch built in 1143 (not 1144 as Brehier so wrong-headedly suggests). And I have a great graw for the Capella Palatine: very special stuff, Latin plan, structure frightfully Greek and the nave plasthered with Byzantine mosaics. And then those incredibly Moslem road-houses (you know—Favara, Menani (Roger II) La Ziza (William I) and La Cuba (William II)! What one finds in Sicily is . . . well . . . Europe . . . but is there ever a word out of me about that? Do you find me . . . parading my knowledge? I think not.

Cefalu, Vespri, Palermo, Monreale, that squat timber-roofed tub— if it weren't for the plan, you'd say pre-Norman. And those very quare-looking gadrooned voussoirs, which really must be Islamic in origin— after all, the earliest example of them is in Bab el Futtuh, Cairo 1087, as every one knows. And those interesting intersecting arcades that give the effect of fourteenth-century English window tracery . . . they at least are Norman in origin, as is the chevron ornament that we find even in Ireland and sometimes on the sleeve of me son's coat that's in the Army.

I hope nothing happens to the Municipio and the Cathedral in Syracuse (some relatives of mine are buried within the walls)—as nice a pair of late Renaissance essays as you could hope to find. I make nothing of this, nor do I shout of my predilections in the newspapers, much as less talented persons might be gently suborned to my lordly standards of taste. If there is one thing I would warn you against it is the baroque style. There you have something that lacks the sternness and strength of truly virtuous and admirable work. It is effeminate—I would sooner have Philipstown. (I hope nothing happens to Philipstown.)

ABOVE IN THE CITY HALL

I read with bitter amusement that the 'scandal' of Dublin's basement dwellings will be raised at the June meeting of the Corporation. This may impress some people, but to me it simply means that the City Vat-Herrs are too fat, too sybaritic, to attempt the climb to the top floor. It is not that basements are luxurious; but compare for one moment, I pray you, the essentially warm situation of the couple in the kitchen with the plight of the widowed lady on the upmost storey. She lives alone with five mahogany sideboards, four beds, an inlaid escritoire, and two upright pianos. Every day she scrubs the stairs from attic to cellar, and do not forget that the only accessible water tap is in the yard, and that she is seventy-three. The gas rationing does not affect her, it is true, since she has nothing to cook; but she does feel it would be nice to use the only bath for some purpose other than collecting rain water, which comes in through the 'roof', owing to the absence of slates. She does not wish to complain, but though twelve of her children are happily married in Cleveland (Ohio) she does not forget that thirteen others slipped through the rotting floor-boards in infancy, and had to be waked in the two-pair back. She feels that if the floor were repaired life would be rather marvellous. She has some bitter words for the Government but feels that, all things considered, Mr Asquith is doing his best. She was born in Dublin, but sometimes would as soon say it's from Injeh she is.

YESTERDAY I marched into the polling booth, happy that the decent

Government had permitted me to take part in the complex quinquennial gestation that culminates in an expression of The People's Will. As usual, everybody looked as if they (yes, I know that 'they' is wrong there) were engaged in some criminal conspiracy. Shifty looks, muttering mechanical smiles. Women trying to look as if they had the remotest idea of the meaning of Irish politics. Youngsters of twenty-one coming in with a face that was intended to mean 'I suppose I'll have to vote but God be with the days of me dead chief, Parnell.' A general air of deceit and pretence, though I'm not sure that there is any difference between those two words. In the corner, a man that looked very like a member of the crew known as 'all right-thinking Irishmen' carefully reading a bound volume of *Irish Times* leading articles in order to find out for whom he should vote 'unless the country is to embark upon another decade of recriminations based upon a civil war that was fought at a time when a large body of the electorate was not even born'. (Needless to say, I dissent from the view that what took place before a man was born can be of no interest to him. I can think of a number of ante-natal occurrences that *should* be of some interest to every right-thinking Irishman: a certain wedding, for instance; or the steps taken in 1914–18 which ended all war forever, the foundation of the G.A.A., the emigration of Bernard Shaw, even my own fight in the eighties for the use of the 'full regulator' in Irish railway practice.)

In the polling booth also I saw evidence of that dreadful pest, the man who is anxious to give the impression that he is personating himself. I will not say that he tries to look like a suspicious character, for the sole reason that I try to write decent English and I will not permit myself (for one moment) to say 'suspicious character' if I mean a character who is not suspicious but whose behaviour provokes suspicions on the part of others. This man manages to sidle into the booth, avoids everybody's eyes, starts searching his pockets and makes no attempt to vote. He is ultimately asked for his name and stammers a name out after some hesitation. No, he cannot find his card. He does not know his number. The agents immediately challenge him. A Guard hovers in the background (using the patent wings devised by my Research Bureau.) Then me dacent man changes his tune, establishes his identity with devastating precision, causes a number of bystanders to identify him, casts his vote (instead of voting) and walks out leaving a very discomfited parcel of officials behind him, all wondering if they will receive solicitors' letters the next morning. A very bad low Irish type.

Leaving the booth myself, I realised that I had once again spoilt my vote by marking Xs opposite the names I had decided to honour. I had also, of course, inserted the usual comic verse but that alone does not invalidate a voting paper. I walked home wondering why all illiterates use the complex symbol X when they put pen to pay up her. Are we wrong in assuming that a stroke or straight line is the simplest and most primitive literary symbol? Is it in fact more recondite and difficult than the X? Or has the X a mystical import for humans, a quality that transcends all considerations of intellect? Naturally, I do not care a thraneen which it is, it is only a self-conscious peasant like myself would raise such issues in a respectable newspaper.

I am glad it is over but for my part I will not celebrate when me man is returned. I am off the bier, as the corpse said when the drunken motorist crashed into the funeral.

I FOUND MYSELF going homewards the other evening, not in a cab but in that odd mobile apartment with the dun-coloured wall-paper, a brown study. Long long thoughts occupied my mind. I was examining myself according to occult criteria which substitute for 'time', 'death' and other gaffes of the frail human intellect that blinding instant of vision which simultaneously begins, explains and closes all. Such insights as I have been vouchsafed give warning that all of us will encounter serious trouble in due time, for the upper limits of our aerial 'existences' bristle with complexities. Your politician will assure you that the post-war world is the great problem that looms ahead, but those of us who do not spend all our time in this universe well know that the real problem will be the post-world war.

Yet going home that evening I was remembering my small self, thinking of all that had happened through the years, re-examining the mélange of achievement and disillusion that I call my life. Praise I have received, blame also: yet how vain are both, how easy of purchase in the mart of men! I feel that one thing at least stands forever to my credit in the golden ledgers—the rather generous provision I made for the widow Manity and her children when her husband—my best friend—died after a long and painful illness. Poor suffering Hugh Manity, I kept the promise I made to him on his death bed.

When I reached home I was in an odd mood. I felt . . . old. Age and achievement hath like brandy a mellowness yet withal a certain languor. My daughter was in the next room humming and putting on her hat. I called her.

'Hullo, Bella. Sit down for a moment, will you.'

'Yes, Daddy. What's the matter?'

A long watery stare out of the window. The pipe is produced and fiddled with.

'Bella . . . how old are you?'

'Nineteen, daddy. Why?'

Another frightful pause.

'Bella, we've known each other for a long time. Nineteen years. I remember you when you were very small. You were a good child.'

'Yes, daddy.'

More embarrassment.

'Bella . . . I have been a good daddy to you, haven't I? At least I have tried to be.'

'You are the best daddy in the world. What *are* you trying to tell me?'

'Bella . . . I want to say something to you. I'm . . . I'm going to give you a surprise. Bella . . . please don't think ill of me but . . . but . . . but, Bella—'

With a choking noise she has jumped up and has her arms about me.

'O daddy, I know, I know! I know what you are going to say! You . . . you're not my daddy at all. You found me one day . . . when I was very small . . . when I was a tiny baby . . . and you took me home . . . and cared for me . . . and watched over me . . . and now you find you have been in love with me all these years . . .'

With a scream I was on my feet. Soon I was racing down the street to the local cinema, clutching in my inside pocket the old-fashioned Mauser, a present from Hamar Greenwood for doing a few jobs for him at a time when it was neither profitable nor popular. I reached the cinema and demanded to see the manager. Soon the suave pink-jowled ruffian appeared and invited me into his private office. Very shortly afterwards two shots rang out and I sincerely hope I will be given an opportunity of explaining to the jury that I had merely wished to suggest to my daughter that as a father of a family who had worked and scraped for years to keep other people in luxury, it was about time I should be relieved of the humiliation of having to press my own trousers.

* * *

DO YOU KNOW it frightens me sometimes when I look at the date. 1943, eh! Getting on, not getting any younger and no use trying to disguise it.

The ears, like grate-black coxswains! I was sauntering down Molesworth street the other day (nothing will do me but try to fix up a merger between that crowd and the Knights, there are difficulties in the way but I am making some progress) and suddenly I found myself looking at the old Molesworth Hall. Will you ever forget the night we did *Broken Soil*, that thing of Colum's? Do you realise that was neither today nor yesterday? The Fays were in their element that time, Frank as the Wise Man in *The Hour Glass* and Willie as the Beggarman in *A Pot of Broth*. And the best fun of all was myself and Starkey as the pupils—I have to laugh when I think of how near we went to making a hames of the whole thing. And Mary scolding the two of us how lovely she looked. I still say it was Joe Hone's fault standing there in the wings making faces at us.

HOW MUCH DO YOU KNOW?

I encountered all the undermentioned expressions (in the course of) last week. Indicate (in your own words, whatever that means) what is wrong with each.

1. An auctioneer's poster which advertises the disposal of a number of things, including a library of books.
2. 'I bought a new pair of shoes today and they are cutting the feet off me.'
3. 'I was down seeing my tailor about a suit of clothes.'
4. 'The jury returned a verdict of wilful murder.'

You will find the answers lower down in this interesting article.

H.M. ENGLISH

In this newspaper recently I noticed a big headline (footlines are prohibited by special orders of the Editor) ESCAPEE GETS JAIL FOR LIFE. One sighs, of course—I mean, surely this man was (if anything) an escaper. The escapee was either the governor of the jail or the State. But I like the scene which takes place in the governor's simply furnished office when me man is caught and brought back again, looking rather foolish and abashed. Present is Mr Kevin Dixon, Attorney General. A blazing mess of wax in the corner indicates that lackeys are sealing an important document. Soon the little ceremony is over and me man is on his way back to the cells, the possessor for life of all that and those Portlaoise Prison with a row of twenty-seven strongly-constructed cottages let to solvent warders, fruit and vegetable gardens, handball-alley, death-chamber, hot linen press, maid's bedroom, garage accommodation for 59 motor cars, well-kept apiary, the whole in perfect working order a unique opportunity for investors. (And all this, mind you, notwithstanding the fact that it is illegal to alienate State property.)

ANSWERS HERE

1. 'Of books' is superfluous. It is not usual to refer to collections of bananas, goldfinches, colza-oil bottles or sewer men's dungarees as 'libraries' of those articles.

2. New shoes do not usually have a restrictive effect on the throat, groin or shoulders but only on the feet. The feet need not therefore be specified.

3. Tailors make suits only of clothes and will not, save in the rarest cases, agree to make suits of ratskin, cocoa-beans or decayed vegetable matter.

4. Homicide is no murder unless it is wilful.

OLD ETIQUETTE BOOKS and the like are not very funny but my honourable lordship has come across a 'National Encyclopedia of Business and Social Forms' published in America in 1882 and assumes that a few extracts from it from time to time will be found diverting. This publication takes the view—quite reasonably—that you are illiterate and gives you the text of your own letters—even your love letters. Naturally, it also gives the replies which you should receive, thus making the whole correspondence rather pointless.

The first example is entitled *A Formal Declaration of Love*. It is too long and embarrassing to quote but in the middle of it the ardent party says, with pauperish dignity: 'I am not, as you know, a man of wealth, but my means enable me to marry, and although I cannot promise you the luxury a wealthier man could bestow upon you, I can promise a faithful and enduring love, and a home in which your comfort will be my chief aim.'

Nice, ah? For 'my means' read 'your means' and possibly you have something nearer the truth. Next comes *A Favourable Reply* and *An Unfavourable Reply*, the latter concluding with 'let me hope that you will find some woman, worthy of you, who will make you the good wife you deserve.' Then comes *A Less Formal Offer*.

'Dear Rosy: On returning from skating yesterday afternoon, and reflecting alone on the pleasant morning we had passed, I was more than ever impressed by my wretched, solitary existence. Will you break for me this monotonous routine of life by saying, "It need not be, Charlie"?

'I have loved you fondly and long; your parents and mine are intimate friends; they know my private character. Will you accept me as your husband, dearest Rosie? Believe me ever your attached, Charlie.'

Then *The Reply:*

' "It need not be, Charlie." I shall be at home this evening. Rosy.

Rosy was a smart dame. But why did Charlie misspell her name? The next letter relates to *A Declaration of Love at First Sight.*

'Dear Miss Logan: Although I have been in your society but once, the impression you have made upon me is so deep and powerful that I cannot forbear writing to you, in defiance of all rules of etiquette . . .'

Mark this villainy—the etiquette of violating etiquette!

'Affection is sometimes of slow growth; but sometimes it springs up in a moment. In half an hour after I was introduced to you my heart was no longer my own. I have not the assurance to suppose that I have been fortunate enough to create any interest in yours; but will you allow me to cultivate your acquaintance in the hope of being able to win your regard in the course of time? Petitioning for a few lines in reply, I remain, dear Miss Logan, yours devotedly, W— P—.'

Now comes the supreme refrigeration—*An Unfavourable Reply:*

'Sir: Your note has surprised me. Considering that you were, until last evening, an entire stranger to me, and that the few words which passed between us were on common-place subjects, it might be called impertinent. But I endeavour to view it in a more favourable light, and am willing to attribute your extraordinary and sudden professions of devotion to ignorance of the usages of society. You will oblige me by not repeating the absurdity, and I think it best that this note should close the correspondence and our acquaintance. By attending to this request, you will oblige, Your obedient servant, Susan L—.'

Here the system broke down completely, for there is no *Forceful Reply to the Foregoing*, such as would give Walter an alternative to immediate emigration.

I could write Miss Logan a pretty fine one myself but as the lady must now be 86 (if she's a day), I will spare her my scorpious tongue.

Here is another model letter from my 1882 American 'National Encyclopedia of Business and Social Forms', being *From a Son, who has Misconducted himself towards his Employer, to his Father*.

'Dear Father—I am in such distress I scarcely know how to commence my letter. Without the least reason, without the least provocation, I left my employer at the most busy season, just for a temporary trifling amusement. He—the best of employers—for the moment was forgotten by me; self predominated. I ran away from my place, and here I find myself disgraced and miserable, and grieve to think how indescribably shocked you will be when Mr Evans communicates with you relative to my absence.

'However, dear father, there is one consolation: I cannot be accused of dishonesty; so I hope my character is not irretrievably ruined.

'Will you see my employer, and tell him how deeply I regret my fault, and entreat him to forgive it, and allow me to return to my place? It shall hereafter be my constant study to perform my duty in the most upright manner, and with the most assiduous attention. Let me hear also, dear father, sending me Mr Evans' reply, that you also forgive Your erring and repentant son, John Thompson.'

FUNNY THING happened the other day. A young friend of mine (I think he is my son as a matter of fact, though we haven't spoken for years) was found 'guilty' following some quaint ritual in that well-known Carpathian hamlet, Kamara. My son is highly educated and has long lost his taste for (those sort of) parlour games, and throughout the proceedings he leant contemptuously on the back wall of the corps, Tauss, pardon me, courthouse. But when the proceedings were over he got a frightful shock. *He was put back*. There he was leaning against a twofootsix masonry wall in coursed random rubble and begob before he knew what was going on he was put back. He tells me (sign language, of course—we haven't spoken for years) that no one except the man who has been (personally) put back through a stone wall by twelve respectable pushing, sweating, cursing pious Irishmen (with the Law behind them) can understand the humiliation of this. He says his ribs are full of mortar yet, he says there are skewbacks under his oxters and a big kneeler at the base of his skull, there's a bondstone still stuffed into the small of his back and his heels are full of external plinth. He says he wouldn't go through it again and I am with him there—once is enough to go through a wall.

D.O. Fogg was in the case.

RESOLVE IN FUTURE to peruse the daily papers thoroughly, particularly the editorial which is always full of current interest, and when you have this course in topical education completed, there will be at least one subject on which HE will be able to say you can 'talk intelligently'.—*Woman's Life*.

It astonishes me that anybody should be so anxious to get married as to go over there ———→* and get a lift on the crossbar in the daily cycle journeys between Kharkov, Bryansk and Orel. And surely the result of such a course would be formidable.

Hello, Jack. There is certainly something brewing on the Orel sector.

Yes dear. Time alone will tell.

Jack, it would not surprise me at all if we were to see a new pincer thrust next week with Kharkov as the nodal point, one claw turning southward through the Donbas to the Dnieper valley.

I agree.

Because, Jack, it is known that the Russians have vast masses of men and material concentrated in that sector.

(What's up with this unfortunate woman?) Yes, dear.

And Jack . . . Do you know the firing power of the new Mark III tank?

'Again, do not ignore the classics as something which bored you to tears in schooldays. Read them again now, when your mind is more cultured and better able to appreciate them, and you will find that they are "surprisingly" fascinating.'

I know. A little of the Oracula Sibyllina, Polyzelus, Lycurgus Orator, a peep into Dioscorides' colourful tracts on physics, Homer, Horace, Virgil, and a very small pinch of Ovid. To describe all this as 'surprisingly fascinating' is to toy with words. And the young lady will get a drop when

* Such references (passim) indicated the editorial columns of the *Irish Times*.

she first mentions the classics to her young man and hears him straight-way deliver a discourse on the plans of Hartigan, Butters and Jarvis and how the books were a better proposition than the tote at the last Junction meeting.

It's many a man they ruined the same horses.

*   *   *

I SEEN that thing at the Abbey—

'My Dear Father.'

Was it any good?

Very well done and well acted but that's all that was in it.

I see.

You couldn't get a laugh out of it.

I haven't been inside that place for two year.

I seen meself sittin there for 2 hours and I couldn't get a laugh out of it anywhere. You like a bit of humour do you know.

I haven't put me head in there since before the war.

It was heavy stuff about clergymen do you know. There's not a laugh anywhere in it. The wife was with me. The best thing I ever seen there was 'Professor Tim'. But this other stuff wasn't much good. One thing I couldn't get a laugh there anywhere.

I'll tell you what my dish is.

Another thing I seen there was Double Trouble be Laurel and Hardy.

I'll tell you what I like. Maritana.

Them's a very mad pair, Laurel and Hardy.

Maritana and the Yeoman of the Guard. You know the one with Jack Point. I-polished-up-the-knocker-of-the-king's-front-door.

The fat lad is a terrible madman. Another time the pair was for bringin a piana up a long stairs.

And-now-I'm-the-ruler-of-the-king's-navee.

Your men got stuck. Your man Hardy is above pullin an sweatin and the thin lad below. Wan was pushing the piana down and the other pushin it up. Begob I nearly passed out laughin. You'd hear the roars of me a mile off. I'd go anywhere for a laugh.

Th'Abbey has new rules out about smokin, Jack was tellin me.

I remember long years ago a Saturday never passed that I wasn't in d'Abbey. There used to be great laughs there in years gone by.

Did you ever see 'Savings Bank' written over the door high up?

That was the old Mechanics Institute, many a time I heard the old man talking about it, workin with blow-lamps there and playin billiards. That was before the Free State.

I tell you what—there's a very queer class of a play put on there now. The sister Annie put on a show there for the orphanage in 1924. There was a lot of lads there with bagpipes.

Well I didn't fancy that 'Father' play. No laughs bar one where a fella slipped goin out of a door. He nearly creased himself. Of course the actors there is very good. There's men there that was over in America.

The sister put on a great play with step-dancers and bagpipes, real Irish stuff. Jack had bottles of stout for the band inside in the pay-box.

Some of the actors was across doin 'Professor Tim' at the World's Fair. All the Irish in America was crowdin in. Take out the green flag over there and you're right. Your men were flyin about in special trains. There was wan particular actor that passed out in the middle of a play.

The sister was very strict about that. She asks Jack what's all the men doin in the pay-office. This is back in '24. Checkin the money for the Revenue, says Jack, fixin up the entertainment tax.

Jack was the boy.

One of the bagpipe lads was found mouldy in Marlboro' St the next mornin, kilts an' all lyin up against a railins.

You could get a good laugh in them days. But that thing the other night there was no laugh anywhere in it bar the wan. I seen meself yawnin in the middle of it.

D'Abbey's gone to hell this ten year.

I didn't get a laugh anywhere bar the wanst.

An' it'll be worse before it's better.

I never seen a play that it was so hard to get a laugh out of. That's wan thing I do like—a good laugh. I'll go anywhere for a good laugh. And that's the truth. A good laugh.

* * *

I LEARNED from a recent news item that my best friend, Mr E. J. Moeran, is 'going to Kerry to write a concerto for 'cello and orchestra . . .'

Well, all I can say is this: it would not be my way, it would not be my way at all and more I will not say. With me, you see, music is an obsession, not a profession. When the feeling for . . . creation . . . suddenly wells up in me . . . like . . . the sea . . . I become—it is fascinating—I become completely passive, the activated rather than the actor . . . and that is why I can be so devastatingly humble about my best oeuvres—I become the vessel, the medium through which something . . . call it what you will but of this world it is not . . . expresses itself. I become almost . . . female. What is it Goethe says? 'Art is the Mediatrix of the Unspeakable.' How true that is! The . . . horrible, really horrible thing is, though, that . . . for the artist . . . art is a humiliation. When one is a genius, one keeps remembering that one's great gifts entail the most frightening responsibilities . . . one is . . . one is simply not as other men. My God the agony of it all, there have been nights when I have nearly gone mad. Mad, do you hear me. But to say quite calmly I am going to write for instance a concerto for Klavier and Orch . . . No, that would be impossible, quite completely out of the question. For I, you see, I, simply . . . never know when this . . . this . . . thing happens to me, I simply never know *what* the result will be. It may, for instance, be a colossal *Kunstfilm* in which the statement of overtonal montage is taken yet a step further in the higher reaches of a rather Russian hierarchy of the spatio-temporal values relating to the metric of colour in the visual-acoustic 'world'—it may be a completely épatant experiment in the grisaille where the contrapuntal possibilities of the tone texture, form and content are balanced against the searing harmonics of sensibility i.e., 'feeling' in the sense of *europäischer Geist*. It may be a poem in which withering humanity, seen in the heartbreaking immediacy of sense-experience, takes on the sweetly occidental aspect of a dying god, terrible yet tender and somehow immaculate. It may be a 'novel' so vast in scope, so perfect in execution, so overwhelming in conception, so sited in unheard-of dimensions that . . . no responsible publisher could risk bringing it before the world. It may be a monumental Minority Report on Some Aspects of the Housing Problem in Europe and the Middle East, with special reference to Occidental Sewage Disposal Its Rise and Fall. It may yet be detailed drawings and specifications for a new locomotive, it may be a modest proposal for the recodification of our somewhat hare-brehon laws, it may be a play so grandiose that the side wall of the theatre has to be torn down to get the scenery in . . . or again . . . it may be a . . . symphony (in Remineur) dedicated to the People of Ireland; *all written so that it can be played on the Perry fiddles now in the National Museum and on no others*. It may be a new brand of porter which can intoxicate but not inebriate. A new elastic guaranteed not to stretch. Grandiose plans for a new National University. A device for buying county councillors. A forte piano. A sacred weapon. An aeroplane suitable for use on land. A pan-knife. An entirely new type of District Justice that hears evidence, announces a decision and says absolutely nothing else.

A machine for rinsing out old stomachs. A plan for repatriating Sudetenland Corkmen. In fact, I mean . . . anything, absolutely anything.

And if you ask me what I am doing now, I reply that I do not know, I only work here.

* * *

ANY READER who feels he or she would like to meet myself and family should write to the Editor asking for particulars as to when I am at home, the best time to call, and whether it is necessary to leave cards beforehand. You will find us, I fear, just a little bit formal. My wife, for instance, keeps her hands in a hand-bag. This, however, need not disturb you. Again, if it happens that you come to dinner, you must be prepared for certain old-world customs—out-moded if you like, but still capable of imparting grace and charm to a gathering of those who knew the vanished world of yesteryear. First a glass of pale sherry, exquisite in its thin needle-like impact on the palate, potent of preprandial salivation. Then fine-tasted *bouillon* in china bowls, served with white rolls, those clandestinely-sieved American cigarettes. My jewelled hand has now strayed to the Turkish bell-tassel and the great triple peal that calls for the dinner proper rings out in the distant servants' hall. This is where the guest who is accustomed to the rougher usage of today may receive a slight surprise. When the dinner is brought in, he will note that it is . . . well . . . in a dinner jacket. Big mass of roast beef in the breast, sleeves stuffed with spuds, sprigs of celery up through the button-holes, gravy sopping out everywhere. A bit formal if you like, but if one does not observe the punctilious regimen of good behaviour, one is, after all, very little better than the beast of the field. Indeed, remembering the execrable manners of a colleague of mine in this great newspaper organisation, I had almost said that one is very little better than the beast of *The Field*.

When the coffee stage is reached, nothing will do my eccentric wife but have it accompanied by an odd confection of her own invention—longbread.

MISCELLANEOUS

The *Irish Times* has been full of grand news these days. 'The Maoris, I read 'are sometimes called "the brown Irish" because they are always smiling and happy.' Fancy! New Zealand I do not know, but strange that it should be the seat of so monstrous a sarcasm. I know that we are morose, crypt-faced, inclined to the view that life is a serious disorder which ultimately proves fatal. But why should these antipodean britishers see fit to send this sneer to us three thousand miles across the sea in the middle of a world war?

Then I read that 'future Croke Park matches may see extremely large numbers of police on duty'. Hmm.

Could the rules not be changed to provide that in every large match at least one of the teams shall be composed entirely of policemen? Alternatively, could not all teams playing there be bound to the peace before they take the field and thus be liable for a stiff jail sentence if they commit assaults on the referee or each other?

Here is another extraordinary news item: 'A pig feeder may slaughter a sick animal, cure it and get a top price. In fact the pig may die and, as an afterthought, be cured.'

There you get, very nicely put, the distinction between a corpse and a carcase.

* * *

I RARELY OFFER my readers a handsome book prize, chiefly because handsome books one dares not dream of parting with; nevertheless, a handsome copy in calf of my own treatise on 'Cockburn's Geared Turbine' I will gladly send to the first reader who sends me the context of the poem in which this rather pidgin phrase occurs:

'. . . his Laodamia it comes.'

Absolutely no chorus pawn dents can be entered into, nor will proof of postage be accepted as proof of delivery. Onus of proof is on plaintiff, though it is not contended that this *dictum* can operate to suspend the rule of law. In Rex v. Beachborough Sea Fisheries Corporation it was contended that defendants were estopped from salvage by trover by reason of non-user of certain jetties, landing stages, slips, causeways, salting-sheds and brine-tubs formerly held under licence from a board not being a harbour board, a board of trustees constituted for the purposes of inland navigation, or a board charged with conserving maritime fisheries: *held* by Palles C.B. that there had been suspensory user *in fructu* and that no escheat or reversionary lapse subsisted by mere reason of effluxion of time, time not being of the essence of the contract, and that the charging order set forth in the third schedule of the Order in Council was properly charged. He quashed the conviction and allowed all parties their costs out of the estate. Continuing, the Chief Baron said:

'Not only must justice be done but it must be seen to be done. It is immediately plain that the Antrim County Council, being a road authority within the meaning of the Grand Jury Acts, the Local Government (Ireland) Act, 1898 (read with the Application of Enactments Order 1898), is not statutorily charged with the maintenance of sea-lanes. Plaintiffs therefore must fail.'

Eh? What am I saying?

Sorry—I pressed the wrong button. It was poetry I meant to talk about.

INTROSPECTION

I often wonder am I . . . mad? Do I take that rather Irish thing, O'Fence, too easily? I go into a house, for instance. My 'host' says 'sit down'. Now why *down*? Why must he be so cautious and explicit. Is there not a clear suggestion there that if he had neglected to be precise, he might turn round to find me seated on top of the bookcase, the head bent to avoid the ceiling and the air thick with fractured cobwebs? How equally stupid the phrase 'stand up!' And how mysterious the sit-down fight as opposed to the stand-up fight!

NI NACH ILLTSIOLLAMHACH

I would like to direct the attention of educated persons to this remarkably elegant little quatrain—a certain Ó Maolchiaráin reproaches parties allegedly responsible for wiping off his son;

> *A lucht do mharbh an ngéig nglain*
> *is do leig fá'n arm a fhuil,*
> *níor cháin an fear, níor aor ibh,*
> *níor libh a thaobh geal do ghuin.*

Apart from the frank implication that a lampoon is recognised as fair grounds for murder, note that the verse, though unpolluted by dissyllables, is dignified and unmonotonous.

SECOND THOUGHTS

The book prize offer above is withdrawn. Too many shrewd Schs. and Mods. and junior ads. in this country, I fear. You guessed the context at once, of course.

> . . . *his Laodamia*
> *It comes ; et iuvenis quondam,*
> *nunc femina, Caeneus . . .*

But I will re-offer the prize to the reader who can tell me when the emergency will terminate.

The Royal Irish Academy of the Post War World

THE ROYAL IRISH Academy of the Post War World (President Sir Myles na gCopaleen (the da)) is making arrangements for turning this country into a limited liability company. Every person who is an existing 'Irish national' will automatically become a shareholder unless he formally opts to be 'an excepted person' within the meaning of Section 10 (b) of the Eire (Incorporation) Act, upon which the draughtsmen are working night and day. The Act will set up a Board which will take over the country as a going concern together with all proprietary messuages, easements, hereditaments and choses in action. Section 104, subsection 3 (iv) will provide for the holding of an annual meeting at which the audited accounts of the undertaking will be considered and at which every shareholder, hereinafter referred to as 'the Irishman', will be entitled to attend and be haired. The members of the board will be 'elected' according to certain mysterious formulae contained in Schedule II of the Act. There will be power to declare a dividend, issue debentures and underwrite industrial risks in other countries. Under Part III of the Act, all persons offering themselves for election to the Board automatically become 'excepted persons' within the meaning of Section 10 (b) and henceforth will be deemed to be 'Irishmen' only if and when elected. On retiring, a member of the Board is de-nationalised but is eligible for re-election to the Irish nation. All very complicated and technical but there you are.

Myself? Where do I come in? I don't quite know but if I am elected to the Board, I can foresee a time when I will have to write certain letters. One, for instance, to the Chairman of the Board (probably J. J. O'Leary) and thus to the head of the State:

> 'Dear Chairman—I write to tender with great regret my resignation from the Irish people. I am compelled to take this step for personal reasons and trust yourself and your co-directors will see your way to accept it. Thanking you for past courtesies, M.'

Then the reply:

'Dear M—The Board and I have considered the contents of your letter and are unanimous in expressing the hope that you will find it possible to reconsider your decision and agree to remain a member of the Irish nation. The Board wish me to stress the importance they attach to maintaining Irish personnel intact in the present serious state of the world.—J. J.'

I cannot agree, of course.

'Dear Chairman—I thank you for your letter but I regret very much that owing to advancing age and failing health, I find it almost impossible to fulfil the manifold duties attaching to the position of Irishman and feel that I should make way for younger men. I am indeed sorry that I cannot meet the wishes of your Board. M.'

But they come back.

'Dear M—While profoundly appreciating the reasons which have led you to tender your resignation, the Board would again warmly counsel you to remain in office for at least a year longer, so that the nation may have the benefit of your advice and guidance in these critical times.—J. J.'

Again I reply:

'Dear Chairman—I have consulted my physician regarding the request contained in your last letter. He has absolutely prohibited the use of alcohol and also stated that he will disclaim all responsibility for my health if I start fighting. Your Board will therefore appreciate that I am by reason of physical incapacity entirely unfitted for the post of Irishman and for that reason must again tender my resignation with regret.—M.'

But they won't take no.

'Dear M—My Board have very carefully considered your last letter. While they are mindful of your enfeebled physical condition, they are still most reluctant to accept your resignation and they have asked me to inquire whether you would be prepared to continue as an Irishman in a part-time capacity.—J.J.'

There you are. *A part-time Irishman!* What an end to a life of patriotic endeavour!

My present hope is that we will be able to get a new section in the Bill providing for persons to retire from the post of Irishman on pension. And they will have to be pretty generous pensions (at that).

* * *

MOST OF MY READERS will recognise the importance of planning. One hears the word mentioned on every side. How good, then, to learn that Sir Myles na gCopaleen (the da) has formed what he is pleased to call the Royal Irish Academy of the Post War World. I defy anybody to exaggerate the importance of this move. It is a move vastly portentous, imponderable and marvellous, its mystical kernel an intellectual epigenesis. Quaternions with cubed vectors are used in the formula, which cannot be evaluated without the use of eighteen differential algebras. The Snodgrass Cycle has been availed of repeatedly in the preliminary calculations. It is all frightfully intricate and subsists intrinsically in a hitherto unsuspected plane of demophysics quite impossible to describe according to the accepted means of communication. Expressed symbolically in its lowest terms, the concept is as follows: $a+b+c-j=a$. Sir Myles (the da), out for a walk, felt the galvanic circuit close and this almost monstrous essay in socio-thaumaturgics is the result. He reached the nearest canal bridge at a run.

One must try, however, to be a little more explicit, even at the risk of misleading. In a word, it is hoped to produce, after an 'interval' of five Planned Years, a Planned Man. This process will be cyclic and Men more and more thoroughly Planned will emerge after each quinquennial gestation. The Planned Man, being himself planned, will occupy his planned brain with plans and planning and will breed children so planned that they will not tolerate anything whatever that is unplanned, half-planned or misplanned. Plan-less occurrences like a shower of rain will be discontinued. Death itself will no longer be the desultory, unpredictable and unsatisfactory phenomenon it has been for so long in this country (notwithstanding the vaunted promises of the Fianna Fáil government) but will be planned and re-planned until an all-party agreed measure can be introduced in the Dáil entitled—with planned irony—the Life (Transitory Provisions) Bill.

All this will not happen in a day. The Royal Irish Academy of the Post War World will have associated with it countless subsidiary planning organisations. The Highways Planning Board will arrange for vast concrete arterial roads to radiate from every centre of population, each road having special lanes for fast traffic, slow traffic, tramways, cycles, pedestrians, invalids, readers of *The Standard*, school-children and Irish speakers. At intervals of two miles there will be rest centres, health clinics, a 'People's Unit' embracing swimming pools, restaurant, cinema, writing and reading rooms, gramophone recital apartments, a home for the aged, a vitamin bureau and two aerodromes.

Meanwhile the National Housing Planning Board will be engaged in erecting ten million vast arterial houses for the Planned People of Ireland, each house complete with steriliser and small operating theatre, a miniature pharmacy for a new planned science of autotherapy, built-in wife, and hot-water on draught from the system already provided by *An Cólucht Náisiúnta um Uisce Galach*, or the National Hot Water Corporation. The Board of Transportation and Communications will lay out and build vast arterial railroads and canals, the railroads traversing only worthless mountain land and being enabled to overcome the unthinkable grades by means of locks. Vast arterial tree plantations will be undertaken by the National Afforestation Trust. Vast arterial hydro-electric, sewerage, waterwork, and mining enterprises will be carried out by direct labour under the auspices and aegis of the National Development Board. A Coal Exploration Company will be charged with the sole take of finding vast arterial coal in this country, and another Company (The National Coal Mining Corporation) will undertake the work of mining it.

That is but an inkling. Further information I must and will give. But surely what I have said is something to be going on with.

* * *

WHAT BETTER to do this morning than to wish Saul my raiders a Happy Christmas sand a brass pierrot's New Ear? Particularly Uncle Paul (the paid) and Uncle Peter (the robbed), Tom, Dick and Harry (most plebeian of trinities, mystical triune prosopopoeia of the commonplace), Billy and Jack (the latter tireless welcomer of the former's ex-friends). Tadhg agus a replica Taidhgin (Mac-rocosm et Mick-rocosm), R. C. Ferguson, Glenavy, Lord Moyne ('Moyne's a Guinness'), Willie Norton, Power, O'Keeffe and Fogarty, then Jelly D'Aranyi, Willie Dwyer, Jack Yeats, and, of course, Hernon. Christmas grey things to myself also. I deserve them as much as anybody—as much as the next, in fact—though I never noticed that they done me much good. What is there in all this seasonable time for me? Just a hunk of Manchester corned beef and a cup of 'coffee' slammed down at 6 p.m. on top of the boiler drawings by my hired slut. I sigh and take off the glasses. Outside in the snow I hear 'Good King Wenky's Loss' being empiped by a small selfappointed choir of juvenile delinquents. Is a straight steam path possible, I wonder vaguely, if we superheat? After a while I 'drink' the 'coffee' and go to bed, feeling very ill.

How tired I am after another year of denunciation!

THE FRIGHTFUL FUTURE

Another year, eh? Nineteen forty-*four*, whaaa? What does it hold in Store Street for us? Come back this time next year and I will tell you. But this much it is permissible to say even now. The Royal Irish Academy of the Post War World has *plans* for 1944. Far-reaching and unthinkable dispositions have already been made. Employment will be afforded to both the stay-at-homes and the returned emigrants, videlicet, the U.A. men and the U.S.A. men. The Academy will without stint pour Phil T. Lukor into (a) the construction of a vast new Cinnamon Theatre; (b) a Ciné-Monotony Theatre; (c) an Ignorarium; (d) a Columbarium (for disused Knights); (e) great new block of Outlaw Courts; (f) an ultra-modern Disease Centre with hot and cold shivers laid on; (g) same old vast arterial roads radiating throughout the length and breadth of Ireland (despite the fact that vast arterial roads which radiate can only proceed radially and without reference to length of breadth). Finally a Greyhound Painting Academy.

* * *

SAY I MAKE a 'joke' and it doesn't appeal to you, you are annoyed rather than amused. Annoyed, simply because you haven't yet found out how to unlaugh. A rather similar problem confronts my Research Bureau. In the Days of the Brown Bread (Lord, how long ago!) a number of disaffected persons, chiefly women, took to illegal sieving operations behind closed doors. Talk to them as you would, you could not induce them to do it behind open doors. Their point was that brown bread did not 'agree' with them and that Willie Nilly (that most reckless person) they must have white. Very well. I did what I could, took the matter up with the Ministers, addressed stern admonitions to the farmers . . . and now . . . everybody can have white. *But including those who want brown*, and with whom white does not 'agree'. Our problem, then is . . . how to unsieve the white flour. See what *you* can do for a change. (Offaly papers please copy.)

But how strange is Nature's chromatic syntax! The more refined a thing is, the whiter it becomes and if you do not believe this do please come round some evening and have a look at my face.

SUCCÈS DE STEAM

But pish! Why should one bother with bread 'problems' and the like when that vast ganglion of multiple brain-nerves, the Royal Irish Academy of the Post War World, is grappling mightily with the task of solving all human troubles *simultaneously*—planning, planning, eternally planning a new world reborn.

Take transport. We all know by now that we will be the laughing stock of the civilised world unless immediately after the war we can build vast arterial roads. Very well. We are all properly ashamed of our winding undulating country roads and we know too well that they are completely without Rest Centres, Rhubarb Dosage Stations, Health Clinics, Dental Hospitals, Vitamin Breweries, Youth Centres—any primitive modern amenity you like to name. But how are we to provide proper vast arterial

roads immediately if the country is full of hills? One way only. The roads must be built on some existing *level* thoroughfare. Of such thoroughfares we have only two—the canals and the railways. The Academy has under consideration a plan to divert railway traffic to the canals and build the vast arterial roads on the railway lines, which are ideally deficient in grades and curves. Reynolds and McCann kindly met the Academy to the extent of constructing an experimental stretch near Dublin. Laugh if you like. At present the rails are laid in the bed of the canal and there is plenty of room for trains and barges to pass each other. There is one snag. Rough stretches of water often mean that the engine's fire is put out and moreover, constant dredging is necessary to keep the rails free of dead dogs and muck. The Academy is now investigating the possibilities of having *floating* trains propelled with the screws of old liners. The advantage here is that the engines could tow barges as well as the adapted coaches and thus make up for the shortage of rolling—or rather floating stock: The position is very fluid at the moment but you may be sure that when you read that the reconstructed G.S.R. concern will be a *transport* rather than a railway company, something like what is shown in aur photograph was contemplated. Why else would My Honour be buying G.S.R.?

AN ENCOUNTER

To come back to bread for a moment, I had an odd experience the other day, met one of my poor relations and asked him how he liked the new white bread. Blank face. Eh, bread? What did I mean bread? White? Hah? Hah? Didn't understand what I was talking about, never heard of it.

(Damn fellow must eat cake.)

* * *

MORE GOOD NEWS! I am in position to announce that the Royal Irish Academy of the Post War World (President, Sir Myles na gCopaleen (the da)) does not intend to dissociate itself from present politico-social trends. Apart from Planning, which is, of course, all-important, the Academy has officially endorsed the new monopolative and amalgamative concept of society. There will be no more *laissez faire* if certain of the Academy's plans mature, nor will profit-making be permitted in relation to any public utility.

The Academy has a rather remarkable scheme concerning Dublin transport. On this subject there is much loose thinking. Reflect for a moment and you will realise that intra-city passenger transport is quite unique and has nothing at all in common with any other carrying business such, for example, as the railway line from Dublin to Cork. The latter is a life-line connecting a number of isolated communities and it is chiefly important because it carries goods and food to sustain them. The carriage of humans, while remunerative, is not an essential element in such a company's affairs; moreover, if isolated individuals insist on travelling long distances, it is right that they should be charged (as undoubtedly they are) an enormous fee for being permitted to indulge this egregious whim. Municipal transport is altogether another matter. The inhabitants of a city survive by perpetual movement within it, darting hither and thither about their occasions like ants on an ant-hill. They may be called the blood of the municipal organism and the public transportation system corresponds to the arteries and veins. *The people have no choice but to move.* It is therefore unconscionable that they should be treated the same as if they were long-distance travellers who undertake a journey possibly once a year, more often than not for pleasure or at least for a purpose that is not essential for economic survival. It is quite ridiculous that a group of individuals should be permitted to extract money from a community for permitting the community to discharge a function essential to its existence.

But municipal transport conducted by private enterprise is not a servile passive thing, dumbly carrying for a price people wherever they may wish to go. It has a dynamism entirely its own, an influence wholly pernicious in the community's development. Teeming city slum centres, for example, cannot be cleared because the depressed classes involved could not submit to the tax levied by the company for the privilege of living on the city outskirts. A transport company can crib and stunt a city and its people.

To approach to the solution of this problem one has only to realise that transport is no less necessary than running water, sewerage, or artificial light. These things are 'free' which means that they are charged for according to the valuation of property. The services are universal and one can use them as much or as little as one likes. There, then, you have the solution of the municipal transport problem. *We must provide a 'bus service that is completely free to all the citizens and maintained out of the Corporation's revenues.* The present system must obviously be changed and a free service would be much better than the only other solution—a flat rate for all journeys. What would the free system mean in terms of money? Why, nothing to scare anybody. The Corporation's annual income is of the order of £3,500,000, of which some £2,200,000 is raised from rates; the rate being about twenty shillings in the pound, the valuation is also about £2,200,000. In 1943 the Dublin Transport Company collected £1,000,000 approximately in fares. Of this sum, it is safe to assume that £250,000 represents either profit or charges that would not arise if the concern were owned by the municipality. If we assume that it would cost the Corporation £750,000 to provide a similar service, it would mean about 7/6d extra on the rates. Is that too much? Consider an average man who lives in a house of £20 valuation; he has a wife and four school-going children, and he is in a two-penny fare situation. The man spends 8d on fares himself, the children 1/4d and the wife 4d; that is a fair minimum daily expenditure of 2/6d. You add another 6d to take care of all unessential journeys and you get a daily expenditure of 3/od or 18/od a week, or an annual expenditure of about £47. If you give this man 'free' municipal transport it will cost him £7 10s od a year.

Reflect on that.

* * *

MUCH INTEREST has been evinced in the scheme my highness propounded yesterday for a system of free municipal transport, the cost to be borne by the Corporation. It is obvious that the scheme is flawless financially, and it will repel only those who take fright at anything that is simple and straightforward and innocent of all bureaucratic complexity. But the idea is sound philosophically also. Consider one point. Why are the present transport company's fares so high? Because, for one thing, the Company's system is not used by all the citizens. This means that a system adequate to carry all the citizens must be maintained by the proportion of the citizens who have to use the trams and buses. Two classes shirk carrying their share of the cost of this essential urban amenity—those who use bicycles and those who use motor-cars. The cyclist is independent of public transport because he has succeeded in becoming a capitalist in a small way; his contribution to a rate-sustained transport system would be individually small but his numbers being great the aggregate would be considerable. The man who prefers to use his own motor-car and thus provides individual transport at enormous cost should not be permitted to do so if this action causes the cost of public transport to rise and thus causes hardship to the bulk of the people, who have not got the money to buy motor-cars. If you increase this man's rates by about one third, he has nothing to complain about; he should provide his motor-car only after reasonable minimum transport has been provided for the public generally.

What would be the effect of the system on business? Assuredly not a bad effect. The coming and going of the citizens would be much more fluid. If I have a shop in O'Connell Street, I must lose thousands of sales in the course of a year because a prospective customer must pay a surcharge of sixpence or eightpence to the transport company in addition to the profit I demand myself. On the other hand, the transport company dumps tens of thousands of customers at my door week after week and beyond making a general payment to the community in consideration of the prominent location of my premises in the city business centre, I make no direct acknowledgement of the fact that public transport is absolutely essential to my livelihood. If my poor law valuation of £1,000 and a municipal transport scheme means that I must pay another £300 annually in rates, that is not unreasonable.

The 'no-fares' system has another big advantage. It would enable the transport system to be operated at costs lower than ever before experienced anywhere. Superficially, labour would be displaced but that problem has been met and dealt with successfully before. The present transport company employs probably a thousand conductors, perhaps fifty inspectors and supervisors and a large countinghouse staff; add to that expenditure on tickets and on the rental of ticket-punching machines and it is not clear that you would have much change out of £200,000 a year. That is an immediate and clear saving. You enter the vehicle at the front and the driver can easily carry out the elementary conducting duties that would remain.

The system introduces into public transport a principle that is well recognised in relation to other essential public services—namely, that everybody shares the burden of the service not according to the use he gets from it but according to his capacity to maintain public services. If a watermain extension to serve a new housing scheme costs £1,000, the tenants do not personally shoulder this crippling burden; it is spread over the whole administrative area and becomes a matter of farthings in the bill of each ratepayer. But the same remote tenants, under the present system, have to pay several thousands poundses to the transport company and will never have the continuing amenity of a watermain laid and working.

There is no real snag in this idea. Yet it will not be adopted because the Corporation and its citizens are too docile: *obedientia civium urbis felicitas.*

POST WAR COPPER PROBLEMS ran a heading I read some tie, McGow. I, superb piece of work, in understanding most like a dog, understood immediately what the article beneath the heading would deal with. (I guess it's the human in me.) Let us pause here to ask what it is that we do in reading. (Pause.) Well, in all reading we *abstract*, we take only some of the possibilities of the words' meanings into account. No matter how concrete (nay, copper) the topic or its treatment seems to be, we are abstracting, we are leaving out some f the possibilities, we are not asking your Aunt Agatha, we refuse to invite those frightful Shaughnessies, we could have young Lynch come and play the xylophone, but no, the hell with it, let's have an intellectual party for once. Obviously, in *reading* (to narrow the thing down somewhat) in different sorts of reading we do this in different degrees but always . . . always keeping as near as possible to standard temperature and pressure. (My little standard joke—Bear with me, as Joe Louis used to say.) Hmmm. We let in (*and should let in*) *less* in reading such prose as this than we let in with most poetry, say . . . (Do you read poetry, de Wrieder, or are you out down town every night drinking your head off? Hmmmm? Drop me a card some time). Now, attention, please.

The important point is that *in all reading whatsoever much must be left out*. Otherwise we could arrive at no meaning and what a beautiful pity that would be! Or—half a moment, Mac!—or if we did arrive at a meaning we mightn't be expected, they mightn't have got our card, there would be black looks, hemming, haw act (since repeeled) and: Of course you're *always* welcome won't you take off those socks? Misther Meaning no sir there was never anny one of that name lived here there was Mick Manning of course the stoker that had this basement before me but he's dead this twenty year. (How *do* you mean, I often ask myself? And should it be done in public? Meaning you know is a thing you can get a lot of praise for—if it's done *well*. (Haha. Sharp dry laugh. Not really amused.) But, look—to get back to the pint (stet it has a head on it) *omission* is essential in the two-fold sense; without omission no meaning would form *for us*; through omission what we are trying to grasp becomes *what it is* (gets its essential being).

The only man that never learnt to omit was Father Dinneen, so that most of the words he has in his book, meaning all things, mean really nothing at all. Putting our point another way, we see that all ratiocinative processes of intellection are addressed, not so much to establishing meaning, but rather to establishing refinements of meaning. Thus the crude uncoloured outline of meaning, familiar even to the lower animals, is of little use to humans, who willingly traffic in nothing that is not recherché and sophisticated.

Example: a piece of steak. To your dog it has the primary meaning—food! This image begets the brother idea—eat! Now attend carefully please. To you, it is not food. You had refined the idea of food before it could enter your mind: you would have refined it to the more particular meaning 'meat' save that the same process forestalled you and you had refined 'meat' to 'steak'. But again you were forestalled, 'steak' had become 'raw steak'—and that really is what you perceived, apparently instantaneously but actually by several steps of reasoning. And of course, each image you admitted as valid excluded countless others you knew to be false: example, 'horse-flesh', 'leather'.

Ah well! Need I say that when I read POST-WAR COPPER PROBLEMS, I immediately refused to admit two 'meanings'. Number wan was the possibility that some of the cute lads in Justice were getting out sketch-plans for . . . brain-new stainless arterial polismen, made of plastic material and 100 per cent prefabricated, to be laid on with th'electhric and the wather afther the waaaar. The other idea was that the men on the Dalkey cars were losing their knight' sleep (they're nearly all Ely Place men) about what to do with all the loose change afther the w. . . .

(There's only one thing to do with loose change of course. Tighten it.)

*

I DISLIKE LABELS—rather I mean it's not that they aren't terribly useful. *They are, old man*. But do . . . do they sufficiently take account of one as . . . a . . . person? There is my dilemma. (How do you like his horns?) But I . . . I . . . (little indulgent laugh) I know humanity, its foibles, its frailties, its fatuities; I know how the small mind hates what can't be penned into the humiliating five-foot shelf of its 'categories'. And so . . . if you must libel me, sorry, wrong brief, if you must label me, if you must use one epithet to 'describe' a being who in diversity of modes, universality of character and heterogeneity of spatio-temporal continuity transcends your bathetic dialectic, if, in short, one . . . practically algebraic symbol must suffice to cover the world-searing nakedness of that ontological polymorph who is at once immaculate brahmin, austere neo-platonist, motor-salesman, mystic, horse-doctor, hackney journalist and ideological catalyst, call me . . . call me . . . (qu'importe en effet, tout cela?) call me . . . ex-rebel. Forget the grimy modest exterior, civilisation's horrid camouflage of the hidden, inner, in-forming radiance. True that . . . economic stresses force one to spend oneself on . . . trifles (what with sherry halfdollar a halfglass and sponge-cake . . . *Sponge-cake?* Me good woman do you realise there's a waaaaaaaaaaar on?). About the valid things, for instance, one must not write; ethics, plastics, authority what is its foundation in the compromise of the diurnal round (This is mine, I think?), the lust for Order (with its glamorous satellites, 'beauty' and 'harmony'—not to mention ancient Hibernians), how to reconcile it with man's unquenchable longing for *Freedom?* (Rather loosely put but you see what a Haeck Reuter is up against?)

I mean one's soul is forgotten but one must be very simple in this kind of thing, and keep frightfully close to the bone, follow the telegraph wires it's about four miles from here. You see, one is . . . one is simply a plain hack journalist, concerned with such prosaic things as . . . getting things across, smoothly, fair play to all, square deal for my masters, and never forget the eager throng of readers (certified) who so instinctively believe in their right to speak their mind that they, they will not be slow to let the Editor person know what they think of one's pitiful work. Very Irish, very traditional, the only difference being that from the poor berated French Revolution onwards we spoke our mind against what poor John Mitchel called 'The Carthaginian' in spite of poison, debt and egg-soil. Now . . . (bitter laugh) . . . now we speak it against . . . writers . . . the Anglo-Irish, Liberals, individualists, children of the Renaissance and other contemptible . . . and unarmed . . . creatures!!!! Of course, when Truth is not paramount, one must cry aloud for Tolerance and free speech. Then as soon as Truth becomes paramount as result of our Tolerance and *Freedom* (!!!!!) . . . there is no longer any need for Tolerance—in fact it would be a crime. Grand. Grand. But . . . just a bit hard on those who . . . do not believe in 'Absolutes', not even in Truth permanent and fadeless. Just a bit hard on those to whom the 'errors' of . . . Plotinus are just as valid, and important as say those molten Iberian lyrics whose sensuous imagery gave Crashaw his melodic line and burning glass.

No, no, no, this is forbidden . . . And still—how wonderful, how indestructible is human nature! and still this man who goes to jail and death will go on saying 'Alas, that Might can vanquish Right, They fell and passed away, but true Men like you Men, are plenty here today!'—the foolish Greek! the silly Renaissance ass!! The comic liberal! By heavens, this time once and for all we'll eradicate from his silly carcass his thousand-year-old folly! . . . But enough! Pass me the strychnine, Mac, it is in the top left-hand corner of the chest of drawers under the old Ph.D (Heidelberg) scroll.

* * *

TODAY ONE of those flashes of intuition again lit me (from within) ignited, fused, shattered me with a light at once agonising in its implication, in its intimation of the loneliness, the sense of isolation, of . . . separation which is the penalty, the glorious, empty penalty, of the modest, harassed, poly-noetic super-person . . . and at the same time exalted and healed the restless, weary intellect, worked to a glistening, scarlet, over-sensitised . . . thread by the tremendous *besogne* of cramming a . . . light-year's thought into three calendar months. I had, at last . . . realised, (in the sense 'felt the truth of') I had experienced in transcendant sense-immediacy a blinding illumination not without its message of goodwill for groping, under-privileged . . . dowdy humanity. I suddenly saw . . . quite clearly . . . sub specie aeternitatis . . . that that . . . strange object, so highly esteemed—(I might almost say esteamed) by our winsome, unscented housewives, even in its essentially knitted, parboiled form, as . . . a table delicacy . . . I saw, I tell you, that that . . . object is pregnant with great possibilities for gallant little Irish industry struggling valiantly to keep its head over the Plimsoll line in a world delirious with the excruciating slap-stick of Free Trade. Yes, I repeat, that odd cephalomorphous object can be made a vital element in our important warp production; from it, I promise you, shall spring a newer, greater and more glorious . . . wool trade, the markets of Cathay and Samarkand shall clamour for our incredible bawneens, the carriage trade of New York, Paris, Berlin shall come to our (intensely half-) door, our ships shall sail H.M. seven seas without Lett or Huendrans, wine shall incontinently bark on the wine-dark waterway, and Ireland long a province be a nation once again. I am, of course, quite serious. This great plastic is for the future and I am confident that given the time, the research, above all the money, our . . . Irish chemists will be more than equal to the task of extracting wool from its resilient, elastic heart. Meanwhile it is a matter of extreme urgency that the Public Real Asians Department of our Ministry for Agriculture should put before the public the dangers inevitably attendance upon the present attitude towards this essentially resinous mineral. Our . . . eager, and no doubt, affectionate, Irish wives must be made to see that though eating is . . . a necessary business, and . . . parboiling is an interesting way to treat objects intended for vulgar carnal provisionment . . . yet, not all sublunar Offal is really suitable for this purpose; alarm clocks, umbrellas, wax flowers, telescopes, carpets, wall-paper and hardwall plaster are instances of a few of such not terribly edible things. Another more obvious one is the interesting worsted bomb of which this evening I have been speaking.

One wonders what absent-minded *colleen* first dimly, myopically dropped one of these valuable reverse-calf objects into the melting pot and then ... obstinate, though charming ... insisted that poor Tadhg ... eat it. The delirious, half laughable, whole lethal recipe spread from wife to wife, from mother to mother, from generation to generation until at the present day there exists scarcely an adult male in this island who has not at some time or other actually performed the intensely music-hall magic of ... *eating a* ... *turnip*! (I mean, it's like drinking that most vitriolic of embrocations, milk!)

I admit it is dangerous suggesting that we do wrong by eating certain things on the mere ground that they can be manufactured into prams, pipe-racks or even newspapers—things obviously more important than grub. I would be personally bereaved if a way were found to convert oysters into policemen's leggings. Such is the persistence and might of industry that ever after there would be no oysters nowhere. And who wants to go up to Jack Nugent for brown bread, stout and half a dozen leggings. As well expect policemen to put shells on their legs—even if it gives you the chance of making some joke about leg-shells.

*

PEOPLE—I suppose they *are* people really—frequently speak to me at some length on the subject of my 'versatility' and—Heaven forfend!—I am compelled to listen to their incomprehensible attempts at communication. On such occasions it is, as you may imagine, simply that I have permitted myself to be lured into making one of my rare appearances in public. (The making or even assembling of such appearances, whether in public or in private, has now been absolutely prohibited by Emergency Powers Order No. 487/e/iv—so do not blame your grocer, he is doing his best in difficult circumstances.) Is it ... is it imagined that this chat ... amuses ... interests or even—O monstrous presumption—*flatters* me? I am quite appalled. It is like ... it is like those rich young baggages who —good heavens, how coyly!—'tell' me that my personal beauty is of an unusually high order. *But of course, of course.* I know. The trivial iteration of facts adds nothing to my ... enjoyment of life. Life ... j'ai ... j'ai seul la clef de cette parade sauvage. And ... versatility? Is the bird of the air, forsooth, to be praised for flying, singing and laying edible eggs in the perilous tree-tops? It is, I think, natural for a person of my stamp (as poor Rowan Hamilton used to say) to embrace all human perfections and accomplishment (but excluding such as may be evil) within the mastery of my superb intellect, gracing not myself but all humanity with an artistic preminence that is withal saturated with an exquisite humility.

'But . . . don't you ever run short of ideas? How can you *always* write so . . . interestingly . . . so . . . so authoritatively about such a variety of things. Seldom, I mean, have . . . so many things been written for so many people . . . by so few a man.'

My reply is simple and, as always, truthful. 'Madam, writing is the least of my occupations. Many other things, many many other things contribute to the sum of my cares. Vast things, things imponderable and ineluctable, terrible things, things which no other mortal were fit to hear of—things I must think upon only when utterly alone. Writing is surely a small thing, indeed. Difficulties Mmmmm. One is not conscious of them. There are, of course, five things and five things only that can be written about and though for me they have lost all interest as problems, I continue to write out of the depth of my feeling for dark groping humanity.'

With a slight bow I am about to turn when I am again assailed by my gross female interlocutor. Will I not tell her what these five things are?

A flicker, just a cup-shake, deforms the austere granite countenance, but true to the traditions of race and caste a courteous answer is forthcoming, courteous but with the sonorous quiver of doom rippling up to the calm word surface of my utterance. 'The fastness of friendship, ma'am, the treachery of one's nearest; the destruction of good by good. Passion which over-rides reason. VIOLENT AND PROUD DEATH!'

Sometimes I smile. I am not of this country, and my agriculture is essentially *altero pede*. But long as I am here I cannot contemplate unmoved the pageant of your great national bilingual revival as it so heroically unfolds itself in a positively promethean agony. The struggle is so unequal. On the one hand one sees massed the degrading influences of occidental Europe, dedicated—one appreciates—to the destruction of everything Irish. The sympathetic spectator like myself, who wishes you all so well, cannot but feel at the same time that this great polyglot . . . un-Irish monster will stop at nothing to achieve its evil ends. Its fearful decivilising influences, dominated by the internal combustion engine and with the anticipation of even greater domination in the world of the future saturated (as it will be) with the anti-gaelic evil of plastics, air-travel, television and mixed cinemas, will not be nullified without a long and bitter struggle.

I APPROVE of those Children's Allowances (of course). For me the family is . . . *everything*. And what more lovely than a family of girls! Any person calling himself a man, any male party being one of H.M. Family Men in the U.K., anyone taking to himself the honourable style of Parent—nay, Guardian—any such jolly defendant leading (how false there sounds the Active Voice!) a life of quiet desperation, knows but too well what resinous high-tensile heartstrings bind the girls to . . . the grandest, finest, best and bravest old . . . Momma in Earl DeWarr, sorry in all the world. How dear to such fellows the familiar scene around the crackling log fire in the vast baronial hall assuming—just for the hell of it—a maximum fibre stress of 1,000 lbs/in (sq.) for each log. (Log tables may be obtained from the superintendent, need I say?)

Candle light twinkles wittily in the gleaming texture of the mahogany polished for many years by the Rt. Honble. Viscount French (himself). Vast elk-hounds sprawl on the tiger-skin pretending to be bored. Nervous under-proof malt pours itself obsequiously into gem encrusted goblets—thence as though by M'Gick into Jem's encrusted gullet. Ha-ho! The festive season is over and grouped demurely around their lady mother's skirt sit the daughters, fairest flowers in all of luxuriant Dublinshire, brightest jewels in Milord's unmortgaged coronet—though of course he also takes ESQUIRE (out of the Club reading-room, egad!)—fifteen lovelier hawsies Herr Kuehls himself could not find in all the Emerald Doyle. And who knows it better than papa himself . . . if it be not his good lady, née Locke (—Lough Neagh is another day's work, Joe). What an old . . . saint she is! Look at her, look at her . . .! Hers is the head upon which all 'the ends of the world are come' . . . and the eye-lids are a little weary. It is a beauty wrought out from within upon the flesh, the deposit little cell by cell, of strange thoughts and fantastic reveries and exquisite passions. Set it for a moment beside one of those white Greek goddesses or beautiful women of antiquity, and how they would be troubled by this beauty, into which the soul with all its maladies has passed. She is older than the rocks among which she sits; like the vampi . . . (O blast, wrong job—get me the works; this means that Flanagan must go.) I must apologise for that break in the programme; it was due to . . . technical trouble beyond our control. We hope to resume in a few minutes and ᵧ. . . in the meantime perhaps you would care to listen to some organ music. (Not merely organ parsley.)

While we're waiting, here's a few jokes. Did you ever look up Thom's Directory under Chatham Row? Do you know what they have—this'll make you laugh. They have THE MUSICIPAL SCHOOL OF MUSIC. Isn't that funny? The last word, of course, should be MUNICH. (Don't münchen it Mac.) Ah, here's the programme back again. Good . . . look at her, gentlemen, positively twinkling with affection and humour under the snowy aureole of her fine-spun white hair coiled in its bower of *petit point*; look at those fine hands, never idle; regard only, I pray, the curve of that exquisite mouth, so pregnant of joy and humour, see but the little droop at the lip's corner . . . Ah yes, this is beauty, not perhaps as the world knows it, but this is the species faciei super stabilem aetatem indeed. And the little jests, the little family quips, how endearing. 'Children!' 'Yes, dear Momma!' The eager loving faces, elfin in the flicker of 20,000 candles. 'Which loves Mother most?' It is little Myrtle, of course, who answers before the pack; not least in beauty she, not greatest in knowledge of the 'world'. 'I, Momma, darling!' 'Right. Get the medicine bottle from the top left hand drawer of the dressing table.' And off goes the young angel, but not without inquiring: 'Shall I bring the vermouth or will you have it neat, dear Momma?'

Ah dear me.

* * *

I AM, of course, terribly interested in matter. We are not the men our fathers were. (A good job, in a way. If we were, we would be . . . terribly old.) It is becoming more and more difficult to grow wheat in this country. The climate yearly grows less frigid. I have not had my skates on for forty-eight years. We have little phosphates. The wild raspberry is now rarely seen.

But this is very confused. This morning I wish to draw attention to a very serious matter. My theme—though difficult, I will endeavour to propound in a number of simple propositions. Attend, please—all!

1. Matter is indestructible.

2. Matter in the raw is apprehended as earth or 'dust'.

3. Matter, through the action of living cells which pervade it, changes itself into many forms. What was clay a while ago now appears for a brief moment as a flower, a tree or a cow. Each of these things ultimately 'dies' and returns to be clay.

4. Everything that the eye can see, with the possible exception of fire and water, is made of clay.

5. It is beyond question that the chemical composition of clay governs

the type and vigour of, say, the crop it will grow, and the Department of Agriculture maintains a Soil Testing Station to advise agriculturists in this regard.

6. Certain manures and fertilisers are known to be necessary for the raising of crops and other dressings are required to combat specific diseases to which certain crops are prone.

No sane person will question the truth of these six propositions. The only other point I wish to make is this—that man also is clay. The mass of the human body (we confine ourselves strictly to the physical here) is made up of the soil where it grows up. The food that nourishes it is the clay, which yields up its salts and substances in the appetising and attractive form of cabbage and beef and spuds. A man born in Ireland and reared here is therefore an Irishman according to far more extreme criteria than the speaking of Gaelic, wearing bicycle-clips at dances, or winning hand-ball medals. He *is* Ireland. He is temporarily a little bit of Ireland walking about on two rather ungainly pink stilts.

To say this is probably to say what everybody knows and admits. Why then do we not *use* this momentous grain of knowledge? For years most of the inhabitants of Glasgow were bandy-legged. This was due, it was discovered, to a deficiency of lime in the city's water supply. Lime was added, and now Glasgow has a straight-legged citizenry. Why cannot regard be had to far more critical deficiencies in soil? Why must tuberculosis flourish in this country, and bad teeth, and rickets, and all manner of respiratory diseases. Simply because the chemical composition of the soil of Ireland is unbalanced. The authorities have the matter in hand, of course. They are talking, I think, of . . . adding calcium to . . . flour! Why not add calcium to Ireland? Flour is only a tiny fraction of Ireland; calcium is also needed in many other fractions.

Even leave aside disease for the moment. We have the name of being a quarrelsome and intractable people. This is due to some unbalance in the composition of the soil. If, many years ago, people who came here with fire and sword to bend us to their will had brought instead great shiploads of, say, sodium bicarbonate and dumped the stuff everywhere, we would now be . . . well, very different persons, with very dissimilar politics. Possibly there would have been less trouble in the past.

What is Ireland? Even the Chief State Chemist would probably reply 'an island surrounded by water'. I suggest that it is about time somebody found out what Ireland is. People keep saying glibly that agriculture is 'important'. If they only knew how important!

How very very enlightening to analyse the soil of the Six Counties! Have you not there a key to the problem of Partition?

* * *

WERE CLEMENCEAU alive today, he would be the first to admit that he and I went rather too far in respect of 'democracy' and 'self-determination' some years back when in a Swiss city, surrounded by the Higher Executive Officers of the European, Asiatic and Eurasian civil services, we sought far into the night to . . . to . . . unmess the peoples of this hemisphere. There was not a man of our obsequious pale-handed advisers who was not on his max., not a few held directorships, not unfee-ed in prosperous mercantile undertakings and some—heavens!—swaggered into the Blue Train on some sort of a Director's Pass. They were very fine, entirely reliable, they had several matters under active consideration. I am convinced that Clemenccau and I listened too much to these people. We were misled on the nature of human happiness. We thought—heaven help our wit!—that happiness could be devised and legislated. We did not then realise that the science of politics—being the name for continual and malicious interference with the primitive structure of society by so-called intellectuals—was the fons et orig O'Malley.

At that time I was ignorant of the Chinese tongue, my knowledge of the Tibetan dialects was imperfect; of Bulgar poetry I knew but little— yet I can now say, after many years of retirement and study, after a perusal of all the literatures of the earth (nor does the last word exclude the hydroïc esquimeau ethos), after an appraisal of all civilisations not incompatible with the Gaelic norm to which all legitimate human sophistication must be related, I have seen it to be universally acknowledged that all sound and stable pre-political communities were composed of peasants and kings—and of nothing else. It seems that the love of a princeling for a commoner was everywhere the beginning of politics, for instantly 'councillors' had to be summoned, a scandal averted, someone whisked out at midnight through the postern gate. At that humble back-door was the civil service born. Yet this mésalliance persisted and the offsprings of it today people the earth. Those who are not kings and not peasants. The egregious, the degenerate, those strayed from two folds. The troublemakers. The War-makers.

Sceptre and crown must tumble down, Shirley said, and in the dust be equal made, with the poor crooked scythe and spade. Observe this same theme in the Gaelic:

> Is mochean in maiten bán
> no taed for lár mar lasán;
> is mochen do'n té rusfoi,
> in maiten buadach bithnái . . .
> Atchí aiged cach tige
> soillsigios tuath is fine . . .

This idea persists in all primitive literatures, even to the exclusion of the love theme. Observe even Horace:

> 'Pallida mors aequo pulsat pede
> pauperum tabernas
> Regumque turres . . .'

It was, as I have discovered, the upset of that antithetical human relationship—the 'progress' of the 'under-privileged', moryaa—that has led to the present mess. I confess I speak as a member of the ruling classes yet I have no bitterness and if all the male members of the tenantry I am, before heaven, entitled to have, are policemen in Detroit, I can say from my heart that I pity them. In me they would have known a loving father.

All this is apropos of what? I read in the papers that some fine Irishmen have declared that we must all live like the good folk in the Gaeltacht, leading that simple life, speaking that far-from-simple language, presumably occupying ourselves with the uncomplicated agricultural chores which distinguish all ethnic groups the world over which have been denied the enervating influence of H.M. English language. Uniquely, a large section of our people wish to be peasants, thus giving hope of a return to the primal balance to which I have referred. To the plain people of Ireland I will make a fair offer. If, gathering together in solemn conclave ye pledge yerselves to be humble unsophisticates unacquainted with English, innocent of all sciences save that of the smiling Irish fields, I, for my part, am prepared to be King. His Most Gracious Majesty, Myles the First.

* * *

No doubt you saw at the Planning Exhibition the big map of Ireland laid out on the floor, you stopped and saw the bulbs go on showing where everything would be in the future. You were very interested in it all and left, reflecting that at no far distant day Ireland would take her place among the nations of the earth. You may have speculated, as I did, on the mysterious alternative that might admit Ireland to that sinister conclave, the nations not of the earth.

In certain of their moments, the planners surprise me. At one point they turned on a little forest, one at every important point in the country. Do you know what these lights stood for? *Great new sanatoria!* Do they ... do they mean to tell me that we are going to have ... *disease* ... in the new planned Ireland. Have they a dastardly scheme under which *pain* will still be possible? Are we—great heaven!—to be permitted to ... to ... *to die* in the new Ireland? If the answer to these questions is yes, then I say all this planning is a ramp. I solemnly warn Pat to look out for himself. Hospitals are being planned for him, clinics, health centres, streamlined dispensaries. I can see the new Ireland all right, in mime-hind's eye. The decaying population tucked carefully in white sterilised beds, numb from drugs, rousing themselves only to make their wills in Irish. Outside, not a stir anywhere to be discerned—save for the commotion of funerals hurtling along the vast arterial roads to the vast arterial cemeteries—planned by architects, need I say—where tombs and tomb-stones are prefabricated in plastics. It is my considered view that Paud keeping step with world hysteria in the belief that he is being 'modern' is a woeful spectacle, is nowise funny. He has got himself a lot of graphs and diagrams and he is beginning to babble about 'built-in furniture'. Give him just a little rope and he will demolish any decent houses he may have and go and live in insanitary 'prefabricated' shells, the better and the sooner to qualify for the new glass-brick sanatorium.

Dublin must do without the boon of an underground because it lacks the density of population that would sustain such a system economically. Similarly, the whole country lacks the population that would sustain even the fraction of 'planning' that is proper to the temperament and economy of this country. Eighty percent of what has been put before us is blatant imitation of what tremendous and strictly local revolutions have thrown up elsewhere and our 'planners' have lacked the wit to dish up even some native sort of jargon. The problem to be addressed here is simply that of the falling birth-rate; time enough to build your—well yes, vast arterial—roads with eight carriage-ways when the day has come in rural Ireland when from every house another house is to be seen, when 'conversation' in rural Ireland no longer means a demented monologue muttered through toothless gums, the old man crouched over the fire nursing the noggin of lethal 'tea'.

What then is the optimum population of Ireland? Nobody can say.

But certain it is that our present population is too low by several millions. To plan so elaborately the material surroundings of the few folk one sees around doesn't make sense, at least to this most rational tanist. As well erect traffic lights in a grave-yard.

I admit, however, that it would be a bit . . . brutal to snatch his plans away from paddy, even if he is holding them upside down. He loves them so much. I hear he'll be getting into long trousers next year. And after that, please God, Clongowes.

*   *   *

GOT A RING from the Central Bank the other day—can you come at once, Brennan and the Board want to see you immediately, something terrible has happened . . . ?

You see? Never a moment to myself (of all people). The daily grind. I must say 'Central Bank' is good. Is it not a little bit . . . undignified to emphasise the 'cent' so much? Or can it be a sly hint that they actually *have* a stock of those mysterious rubies—'roubles', one had almost said—red cents? A great vaulted agglomeration of tossers, preserved in sacred trust for the most honourable Irish nation I had the honour to found back there in '21?

But this summons, I would not care to ignore it, of course. One never knows, I sighed, put on that rather tattered remnant of my cricketing days —my overcoat—and then wheeled out my decrepit insanitary bicycle. Just as I expected—*flat again*! There was nothing forehead but the pump, though none better knew than I that the pump itself was punctured and gave a return for only 2 per cent. of the energy put into it. After twenty minutes' work, involving irreparable damage to the valves (and not those of the tyres, I assure you—but the heart!) I was in position to travel. I managed to get about 500 yards from my house when all the air flew out of the other tyre. It had begun to rain heavily at this time. I had to get down off the bicycle (via the back-step, for I am rather old-fashioned in these matters) and resumed work with the pump in the middle of the downpour. When I had this front tyre reasonably pumped—half an hour of my life had passed by in the meantime—I discovered that the other tyre was again soft. This I remedied, though the palpitations were alarming in the extreme. Another mile's precarious progress and I discovered that the valve-rubber in the front tyre was rotten. Happily I had a spare, but another half-hour's 'pumping' was involved. During all this interval air was escaping from the back tyre, and after another very brief ride the wheel became completely flat. On this occasion my exertions with the pump were so frenzied that the despicable instrument came away in bits in my moist hands. I was now stranded in the rain. I had begun to walk it when a passing small boy consented to allow me to use his pump for a fee of one shilling. For a second shilling he was prepared to supply labour also. By the time I was again in the saddle, the front tyre had begun to evince an ominous bumpiness. I had savagely made up my mind to continue riding with a flat front tyre when—quite suddenly—the two-shillings-worth of air in my back tyre suddenly ran out of it, making further equitation impossible. My heart palpitations were still violent, the pulse quick, temperature up, respiration irregular and painful. I managed to dismount and rested for some time under a sodden tree. I was on my way to . . . the Central Bank, mind you. ?Central!

When I arrived there eventually, wheeling my airless bicycle, I was a much older man. Seventeen attempts to borrow pumps on the way had been fruitless. It is true that one pump was proffered but I had no rubber connexion and it was useless.

I fear I showed my exhaustion somewhat, though I always try to appear business-like and calm in the presence of subordinates. The Board was solicitous, offered the deepest chair, produced the brandy.

'And now, gentlemen,' I asked, 'what can I do for you? What seems to be the trouble?'

The Chairman opened up.

'We wanted to have your advice on an important matter. Frankly, we are very worried about the danger of inflation. Inflation, if by any chance it should become widespread in this country . . .'

I . . . I . . . I ask you! (!!!)

* * *

MAGNUM EST veritas et in vino praevalebit! Some things are bitter but if they be true, should they then be suppressed? A thousand times *no*, nor do I count the cost to purse, fair name or honour, *least of all my own*. I say this with reluctance but say it I must:

Last night I was drunk!

(Sensation.) No, no (makes nervous gestures), do not think I exaggerate, do not whisper that fumes of deadliest spirits were held to my nostrils as I slept. It is absolutely true and I blame nobody but myself. I was simply caught off my guard. There can be no excuses. From myself I demand the high standards I prescribe for others.

Tell you how it happened. Sitting in my offices last night as Regional

Commissioner for the Townships of Geashill and Philipstown Daingean, a servitor enters and hands me a document. You would never—nor did I —guest what it was. A sealed order from the Department of Local Governments . . . *dissolving me*! ME! Wellll . . .!

Extraordinary sensation. First to go is the head, the whole thing falling away into blobs of yellow liquid running down and messing into the liquefacting chest, then the whole immense superstructure seeping down the decomposing legs to the floor . . . a . . . most . . . *frightful* business, nothing left of me after three minutes only a big puddle on the floor!

Happily my secretary rushed in, guessed what had happened and had the presence of mind to get most of me into an empty champagne bottle I had in my desk. Have you ever, reader, looked at the world from inside a bottle? Found yourself laboriously reversing a word like TOUQCILC? Phew! Have you ever, possessing the boast that not once did breath of intoxicating liquor defile your lips, literally found yourself a one-bottle-man? Ever had to console yourself with a bitter jest about your 'bottle-dress'? Ever found what seemed to be your head being hurt by . . . a *cork*? As for the curse of bottle-shoulders, is there any use in talking? Here, though, is a hint. The curvature of the bottle causes violent refraction and if you have any fear that my own fate could one day be yours, be counselled by what I say: *always carry special spectacles*. It pays in the long run!

Let me continue. My secretary, when leaving to go home, placed me for some reason on the mantelpiece in a rather prominent position but first typed out a little label marked POISON—NOT TO BE TAKEN and stuck it on the bottle. A stupid business, really—whence comes this idea that everybody can read or that those who can always believe what they see? Actually I should have been locked away in the bottom drawer of my desk or put into the big press I have marked 'MAPS'. What I feared happened, though it could have been worse. After an hour or so a charlady arrived and began to clean the place up, having first put some of my valuable documents in her bin. She was later joined by an unusual character, a chargentleman, apparently her husband. I do not suppose he was three seconds in the room when he was conscious of myself, on the mantelpiece in the bottle. He calls the wife's attention, then over, whips me down, takes out the cork and begins to sniff at me.

'Portuguese, begob,' he mutters.

'You'll put that bottle down that's what you'll do,' the charlady says severely.

'I'll go bail it's that Portuguese shandy that carried Harry off around the Christmas,' the ruffian mutters.

Next thing . . . *I'm at his head!* Phewwww! It seems, however, that I tasted rather worse than he was prepared to endure because he took only a few sips of me, then bashed the cork back in disgust.

Well, *what . . . an . . . incredible . . . experience*! I managed to get back next day, but it took me all my time and was a most dangerous business. My sole consolation? That if it was I who was drunk, it was the char-gentleman who had the hangover!

* * *

A THING that you might consider when you have time is the wasteful and 'unscientific' structure of language. I mean—say in English—the number of simple economically-devised sounds which are not 'words' and which have no meaning—while gigantic regiments of letters are assembled to form words which have simple meanings and which take a long time to say or write. An example of the latter—'valetudinarianism'. As regards the former, consider the satisfactory syllable 'pot'. Substitute any other vowel you like and you get a 'word'—pat, pet, pit, put. There you have efficiency, economy. Such invention saves everybody's time; even school-children see there is reason there and are not resentful. But 'bat'—that is defective in the 'o' unless you countenance the slang of vintners in letting you have three of 'Beaune' (manufactured from sheeps' offals in a Tipperary haggard) at 55/6 per knock as a personal favour. You can't go all the way with 'get' without having to be cellulose-american and git a gat. Indeed, the efficient three-letter monosyllable is the exception. 'Not' looks good but when you try it out, you find it is, well . . . not. Fan? No. Fag? No. Tan? Yes, by gob, but rather brewish in its less easy moments. Lag? No. Mad is no use without med. and mod., interesting Trinity baubles. Dog is hopeless. Pan is encouraging, but will not fry your fish.

There are four-letter combinations like 'pack', say, which manage the whole five vowels. 'Band' is all right if you recognise the intrusion of German words.

(Flash-back: 'Bag' works in the three-letter group). 'Fall' is fine till you try to put it through the machine. So is 'hell'. 'Pall' might be per-mitted, *gratia* 'mell' and Goldsmith.

What? Is that so? And pray how many four-letter words can *you* find? 'Ball' is another. Still another is . . . (Frowns heavily, regrets bitterly having started such awful nonsense, stares into blazing ESB radiator in watery-eyed perplexity.) Still another is . . . mure. There *is* such a word.

How about five-letter words? There is one good one—hillo. My dictionary says 'int. used to hail distant person or to express surprise at meeting. Cf. hallo'. Cf. also hello, hullo and hollo—'shout; call to hounds'. My whole point is this: You have, say, stamp and stump. Why doesn't stimp mean something? Take the other two missing words . . .

Awful Wife (suddenly): What's wrong with you?

Startled Reader: Me? Nothing.

Wife: You have been staring out of the window and moving your lips.

Reader: What? Me?

Wife: Are you saying your prayers?

Reader (annoyed): I happened to be reading the leading article in today's paper. (Reads aloud.) Manifestly, it would be folly to under-estimate the resources still at the disposal of the High Command and time alone will determine the soundness or otherwise of the strategy adopted in the gigantic issue now being joined . . .

Wife (undeceived): You were probably reading that awful man Chaplin or whatever he calls himself. How any person can sit . . . and read that rubbish is more than I can tell. Did you see my glasses anywhere? And look at the time. Mollie is still out and it's half ten. I've asked you a hundred times to speak to that girl . . .

(I'm sorry for you, reader.)

Begins to mutter. Sorry *for* you. Far, fur, fir, for—O blast!!!

*

FLYING from Lisbon to Foynes the other day, I beguiled (what but?) the time with Hesketh Pearson's book on Bernard Shaw and a recent copy of Mr Sean O Faoláin's periodical *The Boll*. I was interested to see that Shaw has been at his old game of copying other people. In one of his letters (how meticulously composed for publication) he calls somebody a 'whitemailer'. Who, reader, invented this type of jest? Who patented wintersaults, old ralgia, footkerchiefs and a thousand other jewels? (Not that I mind.)

A thing occurred to me about this newly formed Shaw Society. I approve of it, the vice-presidency of the concern I would gladly have accepted had not a false shyness deterred the founders from approaching me; guineas three I would have contributed without demur. It appears that the Society has no headquarters. (Notice how pertly 'footquarters' bobs up?) I was thinking of getting on to Wylie to have the Society permanently housed at the Shaw Grounds in Ballsbridge. It could be done, mind you, given co-operation and goodwill.

Pearson's book on Shaw is not very good. Like the entire breed of biographies, it is too devout. It was precisely this sort of devotional literature, piling mountain-high during Victoria's reign (all uncover, please) that caused the equally distorted portraits of latter-day debunkers. Biography is the lowest form of letters and is atrophied by the subject's own censorship, conscious or otherwise. And when one finds (as one does rarely) that a subject is prepared to take the lid completely off and reveal the most humiliating infirmities without a blush, one usually finds that one is dealing with an exhibitionist who delights in adding on fictitious villainies. George Moore was a mild case. 'Some men kiss and never tell; Moore tells but never kisses.'

There is nothing of much interest in Mr O Faolain's issue of *The Ball*. The only thing that caught my eye was an editorial preamble to an article entitled 'Why I Am "Church of Ireland"':

> *It is part of the policy of* THE BALL *to open as many windows as possible on as many lives as possible so that we may form a full and complete picture of this modern Ireland which we are making . . .*

I discern a certain want of candour in the statement that this is *part* of the policy of the paper. What are the other parts and why suppress them? Would a 'full and complete' statement of policy be embarrassing? Hmmmm. But what I can't get right at all is this question of the windows. Let us suppose that the 'lives' in question are indoor and that the Paul Prys are outside, getting their socks damp in the shrubbery. Surely whatever is to be seen can be seen through *one* window. But forget even that. Why in heaven's name must we go about *opening* windows. The whole point about a window is that you can see in or out when the window is closed. Moreover, it is no joke opening a closed window from outside—though I admit that (even from the inside) a window that is not closed is even harder. And what distinction is implied. I demand, as between 'full' and 'complete'? As to 'this modern Ireland we are making', one can only point out (a) that it would be a queer business if it was a *medieval . . . China* we are making and anyhow, (b) that we are not making any Ireland. We just live here (the travel ban)—some of us even *work* here.

I can almost hear some reader inquiring how I liked flying from Lisbon to Foynes. Well . . . fair. The weather was pretty bad and I found the journey tiring. I have practically made up my mind that next time I will use an aeroplane. Know any cure for aching arms?

* * *

SOMEBODY SHOULD write a monograph on the use of the word 'supposed' in this country. Start listening for it, either in your own mouth or in others', and you will see that it comprises the sum of the national character, that it is a mystical synthesis of all our habits, hopes and regrets. There is no immediately obvious and neat Irish equivalent, and I opine that the discovery of this word 'supposed' may have been a factor in the change over to English. You meet a man you know as you take a walk on the strand at Tramore. 'Of course I'm not supposed to be here at all,' he tells you, 'I'm supposed to be gettin' orders for th'oul fella in Cork. I'm here for the last week. How long are you staying?'

The words occur most frequently in connexion with breaches of the law or in circumstances where the gravest catastrophes are imminent. You enter a vast petrol depot. The place is full of refineries, pumps, tanks, a choking vapour fills the air. The man on the spot shows you the wonders and in due course produces his cigarettes and offers you one. 'Of course I needn't tell you,' he comments as he lights up, 'there's supposed to be no smoking here.'

You enter a tavern, meet a friend, invite him to join you in a drink. He accepts. He toasts your health, takes a long sip, and replaces the glass on the counter. He then taps his chest in the region of the heart. 'As you know,' he remarks, 'I'm not supposed to touch this stuff at all.'

You have been to some very late and boring function. You are going home, you feel you need a drink, you are a gentleman and know nothing whatever about the licensing laws. Naturally you rap at the door of the first pub you see. All is in darkness. The door opens, a head appears, it peeps up the street and then down; next thing you are whisked in.

'We're supposed to be closed, you know.'

Kreisler is not a great violinist, in the view of the Irish. He is supposed to be one of the greatest violinists in the world. Nor is Irish the national language of Ireland, the Constitution enacted by the people notwithstanding. It's supposed to be. You are not supposed to use gas during the off-hours. You are not supposed to change the lie of your golf ball to very adjacent, if favourable, terrain when your opponent is not looking. You are not supposed to use electric radiators, nor are you supposed to own a radio set without paying the licence. Not more than eight people are supposed to stand inside a bus. You are aware that your colleague was at the races when he was supposed to be sick, but you're not supposed to know and certainly you're not supposed to report such an occurrence. You are not supposed to pay more than the controlled price for rationed commodities. You are not supposed to import uncustomed liquors. You are not supposed to use your wife's hair-brush on the dog. You are not supposed to use the firm's telephone for private trunk calls.

And so on. In no such context does the phrase 'not supposed' connote a prohibition. Rather does it indicate the recognition of the existence of a silly taboo which no grown-up person can be expected to take seriously. It is the verbal genuflection of a worshipper who has come to lay violent hands on the image he thus venerates. It is our domestic password in the endemic conspiracy of petty lawlessness.

All that I believe to be true, though possibly I'm not supposed to say it so bluntly.

* * *

I HAPPENED to glance at my hands the other day and noticed they were yellow. Conclusion: I am growing old (though I claim that I am not yet too old to dream). Further conclusion: I should set about writing my memoirs. Be assured that such a book would be remarkable, for to the extraordinary adventures which have been my lot there is no end. (Nor will there be.) Here is one little adventure that will give you some idea.

Many years ago a Dublin friend asked me to spend an evening with him. Assuming that the man was interested in philosophy and knew that immutable truth can sometimes be acquired through the kinesis of disputation, I consented. How wrong I was may be judged from the fact that my friend arrived at the rendezvous in a taxi and whisked me away to a licensed premises in the vicinity of Lucan. Here I was induced to consume a large measure of intoxicating whiskey. My friend would not hear of another drink in the same place, drawing my attention by nudges to a very sinister-looking character who was drinking stout in the shadows some distance from us. He was a tall cadaverous person, dressed wholly in black, with a face of deathly grey. We left and drove many miles to the village of Stepaside, where a further drink was ordered. Scarcely to the lip had it been applied when both of us noticed—with what feelings I dare not describe—the same tall creature in black, residing in a distant shadow and apparently drinking the same glass of stout. We finished our own drinks quickly and left at once, taking in this case the Enniskerry road and entering a hostelry in the purlieus of that village. Here more drinks were ordered but had hardly appeared on the counter when, to the horror of myself and friend, the sinister stranger was discerned some distance away, still patiently dealing with his stout. We swallowed our drinks raw and hurried out. My friend was now thoroughly scared, and could not be dissuaded from making for the far-away hamlet of Celbridge; his idea was that, while another drink was absolutely essential, it was equally essential to put as many miles as possible between ourselves and the sinister presence we had just left. Need I say what happened? We noticed with relief that the public house we entered in Celbridge was deserted, but as our eyes became more accustomed to the poor light, *we saw him again*: he was standing in the gloom, a more terrible apparition than ever before, ever more menacing with each meeting. My friend had purchased a bottle of whiskey and was now dealing with the stuff in large gulps. I saw at once that a crisis had been reached and that desperate action was called for.

'No matter where we go,' I said, 'this being will be there unless we can now assert a superior will and confound evil machinations that are on foot. I do not know whence comes this apparition, but certainly of this world it is not. It is my intention to challenge him.'

My friend gazed at me in horror, made some gesture of remonstrance, but apparently could not speak. My own mind was made up. It was me or this diabolical adversary: there could be no evading the clash of wills, only one of us could survive. I finished my drink with an assurance I was far from feeling and marched straight up to the presence. A nearer sight of him almost stopped the action of my heart; here undoubtedly was no man but some spectral emanation from the tomb, the undead come on some task of inhuman vengeance.

'I do not like the look of you,' I said, somewhat lamely.

'I don't think so much of you either,' the thing replied; the voice was cracked, low and terrible.

'I demand to know,' I said sternly, 'why you persist in following myself and my friend everywhere we go.'

'I cannot go home until you first go home,' the thing replied. There was an ominous undertone in this that almost paralysed me.

'Why not?' I managed to say.

'Because I am the—taxi-driver!'

Out of such strange incidents is woven the pattern of what I am pleased to call my life.

* * *

ONE HEARS a lot of talk about 'Greater Dublin' (most of it unauthorised by me and therefore mischievous) but never a mention of the sticking-out corollary that, according as you increase Dublin, you diminish the rest of Ireland proportionately. This, of course, is a very serious matter. Some fine day the inhabitants of Leixlip will notice something usual about the horizon and, sending forth scouts to investigate, will find it is Dublin. Dublin just down the road today. Tomorrow? The tide will have engulfed ancient Leixlip, the inhabitants will be answerable to Hernon, Keane and Monks. People will write letters addressed 'Main St Leixlip, Dublin, C.98' and you will probably be able to get there on the 16 bus. People in Athlone will say 'You saw what happened in Leixlip. They thought they were safe, that their unborn sons would never be Dublin men. *Hodie Leixlip, Cras nobis.* Let us menfolk take to the hills, let our women-folk be instructed in the art of baking cakes containing keys. To arms!'

'Greater Dublin' is fine if you provide *pari passu* for Greater Ireland. How can this be done? There will be some who will ask that Ireland, sword in hand, should embark on vast imperial conquests. My pledged word to Clemenceau forbids this course, even if other considerations did not make it impracticable.

Two things occur to me. You remember my recent lecture on the export of agricultural produce to Britain, how I explained that with every export of beast, man and great hundred of eggs, we were permanently expatriating a quantum of the essential constituents of the Irish earth, and thus impoverishing the material from which Irish humans are made. Suppose you accelerate this process, some churl will say, suppose you capture the entire British food trade? Would not Britons, nourished solely on Irish bullocks and Irish malt, become as Irish in their physical make-up as the Irish themselves? Develop high cheek-bones, play hurley, fight and become inexorably opposed to compulsory Irish? Write banned books? Become . . . neutral?

The answer is yes and no. First, the process of metabolic hibernicisation would never be complete owing to the fact that it would be difficult for an Irish government to prevent the English people from continuing to drink English water, or to compel them to import Irish water. Water is *most* important since it contains many of the indigenous salts which determine national temperament. You read a lot of nonsense in the history books about foreigners having come to conquer, being 'absorbed' by the Irish. Actually, the poor devils had to eat and drink here, like everybody else. Until chemistry and history are fused in a biological survey of the origins and sustenances of life, there can be no realistic approach to almost any contemporary problem. The other point I must make is this: suppose we went all out to gaelicise the British through the medium of the long gut, suppose we achieved a large measure of success—*what*, *pray*, *would remain here*? If you export all the essential Irish nutriments and if there be 'people' still living here, who *are* they? Hmmmm.

No, additional Ireland must be sought in a different way. It is really quite simple. The present Ireland must first carry out an elaborate survey of its own soil. Thereafter must be sent throughout the known world an army of Irish chemists analysing the soil of every land wherein people dwell. Golden sovereigns will I bet that you will find certain countries, certain areas, wherein the soil is, in structure and composition, identical with that of Ireland. The people of that country—surprised though they be to learn the fact—*are Irish*! Thus can you evolve a world-confederation of Irelands, an empire based on a homogeneity of stomach-trouble. Such an association would long outlast, I ween, anything based on fire and sword. (It would be damn funny if the British turned out to be thoroughly Irish all along. Trouble is they would say (casually, by way of reply to some hon. and gallant member) that the Irish were British all along.)

*

I DO NOT WISH, at this peaceful time, to trouble you with personal matters, still less to obtrude questions affecting my personal honour and prestige. But an item appeared recently in this newspaper which, if allowed to pass unchallenged, might do serious damage. An oddly retrospective condition attached to it, as may be seen. At a Dublin meeting a speaker said (I assume, of course, that newspapers do not lie):

'If Plato had been the Colossus of the ancient world of thought, Shaw was the Colossus of the modern world . . .'

Since apparently he wasn't the whole proposition seems to fall through. But there was more, which pl. note:

'In variety of subject and profundity of thought Shaw equalled Plato; in the staggering boldness of his proposals he surpassed him. Shaw's work,' the speaker added, 'was shot through with two fundamental convictions—creative evolution and a basic income.'

You will, dear reader, doubtless have noticed something rather funny about all this. I'm sure it was unintentional; I like to believe that no insult was intended . . . but . . . *not a word about me in the whole thing from beginning to end*! (!!!) I don't mind, of course—if people choose to make fools of themselves I don't give a damn one way or the other. But in common decency don't you think there'd have been even just a word? But no. No mention whatever.

Ah well! Mind you, it's not that I've anything against Shaw. Shaw is one of the best, we used to see a lot of each other during the old cycling days, many's the fiver he borrowed off me in the Vegetarian Restaurant and to this day I never have an opening in the West End but he comes along and sits there in the stalls munching watercress sandwiches, but . . . *calling him a Colossus of the ancient world*! And then this business of shootings and convictions. Shure . . . how many bullet wounds and incarcerations for the freedom of political thought I have myself and is there ever a word out of me about it? And . . . variety of thought and staggering proposals . . .? Shur, glory be, man, what is that only a mild watered-down specification of my humble daily chores for H.M. Irish Times in the U.K.? And that, be the same token, brings me to the last point—basic income. I said—*basic* income . . . (Editor begins to cough, bites nails, looks out of window). I said the labourer is worthy of his hire. I haven't got the basic income of me good friend George B. Shaw, I may tell you. It's not that I haven't brains—I have more brains in me little finger than your man has in his whole beard. Did you ever see my play, hah? (You had to be quick as it happens.) Ever read my novels, biographies, political tracts? My denunciations of what is evil, meretricious, unworthy? Shure, great heavens, there's no comparison. It's not that Shaw's plays aren't good— the Student Prince is a lovely thing. 'Pig' Malone is fine, and Rose Marie and Charley's Aunt—these are all blooming lovely things—a man doesn't get a reputation for *nothing*, mind you, but a man should have a bit more than that to his credit before you start calling him a Colossus of the ancient world, that's all I say. (Incidentally, where does Professor Joad come into this hasty evaluation of ratiocinative grandeur?) Of course, the basic income is a great help—note that all that unfriendly speech was made at a meeting of the Royal Georgian and Shavian Association of Ireland. Perhaps . . . certain parties have it in their minds that maybe they're mentioned in a certain will . . .?

(Pause. Twilight falls. Voice is heard speaking in the gloaming):

How well the crowd in this town would never think of forming a M na gC Society! It'd be such a . . . a . . . fine tribute to an old man! And with a statue in College Green, my back turned to Trinity! (I *still* say I have the figure to wear a stone beard and stone frock coat!)

*

KNOWLEDGE and learning are funny things if you like. Take for example that old question of the genuineness of the last fifteen words of Plato's *Phaedo*, in the epilogue after Socrates has had his jar. Many commentators hold that the use of the phrase *tón tote* is so odd and out of context that it invalidates the entire passage after *andros*; others hold that it is merely 'a slip' and that the passage is genuine. Hear Hirschig on this point, hear Riddell, Grote, Wyttenbach, Gaisford, Bekker, Geddes, Jebb, Heindorf and Stallbaum—and where are you? Precisely where you were. There is no finality, no *truth*, in such 'learned' disputation. My own view may be stated without reserve. The words between *andros* and *dikaiotatou* inclusive *are quite definitely not an interpolation*. The reason? Why, surely it is obvious. You cannot have an interpolation at the end of a work.

Very well. Leave aside the scholars, forget their hard clashing voices. Is 'the world' the mart of men—is that a garden of noumenal calm, is clarity, precision and finality the benign trefoil that therein grows? Alas, far from it. It is lies, turmoil, chaos, the mother mistaken for the daughter, wealth owned only by the unworthy, the clean of heart in jail, favourites inadequate, money lost, the reek of war stenching the spring. It is . . . (fans out yellow wax-like hands in deprecation) it is . . . heart-breaking.

Take for example the word 'canny'. My dictionary endows it with a tortuous etymology based on the original meaning of 'can', i.e. know. cf. cunning. All that is a lie, of course. The word clearly comes from the Irish phrase *ciall ceannaidhe* (pro. keel canny) meaning shrewdness (of a businessman), i.e. the sort of worldly wisdom that is conferred by experience. Here then we have the wrong thing in the niche, the right thing unknown. (Blows nose.) Take even the pleas that persons in the grip of fear show the whites of their eyes. That too is wrong. That part of the eye is *not white*. See? (Places brown-black tobacco-charred finger on wizened eye-ball, pointing to diseased dull-yellow orbs, blood-flecked and afloat in glistening rheumy wash.) They are as you see quite yellow.

Take what is even a more extreme example. Inebriates, as a class, are despised (chiefly by people who cannot afford to drink) but a more particular derision is reserved for the inebriate's idea that he can see, and has in fact seen pink rats. The incorrigible phenomenalism that is conferred by protracted and malignant sobriety makes the idea of pink rats laughable. But rats are pink. Of that there is of course no doubt whatever. (Roots in 'coat' pocket, pulls out huge squirming black rat, obviously native of Murmansk; the coarse heavy coat and scaly tail almost visibly swarming with bubonic germs.) You see? It *looks* black, even these razor-sharp claws—see?—*are* black. (Rat whistles fiercely and snaps at captor.)

But let us see. We must not be deceived by appearances, here or elsewhere. (Has suddenly plugged in electric razor, pinioned rat on knee and is deftly shaving it.) Now we are getting somewhere. Knowledge is vouchsafing us a glimpse at her treasures. See? The rat is pink. (Rat, plunging wildly, is held up by tail, seen to be half original size, completely devoid of hair, but pink.) There is therefore no aberration necessarily involved in the infra-fur inspection of rodents on the part of vinous zoologists. (Rat emits shrill venomous barks; shorn fur on floor begins to move nearer fire.) None whatever. We have nailed still a further lie and we have done perhaps enough for one day. (Rises, winks broadly, takes up wife's handbag, opens it, stuffs in infuriated whistling rat, closes and replaces bag, which jumps about for a time). I will be in later on tonight if you wish to look in for a game of backgammon. Her nibs if you please is off to a temperance meeting in the Mansion House.

*

A NOTE in my diary says: 'Ten to the power of seventy-nine. Write on this joke.'

Very well. Why not? I wish I had the money to finance *real* scientific research. You remember the worry we had back in the thirties (?this century, I think—or was it?) about the electron, how to determine its mass. Eddington had an amusing angle on the thing. But first let us recall the previous situation where you had the crude journeyman's approach of calculating it as 10 (to the power of −27) of a gramme. Most of us looked on that as a sort of music-hall joke—mass audience reaction makes you snigger but you are not really amused, you are sorry for having forsaken for the evening your monogram on Cicero's *Pro Malony*. Because it really boiled down to this—that if some smartie broke into the place at Sèvres and stole the so-called 'standard kilogramme' your '10 (to the power of −27)' immediately became more obviously the arbitrary unfunny gaffe it essentially was. Very well. The 'scientist', in sum, had been deluding himself that the Heath Robinson experiments which led to that 'discovery' could be solemnly called *observational determination*. Whereas it is just make-believe and whimsy, all essentially feminine.

The 'problem'—as one then thought of it—was to relate the mass of the electron to . . . to something *real* (like, for instance, sleep). The point, of course, about Eddington's handling of the experiment was his realisation that it could *only* give information about a *double* wave system which 'belonged' as much to the electron as to the material comparison standard necessarily used. Very well.

To reach a result it had been necessary to investigate the circumstances where the double wave can be replaced with single waves (really, this sounds like barber-shop talk!)—or in other words, to examine the process where you are slipping from macroscopic to microscopic; call them 'magnitudes' by all means, terminology is unimportant. Eddington, as you know, tied this up with his engaging patent 'comparison aether', a retroambulant nonenity moping about introspectively way below the xx axis, whose mass can be calculated, needless to say, from a formula expressed largely in terms of the fundamental constants of macroscopical physics—the time-space radius, velocity of 'light' . . . and *all* the particles in the universe. Now when this mass is m and the

$$_0$$

electric-particle- proton or electron, it doesn't matter a damn which—is, as usual, m, you have this incredible quadratic:

$$10m - 136mm + m. = 0$$
$$_0$$

What is quite curious is that this new equation and formula for m

$$_0$$

yield (for this velocity) a maximum value of 780 kilom. per sec. per megaparsec . . . which, of course, accords with the 'value' found by observation (!!!!!)

But here is what I am really getting at—the uniquely prolonged sneer that Eddington embodied in the paper he read to us at the Royal Society in the fateful autumn of '33.

'In the maze of connection of physical constants,' he said, 'there remains just one pure number—' (ho-ho-ho, I cannot help interjecting)—'which is known only by observation and has no theoretical explanation. It is a very large number, about 10 (to the power of 79), and the present theory indicates that it is the number of particles in the universe. It may seem to you odd—' (Not at all, not at all, one murmurs)—'that this number should come into the various constants such as the constants of gravitation. You may say, how on earth can the number of particles in remote parts of the universe affect the Cavendish experiment on the attraction of metal spheres in a laboratory? I do not think they affect it at all. But the Cavendish and other experiments having given the result they did, we can deduce that space will go on and on, curving according to the mass contained in it until only a small opening remains and that the 10 (to the power of 79)th particle will be the last particle to be admitted through the last small opening and will shut the door after it.'

Bye-bye, 10 (to the power of 79).
Mind that step!

* * *

I HAVE BEEN INTERESTED in a newspaper report of a lecture given in Dublin recently by a Belfast medical man on the upright posture of man. 'The lecturer said that that posture had been arrived at only in modern man. He showed that it had to be developed by each individual after birth . . .' But not to all modern men does the upright posture come readily. I could give chapter and verse, name the man, the street and the time. I know plenty of . . . old-fashioned gents. Upright, is it? Never heard of it.

Scientists use words oddly. 'Modern' in the above context presumably means about 4000 B.C.; otherwise how could one explain the splayed ungainly feet that have been fashionable for some time. Is the world itself in existence so long? I doubt it and certainly hope not.

But surely it would be more to the point if scientists could explain why man born on the flat, thought fit to stand up. It is true that even the babies of today—one obviously cannot call them modern babies—have to develop the upright posture individually after birth. Presumably attempts to do this before birth were unsuccessful. In other words, all babies learn to walk. The remarkable thing is that they all succeed—or at all events those who fail are rarely seen out of doors in after life. In a way, it is all rather a pity. Man's capacity for mischief certainly did not diminish when he stood up. Consider how the world would look today if he had remained on all fours. Everything would look flattened; houses would be a few feet in height, mahogany counters would be unknown, football would be unheard of, T.D.'s would fight for beds instead of seats, and if one of them managed to rise on a point of order he would be regarded as an acrobat rather than a statesman. And that vertical brawl, the stand-up fight, would be a thing of the future.

Yes, I agree. Not very funny.

TIME: Friday night.

Sets alarm clock for 3 a.m. Saturday morning, dresses hastily and cycles into town. Dismounts at *Irish Times* office, drenched to the skin. Obtains first copy of paper to come off press. Cycles home, pulls wife out of bed to make breakfast, then disappears into back room to study crossword puzzle. Thumbs dictionaries, almanacs, anthologies, thesauri. Begins to get odd words out one by one. Has breakfast. Goes back to work on puzzle. Is still working at it as day wears on. Claws at stubbly face, stares, lies back, grunts, walks to window and looks out. Gives sharp cry and writes down word. Paces room, hunches shoulders, has both cigarette and pipe going simultaneously. Dog yawns noisily, is kicked savagely in ribs. Another word comes. Rolls up trousers and examines knee. Lolls, protrudes denture on tip of tongue, rubs palms together violently. Cracks finger joints. Gives pop-eyed stare at wall, writes down another word. Pares finger nails. Removes slippers and socks and starts doctoring corn. Whistles *The Lanty Girl*. Writes down further word. Has lunch on tray, cannot leave room to have it properly. Sharpens pencil. Gets two words simultaneously. Keeps on and on and on.

Time: Saturday night.

Arrives at golf club clean, freshly shaved, with five half ones on board. Is approached by studious confrère.

Did you see the *Times* crossword today?

No. I didn't see a paper at all today. What about it?

Well, it's pretty stiff this week. (*Produces paper*.) I've spent hours at it and can't get it out at all. Wasted the whole morning on it. I think some of the clues must be wrong.

I thought last week's was easy enough.

You did? Well, look at this one. 'Exhausted at reports,' 9 letters. What could that be?

(Very slight pause.)

Um . . . PROSTRATE, I suppose.

Ohhh! (Sensation.) Begob, *you're* quick at it. And 2 down here, five letters . . .